D1369154

PENGUIN BOOKS

THE KING'S PEACE 1637-1641

Dame Veronica Wedgwood was born in 1910 and educated at a private school in London, in Germany and France, and at Lady Margaret Hall, Oxford, where she gained a first class degree in Modern History. One of Britain's most renowned historians, she was awarded the C.B.E. in 1956, the D.B.E. in 1968 and the Order of Merit in 1969. She holds honorary degrees from both British and American universities and became an Honorary Member of the American Academy of Arts and Letters in 1966, and of the American Academy of Arts and Sciences in 1973. In 1962 she was made an Honorary Fellow of Lady Margaret Hall, Oxford, and in 1965 of University College, London, where she was a Special Lecturer from 1962 to 1970. Her other books include *Strafford* (later revised as *Thomas Wentworth*), *The Thirty Years' War*, *Oliver Cromwell*, *William the Silent*, which won the James Tait Black Memorial Prize, *Richelieu and the French Monarchy*, *Poetry and Politics*, *Milton and his World* and *The Political Career of Rubens*. Her three works – *The King's Peace*, *The King's War* and *The Trial of Charles I* – have received great critical acclaim. J. H. Plumb has written of Miss Wedgwood, 'Her gifts are splendid and altogether exceptional. She is a great craftswoman and a great writer' and *The Times* said, 'Miss Wedgwood belongs to the small band of living historians who write history in the only way that matters, as a living re-creation of the past.'

C. V. WEDGWOOD

THE KING'S PEACE
1637–1641

PENGUIN BOOKS

Penguin Books Ltd, Harmondsworth, Middlesex, England
Penguin Books, 40 West 23rd Street, New York, New York 10010, U.S.A.
Penguin Books Australia Ltd, Ringwood, Victoria, Australia
Penguin Books Canada Ltd, 2801 John Street, Markham, Ontario, Canada L3R 1B4
Penguin Books (N.Z.) Ltd, 182–190 Wairau Road, Auckland 10, New Zealand

First published by Collins 1955
Published in Penguin Books 1983

Copyright © C. V. Wedgwood, 1955
All rights reserved

Made and printed in Great Britain by
Richard Clay (The Chaucer Press) Ltd,
Bungay, Suffolk

942.06

To
GEORGE MACAULAY TREVELYAN, O.M.

ACKNOWLEDGMENT

Although this book has been in my mind for many years it would not have been finished by 1954—if finished at all—without the perfect conditions for work generously given to me by the Institute for Advanced Study, Princeton. I would like to take this occasion of expressing my admiration for the Institute and its work under the humane guidance of Dr. Robert Oppenheimer and my gratitude to my friends there, more especially to the late Professor Edward Meade Earle without whose kindly persistence in urging me to cross the Atlantic I should not have enjoyed those months of exhilarating and peaceful endeavour.

CONTENTS

INTRODUCTION   *page* 13

BOOK ONE
THE HAPPIEST KING IN CHRISTENDOM
JUNE 1637

I.   COURT AND COUNTRY   21

II.   FAITH AND FOREIGN POLITICS   76

III. THE KING'S PEACE AND THE KING'S REVENUE   135

BOOK TWO
CHALLENGE FROM SCOTLAND
JUNE 1637–JULY 1639

I.   THE COVENANT   173

II.   SHIP-MONEY   201

III. THE GLASGOW ASSEMBLY   221

IV.   THE FIRST SCOTS WAR   246

BOOK THREE
AN ARMY IN IRELAND
AUGUST 1639–NOVEMBER 1641

I.   THE RETURN OF THE LORD DEPUTY   285

CONTENTS

II. THE SHORT PARLIAMENT   *page* 307

III. THE SECOND SCOTS WAR   328

IV. PARLIAMENT AND THE CROWN   362

V. THE END OF STRAFFORD   400

VI. THE KING AND JOHN PYM   430

VII. SCOTLAND AND IRELAND   453

BIBLIOGRAPHICAL NOTE   487

INDEX   493

INTRODUCTION

The King's Peace is a narrative history of the British Isles for the four years in the reign of King Charles I which immediately preceded the Civil Wars. I hope in later volumes to describe the course of these wars and the Republican experiment that followed them. The story is not simple; it involves three separate countries, England, Scotland and Ireland, and two civilisations of a wholly different type, the Normanised Anglo-Saxon and the Celtic.

The Scots first revolted against the King because he would have compelled them to religious conformity with England. The Irish next rose, not against the King, but against English and Scottish settlers and the aggressive Protestantism of the English Parliament. They established an independent government at Kilkenny for upwards of eight years. The English, who appealed last to arms, fought—with assistance and diversions from the Scots, Irish and Welsh—a war for religious and political principles which ended in the death of the King on a public scaffold. This, being much resented in Scotland, precipitated a war within Scotland and another between Scotland and England.

European governments, aware of the strategic importance of the British Isles in their own wars, intervened with open or secret help. The French, the Dutch and the Danes offered to mediate between King Charles and his subjects. The Pope sent his nuncio, and the Kings of France and Spain sent their ambassadors to the Irish at Kilkenny. A German prince fixed hopeful eyes on the not quite vacant English throne. English settlements in the Netherlands, Scottish settlements in the Baltic, groups of English traders in Leghorn, Constantinople and Madras felt the far vibrations of the war. So did the young colonies on the eastern fringe of America's vast continent, and the island outposts in the West Indies.

The civil wars of the British Isles had an effect on European politics, on the dominion of the Mediterranean and the rise and decline of colonial empires, but essentially they were the intimate concern of our islands and sprang from the explosive energy, diverse ideals and colliding interests of their inhabitants. The principles for which they fought and the problems that they tried to solve are alive to-day; the conflict between the authority of the State and the liberty of the subject, between public responsibility and private conscience is not, and probably never will be, fully resolved. The doctrines they created, the laws they made or unmade, the sufferings and triumphs of individuals, their nobility and their baseness—all are part of the tradition we inherit and within which we live and think. We are still so much involved with this conflict that passion and propaganda colour all that has been written about it. It is not yet an academic study which we can approach with scientific indifference and cannot become so while a vital current of continuous belief runs through it to us. The final, dispassionate, authoritative history of the Civil Wars cannot be written until the problems have ceased to matter; by that time it will not be worth writing.

A writer approaching a controversial and lively subject on which much has been written owes it to the reader to make his own position at least as clear as it is to himself. The causes of the Civil Wars have been analysed, the rights of the combatants have been judged and weighed by Churchman and Dissenter, Whig and Tory, Liberal and Marxist, utilitarian and romantic. The religion, the political morality and the philosophies of his own time colour the outlook of every writer, however conscientious, although, wise in his own generation, each may add something to our understanding of the past. No historian has ever been, or will ever be, omniscient in his knowledge or infallible in his deductions. None can see the whole and undivided truth.

The contemporary could not do so either. Puzzled by the variety of events which came so confusingly upon him from day to day, and ignorant of much that time alone would bring to light, he steered his way through his own world—as we do now—by the imperfect judgment of an ill-informed mind. But the contemporary knew one thing that the historian can only imagine: he knew what it felt like to be alive at that time, to experience those religious doubts, political fears, and economic pressures as a part of his life. He may not have known or suspected influences which have been later revealed; but he knew what he experienced in his mind or suffered in his flesh, and he knew what beliefs and what interests he admitted to be the motives of his action. "Here we are subject to error and misjudging one another," said Strafford on the scaffold. The day-to-day events of history arise at least in part from error and misjudgment. On this level falsehood itself is a part of truth.

Before history can be put into a coherent perspective it is often necessary to clear away the misinterpretations and the half-knowledge by which contemporaries lived. But the application of modern methods of research, together with modern knowledge and prejudice, can make the past merely the subject of our own analytical ingenuity or our own illusions. With scholarly precision we can build up theories as to why and how things happened which are convincing to us, which may even be true, but which those who lived through the epoch would neither recognise nor accept. It is legitimate for the historian to pierce the surface and bring to light motives and influences not known at the time; but it is equally legitimate to accept the motives and explanations which satisfied contemporaries. The two methods produce different results, but each result may be a fair answer to the particular question that has been asked. They become misleading only if either is accepted as the whole truth.

I have not attempted in this book to examine underlying causes, but rather to give full importance and value to the admitted motives and the illusions of the men of the seventeenth century. I have sought to restore their immediacy of experience.

History experienced is not simple for those who experience it, as every intelligent inhabitant of the twentieth century is aware, and it is impossible to express the full significance of contemporary confusion without sacrificing some, though I hope not all, appearance of clarity. I have tried to describe the variety, vitality and imperfections as well as the religion and government of the British Isles in the seventeenth century in an opening section, deliberately avoiding analysis and seeking rather to give an impression of its vigorous and vivid confusion. Otherwise this book is intended as a straightforward and chronological narrative. I have preferred to describe events as far as possible in the order in which they happened, although this necessarily means a shifting of interest from theme to theme and from place to place. A narrative which sorts out the muddled strands of day-to-day events makes smoother reading, but only a resolute insistence on chronology can make the immediate pressures and confusions which acted on contemporaries clear to the modern reader.

The highest ideals put forward in this generation of conflict were noble; the men who fought or worked for them were less noble than the ideals, for the best of men do not consistently live on the highest plane of virtue, and most men live far below it. The idealisation of certain figures in the Civil War has led, later, to exaggerated condemnations, but a cynical view of human frailty is no help to the historian, and human values can be fairly assessed only if an honest effort is made to understand the difficulties and prejudices of each of the people concerned. These mental acrobatics cannot always be successful, but the attempt to perform them is always illuminating.

This book covers only a few years, and many of the people in it cannot be fully understood until their lives are seen as a whole. It is my aim to show the unfolding of certain characters and the emergence of others and to comment on them, as far as possible, from evidence relating only to the years described. Clarendon's account of Charles I, for instance, together with most of the best known descriptions of the King, belong to a later epoch, are coloured by the knowledge of his end, and are therefore misleading if their evidence is allowed to influence a study of him as he was between the years 1637 and 1641.

The behaviour of men as individuals is more interesting to me than their behaviour as groups or classes. History can be written with this bias as well as another; it is neither more, nor less, misleading. The essential is to recognise that it answers only one set of questions in only one way. Few methods of historical study do more, and no harm will be done by any of them so long as the limitation is understood. This book is not a defence of one side or the other, not an economic analysis, not a social study; it is an attempt to understand how these men felt and why, in their own estimation, they acted as they did.

BOOK ONE

THE HAPPIEST KING IN CHRISTENDOM

June 1637

We have no other intention but by our government to honour Him by Whom Kings reign and to procure the good of our people, and for this end to preserve the right and authority wherewith God hath vested us.

CHARLES I

O thou, that dear and happy isle,
The garden of the world erewhile,
Thou Paradise of the Four Seas
Which Heaven planted us to please,
But—to exclude the world—did guard
With wat'ry, if not flaming, sword:
What luckless apple did we taste
To make us mortal and thee waste ?

ANDREW MARVELL

CHAPTER ONE

COURT AND COUNTRY

CHARLES, King of Great Britain and Ireland, in the thirty-seventh year of his age and the thirteenth of his reign, believed himself to be the happiest King in Christendom. He said as much in the warm June of the year 1637 to his eldest nephew and godson, the Elector Palatine, Charles Louis, who with his next brother Rupert had been on a long visit to his Court. They were the sons of the King's only sister Elizabeth, whose husband, once Elector Palatine and King of Bohemia, had lost in the German wars all that he possessed.

King Charles's claim was not extravagant. He was, to all immediate observation, singularly blessed in the inward tranquillity and the outward peace of his dominions. He had not wished to be involved in the bloody turmoil of Europe even for his sister's and her children's sake. As one of his many courtier poets had prettily expressed it:

> Tourneys, masques, theatres better become
> Our halcyon days; what though the German drum
> Bellow for freedom and revenge, the noise
> Concerns not us, nor should divert our joys;
> Nor ought the thunder of their carabins
> Drown the sweet airs of our tun'd violins.[1]

The benevolent authority which King Charles sought to exercise over his people was reflected in many a noble and civilised achievement of the arts. With the help of courtier-

21

landowners, inspired by the Crown, the embellishment of the capital proceeded apace. The piazza at Covent Garden, surrounded by splendid town houses for the nobility and dominated by the handsome new church of St. Paul, was all but finished. London's greater St. Paul's, the huge, decrepit medieval cathedral, had been purged of the hucksters who used the nave as a market place; the citizens who had for years tipped their rubbish into the crypt had been compelled to find another place for it. A magnificent portico in the Italian manner was being erected to beautify the outmoded Gothic façade.

The King's Surveyor General, the virtuoso Inigo Jones, had some admirable ideas for a new London, spacious, sweet and clean. London Bridge through the narrow arches of which, at high tide, the Thames flowed in dangerous rapids, was doomed to demolition; the crazy structure of houses surmounting it was grotesque and old fashioned, and for the last few years had become dangerous and unsightly owing to a fire which had left, on the north side, only burnt-out shells patched with boards. All this would soon be replaced by a stone structure, modelled on the bridge of Sant' Angelo in Rome, and worthy of a great capital and a great river. In the architectural schemes of Inigo Jones the new London already appeared to be, in outward form as it was in size, the greatest city in Europe.

In practice the King met with irritating opposition. When he decided to demolish the inferior little church of St. Gregory to free St. Paul's from surrounding clutter, the parishioners of St. Gregory sulked; they did not think their church inferior and they too had spent good money on improvements. Other more exasperating incidents interfered with the building of the capital. A fine vista had been planned in the suburban fields of Long Acre, but before work could be started on it, wooden hovels appeared overnight and by morning were full of clamouring squatters.

Apart from opposition there were the usual checks to which building operations are subject—bad weather, delays in delivery of material, mistaken plans which had to be rectified. The superb series of paintings commissioned by the King from Sir Peter Paul Rubens for the ceiling of his new banqueting house at Whitehall was ready more than a year before there was any ceiling to which to attach them. They had to be rolled up and stacked in the workshop of the master at Antwerp. When the ceiling was ready for them they were found to have cracked, and Rubens, who had put his highest efforts into their composition, had to devote some weeks' personal work to them before they were again ready for transportation to England. By the summer of 1637 they were at last safely in their appointed places, and revealed, to those who curiously or admiringly examined them, an allegorical tribute to the late King James of blessed memory.

At each corner symbolic groups illustrated the triumph of peace, wisdom and authority over strife, falsehood and faction: a serpent-headed Medusa writhed under the feet of her conqueror, and Hercules grappled successfully with the Hydra of rebellion. Along each side buxom children, who staggered beneath cornucopias or tumbled among garlands of flowers, conveyed the general idea of prosperity. The three great pictures in the centre showed the late King bestowing order, justice, peace and the benefits of true religion on his people, before mounting to heaven where a throng of Christian angels and pagan gods united to exchange his earthly crown for a celestial one.

In one of these pictures two ample nymphs representing the sister kingdoms of England and Scotland dandled between them a baby boy whose prancing legs and outstretched arms seemed to foretell at once the greatest energy and the noblest aspiration. This child portrayed King Charles himself as an infant. In prosaic fact, he had been a sickly little thing with no resemblance to the bouncing Flemish baby used by Rubens as a model, but the higher truth of allegory is not bound to pedantic details. The pictures illustrated the vision which both King Charles and his father had for their people—peace, order, justice.

A literal-minded critic might have found fault with the whole splendid composition of cloud-capped domes and sky-borne deities. These had little to do with the archipelago scattered out north-westward from the mainland of Europe, the British Isles, with their seven thousand miles of coast, towering crag and jagged reef battered by Atlantic storms, chalk ramparts above the green Channel, dune and quicksand, shelving shingle and crumbling cliff: the beacon on the headland, the bell on the rock, the fishing boats on the beach, the nets drying on the sea wall, the bales unloaded on the busy quays; and inland, the cornfields and the pastures, the sheep on the downs, the cattle in the hills, forest and park, moor and mine, impenetrable mountain and impassable bog; and the King's seven million subjects (more or less) crammed in towns, snug in villages, lonely in moorland farmstead or island croft; or far off on the rocky shore of Newfoundland, the wooded hills of Massachusetts, the warm islands of the Caribbean; or east or west on the world's wide oceans in some *Mary Rose* of Bristol, *Andrew* of Leith, *Patrick* of Galway.

All this was but vaguely comprehended in the vast allegorical design. The painter had not been asked, and had not been expected, to represent the geographical character of the King's dominions or the activities of his subjects. He had been asked to represent certain large and noble ideas, and he had, largely and nobly, acquitted himself of his task. It was not for him to reconcile the vision with the facts. That task fell to the King.

The races, customs, languages, religions and interests of the King's subjects were as various as the landscape of his dominions. The greater number of them lived in England which, with the adjoining principality of Wales, accounted for about five millions; Scotland and Ireland with the islands off their coasts had not above a million each.

A contemporary scholar reckoned that twelve languages were spoken in the British Isles. Only one of these, English, was officially recognised, and the aggressive, conquering language, now in its vigorous golden age, was bounded on the North and West by the older Celtic tongues, once the general speech of the land—moribund Cornish in the extremity of the western peninsula, lively lilting Welsh throughout the principality, and various forms of the melancholy, guttural Irish dialects in the Scottish Highlands, the Western Isles, the Isle of Man, and throughout Ireland. Norse dialects were spoken in the Orkney and Shetland Islands, French persisted in the Channel Islands and French or Dutch among the self-contained communities of refugees who had settled in the south and east coast towns during the last century.

The King's dominions were encircled and invaded by the sea. On the western littoral, jagged headlands and rocky cliffs fronted the stormy onslaught of the Atlantic ocean; on the eastern shores the sandy coastline slowly retreated before the pressure of the North Sea. The sea penetrated far into the interior, up the broad estuaries of Thames and Severn, Humber and Tyne, the Firths of Forth and Clyde and the narrow fjords of Loch Fyne, Loch Long, Loch Linnhe; it grasped whole handfuls from the Irish coast in wide bays and low-shored, labyrinthine loughs. In places the King's dominions were bogged and saturated by the sea, with acres of salt marsh, mud-flat and quicksand.

At least half the King's subjects derived their living directly or indirectly from the sea. Hundreds of fishing hamlets lay along his coasts. The delicacies and riches of the rocks and waters were eagerly sought. On the Cumbrian and Scottish shores the mussel beds yielded pale irregular pearls. The oysters of Colchester and Whitstable were famous; so were Selsey cockles and the shrimps of the sandy Lancashire shores. The Thames estuary had its teeming population of sprats and eels; eels, larger and richer, were the boast of northern Ireland, and lampreys were the speciality of the Severn estuary. Pilchards from Plymouth and Penzance were famous in far countries; mussels were the pride of Minehead. Plump sea-gulls were in demand, and the tiny, naked new-hatched gannet were carried away by the basket load from the Bass Rock to be swallowed, at one succulent, greasy mouthful, by revellers in Edinburgh. Berwick had long been famous for salmon and shellfish but had recently fallen upon evil times; the fisher folk, tempted by the possibility of a record haul, had broken the Sabbath and gone out in their boats. Since that time the salmon had deserted Berwick whose present distress was held up as a warning to all who despised the commandments.

From the North Sea the Yarmouth herring boats brought home by the barrel-load the silvery, living harvest of the deep, and fisher folk came in their cobles from as far north as the coast of Durham and as far west as Lyme to sell their herring on the Yarmouth quays to be split and smoked and marketed. From the ports of East Anglia—Lynn, Southwold, Dunwich, Aldeburgh—the Iceland ships went out for codling. On fish quays up and down the kingdom, housewives bargained for plaice and sole, cod and mackerel, turbot, skate, whiting and " poor John," as they familiarly called the vulgar hake, the Friday fare of the people. Sturgeon and whale, cast up on the coast, were for the King's use.

Far to the north the adventurous Scots were discovering the treasures of the Greenland whale fisheries, but the English Muscovy Company disputed the profitable fishing rights of the icy waters, and English money and resources weighted the scale against Scottish enterprise. Fishing rights in Scotland's own waters were savagely contested, for lowland intruders were opposed by the fierce people of the Highland coasts and the Hebrides, and the aggressive Hollanders fell upon both alike.[2] Round the Orkney Islands the Dutch not only trespassed on the fishing but had, on occasion, fired on the poor coracles of the Orcadians, wilfully damaged the breeding grounds of their seabirds, and plundered their villages.

Where the coasts were low-lying, hundreds of salt pans yielded the mineral wealth of the deep; refineries at Newcastle, Colchester and Chester perfected it. Where the coast was rocky, seaweed was carted inland to enrich the soil. On cliffs and sandhills men gathered samphire and sought for ambergris among the sea-drift on the shore, to sell to the kitchens of the rich. The river delicacies were also prized—fresh-water eels from Abingdon, Severn greyling, and Arundel mullet.

Thousands of small craft plied with goods and passengers from one little port to another. Stubby trows from Swansea carried the coal of South Wales across the Bristol Channel; Minehead and Barnstaple exchanged wares and travellers with Tenby and the ports of southern Ireland, Waterford, Wexford, Youghal, Kinsale and Cork. Fifty sail from these Irish ports would put into the Severn estuary for the Bristol fair in July. The small ships of Perth, Arbroath and Montrose connected the villages of Scotland's eastern seaboard better than the indifferent roads of the interior; those of Glasgow and Greenock linked the western Highlands with the Isles and Ireland. Hull, Yarmouth, King's Lynn, Ipswich and Harwich commanded England's east coast carrying trade. A fleet of three hundred ships carried Newcastle coal to London. Dumbarton and Whitehaven sent colliers to Dublin, and the Irish Mail (wind and weather permitting) went from Chester. Ayr and Irvine traded to France; Leith, Dundee, Aberdeen and Stonehaven to Norway, Denmark and the Low Countries. A cross-Channel traffic from Dartmouth and Exeter brought in the flax and hemp of Normandy and Brittany and exported it again as sail cloth and buckram. Gloucester, queenly among the meads of Severn, assembled the woolsacks of the Cotswold country for shipment to Bristol and beyond. Travellers for France took ship at Dover; for the Low Countries and Germany, at Harwich or from London.

From Bristol, Plymouth, Southampton ships set sail for the Atlantic crossing with a hundred or two hundred men, women and children bound for the American colonies, and supplies of malt and meal, shirts and shoes, cloth and hardware for the settlers already there. Having discharged their cargo they turned northward, bought in Newfoundland fish, sold it two thousand miles away at Cadiz in Spain, and so came home again rich with Spanish wines.[3]

The King's subjects made a living from the sea in other ways besides fishing and merchandise. Lundy Island, the Orkneys, the Scilly Islands sheltered pirates; on the Hebrides, on the Blasket islands, on the Cornish coast and on the black, appalling cliffs of county Clare, delusive fires might burn by night to lure the lost vessel to the mercy of reefs and robbers. The great men of these parts, in return for a share in the profits of piracy and wrecking, would sometimes help their wilder neighbours and tenantry in deceiving and defying the government. A recent attempt to convert Stornoway into a more reputable port by settling merchant folk within it had been stubbornly defeated by the inhabitants. The depredations by sea and land of the Clan Macdonald had been fairly checked on the mainland of Scotland, but it was not two years since the *Susanna* of Limerick, driven against the coast of Lewis by a stormy sea, had been systematically plundered by the Macdonalds under one of their principal chieftains. Between northern Ireland and the Western Isles native coracles plied a traffic in crude liquor and fugitive criminals. They defied alike His Majesty's customs and His Majesty's justice, and preyed from time to time on the English-speaking settlers from London or the Scottish lowlands who were trying to turn the wild Ulster of the O'Neills and Macdonnells into a farming and flax-raising country.

Outside the great ports of the kingdom, foreign ships might be ill received. A Dutch ship damaged by Dunkirk pirates in the Channel had limped into Seaford for help and shelter, but the men of Seaford robbed the crew, ransacked the ship and stood at sulky defiance when the King's government commanded them to make good the damage. The inhabitants of Dunbar turned out with horses and wagons to carry off the cargo of a foreign ship that ran ashore a few miles from their town. A Dutch East Indiaman, storm-driven into an Irish port, forestalled any possible hostility by covering the place with its great ordnance and landing a party to kidnap the son of its richest citizen. The crew of another, which had taken refuge from pirates in a remote Irish haven, terrorised the inhabitants, and refused to pay customs on the goods sold to lighten the burden. As the cargo was of spices, worth two hundred thousand pounds, the King's Deputy in Dublin considered the possibility of forcibly detaining and seizing it all, a design which was foiled because this armed giant of the ocean was more than a match for the English vessels sent to deal with it.[4]

Dunkirk pirates made English waters unsafe. The Barbary corsairs raided the Devon and Cornish coasts and, repeatedly, those of southern Ireland, so that the slave-markets of Africa knew the fair-skinned boys and girls of Plymouth, Barnstaple and Baltimore.

The King was enlarging his navy to protect his people. He envisaged the addition of two major warships to his naval strength every year, while experiments were being made with a new type of ship, the small swift-sailing whelps. At Deptford where Drake's *Golden Hind* still lay at anchor slowly rotting, crowds gathered to watch the amazing progress of the greatest ship ever to be built in England. Still nameless, she rose majestic in the stocks, while the best craftsmen in the country completed the carving, the gilding and the paint which gave elegance and richness to her formidable bulk.

The King's principal shipyards lay along the southern shore of the Thames estuary. A few miles farther up the river, the gigantic London and its satellite villages, the centre of maritime and mercantile England, covered five miles of its northern and three miles of its southern bank with houses, quays and towers. Westward, the buildings ran out along the river bank as far as Westminster; painted barges, cushioned and capacious, were moored at the watergates of the great lords' houses that fringed the Strand. Traffic came and went by water, bearing lawyers to Westminster Hall and officials, servants, courtiers to the King's sprawling palace-village of Whitehall. Eastward from the Tower, the Ratcliff Highway joined Wapping, Shadwell and Limehouse, mariners' villages looking out upon the great ships at anchor in the estuary, with green country and windmills at their backs; they bought in the produce of Essex, coarse hard cheeses and salted meat, to provision the outgoing ships. On the south bank, houses and quays were continuous through Rotherhithe and Southwark; thence they trailed away into the region of disreputable gaiety, the pleasure gardens and bear pits, theatres and brothels of Blackfriars and Bankside. A strip of marshland divided this district from the Archbishop's low-lying red-brick palace at Lambeth and the fields whence, on warm summer evenings, young Londoners went bathing. This great urban conglomerate numbered already close on a quarter of a million souls. In two wide half-circles, north and south, the outlying villages reached inwards to London, as London reached outwards towards them. They grew hay for London horses and vegetables for London tables; their windmills ground the corn for London bread and their innkeepers and dairy maids provided ale and cheesecakes, plums and cream for Londoners on holiday afternoons.

In the recently opened Hyde Park, on London's western perimeter, rich citizens strolled with courtiers and visiting gentry. The occupants of smart coaches showed themselves off in the Ring; there was horse racing and foot racing, two bowling greens, a gaming house and an eating house, and dairymaids walked round with milk for the thirsty. For the humbler citizens of London, Finsbury fields were a favourite walking place although of late years much spoiled by the brick-works which supplied London's builders. Within the city itself Moor-fields was set aside for citizens' wives and maids; here they could hang out their laundry or spread it on the grass; shady trees, specially planted, bore the names of those who had placed them there, and wooden shelters had been put up against sudden rain. It was pleasant by daylight but with nightfall it grew disreputable, even dangerous.

London was first and foremost a seaport. The tidal river lapped at the streets' end; high masts and furled sails closed the narrow vistas of its ancient alleys. Greater than all the other seaports of the realm together, London was the mart of the known world. The Venetian envoy, who had experience in ships and shipping, reckoned that twenty thousand craft, small and great, were to be seen from London in a day. Rowing-boats and ferry-boats carried the citizens upstream and down, or from bank to bank; heavy barges distributed goods from London up river, and brought back to London the produce of the Thames valley. Merchantmen from Antwerp and Amsterdam, Calais and Bordeaux, Lisbon, Leghorn and Cadiz, Bergen, Hamburg and Archangel, Constantinople, the East and the West Indies, rode at anchor in the Pool or unloaded at the wharves. Some were privately owned, others belonged to trading companies— the Muscovy Company, the Levant Company, the West India Company and the Merchant Adventurers. Greatest of all towered the huge ships of the East India Company, " mobile, maritime fortresses " embattled against piracy and storm.[5]

London was a huge port and a huge town and, at its worst, as dark and wicked as such towns are. In the porch of St. Paul's, in the arcaded shopping centre of the New Exchange, the "coney catcher " loitered to ensnare some wide-eyed country rabbit with a little money in his foolish paws. The " jeering, cunning courtesan, the rooking, roaring boy " conspired to wheedle and bully unsuspecting fools. All day the shouts of oyster and tripe women, the swearing of draymen, the creak and clatter of hackney coaches dazed and deafened the newcomer, and after sunset

> " riotous sinful plush and tell-tale spurs
> Walk Fleet Street and the Strand, when the soft stirs
> Of bawdy ruffled silks turn night to day." [6]

London was not a safe place for the innocent, although those accustomed to it, born in " the scent of Newcastle coal and the hearing of Bow bells," knew how to avoid the dangers, and the more experienced revellers who came in for a spree, like Sir Humphrey Mildmay who got home " mad, merry and late " after " playing the fool with two punks in a barge on the Thames," were very well able to take care of themselves.[7] But country boys and girls, driven to the capital by bad times or tempted by tales of easy money, drifted through disappointment and disaster into the criminal depths of the city, to die in the common gaol or of the " Tyburn ague " on the gallows.

As the town grew, and it was growing fast, its gaieties

increased. Bear gardens and pleasure gardens spread along Bankside, puppet-theatres showed *Bel and the Dragon* and other apocryphal matter; peep-shows advertised *The Creation of the World* represented to the life in pasteboard. The two principal theatres, now both covered in and lit by wax candles, attracted the rich and fashionable. Blackfriars on Bankside carried on the Shakespeare-Burbage tradition, with Taylor, thought to be the greatest Hamlet yet seen, and Swanston's much praised Othello; the portly comedian Lowin played Falstaff and the whole Jonsonian gallery of grotesques, and the fair youth Stephen Hammerton drew tears with his Juliet and Desdemona. Christopher Beeston's company at the Cockpit in Drury Lane concentrated on more modern topical works. These two had the highest reputation though half a dozen lesser theatres, more old-fashioned, open-roofed and playing by daylight, still drew large audiences. A French company brought over the neo-classical drama from Paris but the Londoners, taking it into their heads to be scandalised at seeing women on the stage, pelted them with rotten apples. The Queen, who patronised the company, was indignant, and after a little the Londoners forgot their moral views and accepted the novelty.

The tidal Thames, creeping into the heart of the city up many an open inlet, ditch and hithe, did something to purify the town. Fresh water had been brought within reach by the New River Company which had diverted the river Lea to Islington. But rosemary and jasmine were in constant demand to disguise the putrid smells of streets and houses. London children already suffered badly from rickets, and the various epidemic diseases vaguely defined as plague caused ten thousand deaths in the bad year 1636. In the following year, still bad, there was something over three thousand victims.

The respectable citizens of London drew together against the underworld of the criminal, the drunken, the defeated. Their city might be one of the wickedest in Europe; it was also, as a natural consequence, one of the most austerely pious. The virtues of plain living and hard work were extolled and practised;

the Bible and the hundred churches stood firm against the ballads and the playhouses. Religion was a fighting force in the city because it could never cease from fighting, " the miles between Hell and any place on earth being shorter than those between London and St. Albans."

Out of London and into London came and went carriers' carts by road and barges by water. The King's posts started for Edinburgh thrice weekly, but for the most part citizens relied on independent carriers and, except when they found it useful, looked with some resentment on government enterprise. Provincial carriers called at least once in the week, and sometimes more than once, at various London taverns; for Oxford and Northampton the carts left daily. The industrious John Taylor, doggerel poet, scribbler, traveller and busybody, had compiled a *Carriers' Cosmography* listing the available services, but his work had not been easy: the carriers had taken him at first for a government spy collecting information " to bring carriers under some new taxation."

For all heavier goods water-transport was generally esteemed better than the roads, which were rough at best, impassable in bad weather, and not free from thieves. The coastal boats loaded their cargo into barges in the reaches below London and the barges carried goods up the Thames to Reading and up the Lea to Ware. West coast shipping came into Gloucester whence the Severn barges carried the freight to Shrewsbury. The Yorkshire Ouse served northern Yorkshire, the Trent the midlands. The rivers, well-disposed by nature and assisted by the ingenuity of man, had made the English a relatively united and economically interdependent people. Water-transport could not link the wilder country of Wales and had not been exploited in Ireland. The rivers of Scotland, the rapid Forth, the headstrong Tay, the sandy silted Clyde, were beyond the control of seventeenth-century engineering. With few bridges, with troublesome fords often swollen by rain, they emphasised

33

the divisions of Scotland. The elements of unity and prosperity were concentrated in England.

Next after the sea, the King's subjects drew their living from wool and all the industries surrounding it. They herded sheep on the Sussex and Wiltshire downs, in the rich pastures of Cotswold, in the Thames valley, on the Lancashire fells and the Lincolnshire and Yorkshire wolds, in the Scottish lowlands and the Welsh mountains. Wool towns had grown up wherever streams gave water-power enough to drive the mills which washed and whitened it. In manufacture the regions had their specialities. Scotland's plaids protected both highlanders and lowlanders against the rigours of the climate and were exported to all the colder regions of Europe; they were Scotland's principal export and worth more than all the rest together. Wales made coarse friezes, so did North Devon; Carmarthen specialised in flannel. Blankets from Witney in Oxfordshire were famous all over England. Bolton and Manchester wove the soft-textured woollens confusingly called cottons—confusingly because Manchester was already importing Smyrna cotton for her fustians and dimities. (Derby, Macclesfield, Leek and Nottingham, were abandoning wool for the manufacture of silk.) Bradford specialised in rugs and cushions; Kendal in Westmorland, Bewdley in Worcestershire, and Monmouth in the Welsh marshes specialised in stockings and caps. Woodstock and Ilminster made gloves. The best cloth came mostly from the south, although Leeds and Halifax led the way for Yorkshire with fine broadcloth; in general, broadcloth was made round Reading and Newbury and in the Wiltshire towns. Wiltshire cloth was sold over all Europe, and some, shipped by enterprising city merchants to Ragusa, was marketed far within the dominions of the Turk. Coggeshall and Colchester were the centres of the coarse cloth manufacture—the baize and serges—of southern East Anglia; their wares went in bulk to religious houses abroad, and friars of Spain, Portugal and Italy were clothed by the Puritan weavers of Suffolk and Essex. Norwich, once the leading wool town of England, had lost its supremacy and was visibly declining. Gloucester was now, after the all-conquering London, queen of the wool trade strategically placed on the navigable Severn, linked by it to Shrewsbury where the fleeces of Wales were sold, and to Bristol the greatest outgoing port, after London, in the realm. Gloucester also drew to herself the famous fleeces of the white, square-bodied, long-necked Cotswold sheep, the greatest wool-bearers in the country.

York was for the north what Gloucester was for the west; and York claimed also to be what London was for the south. It was the northern centre for the exchange and distribution of raw wool and the finished cloth. But York was also the second capital of England, the seat of an Archbishop, the centre of the King's government in the north parts and, in its own opinion, in no way inferior and in many ways superior to London. Its magnificent walls, its lofty Minster, its forty churches, proclaimed a greatness which defied decline. While the King beautified London, his representative at York, the Lord President of the North, had majestically extended his official residence in the noblest European manner. It was rivalled by the mansion of a private gentleman, Sir Arthur Ingram, whose palatial Italianate house and garden were the wonder of the city. As for good fare York boasted that it could do better than London; northern appetites were hearty and "the ordinary in York would be a feast in London."

The making of cloth was, for the most part, a cottage industry. Women and children sat at their doors carding, spinning or knitting. In East Anglia the big windows of the cottages gave light to the looms which were the livelihood of the family. There were enterprises also on a larger scale, especially in Wiltshire and East Anglia. At Colchester a Dutch settler employed five hundred men and women, and was so hated by the independent weavers that, in a lean year, they burnt his mill.

The factory was not the only enemy of the English weaver. Merchants found it increasingly profitable to sell raw wool abroad, instead of finished cloth. Home fashions too were changing; boots were making long woollen hose superfluous, and linen caps were neater and more comfortable than woollen. Weavers, knitters, spinners everywhere, but especially in Essex, suffered the enforced idleness which brought want and hunger.

High in importance in his subjects' lives, after the sea and the sheep, was the mineral wealth of the King's dominions. In recent years the " Black Indies " of the Durham minefields had begun to yield their riches; coal was mined too in Lancashire, Derbyshire, South Wales and in southern Scotland, and surface workings were frequent over all the English midlands. Some of the northern mines were deep; one shaft went down three hundred feet, reputedly the deepest in Europe, and at Culross on the coast of Fife the workings ran far out under the sea. Coal was a principal export from Scotland, but in England coal was rapidly replacing wood as the favourite fuel, and little went abroad. It came by sea from Newcastle to London and thence by barge inland. At first it had been carried partly in vessels from the east coast ports and partly in London ships, but of late years Newcastle citizens had developed their own coal fleet of over three hundred vessels. With the rising demand for coal the Newcastle hostmen, as the middlemen who transported and shipped the fuel were called, had become rich and powerful. The London faggot-mongers, as their trade in wood declined, had tried to wrest the transport of the new fuel from the " Lords of Coal " in the north, but the King favoured Newcastle and contemplated granting the hostmen a monopoly of the transport. London, now warmed almost wholly by coal fires, envied the rising wealth of the black seaport in the north.[8]

While the quarrel between the transporters raged, the coal miners everywhere remained an outcast minority, a black, savage people living in hovels round the primitive workings. In Scotland men worked so unwillingly in the mines that the old principle of serfdom had been revived by statute in Fife, and the miners were held by law, from generation to generation, in a bondage whence there was no escape. Women and children helped the men, and in some places it was said that whole families camped underground from week's end to week's end, coming up only on the Sabbath for compulsory kirk. In both England and Scotland the absconding felon or homeless vagabond was liable to be forced into this despised and dangerous toil. The miners kept themselves apart from the rest of the population and retained, not unnaturally, terrible and diabolic beliefs. They worked with unprotected tallow candles, and none knew better than they the fearful things that the demons from Hell could do when they unloosed the fire hidden in the depths of the earth.

The miners who worked for metal were more respected, although they too formed a class apart from their neighbours. Often, like the tin-miners of Cornwall, they lived under laws of their own. The lead mines of Mendip were worked by yeomen-miners; by the "custom of the hill" a man might stake his claim to his own small working wherever he struck lucky and set up his windlass. Lead workings pock-marked these hills for miles, causing roads to cave in and creating pitfalls for grazing cattle.

Copper was mined in Westmorland; copper, zinc and silver in the west country where German workers had been brought in by Queen Elizabeth. There were brass foundries near Bristol. King and Court entertained the highest hopes of the veins of silver opened up in South Wales by the indefatigable prospector Thomas Bushell.

Iron, after coal, was the chief mineral wealth of the country. It was a principal industry of Sussex and was worked also in Staffordshire, Derbyshire and Westmorland. Some doubt was felt about the workings in the Forest of Dean; as wood was still used for smelting the ore, the King feared that expansion of the iron works would destroy too much of the forest. The forests of Sussex had already been consumed, and in Worcestershire they were fast disappearing because wood was needed for the salt refineries which had sprung up near the saline springs. Unlimited destruction of timber could not be allowed, English oak being of the first necessity for shipbuilding. Recent experiments in smelting with coal might, it was hoped, solve this critical problem.

English ironmongery lacked distinction. The coarse knives of Sheffield and the cheap swords of Birmingham were widely despised but widely used. The swordsmiths of Hounslow had a higher reputation, and Ripon was distinguished for the excellence of its spurs. A smear of black country ran right across south Staffordshire whose "iron men" returned the hostility and contempt with which the sheep-herding "moorlanders" of north Staffordshire looked upon them. Iron-working was a domestic industry given over to nails and pins, and families worked industriously each at its own small forge. In Staffordshire too there was a local pottery industry, conducted in the same humble domestic manner. But earthenware pitchers and trenchers were not much used outside the clay regions; in general, wooden trenchers and leather bottles were used by the poorer sort, pewter by the better off. The finest harness and leather work was made on the edge of the Cotswolds, at Chipping Norton, or Burford, as famous for saddles as was Woodstock for gloves.

The islands were well supplied with building stone. The quarries of Scotland yielded granite. Marble was worked in Derbyshire and northern Ireland, alabaster in Lincolnshire, Staffordshire and on both sides of the Bristol Channel, at Penarth and at Minehead. There were slate quarries in Wales, Cornwall and Northampton. The Cotswolds had their own beautiful limestone; Devon and Dorset mansions were built from the fine yellow stone of Hamden Hill above Montacute.

The beautiful limestone from Portland in Dorset was coming into fashion and black marble from Ireland was sometimes used for decoration: materials were brought from great distances to produce a sophisticated and European style of architecture. But in much English building local styles and materials still prevailed. Brick was common for large buildings over most of the South although in the North and West timber was much used. A conservative people, the English retained Gothic details of decoration in spite of cosmopolitan Renaissance influence, and English carpenters showed remarkable skill in reproducing the ingenuity of Gothic stonecarving in their decorative woodwork. Inigo Jones, responding to the European fashion, denied to his workmen their individual fantasies; he—like the King in another sphere—decreed that the single mind of the master-architect should plan the entire building with all its ornaments. But outside the capital city medieval freedom of invention lingered yet; the carved lintels of Worcestershire doorways and the plaster ornamentation of Essex and Suffolk houses displayed the simple, gay imagination of the craftsmen who made them. While Inigo Jones conceived of London as a sophisticated European city, John Abell, master architect of Herefordshire, built the last and largest masterpieces of the local style, the elaborate and ambitious timber town-halls of Hereford and Leominster. The masons and builders of Scotland, by tradition and culture more closely connected with Europe and especially with France, had brought to maturity a style in which Renaissance detail was combined with the asperities of the native manner. Turrets, lintels, and doorways, which recalled the softer landscape of the Loire, lightened the harsh architecture evolved in a cold climate and an unstable society, and carved staircases and painted walls and ceilings showed the taste of the richer and more modern lords and citizens.

England was rich in mineral springs, some of only local fame, others famous throughout the land. Bath was the oldest and, though much fallen from its Roman splendour, still a place of considerable resort for health and pleasure. Visitors could enjoy organised entertainments such as dancing and fencing matches, but the chief amusement was to watch the sick people, of all ages and sexes, stark naked but for linen caps, sitting immersed in the great bath. The younger spa, Tunbridge, which offered good public rooms and gaming tables, was temporarily the more fashionable; the fortunate visitor might see " six earls and lords in a morning at the Wells."

The saline springs of Droitwich and the medicinal waters of Buxton and Matlock were locally famous. Physicians spoke marvels of the waters at Knaresborough but they attracted the attention of the curious rather than the sick, because of their petrifying action.

Mining and manufacture notwithstanding, the King's dominions were still essentially rural. His people lived in small communities, were proud of local achievements, prejudiced in the local interest, and very close to the soil.

The countryside offered many simple delights. Izaak Walton and his companions could pass a summer's day in happy argument on the relative merits of their favourite sports, catch trout and chub in the clear streams, listen to the milkmaids singing and watch with tranquil interest the striped caterpillars on the leafy trees and the painted butterflies in the meadows. John Milton in one of his rare idle hours may have seen such dancing in the chequered shade as he attributed to " the upland hamlets." Girls as pretty if not as eloquent as Perdita gave out posies at the sheep-shearing. On winter evenings the young jigged and danced by firelight at Leap Candle or the Cushion Dance; all the year long they had their singing rounds and games, Sellenger's Round, John Come Kiss Me, and Barley Break. Rush-bearing ceremonies, blessing of cornfields and of springs, crowning the May Queen, roasting geese at Michaelmas and sucking pig at Lammas, varied the laborious year. Free beer flowed merrily at Whitsun-ales and harvest festivals, and boys in wigs and petticoats bounced about on hobby-horses to the uproarious delight of all. In strongly Protestant districts traditional Hallowe'en jollities were being ingeniously transferred to Gunpowder Treason Day on November 5th. But religious disapproval so far had had little effect on the celebrations which marked the end of August when London's Bartholomew Fair lasted close on a fortnight, and all over Lancashire and Somerset the wakes were held, usually in the churches, with dancing, drinking, pipe, tabor and fiddle. During the time of general holiday between Christmas and Twelfth Night a Lord of Misrule was still sometimes elected to preside over the festivities, and the old mockery of church ceremonies, permitted in medieval times, was occasionally indulged, but at greater peril. The King, when he came to hear of it, viewed with grave disapproval a swineherd's impersonation of an Anglican priest at a mock marriage. At all times of year, bridals and christenings were an excuse for merry-making and the distribution of gifts, garters, posies, ribbons and—if they could be afforded—gloves. In the lowlands of Scotland the poor people had thriftily invented the " penny bridal," an occasion when each guest paid his penny towards the day's revelling. As anyone could become a guest at such feasts, they were the occasion of noisy mirth, on which the respectable frowned and the Kirk made determined but unsuccessful war.

In the summer months picnic parties from the towns rode out into the country with baskets full of pasties, and London apprentices carried their girls to Islington, Tottenham and Hogsden for cheese cakes and cream. The rich and fashionable favoured the Three Pigeons at Brentford for week-end parties. The sports and pleasures of the gentlefolk were hawking and hunting, and bowls as they grew older; they matched their hawks and greyhounds against each other, and their horses at the local race meetings which were becoming regular events. Sometimes, as at Kiplingcotes in Yorkshire, a piece of plate was the reward of the winner. Newmarket and Epsom Downs were already famous, and horses, like Bay Tarrell, a Newmarket winner, and Toby, whose owner, a London merchant, had gilded his hoofs, were popular favourites. With racing went the bagpipes, and the winner was escorted through the crowds to their shrill music.

Travelling pedlars and mountebanks entertained the villages with their wares and their news; they performed simple operations, drew teeth, cut corns, lanced boils and successfully straightened wry-necked children by cutting the tendons. The crowder, or fiddler, ready to play for any festivity, the rope-dancer, the juggler, and the showman with a bear, or perhaps a monster, were popular figures in the villages and country towns. In Scotland a solitary camel, the King's property, was leased out to a warden who was permitted to show him off, by tuck of drum, at all times of day except during divine service.[9]

In their leisure time students and apprentices competed with the bow; village boys played ninepins, cudgels, or a rough kind of football. In some places local sports were annually held. The famous Cotswold Games, sponsored by jolly Captain Dover, took place every year on a broad-topped down that still bears his name. From miles around came men and boys to compete in running, wrestling, quarter staff and shooting, for a great distribution of prizes and favours. The enterprise enjoyed royal favour and aimed at creating a new Olympia. The King's Court had graced it once with their presence and several poets had celebrated it in rhyme.

The people had the free and spontaneous gaiety of those who live in the moment because the next may bring disaster. The happy lovers who in the summer embraced "between the acres of the rye," would in a famine-stricken winter cling together for warmth before a cold hearthstone. They enjoyed the good times, they endured the bad. Drought, frost, fire, flood were the enemies of all who lived by the land.

With the easy laughter and song went also a primitive delight in violence. Cock-fighting and bull- and bear-baiting were the sports of all classes when they could get to them, and a light-hearted squire like Sir Humphrey Mildmay in Essex would from time to time let out his bull to be baited by the village dogs. Cock-throwing, which meant pelting the poor birds with sticks or stones, was a traditional annual sport among village boys. The ducking of scolds, or leading them through the village bitted and bridled, and compelling their husbands to ride the pole were occasional village amusements. Domestic quarrels were violent in all classes of society; a London regulation forbade wife-beating after nine in the evening because of the noise. Gentlemen who were known to " fling cushions at one another's heads only in sport and for exercise " descended with ease from horse-play to fisticuffs; blows were exchanged on very small provocation and in the most unseemly places. The

Murgatroyds, for instance, annoyed because another family walked into church ahead of them, knocked down and trampled on their rivals, causing a disturbance the echoes of which were several years dying away in the ecclesiastical courts.

The physical conditions of life were not easy for anyone. Few anodynes were known and none were effective; rich and poor alike suffered with little help all the varied torments of the flesh. Familiarity with pain bred, in all classes, a certain stoicism, a deep acceptance of suffering as part of the necessary order of the world and a willingness to inflict it and to see it inflicted.

The King's dominions differed greatly in the quality and character of their soil. In many regions, village communities still endeavoured to be self-supporting in necessities. Small crops of rye, barley and oats, beans and peas were sown in strips in the common field. Hogs pastured on the common or the beech mast in the woods, and were mostly slaughtered at Michaelmas when their lean flesh, smoked, provided the winter meat, and their bladders, blown up, made footballs for the winter's sport. Even in the Scottish Highlands the cattle-herding clans had their sparse crops of oats, sown and reaped by their women. Only in parts of Ireland nomadic communities still existed who scorned the plough and lived, year in and year out, on the milk and flesh of their cattle, such edible grasses and seaweeds as grew without their help, and, from time to time, the plunder of an English settler's barn.

The cattle-farming of the Celtic peoples in Scotland and Ireland survived from early times; their herds of lean and shaggy beasts had the freedom of the mountains and wilds. The Highland clans, ennobling the struggle for provender with the bloody romance of clan feuds, disputed their difficult country among themselves. No one else wanted it. But in Ireland, whose low-lying, spongy meadows provided good pasture, settlers from England and southern Scotland were thrusting the native people and their herds back into the bogs while they introduced better breeds of cattle and more economic methods.

Sheep-breeding in England had, for the time being, reached

its utmost expansion. The towns which had fattened upon it had to be fed with other things than fleeces; experiments were made and methods discussed for increasing the yield of the earth, improving crops, developing wheat and barley in place of the cruder rye and oats. More and more land—for there was still much waste and forest land in England—was used for growing corn and raising cattle. Cattle for milk and meat and hides were being extensively bred in Devon and Somerset, in Herefordshire and the Midlands. The old complaint of the poor in the previous century that the sheep had eaten up the arable land was changed to a new one—that the cultivated land was eating up the common and the forest. The poor man needed the common and the forest so that he could collect firewood and pasture his hogs. Great landowners from time to time enclosed the waste land, but they were not the only encroachers. The yeoman and the labourer also made their surreptitious advances, and small hamlets grew up on the edge of forest and heath, the penurious outposts of landless squatters.

The regions had their specialities. The Sussex wheatear, a tiny bird, was praised as " a little lump of flying sugar equal to the best ortolans of France." In Kent acres of cherry trees provided a favourite fruit for London. In Herefordshire and Worcestershire, and in Somerset, especially about Taunton, and in Gloucestershire, " that rich and fruitful garden-shire ",[10] the far-spread apple orchards filled the autumn vats for cider. Hampshire claimed the sweetest honey in the kingdom; so did Bishop Auckland. Cheddar was famous for cheese, Banbury for cheese and cakes, Tewkesbury for mustard, Pomfret and Nottingham for licorice, and wide fields of crocus round Saffron Walden explained its name. About London for twenty or thirty miles the towns and villages were set in a chessboard of vegetable gardens, cultivated in the Dutch manner, growing asparagus, young green peas, cauliflower and carrots for the luxury market of the capital.

The dairy produce of Devon was gaining reputation, and the fat cattle of Herefordshire ambled along the drove roads, at a comfortable rate of eight miles a day, to their doom in Smithfield market. Northumberland boasted plump chickens and all manner of poultry. There was not much to be said for Cumberland or Westmorland where travellers from the south were shocked at the poverty and smallness of the hamlets, the bare feet and uncouth accent of the people. Carlisle cathedral, to the southerner, was nothing but " a great wild country church," and the city's aldermen wore blue bonnets, like roving Scots, instead of felt or beaver hats. But game birds and venison were plentiful in the north parts and " a huge standing water called Windermere " produced a most delicious fish called a char.[11]

The poverty of Cumberland, which shocked southern travellers, was equalled by the poverty which met the English traveller's eyes when he crossed the Border. Even in a gentleman's house flitches of bacon hung from the rafters in the smoke of the best room, and the lady of the place did not always wear stockings. The women of the one-roomed, turf-thatched, mud-floored hovels wore their petticoats kilted above the knee, but their feet and ankles were clean because they trod their washing instead of handling it.

The best of Scotland was not on the Border. In Lothian, cattle and sheep at pasture, and strips of oats and barley surrounded Edinburgh with an air of modest prosperity. The stone-built capital of Scotland, wedged between rock and loch, its tall forbidding tenements crowned by the airily graceful lantern tower of St. Giles, was like no other town in the islands. It was not, by any but Scottish standards, a rich town; the winds that whistled through its ravine streets blew upon marketing women shrouded in heavy plaids—the material of which, as an English traveller snobbishly remarked, his countrymen made saddle cloths. They were a hard-working, hard-headed people indifferent to outward appearances, very sure of themselves, independent and proud.

West from Edinburgh in the Lennox and in Clydesdale good mixed farming was to be found, orchard, corn and grazing land, fissured here and there with new workings of coal. The city of

Glasgow which commanded at once its outlet to the sea and the system of roads, such as it was, that linked the south-west of Scotland had flourished considerably. It had as yet little reputation as a port, for the sandy Clyde was too shallow to take any but the smallest ships.

The region of Galloway was relatively prosperous because of the steady traffic that passed through its little ports for northern Ireland; it was also famous for sheep and mettlesome Galloway nags. Other regions of good farming, especially for barley and oats, were the carse of Gowrie, the gracious region between Perth and Montrose, and that strangely blest strip of land north of Cairn Gorm, fringing the northern sea, the " golden planure " of Moray. The cattle, deer and small wild animals of the Highlands, otters, badgers and ferocious martens, provided furs and hides which were a valuable export; even the skins of wolves which still roamed the wilder mountains had their price. Beyond the Highlands, the people of the more open northern lands of Ross and Caithness lived upon fish and cattle, a spare, hard existence which did not prevent the men of Caithness from being, in the opinion of the loquacious traveller William Lithgow, " the best and most bountiful Christmas keepers (the Greeks excepted) that ever I saw in the Christian world." [12]

In England and in the more fertile parts of Scotland intelligent farmers and landowners were considering ways of improving their methods and their land. In England the prevalence of common-field farming made large-scale experiments difficult, and in Scotland the system of land tenure, by which leases were terminable from year to year, discouraged long-term planning. But experiment was in the air. New crops and new methods were discussed by the educated. Potatoes and turnips were being tried but had not gained any popularity. Lucerne, clover and sainfoin had been suggested as possible crops to provide winter fodder for cattle, and thus make the wholesale slaughter of beasts every autumn unnecessary. But the ideas put forward by progressive theorists who wished to enclose all the common land and so curtail the spread of cattle diseases were highly unpopular. Occasionally a landowner like Sir Richard Weston at Sutton Place in Surrey conducted experiments in irrigation and the improvement of soil on a large scale. The King had given authority for the draining of some of the fen country, and a successful beginning had been made with Hatfield Chase, a water-logged region between Yorkshire and Lincolnshire which the Dutch engineer Vermuyden had reclaimed. But farmers complained that the local price of corn had gone down owing to the plentiful harvests from the new land.

Vermuyden was now reclaiming the fenlands round Ely, a scheme in which the Court was interested and into which the Earl of Bedford and a number of other distinguished share-holders had put large sums of money. This improvement, and others like it, was bitterly opposed by the fenmen who had long lived by fishing and fowling and had no inclination to see their hunting-grounds turned over to grazing:

> For they do mean all fens to drain and water overmaster,
> All will be dry and we must die, 'cause Essex calves want
> pasture. . . .
> The feather'd fowls have wings to fly to other nations,
> But we have no such things to help our transportations.
> We must give place (oh grievous case) to horned beasts and
> cattle,
> Except that we can all agree to drive them out by battle.[13]

The fenmen decided on battle. They assailed Vermuyden's workmen with showers of stones and repeatedly destroyed the works.

New manures, new methods of sowing and ploughing, the introduction of new domestic animals were also discussed. Richard Childe, with some knowledge of the East, seriously considered the introduction of the elephant: a beast " very serviceable for carriage, fifteen men usually riding on his back together, and he is not chargeable to keep." [14]

New fruits and plants were assiduously cultivated by the

rich. The King's gardener John Tradescant had introduced a small French willow tree, excellent for making baskets, as well as the merely ornamental acacia and lilac. His interesting botanical garden, recently opened at Lambeth, was rivalled by that created for the university of Oxford by Lord Danby. But experimental gardens, beautiful or medicinal, were being made everywhere; Sir Arthur Ingram's at York, ornamented with statues in the Italian manner, was famous and so was the fine garden of Moray House in Edinburgh. Many a country gentleman spent time and trouble introducing new fruits to his orchard and new flowers to his garden—the better kinds of apples and pears and such novelties as apricots, vines and raspberry canes, the Portugal quince, figs, melons, currants and damsons, walnuts, almonds and the edible chestnut. The flowering peach and laburnum were already popular, and Sir John Oglander in the Isle of Wight, recorded proudly in his diary that he had planted "in one knot all sorts of French flowers and tulips . . . Some roots cost me 10d. a root." [15]

Neither the cultivation of their gardens nor wider schemes for reclaiming land could assuage the land hunger of the English or the lowland Scots. The Scots indeed had for generations now emigrated by families to the Baltic shores of North Germany and Poland, there to build up the Scottish–Baltic trade. The number of these foreign-dwelling Scots was estimated at nearly thirty thousand. But for new land both Scots and English looked towards Ireland. Scots and English intruders flourished in Ulster, English intruders in Munster; dairy farming had begun round Waterford and in Wicklow where English cattle had been introduced; good crops of rye and barley grew round Dublin; the government was encouraging the cultivation of flax for linen in Ulster; there was a growing export trade in Irish timber.

Another promised land awaited the adventurous on the farther side of the Atlantic Ocean, where pioneers were planting their English cultivation and their English names—Plymouth, Taunton, Boston, Ipswich—on the shores of a gigantic unknown continent. Not very many of the King's subjects lived in this perilous land, in his opinion too far from his control: from Newfoundland to the Caribbean, not more than fifty thousand. For King Charles it sometimes seemed fifty thousand too many. If his people wanted more land, let them go to Ireland where he could watch over their religion, education and morals. The stream of adventurers went for other causes than the need for land alone; far from his paternal vigilance they practised uncouth religions and strange politics. He was considering whether it would not be wise to prohibit their going altogether.

The structure of society was still hierarchic, although with differences in the nature and the rigidity of the hierarchy in different regions. In England at the topmost level were noblemen of the old school who kept two hundred servants of all degrees, from their Master of the Horse and Gentleman Ushers, their Yeomen of the Buttery and Pantry, to laundresses and grooms, and who went on journeys with a trumpeter to give notice of their coming.[16] At the lowest level was the day labourer with one coarse shirt to his back, earning a night's lodging and a share of pease-pudding, and enjoying from time to time the free spectacle of the great lord and his train passing by. Great as was the distance between high and low, no insurmountable barriers separated, one from the other, the many classes in between. There was unceasing movement up and down. A man might rise or sink by his own good fortune or his own endeavours. Gentility was to be acquired by intellect or valour or wealth; by English custom, all clergy, all university students, all lawyers and any man who had held command in an army might write himself down " gentleman ", no matter who his father had been. In every generation tradesmen and yeomen made their way into the gentry not to mention the clerks and secretaries who rose by service to the great lords or the Court. The last step into the nobility was open to those who could pay the price for it either by direct purchase or by services to the Crown. The older nobility might look with contempt on these sons and grandsons of aldermen financiers and clerks, these earls and barons who had paid cash down for their titles—Middlesex, Portland, Clare, Cork—but they received them in their houses and eagerly sought their daughters in marriage.

The downward movement was as persistent as the upward, and the feckless gentleman who wasted his estates could drop in a few years to the criminal depths of society. The attempt to save the situation by abducting an heiress was made more often than it succeeded. In the summer of 1637 Sarah Cox, a rich orphan of fourteen, was snatched from a party of schoolgirls walking on Newington common and carried away screaming by a young gentleman in a coach. Although she was forcibly married that day, her friends rescued her next morning, and her enterprising husband was thrown into prison.[17]

Love occasionally found a way and if the poor suitor won the lady's heart his chances were usually good. A city heiress, on the eve of her wedding to the dull husband of her guardian's choice, whispered to the handsome younger son of a poor Scots lord that " her affection was more to him, if his were so to her she would instantly go away with him." Receiving the necessary encouragement, she drove to Greenwich with him that night and married him.[18]

The nearness of the Court unsettled London wives and daughters. Courtiers had more persuasive manners than citizens, and the citizen's wife, showing off her new coach in the Ring at Hyde Park, might easily make a flattering conquest of some fine gentleman. An invitation to a Court masque or play might follow, and not all the excited young women who hurried to Whitehall in their best finery brought back an unsullied virtue to the paternal or conjugal hearth. " There is not a lobby nor chamber, if it could speak, but would verify this," declared a censorious writer. It was an insolent common boast of young courtiers that they had cuckolded half a dozen aldermen. In the City of London the moral reputation of the Court stood very low: the Queen was rumoured to be Harry Jermyn's mistress.

or else Lord Holland's, nor was the King held blameless. These scandals were baseless, but jealous citizens repeated, magnified and believed them.

English women enjoyed unusual freedom; the tradition went far back and had much to do with the movement between class and class. When the Reformation closed the nunneries to the younger daughters of the rich or nobly born, they did not remain mewed up, unmarried, because there were no suitors good enough. They married where and how they could: the nobleman's younger daughter married the squire, the squire's younger daughter married the tradesman, the schoolmaster's or vicar's daughter might marry the yeoman, even the labourer, and so on to the lowest rungs of the social ladder. These women were a powerful, secret force, diffusing the pretensions and confidence of gentility in the humblest ranks of English society.

There was no legal and only a limited traditional objection to marriages which outraged the conventions. If the gentleman's daughter ran off with the footman her family might refuse to see her again but it was not an essential point of honour, as it would have been in some contemporary European countries, to wipe out the stain by killing the low-born seducer.

No English tradition prohibited gentlemen from following the professions or concerning themselves with trade. For the small squire it was nothing unusual to practise as a doctor or solicitor or to "get a ship and judiciously manage her." [19] Richer men adopted more ambitious courses. The powerful companies which financed colonial ventures and trade with Russia, Turkey and the East counted noblemen among their directors and shareholders. Many great families were already drawing their fortunes from coal and iron, not merely because these had been found on their lands but because they had themselves opened the mines and organised transport and marketing. The Willoughbies at Wollaton had started glass-furnaces to absorb the produce of the coal mines on their estates. The Byrons, on the strength of a rising fortune in coal, had become *entrepreneurs* and money-lenders on a large scale in the Midlands;

the Robartes family, whose fortune was built on wool and tin, had done the same in Cornwall; the Ashburnhams were the largest iron masters in Sussex; the Lumleys financed the alum works at Hartlepool, and the Lambtons the salt refineries at Sunderland. Sir John Winter, of an ancient Roman Catholic family, leased the iron mines of the Forest of Dean from the King, and with the help of a cousin, Lord Herbert of Raglan a pioneer in experimental engineering, had greatly developed them. He had also acquired interests in the South Wales coal mines, and in the course of the next generation was to foreshadow that marriage between coal and iron from which, in good time, the Industrial Revolution would be born. The Lowthers in Cumberland were developing the mines of Whitehaven, linked with a fleet of ships to transport their produce to Ireland.

England had long since accepted the fusion of the feudal landowner with the industrialist and the merchant. The squire's younger sons were, in the order of things, apprenticed to trades unless their abilities fitted them for the law or the Church. Only the ardently adventurous or irremediably stupid were sent abroad with horse and arms to become soldiers in foreign service.

In all the larger towns, and above all in London, the short-haired apprentices who thronged about the place counted among their number gentlemen's sons, yeomen's sons, the sons of professional men and of citizens. There were distinctions between them of course; gentlemen's sons were naturally apprenticed to the wealthiest and most respectable men. The irascible master worked off his temper on the poor widow's son rather than the baronet's younger brother. But within the framework of the great corporations and before the laws of the city all were alike apprentices, and common interests, hopes and pleasures broke down the barriers of inheritance.

Instructive handbooks enabled the self-made to learn the manners and outlook of the class into which they had penetrated. Richard Brathwaite's *The English Gentleman* and *The English Gentlewoman Drawn out to the Full Body* enjoyed considerable popularity. So did Henry Peacham's more ambitious *The Compleat Gentleman* which aimed at improving the accomplishments of the gentry and instructed them in science, literature and art as well as fishing and heraldry. His *The Worth of a Peny* and *The Art of Living in London* were directed at the many young men who fell a prey to the cheats and temptations of the great city. The anonymous *A Precedent for Young Pen-men* instructed the uneducated, with numerous examples, in the art of polite letter-writing.

The movements and alliances between the classes did not prevent the careful observance of the differences between them; there would have been less point in climbing the social ladder had it been otherwise. None were more anxious to preserve the privileges of their order than those who had but recently risen to occupy it. The merchant who had married his daughter to a lord stood bare-headed in her presence until she gave him leave to cover. The citizen's coach made way for the knight's coach when they met in a narrow place. Relations who had come down in the world often entered the house of their more fortunate kinsfolk as servants and had no more than the rights of servants; the good-natured Ralph Josselin, a country vicar, recorded a generous resolution in his diary: " My sister Mary is come under my roof as a servant, but my respect is and shall be towards her as a sister." [20] Bowing, curtsying, taking off the hat, entering a room, sitting at table were all strictly regulated, although some conventions were declining, and old people grumbled at the free and easy manner of the young.

Some sports were for gentlemen only, special clothes belonged to certain professions. A labourer might play at ninepins but not at bowls, and his wife and daughter must wear petticoats and bodices as separate garments, not gowns like gentlewomen. Lord Stamford was indignant when a sporting vicar trespassed on his land with greyhound in leash and hawk on wrist and a hunting dress of a most uncanonical colour. A blacksmith's wife who ventured forth in a gown suitable to a merchant's wife was hooted back into the smithy by the people of Ludlow.

But some conventions at least were growing slack. A petition had only recently been presented to the King praying him to prohibit the wearing of boots to the lower orders while there was yet time, for "divers inferior persons, both tradesmen and others . . . wear boots as familiarly as any nobleman or gentleman, the which abuse doth not only consume much leather vainly but doth much hurt unto divers poor people which would have much employment by . . . knitting of hose." [21]

The family atmosphere of town and country life was declining but apprentices and sons still shared the house and table of the master and father, servants and family ate together in farmhouses, and in some parts of the country the honest labourer could still count on his Sunday dinner either at the squire's table or at that of a neighbouring farmer. Order of precedence was carefully preserved, and in a few houses the old phrase "below the salt" retained its actual and not merely its metaphorical meaning; the massive salt cellar divided masters from servants. But in the houses of the rich, by this time, separate tables or even separate rooms had become the custom.

Some great houses, particularly in the more rural North, retained the custom of piling the broken meats into tubs and setting them out for the poor, but fashions in food as well as fashions in living were bringing this medieval custom to its end. Foreign dainties, Italian sauces, "French kickshaws," as they were called, and the new elaborate ways of serving food with more emphasis on candied fruit and flowers, on elegance than on substance, were not suited to the old custom. Conservative writers already lamented the roast beef of old England as a thing of the past. Yet solidity had not wholly disappeared from a diet in which, for festive occasions, roast fawn stuffed with suet dumplings, boar's head with lemon, turkey stuffed with pheasant which was in turn stuffed with capon, made their appearance, and the autumn delicacy of all classes was the luscious sucking pig.

Local practice varied greatly, but such in the main was the structure of English society: a clearly defined hierarchy from landless labourer to nobleman, from unskilled journeyman to Mayor—but a hierarchy without barriers, a steep ladder on which men and women passed continually up and down.

This situation was not reproduced in the adjoining lands. The gentry of Wales were as a rule poorer and simpler than the gentry of England. "You can sooner find fifty gentlemen of £100 a year than five of £500," recorded an observer from England, or, as a traditional jingle put it of one Welsh county:

> Alas, alas, poor Radnorshire,
> Never a park, nor ever a deer,
> Nor ever a squire of five hundred a year
> Save Sir Richard Fowler of Abbey Cwm Hir.[22]

But the Welsh gentleman in his stone-built farmhouse, with salmon hanging in the smoke of his chimney, a dresser with wooden trenchers upon it, fixed benches round the fire and about the walls, and a woven cloth for the parlour table on a Sunday, lived a traditional and patriarchal life among servants and tenantry who looked upon him as something more than employer and landlord and felt for him and his a tribal loyalty and pride. Often he still did not trouble himself to have an English surname; knowing well by oral tradition that he was descended from royal stock, he scorned the English insistence on family names; himself he was David Evans ; his son, called Evan from his grandfather, would be Evan Davis. His life, impoverished reflection of the Celtic tradition, had a simplicity and poetry of its own, but even in its decadence Celtic society was more rigid than the competitive, make-your-own-way society of England.

Ambitious Welsh boys sought their fortunes not at home but in England, where their alert faces, quick tempers and musical accent were teasingly accepted. Eloquence and imagination often carried them far in the church or in the law; John Williams, Bishop of Lincoln, was only the most remarkable of the many Welsh bishops in the British Isles, and two of the

King's twelve Judges, John Trevor and William Jones, were Welshmen. Some of these distinguished Welshmen would come home in mature years, settle benevolently among their poor countrymen, patronise and encourage local talent and offer the wealth and fame won in England to swell the diminished glories of their native Wales. More often the emigrant Welsh, successful or unsuccessful, stayed in their adopted country, and the names of Jones and Trevor, Vaughan, Evans and Morgan would be found, sparsely, in parish registers over all the English midlands, the south and west.

In Wales itself the poverty of the people and the patriarchal structure of society made it possible for a few great landowners to wield immense influence and power—families like that of Herbert, carrying half a dozen titles, or Somerset, whose head, the Earl of Worcester, lived at Raglan. Here in Wales the old feudal system superimposed four centuries earlier on the Celtic world had persisted, strengthened by the profound loyalties, rivalries and hatreds of the Celtic tradition.

In Scotland, where the Celtic world, hostile and unsubdued, had been penned into the Highlands, the situation was unlike that in Wales and England. Lowland Scotland, predominantly Anglo-Saxon in race and English in speech, kept perpetual watch on the untamed Highlands, but the feudal organisation imposed on this southern region in the twelfth century had acquired a patriarchal quality from contact with the Celt. The King himself in Scotland was not—as in England—regarded as the feudal overlord and fountain of justice and authority; he was regarded patriarchally as the head of the family. He was King of *Scots* not of Scotland, a ruler with a personal relationship to his people.

The Scottish laird, simply clad in homespun, with his blue bonnet on his head, ruled among his tenantry and servants with the intimacy, affection and arbitrariness of a father. He kept open house for travellers; he relieved the poor at his gate; his people called him by the name of his estate and he called them by the names of their farms. This gave a deceptively friendly air to a relationship which was dictatorial and could be tyrannous. The tenant Scots held their land upon annual lease, and the landlord who found minerals upon his estate, as many now did, might reduce his dependent farmers to landless men overnight at the year's end. The lowland Scots were discovering the mineral wealth of their country and developing shipping and trade of all kinds; compared to England theirs was a harsh and difficult world, where economy and stubborn toil alone yielded rewards. The belief that the Lord had His Chosen People and rewarded them, gave a terrible intensity to Scotland's struggle to establish herself in the pattern of European economics, with her wool, coal, timber and fur exports and her fisheries. The Lord placed coal mines upon the lands of His Chosen; since theirs was the earth and the fulness thereof, it was clear that those who were dispossessed, or forced down the mines in the process, were none of the Lord's people. The belief was not cynical; it was often associated with a strenuousness of austerity and prayer that showed—if in a strange fashion—a deep sense of gratitude and responsibility for the Lord's well-placed gifts.

In the highlands the Celtic clan system generally prevailed, although the ancient clan loyalties were here and there crossed by feudal conceptions of land tenure. The Mackintosh, for instance, was accepted as chief in districts which, by feudal tenure belonged to Huntly, chief of the Gordons. Conversely he was feudal overlord of other regions inhabited by the Cameron clan. This confusion of rights was fruitful of trouble in a land where clan chiefs still in practice had rights of life and death over their people; whatever laws the Crown might pass to curtail this jurisdiction, such men as Argyll, Huntly, Seaforth had a moral and actual power over Campbells, Gordons, Mackenzies which extended to every part of their lives. Among themselves the highlanders were tenacious of their enmities: Campbell slew Macdonald, and Macdonald Campbell whenever they could. The Mackenzies were at feud with the MacLeods, the Gordons with the Crichtons, and every man's hand was against the Mac-Gregors and MacNabs. The land was terrible and bloody, but with a wild beauty dear to those who knew it. In the late summer the clans gathered for the hunting; lesser quarrels were temporarily at rest while for long days over the great hills, they encircled and drove the deer. Sometimes, in the summer days the young men camped together in the meadow land by Tay or Spey, enjoyed the season's sport, swam, wrestled, leaped, danced, through the warm nights when dawn came after sunset with scarce a resting time between. In highland games or highland wars, the sons of the greater chiefs, who had been at the French Court or the English and had learnt the delicacies and graces of cosmopolitan civilisation, slept on the ground among their clansmen, wore—with a cultured elegance—the plaid and trews of their native land, spoke Gaelic, listened to the interminable songs of bards and the sharp music of the pipes, and watched the sword dances and the revels by the long sunset light and the glow of the turf fires.

Some of the southern nobility came north for the hunting; those whose lands lay along the highland frontier—Montrose, Ogilvy, Mar, Eglinton—were usually present. These had adopted some of the highland ways, probably " had the Gaelic," sometimes called themselves chiefs although they were in effect merely heads of families. Their function in the strategy of Scotland was to prevent highland incursions into the richer lands of the South, but over centuries of strife they had learnt to admire and imitate the very things they fought. Sometimes too a foreign visitor was welcomed to the highland hunting; an intruding cockney John Taylor, clad in a kilt lent him by the Earl of Mar, squatted on the unfamiliar, uncomfortable ground throughout the weird dances and wondered why these extraordinary people did not cut down their pine forests and trade them as masts to the shipyards of the world.

Between lowlands and highlands an armed neutrality reigned, broken from time to time by cattle-raiding. The highlanders, who knew that the land had been all theirs until the Saxon came, esteemed it no robbery to steal back something of their own. Lawlessness of the same kind prevailed on the English border.

The late King James, when he succeeded to the English throne, had tried to pacify the borders with a strong hand, and for a time his armed patrols, his hangings and deportations of the border reivers, Scots and English, had brought an illusory calm. But the tradition of valiant robbery and lawlessness was too strong to die in a few years. Under the relaxed vigilance which marked King Charles's reign, the borders had gone back to their old way of life and by 1635 great parts of the country were terrorised by armed gangs who lived by robbery, kidnapping and ransom and revenged themselves so horribly on any who informed against them that few dared do so. The treacherous slaughter of the Laird of Troughend, the subject of one of the finest of the border ballads, was a part of this tale of blackmail and vengeance.

In Scotland the Celtic North and the Anglo-Saxon South were separated by the geographical division of highlands and lowlands. No division so convenient existed in Ireland where alien invaders from England had forcibly thrust themselves upon an angry Celtic land. The first settlers, the Normans, had become in the course of centuries acceptable to the Irish chiefs. The great family of Butler—Earls of Ormonde—were cross-bred with Irish families; so were the Fitzgeralds, the St. Legers, and the de Burghs commonly called Burke.

In the last seventy years new settlers had descended upon Ireland, first from England, then from the lowlands of Scotland. These were calculating, adventurous, competitive, bent on developing the latent possibilities of an undeveloped land, and Protestant, with a Protestant government behind them. The wild Irish were as alien to them as the American Indians to the settlers across the Atlantic. Against these pushful newcomers, the Irish and the Norman-Irish drew together—aristocrats, with their retainers and their clans, a patriarchal society against upstarts.

Apparent peace prevailed, and the royal government, as represented by Lord Deputy Wentworth, hopefully cherished the ambition of seeing Ireland " enclosed and husbanded, beautified with towns and buildings and stored with an industrious well-conditioned people." Dublin at least had been improved with handsome modern additions to the Castle, a pleasant meeting place for coaches and equestrians at Phœnix Park, and a theatre for which the fashionable James Shirley had written the opening play. The Deputy ostentatiously placed his own son at Trinity College (which Queen Elizabeth had founded) as an encouragement to other distinguished residents to do the same. Under government patronage Christopher Syms had composed a new Latin grammar specially designed for use in Irish schools and published recently in Dublin.

Appearances were deceptive. The Irish retained their religion and their unconquered independence of spirit. Their clans remained loyal to their chieftains, whether these were exiles far away, like the Red O'Neill, or friendly to the English government, like Randall MacDonnell, Earl of Antrim, or Murrough O'Brien, Earl of Inchiquin, chiefs respectively of the largest clans in the north and south. Scattered nomadic hordes still lived in the shelter of the hills and bogs, levying blackmail on their neighbours and raiding the settlers when they dared. The worst danger was not from them but from the covert hostility of an entire population. Here in Ireland, sooner than any thought or feared, the struggle of eleven hundred years between the Saxon and the Celt was to burst into a new and terrible blaze.

The same clash of ideas and interests was reproduced in miniature midway between the Irish and the English shores on the Isle of Man. Twelve miles across and thirty-three miles in length, it belonged to Lord Strange, the Earl of Derby's eldest son. He found its lively, loquacious inhabitants faithful to their old customs in spite of benevolent attempts to bring their peculiar system of land tenure into line with that of his other possessions on the English mainland, and to reform their laws. The greatest native family was that of Christian. Its present head was especially powerful because of his many sons; illegitimacy mattered little among the Manxmen and the head of the Christian family bore patriarchal sway over his people. His opposition compelled Lord Strange to modify his policy; for the time being he had accepted Captain Christian as Dempster, which meant that he virtually ruled the island in Lord Strange's name.

The Celtic populations were a significant and possibly a dangerous minority in the King's dominions. They represented an antique challenge to the modern world in a way that the French-speaking Channel Islanders and occasional groups of foreign refugees did not. At the moment, the Channel Islanders were resentfully and jealously guarding their ancient privileges against government encroachment, but they shared with the English and the Lowland Scots much the same outlook on society and the world, although they might have lesser differences of interest and opinion.

Another kind of society, secret and submerged, persisted in the King's dominions: the gypsies. They were known to the people as wanderers and vagabonds, distinguished from the ordinary vagabonds and thieves who roamed the country by a peculiar language and a closer organisation. Ballads occasionally romanticised them but the law persecuted them, and in the lowlands of Scotland to be a gypsy might in itself prove a capital offence.

Such were the peoples over whom King Charles reigned, and to whom he wished to give the blessings of peace, justice, order and true religion, under the unquestioned authority of the Crown. The ideal was constantly before his eyes but the intellectual and æsthetic fashion of the day, strongly bent towards allegory, obscured the practical difficulties of the task. The King lived in a world of poetic illusions and could not but be affected by them. For him and his courtiers, the most ordinary events were swiftly wreathed in pastoral or classical disguise. The Countess of Anglesey gave an evening party for the Queen and at once the poets summoned the goddess Diana and bade the stars shoot from their spheres;[23] Lord Bridgewater's three children made a long journey, and Comus with all his rout sprang eloquently forth to provide a masque and a moral to celebrate their reunion with their parents.

A young poet, hailing a new arrival at Court, cried out:

" What's she, so late from Penshurst come.
More gorgeous than the mid-day sun
That all the world amazes?
Sure 'tis some angel from above,
Or 'tis the Cyprian Queen of Love
Attended by the Graces."[24]

But it was only the Lady Dorothy Sidney with the usual duenna and waiting women.

Arcadian scenes were rhymed and sung, with splendid or with humble staging, in many a school or college hall or private house. Almost every year the King himself acted in a Christmas masque, and, recently, the most expensive masque ever mounted —it cost over £20,000—had been put on in his honour by the lawyers of the Inns of Court. It had represented the Triumph of Peace, and the masquers, about two hundred of them, had ridden through the streets of London by torchlight in the quaint and gorgeous finery designed for them by Inigo Jones.

The King had approved of this masque, written by the skilful and much favoured James Shirley. It too had enacted that same allegory which he had commissioned Rubens to portray. Peace, Law and Justice had, with song and dance, triumphed over folly, faction and idle criticism.

The allegorical trick in poetry and compliment insensibly spreads to other things and becomes almost a habit of mind. The King seemed sometimes to treat administration and politics as though the peace and contentment of the realm were indeed assured because, at his Christmas revels, a golden chariot upon a white cloud had descended against the heavenly backcloth bearing Peace, " in a flowery vesture like the Spring," with buskins of green taffeta, a garland of olives on her head and a branch of palm in her hand.[25]

King Charles had been nourished from childhood in a deep understanding of the sanctity and responsibility of the sovereign's part. His father, long since, had written a book, *Basilicon Doron,* a short impressive manual on the duties of a King, intended for the instruction of his eldest son; that eldest son, Prince Henry, had died, and the younger boy, then his father's cherished Baby Charles, had inherited, along with all else that would have been his brother's, the wisdom and policy enshrined in this book. He must, as a boy, have carefully turned over on his stammering tongue and conscientiously pondered in his mind such sentences as these:

> [A good King] acknowledgeth himself ordained for his people, having received from God a burden of government, whereof he must be countable.

His father, in this book, repeatedly emphasised that the relationship between King and people is that of a father to his children, and that his authority, like that of a father, is founded in the immutable decree of the Almighty. Just as no misconduct on the part of a father can free his children from obedience to the fifth commandment, so no misgovernment on the part of a King can release his subjects from their allegiance. But the King, like the father, has duties and must answer to God if he scants them. This, in essence, was the doctrine of Divine Right as digested and set out by the late King James and as it had been imprinted on the mind of his son. Other writings by the old King were extant, and these too had been studied by the young Charles. " A good King will frame his actions to be according to the law," he had written in his tract on *The True Law of Free Monarchies*, " yet he is not bound thereto but of his good will." In fact it lay with the King to keep or break, make or unmake the laws. In his *Defence of the Right of Kings*, provoked by the rise of certain impertinent theories of popular and clerical rights against the Crown, he had declared:

> " My brother princes and myself, whom God hath advanced upon the throne of Sovereign Majesty and supreme dignity, do hold the royal dignity of His Majesty alone, to whose service, as a most humble homager and vassal, I con-

secrate all the glory, honour, splendour and lustre of my earthly Kingdom."

With a profound sense of his holy office, therefore, and a deep conscientiousness, the earnest and self-disciplined Charles had taken up the burden of kingship, in the early hours of March 27th, 1625, when it pleased Almighty God to call King James to Himself. He was twenty-four. At his coronation he had defied tradition. He had refused to make the solemn rite an occasion for vulgar display and had omitted the customary procession, so popular with Londoners. He had also carefully revised the coronation oath in accordance with his views, swearing to maintain the liberties and laws of the country only in so far as they did not clash with his prerogative. He had eschewed as far as possible the pompous trappings of royalty and had worn white for his consecration. The text chosen for the sermon—it aroused some comment at the time—was *Be thou faithful unto death and I will give thee a Crown of Life*.

The King's ideals were clear from the first. He wanted his subjects throughout his dominions to accept his absolute authority with unquestioning obedience and to belong with uniform and regular devotion to the Church established by law. This was the only just basis of government as he saw it; this once achieved he would—*of his good will*, and not by any legal obligation—protect their traditional rights and freedoms within the framework of the laws, and ensure equal justice, order, and as far as in him lay, prosperity and security to his good people.

No ruler can pursue an effective policy at home or abroad without money, and the revenues of the Crown were inadequate. It lay with Parliament to vote money to the sovereign, and the King had found, within a few months of his accession, that Parliament was very far from accepting his view that it existed and functioned only by his good will. In the first five years of his reign he had quarrelled with three Parliaments in succession. In 1629 he had got rid of the third, in spite of a violent attempt on the part of his principal opponents to prevent the dissolution.

He had committed the leaders of the tumult to prison without trial, made peace abroad, and settled down to conduct his own affairs in his own way.

The King had shelved his problems, not solved them, and the beauty and order with which he had surrounded himself deceived him into the belief that his authority in his kingdoms was as absolute as his authority at Court. He turned away from less pleasing realities, contemplated with pardonable satisfaction his beautiful palaces, his well-behaved Court, his bishops and chaplains, and took this seemly shining surface to indicate an untroubled deep.

His Court reflected his own personality and ideals. He never criticised his father, but he had early perceived the incongruity of King James's theory of monarchy with the jovial squalor in which he chose to live. In his most impressionable years, the young Charles had been for many months at the Court of Spain, wooing the Infanta. The wooing had come to nothing but he had brought back from Spain the memory and the knowledge of a Court ceremonial after his own heart. On his accession the broad Scots jokes and the drunken romps which had amused his father abruptly ceased. Babbling quarrels in ante-room and corridor were stilled. From the Gentlemen of the Bedchamber to the waiters at the sideboard, each man precisely knew where to be and when, at which table to take meat, when to attend prayers, when the King would rise, when sleep, when ride, when give audience, and who, with staff of office in hand or napkin on arm, should walk before him or stand behind his chair. The formality of the Court on all official occasions was rigorous and extreme. The King, alone of European princes, was served on bended knee, and when the French ambassador complained because neither chair nor stool was set for his wife —as was done for the English ambassador's wife in France—he was told that on official occasions no lady of the English Court except the Queen herself, not even the Princess Royal, was allowed to sit in the royal presence.[26] King Charles lived, with no vulgar ostentation, but with elegance and ceremony.

The reform was partial only and did not extend beyond the King's immediate circle. The rabbit-warren palace of Whitehall was a village in itself; in its streets, alleys and outbuildings, a crowded world of dependents, professional courtiers, servants' families and servants' servants lived parasitically on the Court. The Venetian envoy, considering the King's surroundings with a critical mind, condemned his housekeeping as extravagant.[27]

The disorders of such hangers-on were not before the King's eye. He ruled his immediate surroundings with an absolute authority. Had it not been for the licensed gaiety of his French Queen, the Court would have been intolerably strict. She, who loved dancing, masquing, plays and music, enlivened Whitehall and Hampton Court with elegant and innocent frolic. Not only did she and the King take part in the Christmas masques and often bring professional players to Court to perform for royal birthdays or Twelfth Night revels, but she herself, breaking all precedent, had been known to attend public performances at the theatre in person.

The wilder young courtiers looked for additional pleasure, far from the restraint of their monarch's presence; they frequented the gaming tables of Piccadilly, the race course of Hyde Park, the taverns of Westminster and the Strand with their legal or literary gossip, or the expensive, disreputable pleasure gardens south of the river, where, it was said, a single supper with Bess Broughton, or her like, might stand a man in twenty pounds, not to mention what the lady's favours would cost him. But the Court remained, none the less, the focal point of society and the ultimate standard of taste and manners.

It was also an intellectual centre, the meeting place of talent and wit, not less than fashion and beauty. The poets and writers gathered in the gardens of St. James's and Whitehall or the Queen's drawing-room at Somerset House; here they neatly turned their *vers de société* or circulated prose *Characters* and satirical epigrams to amuse the ladies. Suckling risked the mischievous innuendo, Lovelace was frivolous and musical, Davenant musical and courtly. Less talented courtiers with pretensions to poetic gifts circulated their work anonymously and were often mortified at its reception.

The courtiers' talent spilled over into the life of the capital when they turned to drama and mounted their own plays at the London theatres, often with great splendour. The King, as patron, critic and censor, sometimes intervened: he persuaded Suckling to change a tragic to a happy ending, and, with a surprising realism, he discouraged his master of the revels, Sir Henry Herbert, from removing the realistic expletives from the dialogue of Davenant's social comedy, *The Wits*.

The King cultivated music more than poetry; his small private orchestra entertained him as he sat at meat with choice pieces of secular music or, in the Chapel Royal, performed delicate and complex sacred airs, to the scandal of some of his subjects who thought that God's house was no place for Italian fiddlers.

The King's greatest achievement was the superb collection of works of art which he had been accumulating since he was Prince of Wales. Rubens himself had described him as " *le prince le plus amateur de la peinture qui soit au monde.*" His own excellent taste and the advice and gifts of intelligent agents had enabled him to fill his palaces with the rarest and the greatest collection in Europe. He possessed antique marbles and Florentine bronzes, delicate ivories, cut crystal, and the most rich and curious work of the goldsmith and medallist. Many of the noblest works of the Italian masters hung upon his walls—Titian's great " Entombment," Mantegna's incomparable " Triumph of Julius Cæsar," Tintoretto's " Nine Muses," white-limbed on sun-dappled Parnassus, Correggio's " Marriage of Saint Catherine," portraits by Raphael, allegories by Giorgione; the works of the Bassano and Carracci families, of Giulio Romano and the younger Palma filled the gaps. Of contemporary artists, he commissioned paintings from Rubens and possessed those of Rembrandt; he employed in work for his Court and collections Anthony Van Dyck, Daniel Mytens, Gerard Honthorst, Wenceslas Hollar, Francis Klein, the ageing Italian master Orazio Gentileschi with his talented daughter Artemisia; Balthasar

Gerbier, miniaturist, architect and indefatigable busybody of the studio and sale room, assisted and advised him, and he had secured for the chief artist at the mint, the skilled French engraver Briot.

He had bought the magnificent cartoons drawn by Raphael for the Vatican tapestries and sent them to the English tapestry works at Mortlake to be copied, while he commissioned Van Dyck to design appropriate borders for the woven pictures. He had also given encouragement to the Mortlake works by commissioning great numbers of hangings for his palaces. In spite of all, the works had got into difficulties, and Charles, with some idea of making the industry a royal monopoly, bought them for the Crown.[28]

The fashion in tapestries, pictures, and classical decoration set by the King in his palaces at Whitehall, Greenwich, Oatlands and Hampton Court was followed by his nobility and courtiers. Lord Arundel's house was rich in Italian marbles; Lord Pembroke had the famous double-cube room at Wilton decorated by Van Dyck; the splendours of the Marquis of Winchester's Basing House were legendary; at Ham House the King's friend Will Murray had ceiling and wall decorations in paint and plaster work of great elaboration, some of them copied from the architecture depicted in the Raphael cartoons his master had bought.

Although the arts were his chief delight the King respected and encouraged the sciences. The physicians who enjoyed the honour of his patronage included pioneers of the new learning like Sir Theodore de Mayerne, the great exponent of clinical medicine who had probably saved the Queen's life at the premature birth of her first child, and William Harvey, the discoverer of the circulation of the blood.

The numerous lords and gentlemen who meddled with scientific and mechanical matters also felt the attraction and solicited the patronage of the Court, partly, but not exclusively, in the hope of acquiring profitable patents for their inventions. Lord Herbert of Cherbury had rooms in the royal palace to give him easier access to the papers he needed for his projected work on the life of Henry VIII; in the intervals of history he solicited

the King's attention for various practical inventions of his own
—gun-carriages, naval equipment, and a floating bathing establishment to be installed on the Thames. The talented son of the
old Earl of Worcester, Edward Somerset, devoted his ingenuity
to water pumps and hydraulic lifts for his father's castle at
Raglan on the Welsh border, but when business brought him
to Whitehall he gained the intelligent approbation of the King.
Sir Francis Kynaston, courtier and poet, secured the King's
patronage for a school that he founded for young noblemen, but
was less fortunate in getting him to adopt a new kind of furnace
for use in warships. Charles Cavendish, the Earl of Newcastle's
brother, an amateur mathematician who was in touch with
many foreign scholars, doubtless had the King's approbation in
his several attempts to persuade the French mathematician
Claude Mydorge and the French philosopher René Descartes
to make peaceful England their permanent home.[29]

The English Court was the abode of ceremony, elegance
and learning. It was also the abode of beauty. The noble ladies
in silks of pale saffron and coral pink, sky-blue, willow-green and
oyster, their ringleted hair framing plump, oval faces, went by
water to Blackfriars and had their likenesses recorded by Anthony
Van Dyck: Lucy, Countess of Carlisle, bold and handsome;
Lady Ann Carr, pensive, dangling her gloves; Lady Mary
Villiers, with palm and lamb as Saint Agnes.

The courtiers were depicted in masque attire, nonchalant in
buskins with a shepherd's crook like Lord d'Aubigny, or with
appropriate accessories—curly-headed George Digby, Lord
Bristol's scholar son, with papers and a globe, the connoisseur
Lord Arundel with a choice marble statue, Algernon, Earl of
Northumberland, Lord High Admiral of the Kingdom, with an
anchor and a naval battle behind him, Viscount Wentworth,
the Lord Deputy of Ireland, with one of the huge Irish wolf-
hounds which he bred at his hunting lodge near Dublin.

The smaller luxuries which surrounded these men and women
have been etched in loving detail by Wenceslas Hollar, the
Bohemian drawing master of the King's children: the lace

collars and cuffs, the knots of satin ribbon, the fur muffs, the painted fans, the embroidered gloves, the jewelled hat-bands and silver shoe-roses, the fringed velvet and tiffany masks to shield their waxen skins from wind and sun.

The small, fastidious King presided fittingly over his well-ordered Court. By nature reserved, he was isolated still more by that slight impediment of the speech which made him shun all but formal contacts, except with his familiars. Even his friends he kept at their distance, but with a regular and courteous demeanour that all understood and some, who were formal themselves, grew to like. He was constant in his conduct, predictable, disliking steadily those whom he disliked, holding with great firmness to his opinions and his friends, even when the opinions proved mistaken and the friends faithless, and resolute in the fulfilment of his duty.

He was as fine a judge of horseflesh as he was of painting, and in Sir John Fenwick of Wallington he had a trainer and breeder of high repute, one that " bred the best horses ever was in England for coursing, famous over all the world." [30]   In the hunting field the King's formality thawed a little, but never wholly. Deft and lightly made, he rode well; it was necessary that he should. The chase was his passion as it had been his father's, but he was not, like his father, as often in a ditch as in the saddle. " Have I three Kingdoms and must you fly into my eye?" old King James had apostrophised an intruding insect; but the flies, if any, which made this mistake with King Charles were removed without comment. The unseemly, the ludicrous, the merely human were excluded from his public life, and almost all his life was public. Even when he had a hunting accident it was of a high, dramatic kind. Mistaking green weed for a grassy hollow he plunged once in full career into a morass in which his horse floundered irrecoverably. He himself escaped through the prompt assistance of his attendants, and with the utmost coolness, changed clothes with a courtier, mounted a fresh horse and continued the chase.[31]

But though he moved from palace to palace with a restlessness on which foreign ambassadors remarked, he did not know his people well and was a stranger to the greater part of his own dominions. On his journeys he followed always much the same route. He had hunted in the New Forest and visited the Isle of Wight; he went frequently to Newmarket for the races, or to stay with the Earl of Pembroke at Wilton; he had been received at the university of Oxford and he knew the Thames valley and his deer parks at Windsor, Richmond, Oatlands and Theobalds. Once since his manhood, he had travelled to Scotland and back, had seen the wolds of Lincolnshire, had climbed the two hundred and seventy steps of the tower of York Minster to admire the prospect, had crossed the coalfields of Durham, the Northumbrian moors and the hills of Lothian. He had played golf on the links at Leith, and made a progress as far as Perth and Brechin, but, unlike all his ancestors, he had not hunted the deer with the highland clans. He had never been to Wales. He had never visited Ireland. He had inspected his ships of war at Chatham and Gravesend, and had watched, from the sedate summer residence he had built for his Queen at Greenwich, the sails that passed up and down the broad estuary of the Thames to London, but he did not know the seaports of his kingdom or the mariners and merchants on whom the prosperity of his State was so largely built. At his council table, or more informally by conversations in the halls and embrasures of his palaces, he settled a huge number of technical questions relating to taxation, to industry, manufacture and shipping, to the regulation of trade, and the quarrels of his subjects. Through these he had learnt a good many things about the manufacture of salt, soap, pins, and beaver hats, the cloth trade, the importation of wine, the herring fisheries, the oyster beds, the forests, the mines, the foundries and the glass works.

The reports which his Council received regularly from the Justices of the Peace, informed him, if he wished to know, of the general state of the country, the rise or decline of the number of vagabonds, the arrangements for apprenticing orphan children and relieving the industrious poor.

The King had a high sense of duty towards the people whom he regarded as a sacred trust from God, but this was compatible with an open dislike of their proximity and their opinions. It was only, perhaps, when he touched for the King's Evil at Easter and Michaelmas that he allowed the vulgar to approach closely to his royal person, and even then each invalid who presented himself to be cured had to produce a certificate signed by a clergyman, a churchwarden and a justice of the peace before he might enter the palace gates.[32]

He had never had the painful experience from which his father, as a young man, had learnt so much; he had never confronted insolent opponents face to face and had the worst of the argument. No national danger had compelled him to go out among his people and share their perils. He was, at this time, not only the most formal but the most remote and sheltered of all European kings.

Less virtuous monarchs escaped from formality in the arms of low-born mistresses, but for the chaste Charles, no Nell Gwynne, prattling cockney anecdotes, opened a window into the lives of his humbler subjects. What he knew of men, he knew chiefly by report and study. Like many shy, meticulous men, he was fond of aphorisms, and would write in the margins of books, in a delicate, beautiful, deliberate script, such maxims as " Few great talkers are good doers " or " None but cowards are cruel."[33] He trusted more to such distilled and bottled essence of other men's wisdom than to his own experience, which was, in truth, limited; his daily contact with the world was confined within the artificial circle of his Court and the hunting field. He was to say, much later, in tragic circumstances, that he knew as much law as any gentleman in England. It was true; but he had little conception of what the laws meant to those who lived under them.

Admired by some and feared by many, he was not greatly loved. He neither solicited nor gained the affection of his people from whom he expected neither more nor less than duty. In the smaller circle of his Court he was of those who exclude love when they exclude familiarity. His servants knew him to be punctilious and just, a stranger alike to impulses of anger or good humour. In later years the respect which he had from all his household grew into love, but it was his misfortune, not his graciousness, which melted their hearts. In his time of un-questioned power very few felt for him, personally as a man, that unreasonable, human attachment which sweetens service and softens authority.

Yet the King was capable of deep and tender attachment when his secretive affections were touched. His love for his wife, though it had been slow to come, was now the strongest personal emotion in his life.

Queen Henrietta Maria was the opposite of her husband in outward manner and in temperament, and their marriage had opened in storm and rebellion on her side, in a coldness amount-ing almost to cruelty on his. She was nine years his junior and had come to him as an effervescent girl of fifteen, very fond of dancing. He had objected to her gaieties and to the conduct of the French companions who encouraged her. They had been sent away, leaving the tear-stained child to the mercy of her solemn husband and his overbearing favourite the Duke of Buckingham. For three unhappy years she lived forlorn and neglected; only after the murder of Buckingham, in 1628, did she become pregnant for the first time.

She was not strong and her spine was a little crooked. Her first child, a boy, survived only a few hours and she rose from her bed with the bloom of her youth withered. She had always had bad features, with a long nose and prominent teeth; now the freshness of her complexion and her dimpled charm had gone, though the ivory quality of her skin and her large, brilliant eyes still commanded admiration.

The loss of her looks mattered nothing, for Charles, on Buckingham's death, had transferred his devotion instantly and wholly to his wife. He was in love, with the single-mindedness of those who give their affection to few, but to those few entirely. Beloved, the little Queen flowered again; her vivacity, her charm, and a good dressmaker hid all defects. She knew that she was not a beauty but she made the world think that she was. The dancing, on which the King had frowned, was now permitted, and her wit and gaiety made her husband's Court such as she had always wanted. Year by year her mental ascendancy over her husband increased; he sought her advice on every subject, except religion, and had been heard to regret that he could not make her a member of his council. Only in religion was there no understanding between them, for she was as devoted to the Church of Rome as he to the Church of England.

Sufficient to themselves, the King and Queen were not greatly interested in their growing family. Princes and Princesses were born at regular intervals, at cost of great suffering to the Queen. Suitable attendants were appointed to wait on them and they enjoyed every care proper to their station, but although they accompanied their parents occasionally on a Maying party or courtly revel and Van Dyck painted the Royal Pair awkwardly dandling a couple of babies, neither the King nor the Queen was truly at home in the nursery. Not until years later, when they were themselves separated, did either of them indulge in demonstrations of emotional love for their children.

The Queen had not her husband's studious temperament and slow, ruminative mind. She understood things quickly and superficially; he understood them deeply, or not at all. But like many slow thinkers, he greatly admired a quick wit, and like many doubtful and hesitative men, he was easily impressed by the capacity to make a decision, however ill-conceived or impulsive.

The fusion of their two influences—his for stateliness and form, hers for liveliness and style—had made their Court within a few years the " most sumptuous and happy in the world." [34] The achievement was considerable but it was shallow. It bore no relation to the unsolved problem of government.

1. Thomas Carew, *Poems*, Oxford, 1949, p. 77.
2. Lipson, *Economic History*, Oxford, 1948, III, p. 152.
3. *Acts of the Privy Council, Colonial Series*, I, pp. 264–83.
4. *Strafford MSS.* XI, October–November 1637 *passim*.
5. *Relazioni dagli Ambasciatori Veneti*, ed. Barozzi and Berchet, Venice, 1863, ix, pp. 307–8.
6. Vaughan, *Works*, Oxford, 1914, i, p. 11.
7. Ralph, *Sir Humphrey Mildmay: Royalist Gentleman*, New Brunswick, 1947, p. 25.
8. See Nef. *The Rise of the British Coal Industry*, London, 1932, I. *passim*.
9. *Register of the Privy Council of Scotland*, 1633–5, p. 126.
10. *A Short Survey of 26 Counties*, ed. Wickham Legg, London, 1904, p. 83.
11. *Ibid.*, pp. 37, 43.
12. Lithgow, *Rare Adventures and Painful Peregrinations*, Glasgow, 1906, p. 433.
13. Dugdale, *History of Embanking*, London, 1662, p. 391.
14. Hartlib, *Legacie*, London, 1651.
15. *A Royalist's Notebook. The Commonplace Book of Sir John Oglander*, ed. Bamford, London, 1936, p. 84.
16. Brathwait, *Household of an Earl*, London, 1821.
17. *Calendar of State Papers, Domestic Series*, 1637, pp. 422, 547, 565.
18. Knowler, *The Earl of Strafford's Letters and Despatches*, London, 1739, ii, p. 142.
19. Oglander, p. 75.
20. Ralph Josselin, *Diary*, ed. Hockliffe. *Camden Society*, 1908, p. 15.
21. *Bankes MSS.*, 60/19.
22. Rhys and Brynmor Jones, *The Welsh People*, London, 1906, p. 449; Rowlands *Cambrian Bibliography*, Llanidloes, 1869, p. 195.
23. Davenant, *Works*, London, 1673, p. 218.
24. Waller, *Poems*, London, 1893, p. 62.
25. Shirley, *Works*, London, 1833, vi, p. 274.
26. *Calendar of State Papers, Venetian Series*, 1636–9, p. 421; Burnet, *History of my own Time*, ed. Airy, Oxford, 1897, i, p. 28.
27. Barozzi and Berchet, ix, p. 310.
28. W. G. Thompson, *History of Tapestry*, London, 1906, pp. 299, 309, 351 ff.
29. Rigaud, *Correspondence of Scientific Men*, Oxford, 1841, i, pp. 22–3.
30. *Historical Manuscripts Commission, Report X, Appendix IV*, p. 108.
31. *Calendar of State Papers, Venetian Series*, 1636–9, p. 64.
32. Crawford, *The King's Evil*, Oxford, 1911, pp. 165–215.
33. The aphorisms quoted are from his copy of Bacon's *Advancement of Learning*, Oxford, 1640, preserved in the British Museum.
34. Barozzi and Berchet, ix, p. 393: " la piu sontuosa e la piu allegra del mondo."

CHAPTER TWO

FAITH AND FOREIGN POLITICS

THE King, in agreement with most serious thinkers of his time, believed that good government must be founded on true religion. The first essential was that his people should believe rightly and worship God in the manner most acceptable to Him. What that manner was, the Church alone could teach. Unhappily schism in the Catholic Church and vulgar sectarianism with its hundred disputing tongues made it exceptionally difficult in the seventeenth century to know which belief and which form of worship was right.

The overwhelming majority of the King's subjects, whatever their doctrines, their education or their interests, were simply and sincerely religious. They did not doubt that their souls were immortal or that Christ had died to redeem them. Some of them remembered this daily, most of them remembered it on Sunday, and a few perhaps not more than once or twice a year. But it was to them a cardinal fact in life, and in death. From the felon jauntily going to the gallows, with a bold face and a pious word, to the nobleman (of whom there would soon be many) mounting the steps of the scaffold, almost all faced death with an unquestioning belief in a life to come. The nobleman shared with the felon the uplifting and unshaken conviction that the Son of God Himself had, for his redemption, gone the selfsame way. To die without that hope, to die—as men said—" desperately " was an unusual and terrible thing.

The desire to believe and the capacity to believe were still almost equally strong. This was true, with a minority of individual exceptions, of all the King's subjects, in spite of the differences of wealth, breeding and education which divided them.

King Charles counted among his people some of the finest and most cultivated minds in Europe and some of the most primitive. The leading scholars at the universities of Oxford, Cambridge, St. Andrew's, Aberdeen, and the more recently founded Trinity College, Dublin, ranked with the best in the world. Theology dominated the universities but the classics, philosophy, ancient history, mathematics and medicine were also taught. Francis Glisson, lecturing on anatomy at Cambridge, supported William Harvey's new theory of the circulation of the blood, a theory angrily attacked by the Scottish scholar Alexander Ross, who, not content with challenging Harvey and Glisson, was soon to hurl himself with ironical eloquence upon the Italian astronomer Galileo, pulverising him—as he hoped— in a book entitled *The Earth No Wandering Star except in the Wandering Heads of the Galileans*.

London was a centre of scientific activity. At Gresham College, Henry Gellibrand, professor of astronomy, was investigating the magnetic north. The Barber Surgeons company had built an anatomy theatre from designs by Inigo Jones, where public lectures drew distinguished audiences; sometimes banquets were provided, after which the Barber Surgeons, to their chagrin, missed a number of their silver spoons.

Anatomy and all the natural sciences had a great following both amateur and professional. Sir Kenelm Digby was working on an exhaustive inquiry into the *Nature of Bodies* in which he discussed, with other questions, what part of the animal was the first to be formed, whether animals can think and " how the vital spirits are sent from the brain into the intended parts of the body without mistaking their way." Thomas Browne, a physician of considerable reputation who had just settled at Norwich, was compiling an immense and varied store of learning for the book in which he would examine and deal justly with a multitude of common superstitions and vulgar errors in the interests of scientific truth. In Yorkshire, a precocious boy, William Gascoigne, scanned the stars and made improvements in the telescope. It was not three years since the posthumous publication of Dr. Muffet's *Insectorum Theatrum* had opened the way towards the science of entomology.

Mathematicians pursued their solitary calculations. John Napier from his castle tower near Edinburgh had opened the century with the publication of the first tables of logarithms; at another Scottish castle Sir Thomas Urquhart of Cromarty pondered, in his eccentric overcrowded brain, the practice of trigonometry, squaring the circle and the invention of a universal language. William Oughtred had recently published his *Clavis Mathematica*. John Wilkins at Cambridge took time off his mathematical studies to speculate on the habitability of the moon and on an invention, left incomplete, which might have been a telephone. At Cambridge, too, young Seth Ward, poor and studious, wrestled with the problems of geometry. But arithmetic, even in its elementary complexities, was for scholars: in merchants' counting-houses the clerks used the abacus for their sums, although a few now employed an elementary slide rule attributed to John Napier and familiarly known as Napier's Bones. The highly educated and efficient Lord Deputy of Ireland, wishing to reckon fifteen times four, wrote down fifteen four times and added it up. The multiplication table was not at that time taught with the A B C.

The ancient languages of the East and the antiquities of the British Isles exerted a simultaneous attraction upon many scholars. William Bedell, Bishop of Kilmore, the leading Hebrew scholar of the day, had devoted himself since he had gone to Ireland to the study of the Irish language and antiquities and was carefully rendering the Old Testament into Irish. Abraham Wheelocke, Professor of Arabic at Cambridge, who was no less learned in the Persian tongue, after preparing a refutation of the Koran, was translating the works of the Venerable Bede into modern English. Edward Pococke, Professor of Arabic at Oxford, had been granted a sabbatical year to travel dangerously in the Turkish dominions in search of the manuscript treasures of Greek and Syrian monasteries.

The traffic was not all in one direction; Christian refugees from the Turkish dominions sometimes reached England. A Cretan scholar, Nathaniel Canopis, had been brought to Oxford by Archbishop Laud where, from Balliol College, he disseminated his grave learning and amused his colleagues by brewing a black drink from roasted coffee berries.

Scholars in universities and in their homes collected libraries and worked assiduously, together or alone, on problems of history, archæology and etymology never before considered. It was the dawn of the great dictionaries, the surveys, the monumental volumes which laid the foundations of future learning in many different fields. Florio's Italian dictionary, Cotgrave's French dictionary, Minsheu's Spanish dictionary were on the shelves of the learned, as well as Minsheu's remarkable etymological dictionary of nine languages. William Camden's *Britannia* was already a standard work; Dugdale had begun the researches into English ecclesiastical history which culminated in the publication of his *Monasticon*. Henry Spelman had issued the first volume of his glossary of legal terms and was still deeply engrossed midway between M and Z. Dodsworth, Archer, D'Ewes and others were following in the footsteps of Robert Cotton and William Lisle in the study of Anglo-Saxon, revealing the history hidden in place names and the origins of the English language, customs and laws.

The casual tourist had picked up the prevailing intellectual curiosity and would go out of his way to see druidical circles as remote as " Long Meg and her Daughters " in Cumberland. All who crossed the border paused to contemplate the great grass-grown bastion which they vaguely called the Picts Wall. Stonehenge drew travellers to and from the west; Inigo Jones asserted that it had been built by the Romans but other scholars contested this. Visitors to the strange caves of Wookey Hole would play the recorder in order to appreciate the echo.

Lesser, more simply practical or light-hearted speculations

and inventions were discussed. Richard Norwood had paced the distance from London to York, a primitive method of measurement which was surprisingly accurate. " Way-wisers " or small machines attached to the leg, or a coach wheel, for measuring the distance travelled, were a discussed novelty. Rival methods of abbreviated writing, the various new stenographies, claimed public attention. John Babington, one of His Majesty's gunners, had borrowed time from his more serious occupations to write a volume on fireworks in which he described " the manner of making the best sort of stars," and " how to make Fisgigs which some call serpents," with such other skilful wonders as coats of arms correctly blazoned or a fortress of fireworks whence mechanical musketeers emerged to fire off rockets—" which being well and orderly performed will give much content."

The London booksellers and printers, congregated about St. Paul's, had an eager market for their wares, paper volumes displayed on trays before their shops, opened at an interesting page. There were books and to spare, good, bad, indifferent, grave, gay, useful, pious. Each was registered at the King's Stationery Office; the harvest for the year 1637 included a commentary on Aristotle by Thomas Hobbes, translations of St. Ambrose, Symmachus, Virgil, Martial and Petrarch; numerous histories ancient and modern; practical handbooks—*The Complete Cannonier or the Gunner's Art*, *The Attorney's Academy*, *The Husbandman's Practice*, *A Discourse of Bees*; some works on navigation, on medicine, on midwifery; Taylor's guide to the posts called *The Carriers' Cosmography*; the latest plays of Fletcher, Heywood, and Shirley; *The Merry Jests of the Cobbler of Canterbury* and other familiar joke books; a large number of " dainty new ditties," poems, elegies and anagrams; a new issue of *The Wise Men of Gotham* and other old favourites like the lives of Dick Whittington and Old King Cole; St. Francis de Sales' *Devout Life* in English, a new translation of the *Golden Ass* of Apuleius, and *A Posy of Godly Prayers* from an unknown hand.

In the literary haunts of London—Ben Jonson's old Devil

Tavern, or the newer fashioned Rose in Covent Garden, or the Globe, where the walls were painted to represent Arcady—young gentlemen of London and visitors from the provinces talked of the latest books and plays. In country houses, small and great, societies of intelligent men and women met to debate on faith or philosophy, to read their works aloud, to sing or dance together to the pretty music of the virginals or the deeper tones of the small organs which had become popular in many homes. Some have left a name and fame behind, like Great Tew where Falkland's circle met; the pleasures of other great houses are echoed in contemporary letters, Lord Leicester's Penshurst, Lord Northumberland's Syon, Lord Northampton's Compton Wynyates, Lord Newcastle's Bolsover.

Smaller houses, the homes of scholars, clergymen, citizens and gentlemen, offered the delights of good conversation and sometimes also curiosities and things of beauty to look at. The Provost of Eton, Sir Henry Wotton, collected many friends about him in his peaceful old age to talk of painting and literature, to look at the Venetian pictures that adorned his walls, and to examine such curiosities as "a piece of Crystal Sexangular, grasping divers several things within it, which I bought among the Rhaetian Alps."[1] At the house of his friend Izaak Walton, citizen and ironmonger of London, the talk was of literature and the quiet delights of fishing. Samuel Hartlib, another London citizen, collected about him those interested in education, philosophy or the improvement of husbandry. William Oughtred, in his vicarage at Albury, gathered round him his disciples in the study of mathematics, but would from time to time retire to his room for two or three days together, refusing all food and interruptions, until he had solved the insistent problem tracking through his brain. The poet Drummond, at his secluded Hawthornden in the Lothian hills, discussed poetical and political problems with his kinsmen and friends. Dr. Henry King, in his deanery at Rochester, composed verses and sermons and put together a choice library which he intended to bequeath to the Cathedral.

Such were the pleasures to be found among the most civilised nobility, clergy, gentry and citizens. The average level was not so high. The majority of country houses offered coarse entertainment to the mind: the talk was of dogs, hawks, horses, harvest prospects and local quarrels; the books were manuals on hawking or land tenure, a handbook on the law, the Bible, Foxe's "Book of Martyrs", possibly a play-book bought when last the owner visited London, with *Guy of Warwick*, *Palmerin of England* or some other romance.

Education of a kind was widespread at least in England. The grammar schools and ancient foundations like Eton, Westminster, Winchester, Charterhouse and St. Paul's, took the sons of citizens and gentry, of the clergy and the professional classes, sometimes those of the nobility. It was more usual for the nobility to have a tutor resident in the house, and for the richer gentry to send the boys to live with a private schoolmaster where five or six pupils, looked after as part of his family, occupied all his scholastic attention. From such establishments, quite as often as from the ancient and famous schools of the realm, the most eminent men emerged.

Hours were long, and six in the morning the usual time for school to begin. Long before daylight on a winter morning schoolboys would be on their way, breakfasting, as they went, on a piece of bread and honeycomb or a lump of cheese. At school Latin was the basis of all learning; the boys of the middle and upper classes, when they had mastered the language, proceeded to learn all other subjects, including their own religion, in the Latin tongue. The careful, comprehensive and fundamentally simple catechism which had been prepared in the last century by Dean Nowell for the use of older children was composed in Latin so as to fit into the grammar school curriculum. History, philosophy, geography and all appreciation of poetry or great literature came through the study of ancient and modern Latin classics. History written in English, like Holinshed's Chronicle, or the many recent books on European history were for recreation: so was Raleigh's great *History of the World*

—a favourite book among Puritans—which Oliver Cromwell recommended for leisure reading to his idle son Dick.

As Latin was still the universal language of the educated, and modern works both of information and of literature were composed in it, this technique of education did not exclude the boys from contemporary knowledge. On the contrary it brought them into contact with European culture and the greatest of Renaissance and Reformation thinkers. The works of Erasmus, of Melanchthon, of Linacre and of George Buchanan were studied in the grammar schools. Some schools preferred the works of Christian to pagan writers and commended the study of Mantuan, Palingenius or Cornelius Schön, poets and dramatists of the sixteenth century, before those of Lucan, Virgil, Seneca or Terence. The vast corpus of George Buchanan's works, for instance, provided in themselves for English, and still more for Scottish, boys a liberal education; his writings included plays, epigrams and pastorals, a prose history of Scotland as educational as Livy, and, for political philosophy, his *De Jure Regni* which expounded the theory of a strictly limited monarchy.

The immense influence of Buchanan in the schools had been viewed with disquiet by the late King James, and the Archbishop of Canterbury at this present time was trying to popularise in Scottish schools the fluent verse of Arthur Johnston, recently appointed rector of the university of Aberdeen. Johnston, whose religious views were more favourable to the monarchy than those of Buchanan, had achieved a fair measure of contemporary fame by his recent versification of the psalms in Latin.

The basic Latin of seventeenth-century education did not create uniformity of knowledge or outlook. The majority of Latin-educated boys had no more of the pagan classics than a handful of quotations. Their knowledge, philosophy and outlook on life were drawn from the Latin writers of the last century. But a worldly minority among the nobility and richer gentry had studied the pagan classics, had travelled abroad and had tasted the graces and the civilisation of the antique world in its Renaissance revival. They liked the colour, the imagination, the wit, wisdom and nobility of the Latin poets; they quoted the *Metamorphoses* of Ovid, the Satires of Persius and —more rarely—Juvenal, and above all the stoical and republican sentiments of Lucan's *Pharsalia*. Seneca, beloved of the Elizabethans, was going out of fashion, and Virgil was second to Lucan in favour.

Newer methods were discussed rather than practised. Samuel Hartlib was arranging for the publication in English of the important work on education written by the Bohemian exile John Comenius, and some men of learning hoped that the famous educationist might be persuaded to make his home in the island.

The grammar schools did not undertake to teach the elements of reading and writing. The children of professional men and the gentry were taught their alphabets at home by their mothers, but the ability to read and write was not uncommon among the poor in England, especially in the South. Working women left their children to be minded by some stay-at-home labourer, a cobbler, tailor, weaver, or carpenter. To keep them quiet, he made them learn their letters from a hornbook or battledore with the alphabet pasted upon it, which was handed from pupil to pupil. Dame's schools existed in some villages, but the cobblers' " petty schools " were more usual and some of these amateur schoolmasters, the " abecedarians " as they were called, were patient and clever; one carpenter cut out the letters on blocks of wood, others made up little rhymes, invented small rewards, alternated mental and manual work with play. Girls commonly had less of this schooling than boys; they were not so liable to mischief as their brothers, needed less " minding," and were early able to help their mothers at work. The wilder regions, where farmsteads and hamlets were far apart and no such cobblers' schools existed, were served by travelling pedagogues. These vagabonds of the teaching profession would spend a month or two in one small settlement and then pass on, often following a regular circuit that brought them back once in every three or four years to teach a new gaggle of little children to read and write. The craftsmen who kept school had a halfpenny or a penny a week for each child. The travelling pedagogue was given his keep in one yeoman's kitchen or another, and received presents from grateful parents. It was very simple, primitive and unorganised, but it worked reasonably well. Among the country folk the women were usually illiterate but most intelligent men could read.

They could read: but they had little to read. They read the Bible, for that most decent families possessed. They read Foxe's " Book of Martyrs," the most widespread and popular work of history in England, a copy of which was sometimes kept, along with the Bible, in the parish church. They read elementary books of devotion like *The Practice of Piety* and *The Whole Duty of Man*. Reading little, they took the printed word gravely, pondered it much and remembered it well. The more intelligent thought seriously, because the habit of prayer was usual, and concentrated prayer encourages coherent thinking. In respectable families the parents would possess a cheap catechism and would keep their children thoroughly exercised in it. Furthermore, in all the great schools, in some of the petty schools and in almost every home of whatever kind, everyone sang. The women sang at their carding and knitting and spinning, in the dairy and the kitchen; the men sang at the carpenter's bench, at the loom and the forge, or as they followed the plough. A favourite manual of musical instruction, especially devoted to the singing of the psalms, was reprinted two hundred and thirty-five times in the course of the century.

Where the villages lay thickest, where the market towns were busiest, there the psalms and the Bible-reading, Foxe's book and the works of Knox made their strong impression. For simple people, over the greater part of England and southern Scotland, certain ideas and phrases were written deep on the waxen minds of childhood. An astonished Italian reported that " they give their sons Hebrew names and call their daughters after the virtues and have quite abandoned those in use among Christians." [2] The Old Testament was commonly better known to these people than the New, and unconsciously they acquired the outlook, because they acquired the words, of the Chosen People. To the confident, self-reliant and assertive characteristics of the Anglo-Saxon were added tenacious Jewish fatalism and an unyielding confidence in a God who was theirs against the world.

The danger which might arise from the opinions of people who were serious, literal-minded and only in the most elementary sense *educated* was evident to authority. For this reason the Crown insisted on the importance of catechising children in the hope of keeping the speculations of the humble within the disciplined limits laid down by the Church. From time to time efforts were made to establish some kind of uniformity in the books used for instruction by village pedagogues. In theory, if not always in practice, all A B C's were issued by royal authority, so that nothing but the most orthodox and innocuous prayers or sentences could be found in them. King James had attempted unsuccessfully to coerce all the village dominies in Scotland into using a text book called *God and the King*, an obsequious treatise by an English divine.

Where the Celtic languages prevailed the scene was different. The adaptable Welsh had partly brought their native culture into line with English fashions. Welsh, alone of the Celtic languages, could claim a reasonable if not a very large number of printed books. A Welsh-Latin dictionary had been compiled and two Welsh aldermen of London had arranged for the printing of a cheap edition of the Bible in Welsh—at five shillings, to suit the slender purses of Welsh farmers. The Common Prayer had been officially translated and a Welsh poet, Edmund Prys, had versified the psalms. Rhys Prichard, an enterprising clergyman, taught his flock in rhyming Welsh, simplifying and even singing the Bible story. But Welsh was no longer the speech of the educated. The Welsh gentry spoke English and sent their sons to English-speaking schools. They did not trouble much with their daughters, and Vicar Prichard, in an angry outburst at the attitude of his compatriots, exaggerated and underlined the different education of Welsh and English girls: an English tinker's daughter could read, he said, when a Welsh squire's daughter could not. Literacy offered little advantage to those who only spoke Welsh, and the poor rarely troubled to learn their letters. Their crafts, their traditions and much of their literature, they handed on by word of mouth.

What was partly true in Wales was wholly true of the Scottish highlands and of Ireland. No useful comparison can be made between the literate Englishman or lowlander and the unlettered Celt. The two did not represent different levels of the same culture; they represented different ways of life and thought. The highlander and the wild Irishman had skills of hand and eye, and a hardiness lost to the southerners; they had knowledge of legend and history and poetry by memory and oral tradition. They had their own code of honour and respected the laws of their ancient, half-shattered society, older than the Norman Conquest, and older than the English invasion. The Anglo-Saxon thought them barbarous, but they thought him vulgar.

The gentry, in the Celtic regions, sometimes sent their sons to English-speaking seats of learning; the highland Scots to Aberdeen and St. Andrews, the Irish to Trinity College, Dublin. But if they were true to the old religion, as many of them were, they sent their sons abroad. Many a young Irish or Scottish chief had his education in France or Flanders, Italy or Spain. They avoided thereby the crude contamination of the Anglo-Saxons but they hardly preserved the purity of their own traditions: Ireland's most distinguished poet of this epoch, Piers Ferriter, a chief dwelling on the Blasket Islands, wrote Petrarchan lyrics in his native tongue.

Romantics and antiquaries regretted that the Reformation and the printed word had had a deadening effect on the natural imagination of the people. John Aubrey lamented that " the many good books and variety of turns of affairs have put all the old Fables out of doors, and the divine art of printing and gunpowder have frighted away Robin Goodfellow and the fairies." His nurse, he said, " had the history from the Conquest down to Carolus I in Ballad." But the English about the year 1637 had not put fables quite out of doors. While some, aspiring to education and picking up undigested knowledge from the new Anglo-Saxon studies, angrily declared that the common people of England were the oppressed descendants of the conquered Saxons while all the nobility were tyrannous Normans, others still accepted the ancient legend that Brutus, a great grandson of Aeneas, had conquered Britain from the giants Gog and Magog. As the power and energy of their country grew, they were well pleased to think that Britain was now what Rome had once been—the legitimate heir of Trojan greatness.

The people were still in many things, and even in their cities, very close to nature and the springs of life. The voices of wind and water, the signs of sun and moon, stars and clouds, the movements of birds, the baying of dogs, had not lost their messages and meanings. Goblins and fairies flittered in the autumn dusk; Robin Goodfellow had " his creambowl duly set " and sometimes, with human connivance, left threepence in the slippers of industrious maids. Pigwiggin afflicted the lazy with cramps; Billyblind chuckled on the hearthstone of the north country cottage; the water nixies clutched at the ankles of the late traveller wading the swollen burn. The wise, wizened faces of the little folk stared at the lone hunter crossing the moors at dusk. At many a cool spring in a shady hollow, sanctified by the name of a maiden saint, loveless girls and barren wives performed rites which had been old when Saint Frideswide was young. Pagan festivals survived, sometimes crudely Christianised; boys and girls decked the houses of town and country with green branches on May Day and danced riotously round the maypole, though the religious, with some justification, abhorred the practice. Crops and wells were blessed with old pagan rites and at harvest festivals straw dolls were plaited and carried in triumph.

In the wilds of Lochaber from time to time a green man would be seen, one that had been killed between daylight and starlight and belonged neither to earth nor heaven. Some thought these apparitions were only the unhappy dead but others thought them one of the many forms taken by the devil. The strong forces of nature, with the advent of Christianity, had become confused with the devil, and after the lapse of centuries witchcraft had become indivisibly compact of pagan and Christian beliefs. The devil, in many forms, bestrode the islands from end to end. Sometimes he was " a proper gentleman with a laced band," as when he came to Elizabeth Clarke at Chelmsford; at other times you might know him, as Rebecca Jones of St. Osyth did, by his great glaring eyes. He was cold and sensual and rather mean: he offered Priscilla Collit of Dunwich only ten shillings for her immortal soul; she gave it to him and off he went without paying. Respectably dressed in " brown clothes and a little black hat," he spoke in friendly terms to Margaret Duchill of Alloa in Scotland; " Maggie, will you be my servant?" he asked, and when she agreed he told her to call him John and gave her five shillings and powers of life and death over her neighbours.[3]

In England the devil kept low company for the most part. He comforted poor, half-crazed, hungry old women, cackling ill-naturedly at their neighbours and growing foolish over a mangy cat, a tame sparrow or a friendly toad on which they bestowed a comical or high-sounding name, Pyewacket, Jeremary, or Grizel Greediguts. In Scotland he was said to have more distinguished clients. From the spikes on the Tolbooth in Edinburgh grinned the white skull of the Earl of Gowrie, reputed a warlock in his time, as other noblemen had been. The devil drove with Lord Carnegie in a coach-and-six over tracks where no coach could go. The devil had had a hand in it when Sir John Colquhoun of Luss seduced his sister-in-law Lady Katherine Graham, and while the fugitive couple hid in London, their shocked and distinguished families solemnly pleaded witchcraft as the cause of their sin. What witchcrafts flourished among the Celtic peoples it is hard to say, but the English and the lowland Scots viewed their dark powers with apprehension. The Irish, it was certain, could call up vapours from their bogs to the destruction of whole armies.

The frontier between legitimate country lore and black magic was but feebly marked; in general the wise woman or " cunning man " who collected simples and knew how to brew drugs or pronounce spells to cure the ills of men and horses, to take away the toothache, banish warts and ease the pains of childbed, was not likely to be persecuted as a witch, in England at any rate. In Scotland, a more austere religious faith made all rites and jargons suspect, and women who muttered old Latin rhymes or were guilty of touching a sick cow with a blue pebble or other such conduct were within reach of the law though it rarely fell upon them for such things alone.

The " healing touch " was an old English belief. The government sometimes took action against those who claimed to have it, for to heal by touch was the King's sacred prerogative. A seventh son of a seventh son—these were popularly thought to have the power—had practised near London, but his cures were examined by the College of Physicians and dismissed as fraudulent; he turned out not even to be a seventh son. A little boy of five in Somerset, who was incontrovertibly a seventh son of a seventh son, was carried from village to village by his father and made many cures; no money was paid, only fruit and sugar-plums, garters, points and ribbons. The Bishop of Bath and Wells, instructed to look into the matter, was lenient; he let off the father with a caution and sent them both home.[4]

The suppression of superstition and dubious healing rites was but a small part of the King's task. In the matter of witchcraft he had shown himself enlightened, and had intervened to save a group of Lancashire women from malicious persecution. His principal task was the more lofty one of imposing right beliefs and right religious practices on all his subjects, however complex or however simple their minds, however civilised or primitive their way of thought.

To King Charles the Church was the soul of the State, without which the body politic would be inert and lifeless matter. At this tranquil and apparently successful time in his career his feelings for the Church were chiefly apparent in his vigorous determination to destroy its opponents and to enforce upon all his people obedience to its canons. But implicit always in this attitude of his was an inner spiritual passion. His church policy was the outcome not of calculation but of conviction; he was ready to die for it.

In 1637 it seemed impossible that any such sacrifice would be asked of him, yet had the wild hypothetical question been put to him he would not have hesitated in his answer. When he was still a prince, he had been overheard to say to friends that he could not be a lawyer for "I cannot defend a bad nor yield in a good cause." [5]

The sentiment expressed very exactly the King's temperament; when he thought a cause was good he would not yield, and by "not yielding" he did not mean that he would yield on sufficient persuasion, or the day after to-morrow, or the year after next; he meant that he would not yield. This capacity for total resistance showed in these sunnier times as an occasional inconvenient obstinacy: occasional, because the number of things about which the King had completely made up his mind were few. On most subjects his hesitations and indecisions were notorious and embarrassing. But on the question of the Church he was immovable; it was the central pillar of his life, and his attitude to his own royal authority was but a part of his profound conviction of the unique rightness of the Church of England.

He was of the intractable stuff of which martyrs are made— not the swift, ecstatic martyrs who run upon death in a high impulsive fervour, but the sad, thoughtful martyrs who follow over long, patient years some logical sequence of thought and action which always may, and sometimes must, bring them to disaster. It is hard to understand and impossible to do justice to the situation which developed in England unless this peculiar quality of King Charles is seen from the outset as an integral part of it. In 1637 his actions might well be interpreted as those of a King who sought to strengthen the authority of the Crown by extending the authority of the Church. But this was the least part of them; for when it became apparent that their effect was precisely the opposite, that the logic of his policy was leading him not towards a serene magnificence of Kingship but to the mortal hazards of war, to capture, even to death, he would not turn aside.

Charles was the first King who had been brought up from childhood as a member of the Church of England. His predecessors had accepted the Church in maturity, as a convenient framework of belief. Charles had drawn in its doctrine with the innocent acceptance of childhood; the Church of England was to him, as it had been to none of his predecessors, the established order of things.

For the first time, the Anglican Church had as its head a Defender of the Faith who had never considered the possibility of defending any other faith. As if in response to this first monarch, so truly its own, it had flowered into a new beauty, of words, of form, and here and there a shining saintliness. The careful argumentation of Lancelot Andrewes and the menacing thunder of John Donne had been familiar to the King in the early part of his reign, but now a gentler, more pastoral inspiration breathed from the younger generation of preachers, Jeremy Taylor, Henry Hammond, William Cartwright. Many of them wrote poetry; a delicate sensibility to beauty lit up the meditations and prayers which they composed as they contemplated the Infinite from a college study or a vicarage window or the garden of a wealthy patron. They were a minority, as men of sensibility and talent necessarily are, but they set up a vibration in the Anglican community which has not died away. They loved the temperate beauty of their Church, not wantonly glorious like the Church of Rome, nor aggressively plain like that of Geneva. As George Herbert gratefully wrote:

> Blessed be God, Whose Love it was
> To double-moat thee with His grace,
> And none but thee.

The King had at his right hand an Archbishop after his own heart. He had always liked and approved of William Laud, although his father had feared the meddling temperament of the little man and had been unwilling to give him preferment. Under King Charles, Laud had been raised first to the see of London, then to that of Canterbury.

A man of great learning, a profound believer in ritual and hierarchy, Laud was more of a tidier-up and setter-in-order than a true reformer, but he had boundless energy and clear, if limited, vision. His ideal was a Church, rigidly and efficiently organised, its services reverently conducted according to a uniform ritual, its hierarchy sagely established, and the whole population gathered together into one docile flock. This vision exactly matched the King's. It became the corner-stone of a deep personal respect and friendship which made it possible for Charles to overlook the Archbishop's social failings. These were less kindly viewed by many of his colleagues on the King's council who found him troublesome, tactless and ill-bred. The son of a Reading tradesman, he had never acquired the poise suitable to his exalted position, and his appearance—" a little, low, red-faced man "— was much against him. He was irritable, opinionated, apt to shout in argument and to slap about impatiently with his hands. He did not have the sense to avoid the absurd; his enemies can be forgiven for their angry amusement when, at the dedication of St. Catherine Cree Church, the splendid opening phrase, " Be ye lift up, ye everlasting doors: and the King of Glory shall come in," was immediately followed by the entry of stout little Laud. In spite of his shortcomings he had an element of greatness, a selfless and singleminded devotion to his religion and his duty. Like the King, he worked not for what he thought to be expedient, but for what he thought to be right, and, like the King, he would not abandon it.

Under the King's and the Archbishop's influence, outward beauty was much regarded. Inigo Jones designed simple, handsome churches in the Renaissance manner, and re-modelled, on chastely luxurious lines, the chapels of the great. Italianate façades and porticoes were wedded incongruously to older buildings. A hybrid style, later to be called Laudian Gothic, was evolved. There was a revived interest in Church plate, vestments, hangings, screens, lecterns, pulpits, fonts, furniture of all kinds, even in painted glass.

Small organs, many of which came from Germany, beautifully carved and gilded, were introduced into private chapels, churches and cathedrals. Singing of the most elaborate kind was encouraged and cherished; new music was composed for the King's chapel and cathedral choirs. The Church flowered in a new beauty of holiness.

George Herbert, a younger son of a noble house, bred to the Court, had abandoned a wordly career and created during his brief devoted ministry the pattern of the Anglican parish priest. Nicholas Ferrar, of a wealthy family, to whom preferment stood open, had withdrawn from the world to Little Gidding in Huntingdonshire, where with his mother and brother and his brother's children he had created a community devoted to prayer, contemplation, good works and religious studies. Poor widows lived on the charity of this community and village children learned their psalms from the pious ladies with a penny prize for the word-perfect and Sunday dinner afterwards for all.[6]

The good preachers, the sensitive writers, the fine, holy and devout men in the Anglican Church were a minority. The King, who drew towards him divines after his own heart, too easily believed that those he saw were, if not typical, at least dominant in the Church. Factious dissent and criticism seemed to him only the last mutterings of an ancient storm soon to be quiet for ever.

He was wrong in every way. His Church was young and insecure, doctrinally divided, imperfectly organised, open to criticism and but feebly rooted in the affections of the people. At the time of its establishment by law under Queen Elizabeth many points of doctrine had been left vague in order that as many as possible of her subjects might be brought in without offence to conscience. The Church was Protestant because it repudiated the Pope but it was officially spoken of as Catholic and it had retained the episcopal hierarchy. This reformation seemed inadequate to the large number of English Protestants who had come under the Calvinist or Baptist influences which flowed into the country with the Netherlands trade. The first demanded the reorganisation of the Church without bishops, on the model of Geneva; the second demanded liberty for congregations of the faithful to choose their own way of worship. Of the two the Calvinist group was the more intellectual, the more highly conscious and the stronger, for the Baptists and their like declined by their very nature towards an anarchy of subdivision.

Apart from those who fully understood the doctrine and organisation of Calvinism, a great number of Protestants in England tended, by temperament, through the verbal interpretation of the Bible or through animosity to the Church of Rome, to lean away from the Catholic and towards the Protestant elements in the Church of England. The term Puritan, used indiscriminately for all these, had no definite and no official meaning: it was a term of abuse merely. It might be applied equally to a devout cobbler expounding the scriptures according to a theory of his own, or to a dutiful member of the Anglican communion who had done no more than hazard the opinion that the surplice was a remnant of Rome.

For the last half-century the English Church had been striving towards a greater clarity and uniformity of worship and doctrine, but the movement had not been continuously in the same direction. Archbishop Whitgift had compelled the more intransigent Calvinist clergy to leave the Church, and his successor Richard Bancroft had worked with pastoral severity to suppress extreme Protestant doctrines. George Abbot, Bancroft's successor, had reversed this policy. He had favoured the more Protestant clergy and discouraged those whose practices showed too close an approximation to Rome.

The doctrines of Arminius, the Dutch theologian who had challenged Calvinism at Leyden, were at this time gaining currency in England and bringing with them a return to ritual. Abbot detested their tenets, but the intellectual fashion was too strong for him; more and more of the promising young men at the universities adopted Arminian views. When King Charles ascended the throne, the division between the Arminians and the school of churchmen whom Abbot approved was already deeply marked. When Abbot retired, Charles himself put forward William Laud, the most distinguished of the Arminians, to take his place. Laud reverted, inevitably, to the anti-Puritan policy of Bancroft and Whitgift. But he could not undo the work of Abbot. The English Church, from bishops downwards, was full of those who disapproved of the Arminians, and Laud's favour towards them was popular neither with laity nor with clergy. " What do the Arminians hold?" went the ill-natured joke—" All the best livings in England." Both pastors and flock were deeply, bitterly divided.

The crucial question was the relationship of the Anglican Church to Rome. The creed spoke of " one holy Catholic Church " but this meant different things to different men. A man who, like the Archbishop or the King, believed that truth was one and indivisible must necessarily wish to see Catholic Christendom re-united. Certain of the Anglican clergy shared the wish, although the intensity of their desire and the ways in which they would have liked to implement it varied greatly. The sincere and unhappily bewildered Godfrey Goodman, Bishop of Gloucester, was one of the few leading churchmen who doubted the rightness of the Anglican position and would have welcomed a return to the communion of Rome at the price of concessions.[7] Archbishop Laud and his chief supporters saw in the Anglican doctrine and ritual the true Catholic faith, deplored the errors of Rome and were steadfast against them. But Rome, for them, represented an error in Catholicism which might one day be set right. It was very different from vile heresies like Calvinism and Baptism. They would protect their flocks with all their strength against conversion to Rome, but they felt the Roman error to be less fundamental and less dangerous to the souls in their care than the sectarian heresies.

The bishops who survived from Archbishop Abbot's time were essentially Protestant and had no thought at all of undoing the work of the Reformation. Several of them were distinguished for discretion and integrity but they were not fortunate in their leadership. Bishops Davenant of Salisbury and Hall of Exeter, learned and worthy men, were neither of them ambitious for domination. The able and diplomatic Bishop Morton of Durham was equally unwilling to thrust himself forward in Church politics. Leadership of the group who wished to conciliate the Puritans fell therefore to John Williams, Bishop of Lincoln, a super-subtle Welshman against whom the Archbishop waged a continual war. Williams believed, honestly and charitably, that the Church could prosper only through alliance and friendship with the best of the Puritans. But his honesty of motive did not go with honesty of method. Mistakenly meddling in the early quarrels of Charles and his Parliaments, Williams had forfeited the King's favour and laid himself open to the grave charge of revealing state secrets. In attempting to defend himself against this charge, the excitable and over-ingenious prelate had involved himself in an offence even more grave—that of suborning witnesses. The King, dropping the original accusation, had substituted the new one, and Williams, after trying every trick of evasion and postponement, was to face the King's council in the summer of 1637 on this disgraceful charge. So shocking a crime made him at the moment more of a liability than an asset to the conciliatory party in the Church.

The Archbishop, well knowing this, pressed the charge home with the intention of wrecking, at one blow, both Williams and the policy for which he stood.

The division between the best men in the Church was one grave difficulty that the King had to face. Another problem was the inadequate resources and organisation of the Anglican Establishment. At the untidy Reformation made by Henry VIII the economic foundations of the Church had been irreparably damaged. The hierarchy and the administrative framework had survived and been reaffirmed under Elizabeth, but it was another matter to restore enough Church property to maintain the Anglican Church with the dignity of its Roman predecessor. The bishoprics had been so plundered that Elizabethan, Jacobean and Caroline bishops were reduced to the oddest expedients. The Bishop of St. David's tore off and sold all the lead on the episcopal palace. The Bishop of Lichfield recklessly deforested his land to get the profit of the timber. Other bishops converted the short leases of their tenants into life-rents for sums of ready money. This was a help to the bishop who made the arrangement but left his successor poorer than before, and King Charles had vigorously—and vainly—prohibited the practice.[8]

Since the Reformation, tithes had in some places been commuted for money, and in others been alienated to the lay patrons of the living. The value of money had declined in the past eighty years and often changes in agriculture had altered the value and quantity of the payments in kind. Friction over tithes between the clergy and their parishioners or their patrons was frequent, and was intensified by the contention of Puritan dissidents that they did not wish to pay any minister who was not of their own way of thinking, or even that to pay tithes at all was a form of simony, the gifts of the Holy Ghost not being for sale. All these quarrels brought to popular notice the least spiritual aspect of the Church and its ministers.

Patronage of church livings had at the Reformation been greedily swallowed up by laymen of all sorts, landowners or corporations, who had frequently taken a large part of the endowments as well. The smallness of the incomes from preferments led to unashamed pluralism. A churchman who by astute courting of the right patrons had procured several livings for himself could delegate his religious duties to one or two poor curates hired at miserable wages. The pluralist himself, it was said, " weareth cassocks of damask and plush, good beavers and silk stockings, can play well at tables or gleek, can hunt well and bowl very skilfully . . . and can relish a glass of right claret."[9] The absentee was rarely an advertisement for the spiritual qualities of the Church, nor was the starveling curate who filled his place.

The parson's status in the social hierarchy was doubtful; manual labour was frowned on but he had to work his glebe. Parishioners in one village complained because the parson played ninepins with the butcher, and in another, because he undertook odd jobs of thatching in his spare time. No doubt much depended on the reputation and general behaviour of individuals: many of these disappointed educated men, exiled in remote places, found solace in drink and low company, and thatching or playing ninepins with the butcher were only one part of the conduct which was felt to misbecome their office—for when the neatly dressed parson's wife of Fladbury tripped down the village street with her milk pail on her head like a dairymaid she got nothing but indulgent smiles and commendation for her Christian simplicity.[10]

Ordination was inadequately controlled. Orders were sold or forged, or given by bishops on insufficient inquiry into the character and education of the candidate. The Puritan Baxter's account of the Anglican clergy round Kidderminster at about this time—decrepit and doddering or else drunk and immoral—represents the Church as seen by a vehement critic, but these dark colours were true to a part of the reality. The Church had neither the men nor the organisation to meet all the needs of the people. Wales was wretchedly neglected for lack of priests and of those appointed to Welsh parishes few could speak or preach in Welsh. In Herefordshire it was said that in over two hundred churches and chapels there were not twenty incumbents fit or willing regularly to preach a sermon.[11]

Serious-minded men and women, some but not all of whom were extreme Protestants, tried to remedy the shortcomings or the absence of the local clergy by meeting independently for prayer and Bible reading. It was an easy step from this to expounding and preaching. A gentleman living in Exeter, for instance, with a comfortable household employing seven or eight servants, held "a conference upon a question propounded once a week in his own family "—a debate upon the scriptures in which his children and servants joined.[12] However innocently such discussions began, they created a dangerous liberty of argument, and the established Church discouraged them, mildly or vigorously according to the temper of the bishop in charge. Attacks provoked defiance and bred fanaticism; in districts where Puritanism was deeply rooted, family gatherings insensibly grew into conventicles, meeting secretly when they were forbidden. The steady increase in the number of these conventicles was, for all those who had the interests of the Establishment at heart, one of the most disquieting phenomena of the sixteen-thirties.

A group of Puritans, earlier in King Charles's reign, had embarked on a scheme for providing respectable clergy by private enterprise. They bought in advowsons which had become secularised at the Reformation, and presented to them ministers of their own choosing. In this way they planned, little by little, to place men of good morals and sound doctrine—according to their way of thinking—in a great number of parishes. They had not gone far before they were stopped. In Laud's opinion their action was a plot—" in a cunning way, under a glorious pretence, to overthrow the Church government, by getting into their power more dependency of the clergy, than the King and all the Peers and all the Bishops in all the Kingdom had."[13]

From his own point of view Laud was right, but so, from their point of view, were the Puritan gentry who had given time, thought and money to the project. Both wanted to propagate what they took to be right doctrine and both wanted control of the best instrument of instruction and propaganda in the country—the pulpit.

Whitgift and Bancroft in their efforts to reorganise the Church had made great use of one effective weapon, the ecclesiastical Court of High Commission for inquiring into abuses. Under Bancroft clashes with the common lawyers began to arise; the High Commission, as the guardian of public morals, claimed jurisdiction in numerous domestic disputes and also in cases arising on, or in connection with, church land. Disputes over tithes also brought the interests of the Church into contact and collision with the common law [14] and the possibilities of ecclesiastical encroachment on territory belonging to the secular courts yearly increased; the old medieval conflict between spiritual and secular justice was thus revived. The danger to the Church arising from this clash with the common law was immediate and practical, for the pretensions of the High Commission Court created an alliance between the common lawyers and the Puritans.

Archbishop Laud used the High Commission vigorously, both to enforce his doctrinal and ritualistic ideas and to maintain the purity of English morals. Those summoned before the Court were compelled to take the so-called *ex officio* oath before answering the searching questions which might be put to them. Refusal to take the oath or to answer any question was treated as a plea of guilty. This practice above all roused the anger of the lawyers and caused popular critics to compare the High Commission, with sincere exaggeration, to the Spanish Inquisition.

Meanwhile, causes for quarrel with the extreme Protestants both clergy and laity, increased from year to year. Candles multiplied in the churches of the young, fervent Arminian clergy whom Laud favoured; images of saints and of the Virgin were restored or introduced; the Communion table was set up altarwise at the east end of the chancel. The Arminian clergy wore not only the surplice but vestments; a silly woman in Norwich, seeing something red, asked why the Mayor was officiating in church. Music came back to the cathedrals; choir boys were taught to come in two by two and not to turn their backs to the altar; priests bowed towards it; some even used the sign of the Cross.

The more extreme opponents clamoured derisively about these " apish anticks," these cringings and duckings and caperings, and a great number of simple people were truly perturbed and bewildered at what they believed to be a return to Rome. Knowing their Bible and Foxe's " Book of Martyrs," and remembering, in grisly detail, how some of their immediate forefathers had endured martyrdom rather than yield to the idolatries of Rome, they were profoundly unwilling to betray the faith which had thus been sealed and sanctified to them. It was useless to explain to such people that an image is not in itself idolatrous but only becomes so when it is worshipped as an idol; this seemed to them mere sophistry against the forthright words of the second commandment: *Thou shalt not make unto thee any graven image*.

So also with the commandment to keep holy the sabbath day, a commandment notoriously flouted by the Papists. In some regions of the country, where the old religion was still strong, the sabbath-keepers and the sabbath-breakers came into open conflict. In Lancashire and in Somerset wakes and holy days were enthusiastically celebrated by some, in defiance of the pious disapproval of others. King James had attempted to make an end of the people's quarrels by issuing a judgment of Solomon in the matter. In 1618 he had published the *Book of Sports* declaring what games might lawfully be played on Sundays after church: he included dancing for both sexes, vaulting, archery, and maypoles and morris dances in season. The King had prefaced his Book with the argument that if sports were made unlawful, the people would be driven to tipple in alehouses where they would learn to indulge themselves in " idle and discontented speeches."

The Book was, in intention, both politic and humane but it

met with great opposition. King Charles reissued it in 1633 with instructions that the vicar of each parish see that its provisions be thoroughly made known. He was widely reported to have commanded the clergy to read it from the pulpit, and some do indeed seem to have understood his orders in this way, for one, who read the book, followed it with the fourth commandment, adding, "Dearly beloved, you have heard the commandment of God and Man: obey which you will."

The Archbishop's more indiscreet supporters often aroused the animosity of their flock. A vicar of Grantham provoked derision because he genuflected with such extravagance as to lose his balance. A little later, when he tried to move the communion table to the east end of the chancel, his parishioners burst into the church to stop him. The vicar tugged at one end, they at the other, till he gave up the unequal contest, shouting to them to keep their old trestle, he would build a stone altar instead. They would have no " dressers of stone " in their church, they retorted and, led by a couple of aldermen of their city, went off in a party to complain to the Bishop. The vicar followed after, " pale and staring in his looks," pitifully telling the Bishop that his parishioners had threatened to burn his house.

The diocese was Lincoln and the Bishop John Williams, the conciliator. He asked them all to supper and tried to patch up the quarrel. Later he wrote to the vicar: " Whether side soever, you or your parish, shall yield unto the other, in these needless controversies, shall remain in my poor judgment, the more discreet, grave and learned of the two: and by that time you have gained some more experience in the cure of souls, you shall find no such ceremony equal to Christian charity." [15] Not long after he published, anonymously, in a pamphlet entitled *Holy Table: Name and Thing* his own moderate opinion on the place of the communion table in churches. The Archbishop regarded this attempt to propound a calmer view of the controversy with nothing but resentment.

Other church dignitaries were intransigent with their flocks for more secular reasons. At Chester no mayor had entered the cathedral for twelve years, owing to a dispute about the place allotted to him. At last a mayor, who had begun life as a cathedral chorister, tried to heal the breach but no sooner did he attempt to take his seat in the cathedral than the Dean reopened the old dispute and the mayor did not come again.[16]

Sometimes the internal dispute in the Church flared up between members of a cathedral chapter. A prebend of Durham, John Cosin, persuaded the chapter to beautify this most splendid of cathedrals in a worthy manner: great candlesticks gleamed on a high altar of "branched marble" and old defaced carvings of saints and angels were restored. A rival Puritan member of the cathedral chapter, Dr. Smart, in a thundering sermon on idolatry condemned him as "our young Apollo, who repaireth the Choir and sets it out gaily with strange Babylonish ornaments." The Court of High Commission silenced Smart, who lost his place in the cathedral and was fined five hundred pounds. The sentence purchased a temporary victory for Cosin at far too high a price; in the angry Puritan world Smart became the proto-martyr in a new era of persecution.[17]

Whatever the occasional extravagances of the Laudians, the conduct of the English in Church at this epoch stood in need of reformation. Lack of money and the disappearance of endowments had caused many churches to fall into decay and some altogether into disuse. Many were filthy, with unglazed windows, and mud floors like cow byres. Squatters took possession of neglected chapels; in Wiltshire several families were found camping in one, using suitable tombstones as cheese presses.[18] The abhorrence of idolatry taught by the Puritans had degenerated into open disrespect for church buildings. The parish church was often the parish meeting place, not only for sober business but for dancing and drinking parties. Sporting parishioners brought their dogs and hawks to divine service and the poorer sort pastured their hogs in the graveyard. An indignant sexton in Suffolk found the local squire sheltering from a storm with his horse inside the sacred building.

Much Communion plate had vanished at the Reformation and its place was often meanly supplied by wicker and earthenware bottles and vulgar tavern pots. The Calvinist practice of giving the sacrament at a table placed in the middle of the nave was usual; this, in Laud's angry phrase, made the church into an alehouse. He exaggerated, but the central position of the Communion table encouraged the congregation to use it as the common repository for hats and gloves, and to loll upon it with their elbows during the sermon.[19]

Social distinctions were more carefully preserved than reverence towards God. The gentry, and the London apprentices, thought it beneath their dignity to sit bareheaded during the sermon. In Bristol it was customary to wait for the mayor before beginning the sermon, or, if he came early, to begin the sermon immediately, omitting all the rest of the service. The clergy in many towns seem to have thought it right or at least advisable to " give good-morrow to Mr. Mayor, though in the middle of the Lesson." Conversely a respectful ploughman, joining in the responses, was alleged to have answered the vicar's *The Lord be with you* by *And with your worship's spirit.*

Such was the situation which the King and the Archbishop undertook to reform. Not long after the unseemly tumult between the vicar of Grantham and his parishioners, Laud began to insist that the communion table in every church in the kingdom be moved to the east end of the chancel and protected by rails " one yard in height and so thick with pillars that dogs may not get in." [20] The wearing of the surplice, bowing at the name of Jesus, and the churching of women after child-birth (another ceremony repugnant to the extreme Protestants) were likewise to be enforced.

Year after year, by means of visitations and prosecutions in the ecclesiastical Court, the Archbishop pressed on with his counter-reformation, provoking at each new clash and at each new prosecution a deeper resentment against himself and against his King.

The intensity with which his orders were enforced varied

from diocese to diocese. In the south and south-west, the old and cautious Bishop Davenant of Salisbury and the gentle and humane Bishop Hall of Exeter were anxious not to drive good men into opposition for trifles or to provoke animosity among the people. Neither of these bishops was popular at Whitehall, and Charles had had each of them in turn—and Hall more than once—on his knees before the Privy Council for offending his religious susceptibilities. The Dean of Winchester, also, pleaded to be excused from bowing at the name of Jesus because of the offence which this gave to the ignorant and to weaker vessels who might be alienated and lost to the Church.[21]

Very different was the spirit of the vehement Arminian, Matthew Wren, who had been appointed to the see of Norwich in the heart of East Anglia, the stronghold of Puritanism. The vigour of his visitations and the searching character of the questions which were put to the people had, within the space of two years, created a sullen, vindictive resentment throughout his diocese. He inquired not merely into the state of churches and churchyards, the order of services, the dress of the clergy, the existence of conventicles, the employment of chaplains or tutors by private families, but asked whether any man had heard any other speak anything against the King's authority, or if any in the parish did " presume to make matters of divinity their ordinary table-talk." If there were any who took " the liberty of their trencher-meetings . . . rashly and profanely to discourse of Holy Scripture " it was the duty of their neighbours to " name the persons, times and places, as far as you know, or have heard or can remember." [22] This gave dangerous encouragement to informers, provoked suspicion and ill-feeling from many honest, earnest Christians, and instituted a prying, exacting inquiry which was deeply resented. The number of prosecutions in the diocese and the number of the clergy suspended for Puritan conduct or doctrine was, in truth, nothing out of the ordinary. But the anger aroused by the bishop's policy was not assuaged because he was less terrible in deed than in word.

A recently published pamphlet called *News from Ipswich* had given the Puritans of London an exaggerated account of the troubles in East Anglia. Written in a confused but passionate manner, full of rhetoric, but also full of lively details, the pamphlet was widely bought and read before the government could stop it. The source of the publication was never revealed. It bore the statement "printed in Ipswich," but no Ipswich printer had set it up. A popular London preacher, Dr. Henry Burton, the Puritan rector of St. Matthew's, Friday Street, made *News from Ipswich* the subject of two sermons, in which he loudly condemned not only Bishop Wren but all bishops as "upstart mushrumps." This was not the first time that Burton had offended and he cannot have been greatly surprised at finding himself once again the object of government prosecution. In June of the year 1637 he faced his trial before the King's council, with two other opponents of the bishops.

The authorship of *News from Ipswich* had been traced to William Prynne, once a barrister, now a prisoner in the Tower of London. Some years before he had been condemned for the publication of a violent attack on the stage, a work as erudite as it was intemperate, entitled *Histriomastix*. The book was alleged to contain references to the dancing and masquing at Court and thus to offend the King's—and more especially the Queen's—Majesty. Prynne had been fined £5,000, had stood in the pillory, had had his ears cut off, and been sent to the Tower for life. Oxford had taken away his degree, Lincoln's Inn had expelled him, and the Inns of Court, to show their abhorrence of his opinions, had presented Shirley's famous and fabulously expensive masque, *The Triumph of Peace*, as a special compliment to the Court.

Prynne's powerful intellect and massive learning were constricted within the rigid bonds of his fanatical prejudices. He had no interests outside the study, no wife, few friends, and he advocated his Calvinist convictions with the glum ferocity of the professional pedant. He was an exasperating, unloved, unlovable man but his single-minded and ill-placed courage were to make him, over the years, into a popular public character.

Side by side with Henry Burton and William Prynne stood John Bastwicke, one of Burton's parishioners. By profession a doctor, Bastwicke had also been in trouble before and had been imprisoned in the Gatehouse for publishing in the Latin tongue attacks on the bishops. Early in 1637 he had changed his manner, though not his matter, and published an attack in plain English. All three men were thus before the Council for the same offence: a deliberate attempt to undermine the hierarchy of the Church. Prynne, Burton and Bastwicke might each individually be dismissed as a cantankerous eccentric. But they voiced an opposition which was steadily growing.

The opposition was serious, although often expressed in an ignorant, factious and ridiculous manner. Henry and Susan Taylor, from a Norfolk village, had, for instance, loudly babbled that bishops were lazy fellows, that tithes were unlawful, that the Anglican service was no different from the Mass and—with an unexpected veering from Protestantism to Popery—that the clergy should not marry.[23] The vicar of Llanidloes, who let his parishioners shoot birds in the nave and cut up his surplice for towels, was of much the same mettle as the Essex woman who pegged up her laundry in the chancel, crying that if parson brought his old linen into the church, so would she; or the good wife in Wolverhampton who, on being told to wear a veil for her churching, impudently clapped a dinner napkin over her head. Now and again the extremist fringe showed signs of mental derangement; the crazy Lady Eleanor Davies, who had the reputation of a prophetess, marched into Lichfield cathedral with a bucketful of pitch and splashed it over the altar hangings; she was assisted by the town clerk and his wife, both of whom seem to have been sane.[24] All this was ridiculous; but the popular emotions and the deeper convictions which underlay these incidents were not ridiculous.

The King's attitude to sermons stirred the Puritans more deeply than his attitude to ceremonies. The sermon, the ex-pounding of the scriptures, was their great strength; when a parson was himself weak in this kind of eloquence it was not unusual for him to engage, often at the expense of the parish, a lecturer to do the preaching for him. The great majority of these were Puritan clergy who, in present circumstances, were unlikely to get any higher preferment. Where Puritanism was strong, parishioners sometimes joined together for the godly purpose of paying for extra sermons, usually mid-week lectures. In this way, without any direct contravention of the authority of the Church, extreme Protestantism was poured forth from a great number of pulpits.

The King and the Archbishop, determined to stop the abuse, decreed that one sermon on Sunday, on a strictly uncontroversial topic, was alone to be permitted. Suitable sermons for general use were available, to help the less eloquent, in the *Book of Homilies*. At afternoon service a general catechism was to take the place of the sermon. As for the mid-week sermons, they were only to be allowed under strict diocesan supervision. Two more Puritan devices were forbidden: the church bell was not to be rung in a special manner to distinguish a service with a sermon from one without, and popular preachers were no longer to hold their services either later or earlier than those of neighbouring clergy, to enable people from outlying parishes to combine them, on a Sunday, with compulsory worship in their own church. In future there was to be no question of sermon-hungry parishioners straying into other folds to taste forbidden fruit.[25]

Apart from this general prohibition, the Archbishop and the bishops who supported his policy, from time to time suspended individual clergy or prohibited them from preaching. In Wales, the ignorance of the people and the isolation of farms and hamlets caused a few conscientious clergy to preach out of doors, in farm houses, or at irregular hours. William Wroth of Llanfaches, accused of such practices before the High Commission, pleaded with Celtic passion. He had seen " thousands of immortal souls around me, thronging to perdition, and should I not use all means to save them? " He was deprived of his cure none the less; so was William Erbury, of St. Mary's Cardiff and his curate, Walter Craddock. These three devout evangelists were strongly marked with Puritanism and, on losing their cures, continued to preach privately in despite of the law; Craddock ("a bold ignorant young fellow," said the High Commission) took his staff and scrip and roamed the hills of South Wales expounding the word of the Lord to the people in their own tongue. But even the gentle Rhys Prichard, who was no Puritan, was in trouble with authority for his unconventional practice of teaching the scriptures by making and singing Welsh songs with his flock. The Archbishop, whose first bishopric had been the South Welsh diocese of St. David's, was willing enough that the light of the gospel should shine in Wales, but it must shine only as he directed.

Clergy who had clashed with the Archbishop did not easily escape his vigilance. Thomas Shepard, a young man who shortly after his ordination had been chosen as their lecturer by the people of Earl's Colne in Essex, was one of those forbidden either to preach or to exercise any other religious function. He vainly argued his case in an interview with Laud, but the Archbishop trembled with rage and looked, Shepard recorded, "as though blood would have gushed out of his face." Shepard and his friends, who were no more courteous to Laud than he to them, spoke of him among themselves as the swine sent "to root up God's plants in Essex." Uprooted, Shepard fled to Yorkshire where he took refuge in a private household, but his retreat was discovered and he sailed for the wider freedom of New England.

New England and the other settlements far across the Atlantic were a source of nagging annoyance to the Archbishop and the King. It was difficult to know for sure, and almost impossible to stop, what was going on in those places. The Archbishop did his best by persistently interfering with the efforts of Puritans to raise money for "godly ministers" to go out to the congregations across the Atlantic. The stream of emigration of Puritan congregations and their clergy went on none the less and the

King was now seriously considering a total prohibition of all further sailings.

An annoyance of another kind came from the Protestant shores of Europe. English clergymen ordained by Calvinists in Holland somehow made their way into the English Church, and several protests to the Prince of Orange not to permit this irregular ordination of Englishmen had hitherto been in vain. Enclaves of foreign Calvinism also remained within the King's dominions. The Channel Islanders had received the Reformation from France and were indifferent to the English-speaking version of it later dispensed to them. Allowances had to be made for the Channel Islanders; they enjoyed a good many separate rights, owing to their status as part of the lost Duchy of Normandy. Administrative quarrels, bitter and frequent at this time, were not Laud's province: religion was. He went to work with more restraint and wisdom than usual. The difficulty was that all instruction in the islands had to be in French, and teachers were usually trained at the Huguenot academy at Saumur. Laud endowed three fellowships for Channel Islanders at Oxford in the hope that good education and pure doctrine would flow forth together from his own university.

The refugee churches, founded by fugitives from the Spanish Netherlands or France, and scattered over the south and south-east—at Norwich, Colchester, Maidstone, Sandwich, Canterbury, Southampton and London—came in for rougher treatment. Wren attacked them in the Eastern counties, Laud in the diocese of Canterbury. Their reason for existence as communities was questioned and they were commanded to attend the English parish churches and dissolve their separate organisation. Their English fellow citizens took their side; quite apart from the religious aspect of the matter, the towns which sheltered them did not want their own parishes to become responsible for the poor and infirm of communities which had hitherto always looked after their own.[26]

The English Church covered England and Wales and enclosed at least two-thirds of the King's subjects, willingly or unwillingly, within the fold. The Churches of Ireland and Scotland, which also engaged the King's attention, offered different problems. The Church of Ireland was, in organisation, doctrine and liturgy, the same as that of England, and the King usually sought the advice of Laud in making appointments to Irish bishoprics, in spite of the primacy, over the Irish Church, of James Ussher, Archbishop of Armagh.

Ussher's Anglican flock consisted chiefly of settlers and their families. Ineradicable and all-pervasive, the Old Religion commanded the allegiance of the Irish; the Roman priests and bishops had their loyalty although cathedrals, churches, chapels, and episcopal residences and revenues were in the hands of strangers, and their own clergy lived on the charity of the faithful by the sufferance of the government.

Abroad, in Rome, in Spain, in the Spanish Netherlands, Irish friars kept in constant touch with their brethren at home. Plots for the return of Ireland to the Church, with the help of Spain, were continuously in the air. A mysterious figure, the titular Archbishop of Cashel, moved secretly between Ireland and Spain; it was said that the Spaniards paid him a thousand ducats a year for his services, and the Lord Deputy Wentworth had hitherto been unsuccessful in identifying and seizing upon him.[27]

The Church of Ireland was adrift like a raft on an alien sea, and had not even the universal approval of the settlers who were inclined, especially in Ulster, towards the anti-episcopal doctrines of Calvin. It was at least fortunate in the Primate, James Ussher, Archbishop of Armagh. He was " a tall, proper, comely man," of a fine but austere presence, studious and frugal habits and simple, courteous bearing. Ussher's Protestantism was enriched by great learning, guided by a high intelligence and informed by a genuine, though concealed, warmth of heart. He was a man of strong, unbending character but he was not provocative. Laud, who did not agree with him, respected both his knowledge of Ireland and his integrity; he never willingly went against him either in his appointments or his policy, and the Irish Church had been allowed to retain an essentially Protestant character. The English Church in Ireland had, however, suffered no less than the Church at home from the unscrupulous plundering of its revenues since the Reformation. The ceaseless law suits about property and endowments between the clergy and the laity made it unpopular with the wealthy settlers and sometimes contemptible to the pious.[28]

In Ulster the Lowland Scots who had come over in the last twenty-five years were emphatically Calvinist, often gave trouble to their bishops and were sometimes abetted in it by their own clergy. Since defiance of authority could not in any circumstances be tolerated, Archbishop Ussher, though not altogether happy about the matter, was at one with the Lord Deputy Wentworth in disciplining the recalcitrant. A number of the more stubborn had been deprived of their livings and made to leave the country. The Bishops of Down and Derry were the firmest in carrying out this policy, a circumstance which (because of the refrain of the old song—*hey derry down derry*) provoked a grim smile even among the Puritans.

Some of these expelled Scottish clergy had set sail for New England, but contrary winds had driven them back to the Ayrshire coast, where they were joined by others who had had to leave Ireland. Their forlorn condition touched the good people of these parts, especially the women, and the strong-minded housewives of Ayr came to Edinburgh to plead their cause. When the King's councillors tried to pass them by, their spokeswoman laid a muscular hand on the arm of the foremost with " Stand, my lord, in Christ's name, till I speak to you."[29]

Most of the King's councillors in Scotland were anxious to yield to Calvinist opinion whenever possible, for the religious situation, complicated by economic anxieties and national pride, was more immediately dangerous there than in either of his other kingdoms. Seventy years before, Scotland had been the scene of a violent Calvinist Reformation. The bitterness of feeling between Calvinist and Catholic had been further intensified by the racial antagonism of Saxon and Celt; the old religion survived in the restless highlands but the industrious people of the lowlands turned to the new.

King James VI had sidled his way through the savage factions of his nobility until he achieved effective authority over the warring elements in the Scottish state. Catholicism survived illegally in the wilds, but he made the nation's official religion Protestant, while steadily discouraging its more extreme manifestations. By the exercise of patience and ingenuity and the offer or distribution of bribes, King James had persuaded succeeding Assemblies of the Kirk to accept the return of episcopacy and to pass orders for church worship and organisation—the famous Five Articles of Perth—by which kneeling to receive the sacrament, confirmation by bishops and the principal fasts and feasts of the Church were restored. Further he had not tried to go, and he had been constant always to one important principle of policy: to do nothing likely to unite the interests of the nobility with those of the extreme Calvinists. He had been careful, when restoring the bishops, to make no attempt to restore also the episcopal revenues seized by Scots lords at the Reformation. The Jacobean bishops were humble and cautious men careful to placate the secular lords. King James had, moreover, left the parish organisation of the Kirk intact, so that the system of moral and religious control in each village and community was on the Geneva model, with elders and frequent meetings to maintain discipline and to control alike the minister and the people.

King Charles was unwilling to acquiesce in this middle part. When he visited Scotland—which was not until the ninth year of his reign—he introduced the full Laudian ceremony at the chapel of Holyrood. The coronation was marked by a clash of wills with the Lord Chancellor, who threatened to resign rather than give precedence, at the King's request, to the Archbishop of St. Andrews. "I will not meddle further with that old cankered goutish man," said the King angrily as he yielded the point. In outward form the coronation was, otherwise, according to the King's desire, but the hearts of his nobility did not go with their hands. Lord Rothes, who carried the Sword at the ceremony, attempted some days later to present a petition against the bishops.[30]

Parliament, meeting during the King's visit, passed some further reforms in ceremonial with only a narrow majority—some said with no majority at all, but by the juggling of the clerk who was a King's man. Charles noted the names of all who had voted against the measure and when, not long after, one of them, Lord Balmerino, was found to be in possession of a draft of another petition against prelacy, the King had him arrested on a charge of high treason. Tried by the King's council and condemned by a casting vote, Balmerino was then graciously reprieved by the King. He felt no gratitude, only a smouldering resentment at a monstrous proceeding.

The passions raised by the Balmerino trial and the unwillingness of so many of his lords and people to accept further changes in ceremony and ritual should have opened the King's eyes to the difficulties which lay before him in trying to make the Scottish Church as like the English as possible. But the King was in no position to make dispassionate judgment. The courtier-Scots whom he kept about him in England were willing and obedient Anglicans; those who had been most forward and most favoured in Scotland during his visit had also been, either from conviction or from policy, episcopalian in sympathy. Drummond, the poet-scholar, who had composed the official welcome to the King, was a convinced episcopalian; so were several distinguished scholars and clerics, expecially those from the university of Aberdeen. The distinction and eminence of these Scottish episcopalians concealed from the King the relative smallness of their numbers. A Court religion will always be in some degree a fashionable religion, and in Edinburgh in the thirties persons of rank frequently attended the Anglican service at the Chapel Royal. The Anglican service was also used by one or two of the younger bishops in their chapels and at New College, St. Andrews—all this with no noticeable protest, or none that reached the King's ears. He came to believe, on evidence all too slight, that the old stubbornness of the Calvinist Scots had weakened, and continued firmness would break it down altogether.

More truly religious and less wary than his father, Charles had from the outset abandoned political caution when faith and the honour due to the Church were in question. His attempt to make the Chancellor give way to the Archbishop, and his regular appointment of bishops to the vacant places on his council in Scotland, was deeply disturbing to the Scots. When in 1635 the Chancellor died, the Archbishop of St. Andrews was appointed in his place. The nobility, who were willing enough to tolerate bishops as inferiors, were indignant at this new elevation. They saw in it an attempt by the King to govern Scotland by means of his own prelatical nominees. The situation was not improved by the character of some of these. The Archbishop was old and careful to placate when he could. But the younger generation of bishops were bolder men, more zealous for the King's policy; they were prepared to outface the nobility and to respond to rudeness, not with Christian resignation but with episcopal dignity. Personal quarrels occurred even at the council table. So far from strengthening his council in Scotland by appointing bishops to it, the King weakened it by multiplying causes for hostility and division among its members.

The Scots nobility, on and off the Council, had another reason for resenting the King's religious policy. He had already proclaimed his intention of restoring to the Church some, if not all, of the property which they had seized. His two principal Scots courtiers, Lennox and Hamilton, had agreed to sell back to the Crown, for the Church, lands that their fathers had taken. The good example was not followed by other lords, who felt a growing apprehension for the safety of their property.

The King had not revisited Scotland, but in the four years since his coronation he had continued, undeflected, in his church policy. The clergy who supported him, mainly in the region of Aberdeen, moved further in the direction of English practice and ritual. A Jesuit missionary reported the appearance in Scottish churches of organs and altars, the wearing of the surplice and the singing of matins and evensong. The form of worship seemed to him "an imitation of the Mass."[31] The powers of a High Commission Court were now conferred on the Scots bishops, who thus, like the English, acquired the right to discipline the unruly. A new Book of Canons, something on the English model, had been sent to Scotland to replace the *Book of Discipline* of John Knox. These things aroused a muttering resentment, but the opposition had as yet no organisation; the alliance between the nobility, who felt their power and property in danger, and the discontented clergy and laity had not fully come into being.

The Book of Canons, which brought the organisation of the Scots Church into line with that of England, was to be followed by a new Prayer Book which should do the same for the order of worship. It was ready by the year 1636 but on the advice of the King's council in Scotland its introduction was postponed for several months.

The council was divided in opinion. The bishops naturally approved of the Book; several of their fellow councillors did not, and most of them foresaw serious opposition. The Book was presented in a manner bound to offend the sensibilities of the Scots. No Assembly of the Kirk and no Parliament had been called to discuss it, and although it had been drawn up by Scotsmen, they had gone to London to draft it in consultation with the English Archbishop. Furthermore, the King had prefaced it with a royal command to all ministers to use it and a sentence of outlawry on all who refused. A beautiful and dignified liturgy thus reached the Scots in a manner and in a form which could not but be offensive. It looked like an assault on their political as well as their religious independence.

The danger, as the King's council knew, lay as much in the ambitions of the discontented peers as in the religious fervour of people and ministers. What would Rothes and Balmerino do, given the opportunity? Their religious feelings might not go very deep, but suspicion of anything that smacked of Popery touched at once their prejudices, their dearest interests and seventy years of continuous tradition. As a ruffianly old nobleman said, when religion was discussed: "If I have lain with never so many whores, I'll never lie with the whore of Babylon." If the bigotry, greed and ancient feudal authority of the nobles should come together with the fervour of the people, great trouble would certainly follow.

For this reason the council asked for postponement, and only at the repeated instance of the King, at last, and with trepidation, fixed a Sunday at the end of July 1637 for the official introduction of the new order of worship throughout the country.

In Scotland and in England dislike and suspicion of Catholicism went with certain simple and far-reaching political prejudices. Both countries had experienced, to a greater or lesser degree, the reverberations of Europe's religious wars. Both had recollections of attempted foreign interference in the Roman Catholic interest, but in England the prejudice against Catholicism was closely linked with the hatred of Spain. It was the heritage of the Armada and the Elizabethan seamen. When the King had visited the Isle of Wight as a young man he had been surprised to see an inn sign representing a friar clawed by a lion. When he asked its meaning, his host, the genial John Oglander, boasted " we serve all papists and priests in that manner." [32] John Oglander was far from being an extreme Protestant, still less a Puritan; he spoke from the fulness of an Elizabethan heart.

King Charles made little allowance for such prejudices, and did not understand the confusion of thought in many of his subjects' minds. At York he had carefully arranged for the restoration of the shrine of Saint William; both he and Laud spoke respectfully of the saints, and it was alleged that a cleric who had referred disparagingly to Saint George had been made to apologise for his irreverence. The Archbishop had certainly prosecuted a man for publishing an almanack in which the names of Protestant martyrs from Foxe's Book were substituted for those of saints.

Side by side with the harassing of Calvinists, Baptists and other Protestant critics of the Church, went a policy of comparative toleration for Roman Catholics. In his marriage treaty the King had undertaken to repeal the more oppressive of the laws against them. Parliament had compelled him to break this promise, but in the long intermission of Parliaments after 1630 the King had found a way out. He did not repeal the laws but he exempted his Catholic subjects by individual letters patent, in return for a sum of money; this policy was advantageous as well as tolerant.

In other ways, the laws rusted. It was by law a capital offence for an English priest to be found in the country, but priests went openly about London. The Franciscans had returned, theoretically in secret, although their presence was generally known; the English province had been re-founded, and the Jesuits, who were jealous, spoke of them as Archbishop Laud's trencher-flies, a term which seems to have arisen from Laud's purely intellectual interest in the suggestions put forward by one of them, Franciscus a Sancta Clara, for the reconciliation of the Anglican and the Roman Churches. Another eminent exile, Mary Ward, the founder of a new religious order in Germany, the *Englische Fräulein*, came home with a small band of nuns and found a temporary resting place for them in Yorkshire.

The Catholic, or potentially Catholic, minority in the country was still in some districts a large one, able to give help and protection to the priests. In London, the bulk of the respectable population was strongly Protestant; the priests worked among the poor, the outcasts and the plague-stricken. Sometimes these London priests were under arrest and lived in prison awaiting trial, but by day they were allowed out on bail to perform their priestly functions. The further course of the law against them was held up indefinitely by the mercy of the King. This curious situation aroused some critical comparisons with the plight of one or two Protestant preachers and writers whom the King's justice had confined to prison without such unofficial privileges.

In Ireland the penal laws had been temporarily suspended in return for a large sum of money. Roman Catholics were allowed to practise at the bar and to hold positions of public trust. No obstacles were put in the way of the private practice of their religion although public services and large gatherings of the faithful were expressly forbidden, as were also pilgrimages, processions and all open demonstrations of faith.

In Scotland, where the majority was strongly Calvinist, the King's attempts to alleviate the persecution of his Catholic subjects were less successful. The Catholic cause was, for one thing, closely connected with the Gordon clan and its chief the Marquis of Huntly, a circumstance which confused the religious problem with the enmities of the clans and the traditional hostility between highlands and lowlands. All that the King had contrived to do was to grant special privileges to Huntly and his family.

Jesuit missionaries were active in Scotland, and, in the region round Aberdeen where Huntly's power was greatest, they conducted a regular ministry among the faithful. The air of secrecy and conspiracy which surrounded a religion carried on in so limited and dangerous a manner was especially strong in Scotland. In 1630 a principal member of Huntly's family had perished with several companions in a fire at Frendraught, a house belonging to the Crichtons. The Crichtons, though apparently reconciled, were hereditary enemies of the Gordons, and foul play was suspected. If the horrible business had indeed been a murder and not an accident, it was probably the result of personal enmity and nothing more, but a religious motive was half suspected. The Catholics told a tragic tale of the heroism of the young victim who had expounded the true faith to his companions as the flames crept up the tower in which he was trapped. This, with the evident unwillingness of those responsible for justice in Scotland to bring the crime home to the Crichtons, suggested that religious feuds were involved and that

Protestant sympathisers were determined to shield the murderers of a prominent Catholic, in spite of all that the King could do to have the culprits punished.[33]

The King's concessions to Catholics might not have provoked so much unfavourable comment from his Protestant subjects had not the open practice of Catholicism at Court attracted general attention. The Queen was the focus of fashionable Catholicism: a new and elegant allure lit up the old religion, and many lords and ladies flocked to the services in the Queen's chapel at Somerset House. Some went to be in the fashion but some were potential converts. The Queen's confessor, a charming and cultivated Scottish Benedictine, Robert Philip, often debated religious points with interested courtiers, and the existence of what was almost a Roman Catholic mission at Court made a bad impression on Puritan Londoners. The King, although he was indignant when any of his courtiers became converts, encouraged the intelligent and cultivated priests who surrounded his wife. He dearly loved a theological argument, and these men, unlike the Calvinists, talked a language which he approved and understood. He felt himself in many ways very close to them.

When the Queen had shown him a beautiful diamond cross, a gift sent to her by her godfather Pope Urban VIII, he had smiled and said that he must change his opinion of Roman priests: he had until this time believed that they would take but never give. The innocent jest gave rise to malicious speculation as to what the King had meant by the promise to change his opinion.

With his ideal of unity and uniformity, Charles truly wished to see Catholic Christendom made whole again. But, like the Archbishop and the Laudian clergy, he was convinced that this could only be through concessions made by the Pope to the Anglican communion. He stood out with resolute firmness against the appointment of a Roman Catholic bishop to look after the faithful in England. The establishment of a dual system of bishoprics, Roman and Anglican, would have implied acceptance of schism. Compliments between his Court and the Vatican were, however, frequent, and the Pope presented him with a splendid bust done by the famous Bernini from Van Dyck's painting.

The Vatican had exchanged agents with King Charles's Court in 1636. The King had sent to Rome the Scot Sir William Hamilton an optimistic Roman Catholic who talked hopefully of the coming return of Great Britain to the Church. Father George Con, the Vatican agent in England, was also a Scotsman but of a more realist temperament: he recognised the ultimate intransigence of both sides and he was alive to the strength of Puritan opinion in England. An intelligent and highly educated man, Con had a threefold attraction for the King, as a fellow Scotsman, a connoisseur of the arts and a cultivated conversationalist. Although he had no intention of changing his religion, Charles received and welcomed him with friendly familiarity and on one occasion had kept the chapter of the Knights of the Garter waiting for more than half an hour while he showed Con some new acquisitions to his collection. The slight to the greatest knightly order in the kingdom naturally provoked comment.

In other ways the King's affection for his wife and her friends made him indiscreet. He once accompanied her on a visit to the small community of Capuchins under her protection at Somerset House, inspected their chapel and their cells and stayed to share their humble and friendly supper.[34]

Charles himself, strong in the consciousness of his innocence, had no patience with the foolish misunderstandings to which his conduct gave rise, and punished with severity those who propagated slanders. A man who asserted that the King attended Mass with the Queen was fined £5,000, but while the King continued his favours to Roman Catholics, such harshness was in vain; his critics merely assumed that he chose an occasional victim to gloss over the awkward truth. Archbishop Laud, who fully recognised the danger, regretted the King's encouragement of Con and implored him to restrain the influence of some of the Queen's other protégés. Two of her courtiers troubled him especially, Toby Mathew and Wat Montagu; the former was the son of an Anglican bishop, the latter of the pious and sternly Protestant Earl of Manchester. Both were recent and eloquent converts to Rome, and both were clever men. Montagu was the more serious, Mathew the more amusing. He delighted in and played up to a reputation for entertaining silliness—as, for instance, when he offered to make some of the new drink, *chocolate*, for the Queen and did indeed do so, but absentmindedly drank it all up himself. Under this mask of levity, he was a man of a keen, inquiring mind, widely read and alert to all the latest explorations in the sciences. Not the least charm of fashionable Roman Catholicism at this time was that it represented also the *avant-garde* of intellectual life. Lord Herbert of Raglan and Sir Kenelm Digby, both Catholics, stood with Toby Mathew among the foremost amateur scientists of the age, and it was a group consisting principally of Catholics who a few years before, had tried to found a society devoted to the new learning.

The Archbishop was aware of the impression made by the King's encouragement of Roman Catholics. The popular argument was ignorant, incorrect, but deadly: if the King, the head of the Anglican Church, persecuted honest Protestants and smiled upon the Papists, it followed that the Church itself was being led back to Rome. The King's indiscreet and harmless relations with his wife's friends made his, and Laud's, religious policy suspect, not only to extremists and fanatics, but to the substantial majority of his Protestant subjects.

The misapprehension was deepened and embittered by the part which England under King Charles had come to play, or rather *not* to play, in the politics of Europe. Educated men had certain broad conceptions of foreign policy and of England's position and part in European affairs. For the last seventy years western Europe had been divided into two warring camps: the intense struggle between the Habsburg dynasty, ruling in Spain and Austria, and the Bourbon dynasty, ruling in France, had extended and confused the religious wars arising out of the Reformation. The Habsburg dynasty had taken upon themselves a crusade against the heretic; as a result, the French King, although officially Catholic, usually found it wise to sustain the Protestant forces with advice, money and arms, while the Vatican, which also had political interests to consider, tended to support France against Spain. In England this criss-cross of dynastic and religious interests was not widely understood, and the war appeared simply as a religious struggle or as a fight against the dominance of Spain. When, in Elizabeth's time, the English had entered the conflict they had fought against Spanish sea-power which barred their own adventurous expansion in the Americas, and with equal if confused zeal against the Church of Rome and the Spanish Inquisition. The fact that the Roman Catholic powers were not all on the same side in the war, and that the Vatican had moved steadily into alliance with France against Spain, meant very little to the average uninformed Englishman.

The last twenty years had been marked, in Europe, by a resurgence not of the Spanish but of the Austrian Habsburgs who, in the first decade of the Thirty Years War, had regained a large part of central Europe and of the German states for the Catholic Church. The plight of their co-religionists was brought home to the Protestant English by the presence in their midst of refugee German and Bohemian divines, often in such want that they sent their children in quest of alms from door to door. The words " the Protestant Cause " had become a catch-phrase in political discussion. Without very much conception of what the King could do to help the Cause, alehouse politicians—and a fair number of intelligent critics as well—blamed him for doing nothing. In Europe the Protestant Cause was sustained against Spain and Austria in the fields of Germany and Flanders by the Dutch and the Swedes, on the Rhine principally by the French, and at sea, against the Spaniards, by the Dutch alone. The King of England's great ships did nothing more distinguished than squabble with neighbouring Protestant powers about fishing rights.

Clashes with the Dutch in the Narrow Seas and in the Indies, where the merchants of both nations competed for trade, were becoming yearly more violent. But the average Englishman's feeling for the Protestant Cause was stronger than his feelings of rivalry so long as the Dutch were at war with Spain. The Hollanders could still therefore count on English volunteers for their armies and on sympathy from most, if not all, the English people. King Charles's subjects were not so deeply gratified as they should have been when the King, instead of assisting the Protestant Cause, turned his naval guns against the Dutch and with a show of force compelled their government to accept England's prior rights over the herring fisheries. The King, who was anxious to silence critics and to impress on his subjects the importance of what he had done, had a silver medal struck for the occasion. It was a most beautiful piece of work by Briot and bore the lovely text: *Justice and Peace have kissed one another*, but the symbolism represented the intention rather than the achievement of the treaty. The Dutch took little notice of the agreement, and incidents between their fishing boats and the Navy continued much as before.

A Court which favoured the Catholics, a Church which persecuted the Calvinists, a navy which fired only on the Dutch—the simplified picture was open to a dangerous interpretation. Neither at home nor abroad did the policy of King Charles appear Protestant. In the opinion of many it was not even neutral: in 1630 the King had made a treaty with Spain by which Spanish silver was to be minted in England and transported in English ships to Antwerp, where it was needed to pay the Spanish armies which were fighting the Dutch. To Spain the advantage of this arrangement was that the money, shipped by a power which was technically neutral, was safe from interception by the Dutch navy. The advantage to King Charles was that he received a share of each load of bullion for the English mint. This, as the Dutch complained, was a very odd kind of neutrality. In effect the King had become the pensioner and helper of Spain.[35]

The Protestant critics of the King's policy were bound together by the sentimental cult of the King's only sister Elizabeth. She had been married in 1613 to the young Elector Palatine, a Protestant and Calvinist alliance which had been extremely popular. Her husband had some years later accepted the crown of Bohemia from the insurgent Protestants of that country, an action which had precipitated the Habsburg crusade against Protestantism in the imperial dominions. In the course of the struggle the unhappy man had lost not only Bohemia but his title of Elector and all his hereditary German lands. Elizabeth had left behind in her own country a pleasing impression of her youth, liveliness and beauty. This had since been overlaid with visions both noble and tragic: Elizabeth, crowned Protestant Queen of Bohemia; Elizabeth, "our blessed undaunted lady," sharing the rigours of her husband's wintry flight from Prague; Elizabeth, Queen of Hearts, rallying to the drooping Protestant Cause the chivalry of northern Europe; Elizabeth, a fertile mother of many beautiful children (cheap woodcuts of her with an increasing troop of little ones were very popular in London); finally, Elizabeth the tragic widow defending the forlorn rights of her eldest son. At the core of these visions was a living woman of charm, character and considerable beauty. Those who troubled to make the short journey to The Hague, where she lived as a pensioner of the Dutch government, found their fervour for her cause stimulated by her conversation. A few of the more austere Calvinists were shocked by the frivolity of her family, who were greatly given to acting plays, but most visitors were impressed by her courage and high spirits.

The Queen of Bohemia herself was attached to her brother, King Charles, and was grateful for the help which he sent her. But it was known—how could it be otherwise?—that she regretted his inability or unwillingness to take on her behalf any effective action in war or diplomacy. The visit to the English

Court of her son, the Elector Palatine, Charles Louis, had strikingly emphasised the King's failure in this respect. The young man had come seeking help from his uncle, hoping that the King would find the time ripe for intervention in the European war against the Spanish-Austrian power. It was plain for all to see, in the summer of 1637, that he had been turned away, if not quite empty-handed, at least gravely disappointed. He had hoped that a defensive and offensive alliance might be signed with the King of France, now fighting the Spanish-Austrian power on the Rhine, in Flanders and on the Pyrenees, that the English navy would join with the Dutch in the attack on Spanish sea-power, and King Charles take up the part once played by Queen Elizabeth. As nephew of the King he would then have had the help and prestige he needed to regain his father's forfeited lands in Germany.

The King had, however, made difficulties even about recognising the precedence to which, as an Elector, his nephew thought himself entitled, and on one occasion he had had to listen to a Court sermon denouncing the Calvinist doctrines in which he had been educated and for which his father had fought. The King, after a brief wavering in the direction of an alliance with France against Spain and Austria, had sunk again into his uncertain neutrality. " Mutability and confusion reign here," lamented the Venetian envoy, while the Spaniard, in a burst of rage at the King's vacillations, declared to a fellow ambassador that no Court in the world conducted diplomacy so strangely as did the English; they did not listen, they did not understand, and they changed their opinions at every moment. A wild scheme by which the Elector's younger brother Rupert was to command a fleet for the conquest of Madagascar was all the talk of the Court for some weeks, and Davenant celebrated the imaginary venture in a poem. At another time the King spoke of placing fifteen warships at the disposal of the Elector. But in the end Charles continued to devote his naval energies to the herring quarrel with the Dutch, while all that he gave the young Elector was advice to go to the wars himself and make a reputation. He was, at least, generous about personal allowances to both the princes, and added a sizeable lump sum with which the Elector could hire some soldiers, but, as his courtiers said, he was willing to pay to get rid of his poor relations.[36]

The Elector had a cool head and a cool heart. Early in the proceedings King Charles had had to reprimand the young man's secretaries for putting too many military and diplomatic schemes into his head. The reprimand may have been intended for the Elector himself, who was thereafter no less active but more discreet. He privately canvassed the opinions of the Venetian and Dutch ambassadors in London on his own affairs and his uncle's policy.[37] He also cultivated the friendship of the more eminent Protestant critics of the King, especially those with naval and colonial interests.

The alliance of colonial adventure with militant Protestantism, which had sprung from the first clashes of English seamen with Spain, had grown stronger when the policy of the Crown became favourable to Catholics at home and to Spain abroad. English naval enterprise of late, had developed in a manner likely to prove dangerous should it come to an open conflict between the Court and its critics. By the peace with Spain in 1604 King James I had relinquished the claim of Englishmen to trade in the West Indies. Undeterred, English captains continued to trade under foreign flags. They used as their bases ports in the Netherlands, in southern Ireland and in North Devon. The illicit nature of their traffic made them bold, self-reliant and unscrupulous. Fiercely conscious of their English race, reputation and religion, they were at the same time indifferent to and contemptuous of the authority of the royal government, which neither recognised nor protected them. One of England's major commercial interests and one of the chief sources of national and local pride thus eluded the royal authority altogether. A new tradition, which had ripened through a long generation, had created something like an opposition, rather than a loyalty, between the most adventurous English seamen and the Crown. While the King struck pretentious medals about herring treaties, his subjects defied Spain, the traditional enemy, at their own expense and under any flag but their own.

Foremost of the men who financed and sometimes took part in this underhand expansion of sea-power was Robert Rich, Earl of Warwick. He was the son of Penelope Devereux, immortal as the *Stella* of Sir Philip Sidney's poems. By her unloved husband (" that Rich fool, who by blind fortune's lot, the richest gem of love and life enjoys ") Penelope had been the mother of two sons—this Robert, and a younger, Henry, now Earl of Holland and a favourite of Queen Henrietta Maria. By her lover, the Earl of Devonshire, Penelope had had a third son. Mountjoy Blount, now Earl of Newport and a prominent man at Court. These three men were on friendly family terms with their cousin, the living Earl of Essex, Penelope's brother's son. Another friend, the Earl of Hertford, had married the Earl of Essex's sister. Of this family group Holland and Newport alone were figures at Court. Warwick, an active seaman who had himself once led an expedition to the West Indies, preferred his country houses and the ships and dockyards to Hampton Court and Whitehall. Essex and Hertford had both as young men suffered humiliation and unhappiness at the hands of the Court. Essex, at twenty-four, had been compelled by King James I to allow his wife, whom the King's favourite wished to marry, to divorce him on the score of impotence. He had served in the Low Countries since then and had the reputation of a good soldier, a good Protestant and an honest unpretentious fellow. Hertford had in youth loved and secretly married the Lady Arabella Stuart, cousin of King James. The alliance had been thought to endanger the throne to which Arabella and Hertford had each a tenuous claim. The lovers were parted, Hertford fled the country and Arabella died, mad, in the Tower. At fifty his tragic romance was a thing of memory; he was comfortably re-married to the sister of Essex, and the father of a family—a stodgy, uninspired gentleman of Protestant views, neither in nor out of favour with the Court, but not particularly attached to it.

These kinsmen had other associates and friends, Lord Saye and Seal, Lord Brooke, John Hampden a rich Buckinghamshire landowner, and John Pym a West country squire of great business ability. Both these latter had been prominent opponents of the King in the last Parliament and all were active in advocating and financing colonial ventures.

The Elizabethan wars with Spain had created the alliance between strong Protestantism and colonial expansion of which these men were the most outstanding representatives. At home, they protected and encouraged the Protestant clergy. In the settlements across the Atlantic they placed ministers of the same kind. New England was becoming a refugee centre for laymen and clergy unwilling to accept the Laudian rule; astonishing in its religious and intellectual vigour, the little settlement of Boston had already in 1636 founded a college for Puritan theology and Puritan learning in the New World. John Harvard, graduate of Emmanuel College, Cambridge, the chief centre of Puritan thought at home, had left four hundred books and seven hundred pounds to create a second Cambridge by the Charles river in Massachusetts.

But the ideals and interests of the leading Puritan-adventurers and their antagonism to the Crown were concentrated in particular in the Caribbean settlements controlled by the Providence Company of which Warwick, Saye, Brooke and Hampden were all shareholders. Warwick's courtier brother Lord Holland, another shareholder, protected the company's interests at Whitehall. Oliver St. John, a leading Puritan barrister, was the company's solicitor and its secretary was John Pym.

The Company had founded the settlement of Providence, on the small Caribbean island now known as Santa Catalina, with a two-fold intention. The outpost, with its two neighbouring islands Association and Henrietta, was well placed as a naval base for the harrying of Spain; but the new settlements were also to be models of primitive virtue. In Providence, Henrietta and Association sin would be unknown and simple purity reign supreme. The Company drew up regulations, forbidding cards and dice and permitting only chess as an evening recreation for the people, with other stern and simple rules. Whoring, drunkenness, profanity would not be tolerated. A carefully chosen minister—a German Calvinist refugee from the Palatinate—was brought home in disgrace for singing catches on a Sunday.

The business of these three godly settlements was chiefly to keep watch on Spanish ships and prey on them when possible. The Earl of Warwick and his friends were sincerely trying to create three nests of pirates with the behaviour and morals of a Calvinist theological seminary. Other difficulties beside moral ones afflicted the Providence settlements. Only negroes could work effectively in the climate, but this involved the company in the African slave trade; moreover the negroes grew mutinous and further importation had to be stopped. There was little water. A plague of rats swept the settlements. The cultivation of tobacco and cotton both failed to pay—tobacco because of the King's interference with the trade, and cotton because the means to dress the raw material for export were lacking. Fruit and sugar canes alone seemed to do well, and hogs throve. But Spanish, French and Dutch hostility menaced the islands on every side, and in 1635 the Spaniards raided and totally destroyed the settlement at Association.

The shareholders of the Company met in London, either at Lord Brooke's house or at Warwick's; John Pym was at one or other of the houses more often than the rest, for the main burden of organisation rested on him. He was an efficient manager and administrator, with a quick, resourceful wit, a good memory, and an astonishing capacity for acquiring, digesting and using information.

The shareholders of the Providence Company undoubtedly talked politics together. They could hardly have avoided it, since their religious and colonial interests were so much affected by the King's church policy and by his friendship with Spain. Some or all of them certainly paid their respects to the Elector Palatine during his long and disappointing visit to his uncle's Court. At one moment during that visit, the King, in a tentative movement towards a change of foreign policy, went so far as to give verbal consent to a war of reprisals on the Spaniards in the Caribbean—a war to be waged at the Company's expense and with its own ships. Faced with a continual tale of loss and disaster, the Company had considered moving the colony to the mainland but the possibility of recouping their losses through licensed piracy brightened the outlook, and in the summer of 1637 the shareholders sank another £100,000 in the enterprise and decided to go on with it.[38] Their original ideals had dismally faded and an enterprise which had began with the genuine intention of planting a godly commonwealth, had deteriorated into a scheme for licensing pirate captains in return for a share of the profits. The records of the Providence Company are depressing, but it was, for all that, the heir of the Elizabethan tradition.

The King's private permission to the governors of the company to pursue their own war on Spain did not in their eyes counterbalance the rest of his foreign policy. Saye, Brooke, Warwick, Hampden, Pym and their friends felt as strongly as any in England that in failing to support the Elector Palatine the King was betraying the Protestant Cause and losing the opportunity of a war both profitable, honourable and just.

The King's religious policy and his foreign policy worked together to increase the misgivings of his opponents about the future of their country under his unquestioned rule. A small fact, a mere accident, to which Prynne had drawn attention in his *News from Ipswich*, seemed to clinch the matter. In the reissue of the Prayer Book for the year 1636 the prayer for Elizabeth, Queen of Bohemia, and her family had been omitted. Prayers for the King's sister had been said as long as Charles was childless and she was heiress-presumptive to the throne. By 1636 he had five living children: the number of his relations who could reasonably be included by name in a prayer was naturally limited, but the exclusion of Elizabeth was loaded with dark significance by her brother's critics.

The King treated such follies with contempt, but he was

mistaken in doing so. The various parts of his policy were open not simply to misinterpretation, but to the *same* misinterpretation. There lay the danger: his religious policy and his foreign policy united too many of his subjects in the same resentments and the same fears.

BOOK I CHAPTER II REFERENCES

1. Logan Pearsall Smith, *Life and Letters of Sir Henry Wotton*, Oxford, 1907, i, p. 218.
2. *C.S.P. Ven*, 1636–9, p. 305.
3. Matthew Hopkins, *Discovery of Witches*, London, 1647; *Scottish Historical Review*, IV, p. 42.
4. *H.M.C. Report VII, App. II*, p. 229.
5. Laud, *Works*, Oxford, 1847, iii, p. 147.
6. *Ferrar Papers*, ed. Blackstone, Cambridge, 1938.
7. See Geoffrey Soden's *Godfrey Goodman* (London, 1953) for a refutation of the belief that this unhappy man was in fact reconciled with Rome while holding an English bishopric.
8. Cardwell, *Documentary Annals of the Church*, Oxford, 1839, ii, pp. 195–6.
9. *The Curates Conference, Harleian Miscellany*, London, 1808, i, p. 497.
10. *C.S.P.D.*, 1637–8, p. 539; *Ibid.*, 1639, p. 108; Symonds, *Diary of the marches of the royal army*, ed. C. E. Long, Camden Society, 1859, p. 27.
11. *H.M.C. Portland MSS., III*, p. 79.
12. *Chronicles of the First Planters*, ed. A. Young, Boston, 1846, p. 346.
13. Laud, *Works, IV.*, pp. 303–6; see also Isobel M. Calder, in *American Historical Review*, LIII.
14. See *History*, XXVI (1941) for M. James's full and lucid exposition of the tithes question.
15. Williams, *Holy Table: Name and Thing*, Lincoln, 1637, pp. 7–9, 20.
16. *C.S.P.D.*, 1638–9, pp. 141–2.
17. Fuller, *Church History*, London, 1655, Book IX, viii.
18. *C.S.P.D.*, 1637, pp. 298, 484–6, 491, 499, 518.
19. Hessels, *Ecclesiae Londine-Bataviae Archivum*, Cambridge, 1897, III, ii, p. 1681; I. S. Williamson, *History of the Temple*, London, 1924, p. 393 n.
20. Cardwell, p. 202.
21. *Winchester Cathedral Statutes*, Oxford, 1925, p. 92.
22. *Articles of Visitation of the Diocese of Norwich*, 1636.
23. *C.S.P.D.*, 1637, p. 582.
24. *Ibid.*, p. 531; 1637–8, pp. 219, 382.
25. *Ibid.*, 1637, p. 519.
26. Hessels, III, ii, pp. 1645–1749 *passim*.
27. *Strafford MSS.*, XI, folio 322–3.
28. The MS. *Memoirs* of Richard Augustine Hay in the Advocates Library at Edinburgh

contain an illuminating account of a lawsuit by the bishop of Clogher; the *Lismore Papers*, ed. Grosart, London, 1886, throw light on some of the conflicts of the Irish Church with the Earl of Cork.

29. Blair, *Life*, *Wodrow Society*, Edinburgh, 1848, p. 154.

30. Balfour, *Historical Works*, Edinburgh, 1825, II, pp. 141–2; Guthry, *Memoirs*, London, 1702, pp. 10–11; James Wilson, *History of Scots Affairs*, Edinburgh, 1654, p. 8–9.

31. Forbes Leith, *Memoirs of Scottish Catholics*, London, 1909, i, pp. 164–72.

32. Oglander, p. 15.

33. Forbes Leith, i, pp. 57, 92, 97 ff.

34. See Gordon Albion, *Charles I and the Court of Rome*, London, 1935; A. O. Meyer, *Charles I and Rome*, *American Historical Review*, 1913, p. 23; *C.S.P. Ven*, 1636–9, pp. 70, 120, 149–51, 217–18.

35. Feavearyear, *The Pound Sterling*, Oxford, 1931, pp. 82 ff.; see also *Clarendon State Papers*, Oxford, 1767, ii, pp. 712–80.

36. *C.S.P. Ven*, 1636–9, pp. 108, 130 f, 140 f, 184 f, 220, 234–6.

37. *Ibid.*, pp. 94, 107.

38. *C.S.P. Colonial*, 1574–1660, pp. 249, 255, 264–5; see also A. P. Newton, *Colonising Activities of the English Puritans*, Yale, 1914.

CHAPTER THREE

THE KING'S PEACE AND THE KING'S REVENUE

T HE distrust created by the King's church policy would have been less damaging to his prospects had he been successful in practical administration. A government which is not trusted can be effective only if it is feared, and Charles might have achieved something of what he wished to achieve had his administration been conducted in such a manner as to command respect and compel obedience.

England was the richest, most influential and most valuable of his dominions, and on English administration his true power was based. No reputable English lawyer would at this time have contested the proposition that " the law of Royal Government is a law fundamental."[1] But the way in which this government was to be exercised gave rise to argument. The King believed that it rested with his good will alone to respect and uphold his people's liberties, but a contemporary legal work aptly expressed another view, " English laws are rather popular than peremptory, rather accepted than exacted."[2] In practice the administration of the laws rested on the consent and co-operation of the King's subjects, countrymen and citizens, justices of the peace, constables, sheriffs and lords lieutenant throughout the country, to whom power was delegated. " The authority of a King is the keystone which closeth up the arch of government," one of the King's principal supporters had said. But the arch was made up of many other stones beside the keystone. To change the metaphor: the King was the fountain of justice. But the river of justice which flowed from the monarch divided into multitudinous smaller streams and canals irrigating the whole country, with, as it were, their own locks, weirs and fishing rights: they retained only a theoretical and remote consciousness of the fountain whence their waters came.

The King personally appointed the judges, whose first duty, as he saw it, was to maintain his authority. Francis Bacon, his father's Chancellor, had described the judges as "lions under the throne." If the lions roared in such a manner as to shake rather than support the throne, it was plain sense, and plain duty, to silence them. Neither James I nor Charles I had hesitated to do so. James had removed Lord Chief Justice Coke, the loud-mouthed champion of the common law, and Charles dismissed Lord Chief Justice Crewe when he refused to uphold the legality of one of the royal demands for money. To make his authority over the judicial bench clear beyond doubt the King had altered the formula by which judges were appointed. In the past judges had held office *quamdiu se bene gesserint*, or as long as they behaved rightly. In King Charles's time the judges were appointed *durante bene placito*, or during the King's good pleasure.

The King was careful to discourage all studies which seemed likely to produce a wrong attitude in lawyers. The antiquary Sir Robert Cotton found warrant in Anglo-Saxon institutions and in the baronial wars of Henry III for doctrines of government unfavourable to the King; his library was impounded and he himself excluded from Court favour. The King also prohibited further publication of Sir Edward Coke's commentaries on the laws, seized his papers and relegated the ex-Chief Justice to apoplectic silence in a country exile.

Such actions would have been politic had the King found nominees of worth and character to fill the Bench, but his choice fell too often upon the merely ambitious, the complaisant, or those with money to offer. John Finch and John Bramston, who had 1 een the Chief Justices since 1635, were learned and ingenious lawyers, but Finch was too unscrupulous, vain and ambitious to command respect, and Bramston was weak and malleable. Edward Littleton and John Bankes, respectively Solicitor-General and Attorney-General, were men of greater integrity; these were respectable appointments. But as a rule the prices of remunerative places were whispered round Whitehall and the prospects of the bidders openly discussed for months at a time.[3]

While, as lions under the throne, the judges grew to look like sheep or even jackals, respect for them declined. This did not affect the popular esteem in which the law was held, for the law had an existence independent of the King's theories or the corruption of the Bench, and therein lay its strength.

Justice was administered throughout the kingdom in a multitude of small local courts, and the governors of England, in all that affected the daily life of the subject, were the local justices of the peace—small gentry in the countryside, aldermen in the cities. At Quarter Sessions the justices, gathered together in the county town, fixed the rate of wages and discussed the state and needs of the county. They were competent to try all crimes except treason or offences by the King's servants. These cases, together with a few which presented exceptional problems of law, would be reserved for trial by the King's judges at the Assizes.

Between sessions the justices saw to the daily affairs of the village, apprenticed boys to trades, disciplined unruly servants, ordered idlers into the fields at harvest time, licensed or suppressed alehouses, punished rogues and vagabonds, put bastard children out to nurse, sent lewd women and incorrigible beggars to the house of correction, relieved the sick, poor and disabled, encouraged lawful and discouraged unlawful sports, and saw to the maintenance—such as it was—of roads and bridges.

The innumerable petty disputes over boundaries and trespass, which occurred in a countryside very little enclosed and cultivated on the strip system, were mostly settled by the old manorial courts—the Court Leet or the Court Baron—both of which still survived. Here the lord of the manor or his steward sat in the chair of justice, to deal with trespass, poaching, and injury to park land, but also to rebuke eavesdroppers, scolds, drunkards and trouble-makers.

Neither lords of manors, stewards nor justices of the peace in town or country were by custom or necessity deeply versed in the law, though many of them had been for a while at the Inns of Court in London. The little learning they had then acquired, and one of the many convenient handbooks specially written for them, gave them all the technical help they needed in a task in which experience and common sense were fully as important as knowledge of the law.

This widely delegated judicial system had its focal point at Westminster, in whose ancient hall and in the buildings which abutted against it, the four courts of King's Bench, Common Pleas, Exchequer and Exchequer Chamber held their sessions. The boundaries between the first two courts were indistinct; the King's Bench was supposed to deal in general with actions of the Crown against subjects, the Common Pleas with actions between subject and subject. Each had a Lord Chief Justice and three judges attached to it, and had power to rectify the errors committed by the inferior courts of the kingdom. The Exchequer Court, whose four judges were confusingly called Barons of the Exchequer, dealt with cases arising out of taxation. The Court of Exchequer Chamber, so called merely from the place in which it met, was used when the judges of all three courts assembled to decide on some particularly difficult case.

The hearings of all these courts were open. Justice in England was conducted in a bustling, public manner. Westminster Hall was divided into smaller courts by partitions shoulder-high; several cases might be going on at once, within sight and earshot of each other and of the crowds who sauntered past. What was true of Westminster Hall was equally true of lesser courts in cities and villages. The administration of English law was a familiar, instructive and entertaining spectacle in the midst of ordinary life, and the audience followed it with the half-professional interest of those who were sometimes actors themselves in the daily drama. As plaintiff or defendant, as witness or surety, or as a minor official of the court, the great majority of the population would be at one time or another directly involved with the law. Not only the wealthy and powerful knew and used it; the journeyman and the wagoner, the labourer and the boatman larded their alehouse conversation with the mis-remembered jargon of the courts and had a crude conception of the law's logic and of their rights under it. " Every plough-man with us," wrote a contemporary lawyer, " may be a senes-chal in a Court Baron: he can talk of essoins, vouchers, wither-nams and recaptions." [4]

Familiarity bred not contempt but affection. There is little evidence at this epoch in England of any real fear of the law. Its purpose was to uphold the rights of Englishmen, and on the whole Englishmen saw to it that the law did so. Certainly there was corruption of many kinds, bribery and intimidation being the most common; certainly the law, administered entirely by men of substance and property, bore harshly on the outcasts of society. But society was composed of interlocking, inter-dependent groups, and it was in the interests of all parties, squires, tenants, yeomen and hired servants, to maintain equable if not always equitable relations. Vagabonds and " masterless men "—a term still much in use—were the only constant victims of the law, and they were not always helpless. Tradition told of a rogue who had brought and won an action for damages because the pillory had collapsed under him and nearly caused him a fatal injury.[5]

For the rest, the English passion for litigation, common to all classes, reveals the general attitude to the law. It was an attitude at once proprietary and resolute: the law existed to defend and confirm each man in his proper station; it was a servant or a guard, but not a master. In England, furthermore, lawyers and laymen were not sharply divided into hostile groups. This was true even of the humbler sort, since the labourer knew, understood and sometimes played a part in his local court; but it was far more true of the educated classes. West of London, straggling down both sides of Holborn towards the river, lay the Inns of Court—Lincoln's Inn, Gray's Inn, and the Inner and Middle Temple. Hither, more often than to Oxford or Cambridge, the country gentleman or the rich citizen sent his sons to see a little of life and to learn a little law. Rich young men and poor young men lived together in this district; rowdies like Augustine Garland and Nicholas Love of Lincoln's Inn who had just been disciplined for holding the porter under the pump,[6] solemn students like Matthew Hale who read for sixteen hours a day, intellectuals discussing music, philosophy, literature and the fine arts, like John Hutchinson and Edward Hyde. They shared the same lectures, ate in the same halls, attended the same chapels, and participated in some of the same hilarities at the Christmas revels. The Inns of Court were the third university of England, and in point of influence the first. Here above all, through innumerable youthful friendships, was forged that alliance between the men who made, the men who interpreted and the men who administered the law, which opposed a solid bulwark against royal or clerical encroachment on the law's authority.

The King controlled the appointment of Judges, but he could not control the operation of the law: the machine had a life of its own. At the Assizes the King's Judges instructed the local justices of the peace on the royal policy, issued general recommendations for the future and reprimanded them when the King's policy had not been properly carried out. But in the last resort the King's commands were obeyed only if the justices wanted them to be obeyed; and no effective means existed whereby the justices could be coerced into carrying out any measure which was generally unpopular. The King's council could prosecute, reprimand or remove a few recalcitrant justices but if the majority were to oppose him he could not reprimand or remove the entire bench; who, then, would be left to carry on the necessary affairs of the countryside?

Queen Elizabeth had kept her justices in salutary fear of the royal authority by calling the incompetent to order before the council; but her fingers were on the pulse of the country and she had avoided collision with public opinion. In this way she had created and maintained a delicate equilibrium between the authority of the Crown and the demands of the subject. She had been respected and feared, but she had also been popular, and she had never allowed any crisis to arise in which her power was pitted against the will of her justices or her people.

King Charles had too high an opinion of the Crown's authority to consider the necessity of maintaining this equilibrium. At the outset of his non-Parliamentary rule he had determined, wisely enough, to bring the justices into regular contact with the Crown by requiring them to make semi-annual reports to the royal council. This plan for more regular and stricter control had coincided with a number of interesting royal proclamations designed to improve the administration of the Poor Law, to prevent the spread of epidemics, to avert famine or a shortage of corn, to control unhealthy and ill-considered building and to relieve the distress of debtors or the chronically disabled. This double move foreshadowed what might have been a benevolent social policy directed and controlled by the Crown, and intended to increase the central power of the King's council at the expense of local and parish authorities.

But the success of the experiment depended on the vigour with which it was prosecuted. After a year or two the social legislation ceased, the proclamations were neglected and surveillance flagged. When, for instance, the King attempted to relieve distress among cloth workers by a government scheme for buying in raw wool and redistributing it to the spinners and weavers of each district, it was found that the central government lacked the administrative skill, the authority and the expert knowledge either to compel or to persuade the full co-operation of the justices. The misconceived scheme was allowed to drop but it damaged the prestige of the central government and strengthened, in the justices of the peace, feelings of resentment and contempt.

Although administration thus eluded the King's control, he

was still the fountain of justice. He exercised, through the Privy Council and through his Court of Chancery, the power to rectify the errors of any court in the realm, and the errors were many.

High costs and corruption were the prevalent diseases of the courts. Lawyers had their fees and documents cost money; every Court swarmed with hangers-on, clerks, copyists, doorkeepers, each expecting something for his pains, each ready to give extra assistance to the litigant who paid him most, and to do an ill turn to the litigant who forgot to pay him at all. Round Lincoln's Inn and the Temple false witnesses hung about for hire.[7] Suits could be endlessly delayed by the ingenuity or malice of clerks bribed for this purpose, and the delay might be as bad as loss. No one doubted that a rich and powerful man could win a case against a poor man, if by no other means than by spinning it out until his opponent fell into debt and cried for mercy. The deliberate ruining of some unhappy victim by this means was a frequent subject of contemporary plays, and surviving records give examples of it. Vindictive and false prosecutions occurred; a great landowner might have half the justices of a county in his pocket. Most of those in authority took bribes and, according to the Venetian ambassador who was shocked at the practice, regarded it as harmless and natural.[8]

The law remained serviceable in spite of all. The majority of cases before the courts were not between ill-matched litigants, nor did every powerful man in England abuse his power. For the most part, cases were between equals, where the difference between a fourpenny or sixpenny bribe did not grossly affect the scales of justice. Corruption, intimidation and general dishonesty were held in check by the practical conviction that, within certain limits, the law must be made to work.

When so much was known to be amiss with the ordinary courts of the realm, the King might have strengthened his position and undermined the influence of the common law by demonstrating the superiority of justice directly dispensed by the Crown. He did not take this opportunity. Widespread as was criticism of the ordinary courts of justice, few if any were heard to praise the superior honesty, speed and cheapness of those directly controlled by the King.

The Court of Chancery, which existed specifically to give a remedy to the subject when there was no remedy at Common Law, was at this time admittedly the most expensive, slow and corrupt court in the Kingdom, and was used quite as frequently as any other court in the realm to forward the interests of the great, more especially those with influence in the royal circle, against those whom they wished to weaken or ruin. The Court of Wards, for several generations the most unpopular court in the Kingdom, was feared and hated by the gentry because it had insensibly become nothing but a means of raising revenue for the Crown at the expense of any estate inherited by a minor, any disputed will or inheritance. Both these Courts were famous for interminable and expensive delays, for the number of their predatory clerks and their extortionate charges.[9]

The reputation of the King's Court of Star Chamber, the most important of the prerogative courts, was better, although it was not free of taint. The Star Chamber was simply the King's inner council, with the two Chief Justices in addition, acting as a court of law. The Council's functions had been developed in this way since the time of Henry VII for the express purpose of defending the King's humbler subjects against the unscrupulous powerful. The Star Chamber could and did punish bribery and intimidation; it intervened to stop the deliberate persecution of a small man by a wealthy enemy in the law courts; it called incompetent country justices to order. For more than a century it had held in check the bribing nobleman or the corrupt magistrate who flouted justice too outrageously. But a court created to check abuses had developed abuses of its own, and malicious prosecutions in the Star Chamber were not unknown. King Charles, moreover, had used it to silence critics of the Court, Church or government and, on occasion, critics or libellers of his friends and ministers. Intending to make his subjects fear his authority, he had in a few cases authorised very heavy fines and humiliating punishments. His subjects were not intimidated; they lost faith in the Star Chamber as a source of protection and became suspicious of it.

Three other courts depended on the King's council: the Court of the North at York, the Court of Wales and the Marches at Ludlow, and the Court of Castle Chamber in Dublin. These too were designed to extend the punitive and protective powers of the King to the furthest parts of his dominions, and to open for the subject a direct path to the justice of his Sovereign or his Sovereign's immediate Deputy. Placed in York, Ludlow and Dublin, they were intended to give the Lord President of the North, the Lord President of Wales and the Marches, and the Lord Deputy of Ireland the necessary powers to control the pretensions and possible violence of the over-mighty lords who in these remoter regions might overawe and oppress His Majesty's lesser subjects. Of the three the Court of Wales had the least to do and was the least criticised. It performed its functions effectively under the mild and pompous guidance of the Earl of Bridgewater whose chief concern was to keep clear of political quarrels.[10] The Lord President of the North and the Lord Deputy of Ireland was one and the same man, the Viscount Wentworth, a governor of a sterner vision than Bridgewater, and facing both in the North and in Ireland a harder task. He had striven manfully to combine the defence of the humble against the mighty with the disciplining of the King's critics. In York, and more especially in Dublin, Wentworth had on occasion defended the interest of this or that inarticulate farmer or weeping widow against the tyranny and dishonesty of the great landowners. In Ireland at least, the King's justice had gained with the smaller men a popular reputation for speed and efficiency. But in England the benefits Wentworth had bestowed were disregarded, and the severity with which he had punished his opponents was common talk. Sometimes, and not always on the happiest occasions, these Courts worked together. Wentworth, had for instance, condemned a man named Esmond in Dublin; Esmond died soon after, and some of Wentworth's enemies put it about that he died from the after-effects of a blow struck by Wentworth's own vice-regal hand. To crush this libel Wentworth prosecuted the scandalmongers in the Star Chamber. The malicious or ill-informed at once suspected that the Court of Star Chamber was being used to cover the tyrannies committed in Dublin.

The worst characteristic of the prerogative courts was that they encouraged informers and were by no means always competent to distinguish between false information and true; the innocent might be wrecked in the Star Chamber as well as the guilty. Certainly of late years high words at the village pump or a quarrel in an alehouse could, through the malice of an informer, bring a frightened victim before the Star Chamber: Will Brown heard Tom Smith say, " Let the King be hanged " but Tom Smith says he said, " You be hanged," and no word concerning the King's Majesty. And so on and so forth, until a sensible justice at Ipswich reporting the case of Ann Dixon, aged fourteen, accused of treasonous words by a neighbour, remarked that if informers continued at this rate every scold's quarrel in the land would come up before the King's council.[11]

Another recent development aroused criticism both in lay and legal circles. The ecclesiastical Court of High Commission had begun to act in very close co-operation with the Court of Star Chamber; they sometimes appeared to function as the spiritual and temporal arms of the same fierce justice. When Dr. Alexander Leighton wrote a virulent attack on the bishops, the Court of High Commission unfrocked him, but the Court of Star Chamber had him flogged and imprisoned for life.

In an age when branding and whipping were common punishments, the prerogative courts had no monopoly of cruelty, but public opinion distinguished very clearly between permissible and impermissible barbarity in criminal sentences: in that steadfastly hierarchic society much depended on the social position of the victim. It was strongly felt that lawyers, physicians and clergymen, persons of university education, who wore black gowns, clean linen, hats, cloaks and gloves, and wrote

" gent " after their names, ought not to be subjected to the physical punishments reserved for screeching harlots or drunken vagabonds. The Court of Star Chamber, occasionally, passed such inappropriate sentences and half a dozen of them over as many years were enough thoroughly to perturb the conventional. When the public executioner, making ready to apply the lash, politely addressed his victim as " Sir," it was evident that a very singular situation had arisen.

The prerogative courts had one other sinister peculiarity. In England torture was unknown to the Common Law; its application was the King's prerogative. As the distinguished lawyer John Selden reflectively remarked: " The rack is nowhere used as in England. In other countries 'tis used in judicature, when there is a *semiplena probatio*, a half-proof against a man: then, to see if they can make it full, they rack him if he will not confess. But here in England they take a man and rack him, I do not know why nor when: not in time of judicature, but when somebody bids." " Somebody " was one of the King's councillors, using the royal authority to apply the torture. King James had used it several times, King Charles once only—unfortunately on an innocent man.[12]

Had the King made the prerogative courts the object of respect, had he asserted a watchful control over the justices of the peace, he would have gone a long way towards making his vision of authority into a reality. But he lacked concentration of purpose. He was too often deflected by immediate considerations of convenience or profit. He had been on the throne twelve years, seven of them without either Parliaments or wars to distract him, yet it was evident to any perceptive observer that he had neither won popular favour for his government nor built up enough strength for himself to make that favour unnecessary.

The reason for this mismanagement—or, more exactly, this absence of management—was to be found at the centre of the administration. To help him to realise his vision, the King had need of such ministers as Elizabeth had had—wise, wary, judicious and vigilant, single-minded in their devotion to the task of government. But the very core of King Charles's government, his own council, was feeble, factious and corrupt.

The central government of England was discharged by the King's council, chiefly by an inner group with no official title although it was sometimes referred to as the Junto or the Cabinet. At moments of crisis, or on special occasions—when the Lord Deputy of Ireland came to report on his government—the King presided; at ordinary times he rarely attended. As the council consisted of men who were constantly about the court or held important offices in the Royal Household, it was easy for him to consult with individual advisers at any convenient moment, and since ultimate decisions rested with him alone, the most important were often taken in private.

The council was essentially a council of courtiers. Little attempt was made to find the most experienced man for any special task or to make use of his ability; the King preferred to choose from his friends and servants those who were most congenial to him, in the ill-grounded belief that he would find in them the knowledge and technical skill that was wanted. The principal members of this almost fortuitous group of noblemen and court officials were few of them remarkable. There was William Cecil, Earl of Salisbury; one of the least distinguished men of a distinguished family, he had a reputation for caution and parsimony and for having no will of his own. There was Philip Herbert, Earl of Pembroke, who concealed his natural craftiness under a mask of buffoonery; he was a bad-tempered, overbearing man who swore " God damn me " and boasted of being illiterate—a singular figure in that cultured society; he retained the King's favour partly because he could offer him the best hunting in England, partly because his eccentric pose appealed to Charles's slow-moving sense of humour, and chiefly because as a youth he had been a favourite of the late King James. Charles was always good to those whom his father had loved. Another of his councillors, who had risen in the same way, was Henry Rich, Earl of Holland, whose flashing dark eyes and glossy black hair had earned him the nickname of *El Conde*. Vapid, vain and silly, his thoughts were mostly of dress and of past and future conquests in the lists of love, but under a surface charm he was stubborn, arrogant and vindictive. Holland was younger brother to the Earl of Warwick, the Puritan pirate and the most prominent of the lords in opposition to the Court. Although he resembled his energetic and capable brother in very little, he was known to further his brother's interests whenever he could, which did not make him a disinterested counsellor for the King. By comparison with these three the Earl of Northumberland stands out for his intelligence; his letters show him to have been a man of reasonably shrewd observation and judgment, and he had enough knowledge of naval affairs to acquit himself creditably in the office of Lord High Admiral.

Two Scots also sat on this English council, the Marquis of Hamilton and the Duke of Lennox. Hamilton, a favourite with the King from boyhood, had a kind of slow-witted cunning and more confidence in his own judgment than it deserved. The character of Lennox can be read from Anthony Van Dyck's different versions of his fair, aristocratic, equine features: he was a good young man, loyal, sweet-natured and simple-hearted, but not clever.

The Treasurer was William Juxon, Bishop of London, an urbane prelate and a very upright man. The Chancellor of the Exchequer was Francis, Lord Cottington, an irresponsible, irrepressible good fellow, with a shrewd head, a witty tongue and few moral scruples; a man whom everybody liked and no one altogether trusted. There were two secretaries of state; plodding old John Coke, honest, painstaking and slow, but quite incapable of checking the corruption of his clerks,[13] and the lively Francis Windebanke, with a finger in every intrigue and a family of up-and-coming sons to place in the world. As makeweight there was the Comptroller of the Household, Sir Harry Vane, a jaunty little man bursting with personal ambition and his own importance.

Holland, Hamilton, Cottington, Windebanke and Vane were all, by taste and temperament, schemers who used their influence to get profitable places for themselves, their families and friends. The Queen, whose busy and gay nature overflowed easily into such petty conspiracies, encouraged them, and they found other willing friends in the many idle courtiers. Lord Northumberland was not himself a natural plotter, but he had for brother and sister a pair of notable intriguers, Harry Percy, and the beautiful Countess of Carlisle, the Queen's closest friend. The King had friends no less dangerous: his two most trusted Gentlemen of the Bedchamber, Will Murray and Endymion Porter were inveterate wire-pullers. Through these people and their like, the council became the heart and centre of Court intrigues rather than the heart and centre of government.

The King's council in England had its exact parallels in Scotland and Ireland. In Ireland it was under the control of the King's Viceroy, the Lord Deputy, who being a strong man and an energetic ruler guided it pretty well as he pleased. Scotland had no Viceroy; the King governed his native country direct from England, but he governed it personally with no reference to his English council which, naturally, had no right to meddle in the affairs of the other nation. The King's Council for Scotland was too far away for the King to be able to discuss matters with them in any effective manner. The connecting link was the Secretary of State for Scotland, Lord Stirling, who followed the Court and communicated the royal wishes to the council at Edinburgh. Their task was mainly to carry out those wishes. King James had developed this peculiar form of government. "Here I sit and govern Scotland with my pen," he had remarked with satisfaction, but he had been able to do so only because by twenty years of astute intrigue and policy he had reduced Scotland to a state of unprecedented docility. In his son's time this was no longer so. What counted in Scottish administration was the authority of Highland chiefs and southern nobles and lairds; early in the century the English system of justices of the peace had been introduced, but it had done no more than confirm the authority already wielded by these men. What counted in Scottish Law was the opinion and influence of the judges, the Lords of Session. King James's Council had represented their interests, made use of their opinions and commanded their respect.

King Charles's Council did none of these things. In the attempt to make it more amenable to his will he had eliminated the Lords of Session altogether from the board and when vacancies were to be filled, he would pass over the great and powerful nobles and place on the Council instead lesser men, in the belief that they would serve him more obediently. It was only a matter of time until he should discover that the authority he exercised through his Council in Scotland had ceased to be any authority at all.

The Scottish Councillors had fewer opportunities for corruption and intrigue than their English counterparts, though they used all that they had, and Lord Traquair the Treasurer was generally regarded as having made a fair part of his fortune out of his office.

The councillors in both countries were open to a certain moral corruption not wholly of their own seeking. Conciliar government in their time was midway between modern cabinet government and the personal system of the Tudors. A modern minister who finds himself in disagreement with government policy resigns his place. A Tudor minister who persistently disagreed with the sovereign's policy would not long have remained in his (or her) confidence. The position of several of King Charles's ministers, both in Scotland and in England, was not only unprecedented but unique in the history of the British Isles. Their advice and opinions were systematically overruled or disregarded by the King, but he kept them in his council and expected them loyally to support and carry out his policy. They could not resign because resignation from the King's Council would have been tantamount to self-inflicted political disgrace. Men like Northumberland in England and Lord Lorne in Scotland were therefore compelled to serve, although it grew yearly more difficult for them to serve with sincerity, honour or loyalty.

The King's two most intelligent ministers, the Archbishop of Canterbury and the Lord Deputy of Ireland, stand out head and shoulders above their corrupt or feeble colleagues and were single-minded in their devotion to the King's ideals. But Charles was as much inclined to pass over their advice as he was that of lesser men.

He supported his Archbishop in his plans for the Church but in most other spheres he resented his interference. Laud was greatly disliked by the Queen and, as if to make up to his wife for his partiality to the Archbishop's views on the Anglican Church, the King opposed him on almost all other matters. He went clean against his advice, for instance, in the favour he showed to Roman Catholics, and was disposed to be irritable when Laud drew his attention to the more difficult and problematical aspects of his home policy. After one discouraging effort to explain to his master certain worrying aspects of the political situation, Laud lamented to his friend the Deputy of Ireland, " The King is more willing *not* to hear than to hear." [14]

The Lord Deputy of Ireland, the King's only other outstanding adviser, owed his position largely to the Archbishop's judgment. It was probably Laud who had persuaded Charles to offer a seat on the council and a title to one of the most troublesome members of the House of Commons in the Parliament of 1628. Laud had seen that the fervour which moved Thomas Wentworth to oppose the King was a fervour for strong government rather than a factious resentment of royal authority. The offer had been accepted, and the leader of an angry House of Commons had been transformed into the most zealous of the King's servants. Wentworth was a tall, spare, formidable Yorkshireman, with a notoriously bad temper and no personal charm. His dictatorial manner, which reflected his sense of his own position, generally inspired dislike and his ostentatious display of the wealth he had acquired in the course of his career provoked envy. But he had strong and tender affections and depths of simple loyalty and gratitude in his nature which made him truly beloved by those who knew him best. As a practical administrator he had done well in the North of England, and more than well in Ireland. He was efficient and fearless, and he worked with a violent methodical energy at every task he took in hand. Like the King, like Laud, he believed in the establishment of unquestioned authority as the foundation of good government.

Charles, Laud and Wentworth had each of them the desire, and, acting together would have had the skill, to make a reality of that ideal vision of authoritarian government pictured by Rubens or set forth in the masques at Whitehall. But the King wanted the thing to be done without the strenuous effort of doing it; he deflected the energy and discouraged the efforts of his two best ministers, and believed that he had mastered the problems of the political situation when he had done no more than postpone their solution. He was encouraged in this delusion by optimistic, flattering or ignorant voices at Court, and he became, as each peaceful year went by, ever more willing to be deceived.

The friendship of Laud and Wentworth was cemented by their common frustration. Both were deeply loyal to the King but critical of his behaviour. In their lengthy correspondence each detailed to the other his views on the events of the day and deplored the intrigues of Court and Council. These letters reveal in both Laud and Wentworth a grasp of essentials, an analytical sense of the situation and a sharpness of judgment which are impressive. The alliance of the two, had it ever become effective, would have given to the King's government the strength it so gravely needed. But Charles, following an old, sly, unwise maxim of his father's, did not care to encourage men who were stronger than he.

The King was serious-minded, but he was not industrious. His gravity of manner, and the solemn character of many of his pleasures, have done much to conceal the disarmingly simple truth that he was lazy in all matters of government. His casual attitude to his council, his unwillingness to listen to disturbing information, his hunting three or four times a week, the long hours spent in pursuit or enjoyment of works of art, or in theological discussion—all tell the same tale: he was not interested in practical administration. He idled away the opportunities of his reign, while his two ablest ministers—Laud confined to Church matters only and Wentworth virtually in exile—exchanged their troubled letters, and the rest of his ill-chosen councillors concealed from him anything likely to disturb his equanimity [15] and played at pitch-and-toss with the reputation and resources of the Crown.

The reputation of the Crown was deeply involved with its resources because the measures taken to increase the royal revenues were a principal reason for the dwindling respect in which the government was held. A constant need for money hampered and deformed the King's policy, and the methods he chose to raise it were unpopular and corrupt.

Charles was not himself responsible for the financial difficulties of the Crown. He was by nature careful but he had certain costly obligations—the help he gave to his sister—and he had at least one very expensive taste, his collection of works of art. It was no fault of his that the value of money had declined while the demands made on the Crown had grown. Out of dwindling revenues he had to meet the expenses of the central government, and the efficiency with which that government was carried out depended on the amount of money forthcoming.

The lands from which, in the Middle Ages, the Crown had derived its chief revenue had some of them been sold in the last century to raise ready money. The rents from those which were left were still considerable, but the cost of collecting them tended to rise; these rents formed the most calculable part of the royal income, and were therefore often mortgaged in advance. The net revenue from land, after payment of all expenses and of the assignments which annually accumulated against it, was by King Charles's reign only about £25,000; in the early part of his father's reign it had been three times as much. The steep drop was symptomatic of the rate at which rents had been alienated for ready money and of the accumulating demands made on the remainder.

The bulk of the King's income was derived from import taxes levied on various commodities. The amount of these taxes, collectively known as Tonnage and Poundage, was fixed by Parliament at the beginning of each reign. But the first Parliament of Charles I had taken the unprecedented step of refusing to fix the rate of Tonnage and Poundage for more than a year at a time. From the King's point of view, this was unpardonable and insulting conduct for which the laws and customs of the realm gave no authority. From the point of view of the House of Commons, it was a justifiable attempt to exert control over the royal policy, justifiable because the Commons distrusted both the policy and the advisers of the King. Failing to come to a satisfactory agreement with any of his Parliaments, the King had in the end fixed Tonnage and Poundage at a rate that he considered reasonable. Although some defiant merchants had refused to pay and been imprisoned by order of the royal council, the bulk of his people had yielded rather than dislocate the trade on which they and the country depended.

The collection of taxes had grown more complicated with the extension of commerce and the increase of the King's demands. A central office, the Exchequer, existed through which the royal revenues were supposed to pass, but there was no government organisation for the collection itself, or at least none large and effective enough. Taxes were therefore farmed to courtiers and financiers; they bought a lease of the tax for a period of years, paid an agreed sum to the King, and organised the collection to allow a reasonable profit for themselves. The King, in straits for ready money, complicated the situation further by anticipating the returns on the taxes and making grants on them in advance. He also borrowed from the tax farmers, creating double and treble confusion. The receiving officers of his Exchequer complained that these assignments and anticipations meant that less than half the King's supposed revenues passed through the Exchequer. The debts contracted on the yield of the taxes were often paid out direct by the tax farmers, and this by-passing of the Exchequer made it impossible to keep track of the King's money. It might well be that some grants of money or debts were paid twice over.[16]

Besides these two major sources of revenue, the Court of Wards provided a discreditable third source. For a gentleman to leave a minor as his heir was often a real disaster; the administration of the estate fell to the Crown which sold it back to a guardian of its own choosing. Admittedly the Crown usually chose the nearest kinsman, but even so the charges connected with wardship and with the final freeing of the estate when the heir came of age were heavy, and by the time the Crown and the guardian had each made a profit the estate was often, in the expressive contemporary idiom, " tottering." The wardship of some great heir or heiress might yield fat returns to the guardian who administered the estate largely for his own profit during the child's minority, and he could sell the hand of his ward, male or female, for a high price in the marriage market. The guardianship of a wealthy lunatic was also profitable, and to " beg a fool " of the Crown was an accepted procedure among grasping courtiers. The King intended well by the wards of the Crown, but he needed the revenues brought in by the Court of Wards too much to work any reform in its organisation. The Court was at the moment under the control of the cheerfully unscrupulous Cottington who had immensely increased its yield, to his own advantage and the King's. In the year 1637 it brought £61,972 to the royal coffers, an increase of more than £25,000 since the beginning of the reign.[17]

The King's financial advisers, like those of his father before him, were indefatigable in their efforts to find new sources of income. Two principal methods were employed: the revival of obsolete medieval practices, and the exploitation of the expanding world of industry and trade. In both of these the King's principal adviser for several years was the ingenious old lawyer, William Noy. An anagram of his name—" I moyl in law "—fitly described his activities: his moylings unearthed a number of interesting possibilities, for many of which the King found immediate use.

In feudal England every landowner of a certain standing had been required to do a knight's service for the King in war, or to compound in money if he could not. This practice, to the acute annoyance of the gentry, was now revived and all those who came within the prescribed income limit were required to receive—or, as they put it, to " endure "—knighthood, paying the necessary fee to exempt them from military service. Those who refused the unwanted title were still liable for the fee.

More profitable still was Noy's revival of the old Forest Laws. When the King had in very truth depended on the game that he killed in the hunting season to feed himself and his retinue, it had been an offence to enclose or encroach on the great stretches of royal forest which were scattered over the kingdom. Gradually, as the King's need for game grew less urgent, much of what had once been royal forest had been brought under tillage or pasture and had passed into private hands. This made it possible for the King suddenly to institute an inquiry into enclosures of forests within the last fifty years. Those who had offended were fined large sums—or at least they were condemned to pay large sums, although the King often subsequently reduced the fines. The reduction rarely consoled the victim for the inconvenience, interference and fright to which he had been subjected.

Noy's next revival was the Elizabethan tax of Ship-Money, a contribution levied on seaports and coastal regions for the building and maintenance of the navy. The sums were fixed by the King's council, collected by the justices of the peace and sheriffs, and paid direct to the treasurer for the navy. This was in many ways the best managed and most economical of the King's plans, for relatively little of the money leaked away in the expense of collection and the tax went direct to the purpose for which it was intended.

Noy's masterpiece was his evasion of the legislation against monopoly. Queen Elizabeth had made the happy discovery that the Crown could raise money by granting the sole right of trade in certain commodities, or the sole right of manufacture, to some rich and favoured person. The abuse of such monopolies and the source of extra-Parliamentary revenue that they gave the Crown, had caused the House of Commons to attack them, and the Parliament of 1624 had finally made them, one and all, illegal.

William Noy found a legal way out of the difficulty. In future, monopolies were granted only to those who had found and wished to develop some new form of manufacture: in order that invention and valuable new processes might be given every encouragement, it was only fair that such people should enjoy special favour and protection. The word *monopoly* was replaced by *patent*. The King granted patents to the *projectors* who wanted sole rights of manufacturing beaver hats or copper pins because they had a specially efficient method which stood in need of protection from competition until it should be established. Some patents were justly given for interesting experiments; the majority were given on the most trivial pretexts. Monopolies, expelled by Parliament, came back fourfold in this transparent disguise. A further ingenious plan was to grant, not the sole right of manufacture, but the sole right of transport of some particular kind of goods. Occasionally the complications went even further, and the King would sell to one projector rights of manufacture and transport, and to another the right to grant, for a consideration, licences to individuals to infringe the privileges of the first projector.

Besides patents, and licences to evade patents, the King also made money out of the so-called incorporations. For a sum of money, he was willing to incorporate new companies of craftsmen—the leather-workers, for instance, the beaver-makers and others—granting them the right to organise their own industry. The inspiration for patents and incorporations was chiefly financial, but there was an element of policy behind these expedients. The granting of patents could be used to bring certain industries very closely under the supervision of the Crown, thus creating a primitive nationalisation of manufacture. The incorporations arose from a genuine economic grievance and did something to alleviate it. Many of the older companies had ceased to be corporations of craftsmen and become corporations of merchants: they merely *sold* the goods which were made by others. Already the social revolution had turned its quarter-circle; craftsmen were being driven down, by the united pressure of these companies of merchants, into the position of mere suppliers, whence it might be a short step to being hired labourers. The independent craftsmen therefore strove to band themselves together into companies which could negotiate on equal terms with the tradesmen who bought and marketed their wares. Charles's grants of incorporation were a reasonable attempt to improve the conditions of the craftsmen, to stem or alter the course of economic and social changes, and to create a firm attachment between the Crown and the artisan, against possible exploitation from entrenched companies of middlemen.

Charles's policy provided the ground-plan of a politico-economic programme which foreshadows that of Colbert in France fifty years later and which, had it been firmly pursued, might have established the Crown in the affections of the artisan population and set England on the road to an enlightened *étatisme*.

But long-term and constructive economic plans were in pawn to the King's immediate needs. The exaction of fines, not the protection of the poor man's rights from the wealthy encroacher, was the first consideration in applying the forest laws. The somewhat wider laws originally intended to prevent depopulation, and enforced against those who enclosed common and waste land, were used with the same financial purpose and social inconsistency. The King himself enclosed common land and encouraged enclosure when it seemed profitable to do so; he supported the great drainage and enclosure schemes for the fens, and he turned over to tenant farmers a part of the once common land on the royal estates near Berkhampstead.[18]

In the same way, the money that flowed into the treasury, and not the intrinsic merit of patents or of commercial schemes, governed the grants to projectors, and if there was money to be made out of the struggle between a new incorporation and an ancient company, as there often was, the King was prepared to let the quarrel fester, with a concession now to one side, now to another. Four patentees shared the right to trade wholesale in tobacco in the county of Durham; one, the most powerful, took proceedings against the retailers, mostly alehouse keepers, who were buying from the others. Small men were harried, accused and persecuted about twopenny screws of tobacco, and, whoever was to blame, the affair did not make the King popular in Durham.[19]

The King's ingenious bullying of the London Vintners' Company had aroused some ill-feeling in the City. He had demanded from them payment of £4 on every tun of wine. When they refused the Star Chamber issued a decree forbidding Vintners to cook and serve meat to customers. As most of the Vintners had long practised this auxiliary trade the prohibition hit them hard. They paid £6,000 to the King in the belief that he would proceed no further with the decree. Soon however prosecutions began again and the Vintners learnt that these would be stopped only if they agreed to pay 1d. to the King on every quart of wine sold. Some of them were for resisting and letting the matter go before the Star Chamber, but the Master of the Company, Alderman Abell, was rather a man of business than a man of principle. He saved the Company from further trouble by negotiating a deal through the King's Master of the Horse, the Marquis of Hamilton. The Company would pay £30,000 a year (£4,000 of it to Hamilton) for the privilege of serving meals as well as selling wine.[20]

The King, inspired by a salt shortage early in his reign, had considered making salt into a royal monopoly, as it was in France, thus taxing at the source a prime necessity of life and securing a steady income. The need for immediate funds caused him to grant not one, but two, patents for the production of salt. The two patentees naturally came into collision; with the Crown behind them, they also collided with the people of Yarmouth when they tried to set up salt pans on what was time-honoured common land, and they annoyed fishermen and fish merchants throughout the country by interfering with the production and distribution of that absolutely essential commodity, saltfish. Not content with the working of the rival patents, Charles next revived an old tax on salt in order to farm it for a substantial sum; the monopolists claimed exemption and Charles prosecuted them in the interests of the tax farmer; but the tax farmer complained that, as everyone now used Scottish salt, he had lost on the transaction. The Scots added a contradictory note, by claiming that the English monopoly had ruined their trade. Not all the complaints can have been true, but this much at least was true: that the Crown was very little richer and a great deal less liked for the whole business.[21]

More absurd and quite as irritating as the salt business was the trouble over soap. In 1631 the King granted to a group of projectors, several of whom were Roman Catholics, the exclusive right to make soap of vegetable oil for fourteen years. They agreed to pay the King £4 a ton and to make five thousand tons a year at 3d. a pound; they were permitted, in view of the supposed superiority of their soap, to examine all other manufactured soap and impound or destroy any that they thought below standard. At a test held in private in London, their soap was certified better than that of the London soap-makers. It did not fare so well at Bristol where a tavern maid and a laundress lathered away in public at some soiled linen napkins with the projectors' soap and with soap made by the Bristol soap-makers; they demonstrated that the Bristol soap washed whiter and more economically than the projectors' soap. In spite of this the King ordered the closing down of seven out of Bristol's eleven soap-boiling workshops.

In London the struggle went on with unabated venom. The King's projectors prevailed on the King to prohibit the use of fish oil in soap altogether; on the strength of this they seized the stock of the London soap-makers and prosecuted them in the Star Chamber, following this up by an offer to buy them out of business. The London soap-makers refused the bait and some of them were imprisoned. Murmurs were now rising on all sides. While fishing companies were affected by the prohibition on whale oil, the people in general declared that the projectors' soap was bad. The projectors mobilised the Queen's ladies to write testimonials to the excellence of their soap but laundresses and—more important—cloth-workers throughout the country continued to condemn it. In response the King prohibited the private making of soap altogether and gave the projectors the right to enter and search any private house. All in vain. By the summer of 1634 illicit soap was being sold at a shilling the pound or six times its original price, so low was the general opinion of the projectors' soap. At this point the projectors gave up their plan of using only vegetable oil and took to using the fish oil, which they had made illegal for everyone else. In a final effort to drive their rivals out of business the King put a tax of £4 a ton on Bristol soap. The Bristol soap-boilers refused to pay, and fourteen of them followed the London soap-makers to prison. The farce could not continue much longer and in 1637 the King wound up the project and bought in the projectors' rights for £40,000 of which he made the London soap-makers contribute half. He then allowed the London men to go back to their interrupted manufacture on payment of a tax of £8 a ton to the Crown.[22]

The intermittent bullying and imprisonment angered and injured a minority. It was, in the long run, the constant prying interference arising from the King's financial projects which alienated the majority, an interference so marked that quite innocent strangers who asked questions would suddenly find themselves the object of insulting hostility, because they had been taken for government spies.[23]

The salt trouble and the soap trouble had irritated the Scots as much as the English. The poorer nation felt and feared the effect of the King's financial tamperings more than the richer one. England had already a well-established position in the economy of Europe. Scotland was struggling for a place and what was in England an irritation might in Scotland be a disaster. Salt was, after plaiding, the principal export of Scotland, and although the King's planned salt monopoly had in truth done little, if any, damage, it had caused grave anxiety while it lasted. The soap business was more serious, because by restricting the use of whale oil for soap the King had injured the Arctic fishery interests of the Scots. Further injury was done to Scottish trade by doubling the export duty on their coal, in spite of energetic protests;[24] worst of all was the scandal of the copper coinage.

Scotland, where the people still resorted to barter in many transactions, was perpetually short of small coin. The King had therefore granted to the Earl of Stirling the right to mint copper tokens. This patent was to serve a double purpose: the coins were to solve the problem of small change in Scotland and the profits made by Stirling were to be written off against a considerable debt which Charles had incurred towards him. Stirling was suspect in his native land because he belonged to the large group of courtier Scots who had followed their King southward and associated their fortunes with his, to the neglect of their own country. A poet, a scholar and nothing of a financier, he so managed the copper coinage as to create a noticeable inflation, to bring the quality of the King's money into disrepute and yet not to cover his own debts. The King, who had no other means of paying him off, remained deaf to repeated protestations from the Scots, and left Stirling, year after year, to bedevil the currency of Scotland.

William Noy had died in 1634, leaving his taxation schemes for others to operate. He had claimed to be a lawyer rather than a financier, and it is possible that if the King had had a Treasurer who was also something of a statesman and an administrator, Noy's ingenuity might have become the basis of an effective policy. A man who controlled and organised the collection of taxes so that the maximum came in to the King, and kept the scheming and corruption of Court speculators within bounds, could have given the King's government a steady income. A man who could develop the elements of policy embedded in the King's financial plans might have saved the King's government. No lack in the King's Council was more disastrous than the lack of a clever man at the Treasury.

The lack was the more regrettable because it was unnecessary. When the King's first Treasurer, the adroit and dishonest Portland, died in 1635, Archbishop Laud had used all his endeavours to have Wentworth appointed to the place—a man of ability and statesmanship, with a marked gift for financial administration. But he would have severely checked the courtiers who filled their pockets at the King's expense, and they, knowing this very well, had combined to oppose the appointment. The King did not wish to be surrounded by reproachful and indignant faces, which he must certainly expect if he placed Wentworth at the Treasury; he kept him in Ireland instead. Let the reproachful and indignant faces, which Wentworth's methods invariably created, be out of his sight, in Dublin. First he put the Treasury into commission between several councillors, which greatly increased the chances of delay, loss, confusion and corruption; then he gave the post to the Bishop of London. William Juxon was honest and careful as far as his eyes and hands could reach: he did his best. But he could not attack the trouble at the root, expose the corrupt, control the projectors and licensees, buy out the tax-farmers, and institute thorough-going reform. He had been appointed to the task because it was known that he would not do or want to do such troublesome things.

Wentworth, exiled from the Treasury for which he had hoped, set himself to improve the King's finances in the way still left open to him. He determined to make Ireland a valuable source of revenue to the Crown by making it prosperous and developing its resources. Prosperity could come by encouraging the Irish to work hard and—as even Wentworth anticipated difficulties in that plan—by bringing over industrious settlers in large numbers. He set his face resolutely against any short-term policy that would prevent the realisation of his plans; because it would have damaged Irish trade in saltfish, he opposed the King's attempt to extend the salt monopoly to Ireland, and he argued as firmly against the imposition of vexatious taxes on settlers who had not yet established themselves. "The Kingdom is growing apace," he wrote, "and a thousand pities it were, by bringing new burdens upon them, to discourage those that daily come over . . . especially when, but by a short forbearance, till they have taken a good sound root, his Majesty may at after gather five times as much from them without doing any hurt, where a little pulled from them at first breaks off their fruit in the very bud." [25]

He had to argue unceasingly with the King, who, when he was not expecting quick returns from taxes, was granting away Irish land for ready money. This, too, Wentworth strove hard to prevent by pointing out that only the right kind of settler could make Ireland permanently prosperous and a permanent asset to the Crown. In the meantime he did for the Irish taxes what he had longed to do in England: he bought out the tax-farmers and, refusing all outside requests for a share in the booty, farmed the principal taxes himself. He made his own profit on them and needed it, because he considered that the King's dignity ought to be fitly maintained by his Deputy in Ireland; he bought land, built hunting boxes and gave fine entertainments in Dublin castle, which he had greatly enlarged. His enemies —all those whose grants of land he had stopped or whose profits in the taxes he had curtailed—declared that he grew "monstrous rich" and hinted to the King that Wentworth enriched himself and not the Crown. But the King's revenue from Ireland rose from year to year, and the growing prosperity of the country promised even better things for the Treasury. The King, rightly, trusted Wentworth, although he deplored his capacity for annoying people. The disquieting energies of the York-shireman had been diverted to Ireland, but they overflowed none the less. Whitehall and St. James's were soon full of irritated courtiers whose hopes for profitable grants of Irish land had been dashed.

In this summer of 1637 the King and Wentworth were corresponding chiefly about the great affair of the Londonderry Plantation. About twenty-five years earlier, the City of London had entered into a contract with the Crown to farm and develop an indefinite area of northern Ireland in the region of Derry. There had probably been *bona fide* errors in the original charter, and ambiguities deliberate or accidental. The acreage of the land taken over by London was nearer 400,000 acres than the 40,000 mentioned in the charter. King James, before long, felt he had given away too much, and surveys set on foot by the Crown had shown that the City was failing to fulfil its obligations under the Charter. Early in 1635, the City was finally tried before the Star Chamber for wilful neglect; they pleaded that they had been faithful to the spirit and intentions of the charter but lost their case. Justice, of a kind, was probably done in this matter but its purity was suspect because it was evident from the first that the Crown intended to revoke the City's charter and resume control of the land.

Following the usual procedure, the Star Chamber not only deprived the City of all its lands, but added a fine of £70,000. " Londonderry hath almost undone London," it was said, but the City did not accept this without a struggle, and after two years of argument and numerous counter-propositions the fine was reduced to £12,000.

Wentworth, who had worked out the potential value of the land and the actual value of its excellent fisheries, was anxious to retain it all as a part of the royal possessions, and suggested it should be settled on the little Duke of York, the King's second son. To Wentworth's profound annoyance the King seemed more inclined to snatch at immediate profit by leasing it away.[26] Whatever he did with the land it was questionable whether either the King or Wentworth had done wisely to alienate the richest and most influential city in the three Kingdoms for £12,000 and the lands and fisheries of Derry.

The King's ambition was so to organise and develop his resources that he would never again be under the necessity of calling Parliament in England. Although he naturally made no public declaration of this purpose, it was unmistakably implied and was well known to foreign ambassadors as well as to the King's own councillors, who took care, as far as possible, not to mention even the possibility of a future Parliament.[27] He recognised that patents and fines were no permanent solution, but he felt, not without reason, that a permanent solution was within his grasp. He had enforced Tonnage and Poundage after Parliament's dissolution in spite of their refusal to grant it and, after the initial outcry, his subjects had accepted the situation. In the year 1636 by the issue of a new Book of Rates compiled by his authority alone he adjusted in the interests of the revenue all the customs duties payable in the Kingdom. This too went through without undue clamour. The King had thus arrogated to himself the right to settle this very important part of his income without having recourse to Parliament.

If he could also exercise and enforce the right to impose new taxes on his subjects without recourse to Parliament, he would have finally and effectively emancipated the Crown. It was therefore with a double purpose, political and financial, that he adopted Noy's suggestion of reimposing the Elizabethan tax known as Ship-money. This was a levy on the coastal counties and seaports of the realm for the express purpose of strengthening the navy. The tax was well-selected for the King's purpose because the expansion of sea-power was usually popular with the English, and the raids of Barbary corsairs on the south coast and of Dunkirk pirates in the Channel fully justified an increase in the navy. The tax, unlike so many of the King's financial plans, was in itself profitable and economical: the money was collected direct by justices of the peace and delivered to the sheriffs of counties who paid it over at once to the Admiralty. Very little leaked away in the process.

The revival of the Elizabethan impost was calmly received, and in the following year the King tried the critical experiment of extending the tax to the inland counties. This was an innovation, and at once—as he had expected—the critics of the government began to argue that he should have consulted Parliament first. Lord Danby gave the King a written protest, asking that Parliament might at once be called. The King had accepted the paper and begun to read it before he saw what it was. He went pale and paced the room angrily and in silence. For the next week he gave up his usual hunting expeditions and spent long hours in council. As a result he strengthened his policy against the Dutch, grew more insistent in his demands that the herring treaty be respected, and officially republished a book called *Mare Clausum* by John Selden, which claimed that the English had exclusive rights in the Narrow Sea. He hoped by this demonstration to stimulate enthusiasm for the navy and willingness to pay Ship-money. But although Selden, whose book was thus singled out, was a popular and influential man in the very party which most opposed the King, the demonstration had almost no effect. Spanish rivalry, and the poor figure cut by their country in the struggle for colonial power and the Protestant cause, interested English seamen more than this lesser dispute with the Calvinist Dutch. The Earl of Warwick, making one of his rare appearances at Court, told the King, openly and in public, that he would not raise a finger to make his tenants pay Ship-money against their consciences, but that if Charles would call a Parliament he would find his subjects ready, nay eager, to grant all he wanted for a war on Spain and Austria in the interests of the Elector Palatine. The King listened with an absent smile until Warwick had finished and then, brushing all he had said into oblivion, told him that he hoped he would set an example to all by his own obedience and promptitude in meeting the tax.[28]

All the same the King took the precaution of propounding a critical question to the judges. In time of national peril and imminent danger, he asked, could the King demand, without further ado, financial or other help from his subjects? All except two of the judges, Sir George Croke and Sir Richard Hutton, agreed that the King had such a right, and was furthermore " sole judge both of the danger, and when and how the same is to be prevented and avoided." [29] In the belief that they were bound to yield to the majority, the two dissident judges signed the general statement. The King thenceforward considered that he had a unanimous judicial ruling in favour of Ship-money.

Notwithstanding the ruling of the judges some of his subjects refused to pay. Sometimes resistance became violent; high words and cudgel blows were exchanged between Thomas Cartwright, the squire of Aynhoe in Northamptonshire, and the sheriff's men. Much of the resistance was, noticeably, in the districts where the leading opposition peers were powerful. The Earl of Warwick had said that he would not compel his people to pay; he went further for he strenuously encouraged them not to do so. It was clear to the King and his Council that those who openly refused were hoping to be prosecuted. Prosecutions for non-payment would provide the King's opponents and their lawyers with a chance to argue the constitutional merits of their case in public. Next to a debate in Parliament, this would be the most effective method of attacking the policy and actions of the Crown.

The King saw the danger and at first evaded it. To the undisguised annoyance of Lord Saye and Seal, he took no notice of the crafty peer's repeated and rude defiance of the sheriff's demands for money. The constable was sent to distrain his goods, and drove off some cattle that the rich old man could well spare; Lord Saye, drawing attention to himself again, brought an action against the constable. The King, disregarding the Ship-money business, retaliated by prosecuting him for infringing the forest laws—proceedings which gave Lord Saye and his lawyers no chance to open their mouths about Parliament or taxation.

The defiance of subjects could not with safety be tolerated, and although the King was determined not to gratify Lord Saye by prosecuting him, he had to find means of settling effectively with his opponents. In the summer of 1637 the case of Rex *v.* Hampden came up in the Exchequer Court. John Hampden of Great Missenden in the county of Buckinghamshire was only one of many who had refused to pay Ship-money on principle. At this time about forty-three years of age, a man of high intelligence and great charm, he was an influential landowner, a shareholder both in the Providence and the New England Companies, and a friend of the Lords Warwick, Brooke and Saye, and of John Pym.

English law ran its course with due deliberation. Hampden was not cited before the Exchequer Court until May 1637 to show cause why he should not pay an assessment of 20s. on his lands at Stoke Mandeville. What with preliminaries and delays, it was evident that the case would not be tried until after Michaelmas.

In the summer of 1637 King Charles had projects and problems in plenty: the Hampden case, the reform of the Scottish Church, the prosecution of the Bishop of Lincoln in the Star Chamber, not to mention Prynne, Burton and Bastwicke, the rebuilding of St. Paul's, the extension of the fleet, the draining of the fens, the development of the Welsh mines, the improvement and colonisation of Ireland, the purchase of new pictures for his collection, the enlargement of his deer park at Richmond. Although anxieties were inseparable from the office of a King he viewed most of his projects with hope and confidence. He spoke with a deep and grateful sincerity when he described himself to his nephew the Elector Palatine as " the happiest King in Christendom."

The Elector, young in years but already old in disillusion, had seen and heard enough during his sojourn in the country to make him doubt his uncle's judgment. The present happiness of King Charles, like the painted ceiling of his banqueting house at Whitehall, bore no relation whatever to the political reality.

BOOK I CHAPTER III REFERENCES

1. David Jenkins, *Lex Terrae*, 1647.
2. Fulbecke, *A Parallel or Conference of the Civil Law, Canon Law and Common Law* London, 1602.

3. Holdsworth, *History of English Law*, London, 1922, v, p. 353.

4. Fulbecke, *op. cit.*

5. *Anecdotes and Traditions*. ed. W. J. Thomas. *Camden Society*. 1839. p. 53.

6. *Records of the Honourable Society of Lincoln's Inn*, London, 1897, II, p. 326–7.

7. See *Hudibras*, Cant. III, Part III, ll. 760–5.

8. *Cal. S.P. Ven*, 1636–9, p. 165. The very great emphasis put by Shakespeare in *The Merchant of Venice* in the trial scene on the incorruptibility of Venetian justice is interesting in this context; the idea needed to be hammered home to an English audience.

9. Spelman, *History of Sacrilege*, London, 1698, p. 233; for a full account of the Court of Wards see H. E. Bell, *Court of Wards and Liveries*, Cambridge University Press. 1953.

10. Skeel, *Council of the marches of Wales*, London, 1904, p. 151.

11. *C.S.P.D.*, 1637, pp. 417, 463–4; 1637–8, p. 140.

12. Selden, *Table Talk*; Jardine, *A Reading on Torture*, London, 1837, pp. 53–4, 108.

13. *C.S.P.D.*, 1639, p. 181.

14. *Strafford MSS.*, X, Laud to Wentworth, December 19th, 1637.

15. *C.S.P. Ven*, 1636–9, p. 125.

16. *C.S.P.D.*, 1639–40, p. 61; see also Dietz, *English Public Finance*, New York, 1932.

17. H. E. Bell, *Court of Wards*, Appendix.

18. *C.S.P.D.*, 1639–40, p. 71.

19. *Ibid.*, pp. 89–90.

20. Rushworth, III, p. 277; Knowler, I, p. 507.

21. Hughes, *Studies in Administration and Finance*, Manchester, 1934, pp. 88–115 *passim*; Hist. MSS. Comm. *Rep. XIII, App. IV*, p. 206–7.

22. *A True relation of the State of the Business of Soap*, London 1643; H. E. Matthews, *Company of Soapmakers*, Bristol Record Society Publications X, Bristol, 1940, pp. 122, 194–5, 207–10.

23. *Short Survey of 26 Counties*, pp. 8–9; *Carriers' Cosmography*, Preface.

24. *Register P.C. Scot.*, 1633–5, pp. 223–4, 258–60.

25. Knowler, II, p. 89.

26. See T. W. Moody, *The Londonderry Plantation*, Belfast, 1939, for the details of this complicated case; Knowler, II, 91.

27. *C.S.P. Ven*, 1636–9, p. 124.

28. *Ibid.*, pp. 110, 124–5.

29. Rushworth, II, 608.

BOOK TWO

CHALLENGE FROM SCOTLAND
June 1637 - July 1639

Subjects ought with solicitous eyes to watch over the prerogative of a crown. The authority of a King is the keystone which closeth up the arch of order and government, which, once shaken, all the frame falls together in a confused heap of foundation and battlement.

THOMAS WENTWORTH

Let God, by whom Kings reign, have His own place and prerogative.

ALEXANDER HENDERSON

CHAPTER ONE

THE COVENANT

June 1637 – February 1638

A FAVOURABLE decision in the Hampden case and the imposition of the new Prayer Book on Scotland would carry the King a long way towards realising two of his ambitions: the financial independence of the Crown, and uniformity of religion in his dominions. In the meantime the Court of Star Chamber dealt drastically with the three men who had written and preached against the bishops in general and Bishop Wren in particular. Prynne, Burton and Bastwicke were small fry but their punishment was of importance in the royal scheme of things. "The intention of these men," Laud declared justly enough at their trial, "was and is to raise a sedition, being as great incendiaries in the State as they have ever been in the Church."[1] Lord Chief Justice Finch, the principal pillar of the King's judicial system as Laud was of the Church, fully concurred in this view. He led the councillors in imposing a sentence of extreme severity. All three men were sentenced to pay fines which amounted to more than all that they possessed; all three were to be confined for the rest of their lives in the remotest parts of the King's dominions. Before they disappeared for ever from public view they were to stand in the pillory and lose their ears. Prynne was also to be branded.

On June 30th, 1637, a hot bright day, the victims were led out to suffer in Palace Yard, Westminster. Sympathetic crowds had gathered to watch. Rosemary and sweet herbs were scattered before the martyrs' feet, and cups of wine and *aqua vitae* were offered to refresh and strengthen them. When they were uncomfortably wedged in two pillories, Mrs. Burton climbed on a stool and kissed her husband. The crowd cheered. Burton was in his best clothes, with new white gloves and a little nosegay in his hand, on which a curious bee alighted; the incident inspired him to utter a short sermon. The sufferers stood in their awkward pulpits for two hours, in the glare of a hot sun, and had plenty of time to preach, Prynne speaking loudest and longest. When the executioner approached to cut off their ears, Bastwicke, the doctor, produced a surgeon's knife and instructed him how to perform his task. The man, none the less, treated Prynne very roughly because—so the Court said afterwards— Prynne had undertipped him, only half a crown and all in sixpences.

The crowd surged about the victims, and relic-hunters strove to dip handkerchiefs in their blood; Burton, who was over sixty, fainted for lack of air and it was almost impossible for a surgeon to get through the press to attend to their wounds. Prynne, meanwhile, with astonishing fortitude, repeated a Latin epigram which he had composed on the subject of the letters (S.L. for Seditious Libeller) with which his face had been branded. Someone in the crowd drew a growl of agreement by remarking that if these three men had been Papists no harm would have come to them.[2]

The Archbishop's annoyance when he heard of the demonstration was mixed with anxiety which he confided to Wentworth. Both of them recognised the dangerous force which lay behind this outburst of enthusiasm for the fanatics. Such feelings were not confined to the Londoners. On their way to prison the three were followed and helped by crowds of sympathisers. Prynne especially was warmly welcomed at Chester, given dinner by the mayor and presented with a set of hangings for his prison room at Carnarvon Castle. With praiseworthy resignation to his fate, he had procured a Welsh Bible and was studying the language.

The Star Chamber had one more important case to decide before the summer recess. On July 15th, 1637, Laud's antagonist, John Williams, Bishop of Lincoln, was sentenced for perjury. Williams's guilt in this unhappy and extremely complicated case is not in serious doubt. But his reputation as a conciliator and an opponent of Laud was well known, and the popular belief that he was being deliberately victimised was not quite groundless. His crimes provided a means towards his ruin which was extremely welcome to the King and the Archbishop.

The Star Chamber and the High Commission worked hand in hand over this significant prosecution. The Star Chamber condemned Williams to pay a fine of £10,000, deprived him of all his ecclesiastical revenues, and sent him to the Tower during the King's pleasure, and the High Commission suspended him from the exercise of all episcopal functions. Perjury and bribery were not offences for which Williams could be deprived of his various preferments. An unashamed pluralist, he held both the bishopric of Lincoln and the deanery of Westminster. Laud hoped that, discredited as he now was, he would humbly buy his release from the Tower by resigning both and creeping away to whatever desolate small diocese in Ireland or Wales was pityingly assigned to him.

John Williams was no fanatic martyr for religion's sake, nor was he an innocent man deeply wronged; he was a politician of irrepressible tenacity and optimism, convinced that his judgment in Church matters was right and that Laud's was wrong. He had no intention of relinquishing two key positions in the Church merely because of a conviction for perjury. Laud had assumed jurisdiction in the see of Lincoln, but as long as Williams refused to resign, some turn of fortune might always restore his power; he held out, waiting for the change of affairs which should undo Laud. Harried by threats of further prosecutions, deprived of almost all his means, reduced to a single square meal a day—at which, however, he often entertained guests—he continued in the Tower, voluble, obstinate and unafraid.[3]

One or two lesser matters marked the end of the summer.

The Attorney-General, John Bankes, considered what should be done about a pamphlet with the offensive title "A Breviate of the Prelates' Usurpation" which had been slipped into his hand together with a reproachful personal letter declaring that it was a pity to see "a religious and godly gentleman" like Bankes associating himself with the persecutors. Bankes was in truth one of the milder of the King's legal advisers and he disadvised a Star Chamber prosecution in this case.[4] Meanwhile the King's Council reprimanded two unruly young noblemen who had come to blows in a narrow street, and reversed the action of a London jury which had acquitted a couple of draymen who, after colliding with a nobleman's coach in a traffic block, had used abusive language to him. The saucy fellows were flogged and sent to Bridewell by direct order of the Council, which severe and high-handed action in defence of the social order called forth no protest from anyone.[5]

Vacation silence had descended on the law courts, and King Charles was enjoying the season's sport at his favourite country house of Oatlands, when, in the first week of August 1637, unwelcome news reached him from Edinburgh.

His council in Scotland had fixed Sunday, July 28th, for the introduction of the new Prayer Book throughout the country and announced that they themselves would mark the occasion by going in procession to St. Giles' Cathedral for the morning service. One councillor, Lord Traquair, who was never afterwards able to explain his conduct satisfactorily to the King, remembered a pressing engagement on the other side of the kingdom; his more astute colleague, Lord Lorne, had a sudden indisposition. For the rest, the councillors attended.

As soon as the Dean, Dr. Hannah, began the service, the crowd at the back of the church set up a shout and followed their words by hurling clasp Bibles and folding stools at the Dean and councillors. The rioters were with some difficulty put outside by the guards, but a great crowd round about the cathedral battered the doors and pelted the windows for the rest of the service. Demonstrations of the same kind had taken place in other churches that day, and in the afternoon roving gangs in the Edinburgh streets set on some of the King's supporters to the peril of their lives.

The demonstration had been premeditated. For the past three months the principal ministers, gentry, citizens, and lords who objected to the Book had been considering what to do when the crisis came. The religious fervour of the populace was genuine; they had only to give it guidance. The King's councillors, knowing both the zeal of the populace and the intelligence of those who were directing it, realised how great was the threat to the King's authority in Scotland, but they also realised the peril in which they themselves stood. Consequently, although they declared the rioters guilty of treason and worthy of death, they also suspended the Service Book, and removed the seat of their session from the heart of incensed Edinburgh to the defensible seclusion of Holyrood. By their words they proclaimed the King's unshaken authority, but by their acts they revealed themselves unable, and perhaps unwilling to support it.[6]

This was the news which reached the King at Oatlands. He was coldly and fiercely angry, as much at the cowardice of his Scottish council as at the insolence of the rabble. He sent a peremptory command that the use of the Book be immediately resumed and the principal rioters forthwith arrested and sentenced for their crime.[7] He acted with majestic indifference to common reality. Rebellion was still to him no more than a painted hydra, something not yet experienced in the rough and personal manner known to his councillors as they apprehensively traversed the narrow streets of Edinburgh.

They could not carry out the King's orders because they had not the strength to do so. Even the ministers willing to use the Book could do so only if their congregations allowed them. William Annand, a Glasgow minister, who boldly continued with the new service, was all but torn in pieces by a crowd of women, and the Bishop of Brechin, tough and formidable, who glared at his congregation over a pair of loaded pistols while he conducted the service, barely escaped the rabble which lay in wait for him afterwards.[8]

Petitions against the Book poured in from all the southern parts of Scotland. Crowds from Fife and the Lothians began to gather in Edinburgh. The first outbreak was followed and sustained by burghers, by men of learning, by lairds and noblemen from all the south. National as well as religious fervour fed their anger. Thirty-five years of resentment lay behind this movement; the King was paying for his own and his father's neglect, for the long absence in England, for the attempt, once too often, to govern Scotland from Whitehall with a stroke of the pen.

In England meanwhile the King attended the wedding of his cousin the Duke of Lennox to the only daughter of his one-time favourite, the murdered Duke of Buckingham. The young people, who were thought to be much in love, were married by the Archbishop at Lambeth Palace on a thundery wet day in August, the King coming in person to give away the bride. A reception at the house of the bridegroom's aunt was the occasion of much innocent mirth and the presentation of splendid gifts, including a white satin purse containing five thousand pounds in gold.[9] The King and Queen left late and called again on the following morning, early. They were genuinely attached to Lennox and his lady and wished to see them happy before leaving London for another visit to Oatlands. Both husband and wife were their personal attendants, but had leave of absence from Court for a brief honeymoon.

The honeymoon was shorter than had been intended, for just at this time the Duke's mother died in Scotland and he had to hurry north to attend her funeral and settle her affairs. Lennox was little acquainted with politics, but he was the King's cousin and a chief nobleman of Scotland, and it was natural for Charles to expect from him a personal report on the situation in the troublesome North.

He reached Edinburgh about the third week in September 1637 and the Council courteously asked him to be present at their session of the 20th of that month. Lennox, as he walked through the streets to his appointment, was impressed and disquieted by the great crowd of people who lined his path, with suppliant, expectant gestures, " saluting very low." [10]   Both the populace and the Council hoped much from Lennox: he was the King's nearest kinsman of the Stewart family; he was thought to have influence, and he had the reputation of a good-natured, honest, conciliatory gentleman.

As witness to the deliberations of the Council at this critical time, the King's cousin got no very happy impression. On the council board lay a handful of typical petitions against the new form of worship, and the lengthy text of a Supplication, drawn up and signed by a great body of the clergy supported by some of the nobility. " This new Book of Common Prayer," so ran the Supplication, " is introduced and urged in a way which this Kirk hath never been acquainted with, and containeth many very material points contrary to the Acts of our National Assemblies, his Majesty's laws of this Kingdom and to the religion and form of worship established and universally practised to the great comfort of all God's people, His Majesty's subjects since the Reformation . . ." The Council asked only one thing of Lennox: that he would explain the pressing danger of the situation to the King and take with him two or three of the more violent petitions to prove that they were telling only the truth when they humbly entreated His Majesty to believe that they could proceed no further with the Book.[11]

On his return to England Lennox found the King in no mood to yield to insolent rebellion, and had not himself the firmness of character to change his master's set opinions. The King's plans for improvement at home and abroad, in small things and in great, still appeared to make steady progress. He had just peremptorily prohibited corporations and city companies from voting by ballot at their meetings, a secretive process, introduced from Venice some years earlier, of which his father also had strongly disapproved.[12]   His attention was drawn, at the same time, to a new silver mine in Wales. It would produce, it was estimated, three hundred pounds worth of the precious ore every week, and the King had granted its enterprising exploiter, Thomas Bushell, the right to set up an additional mint for this bullion at Aberystwyth.[13]   Among the schemes for reclaiming land, a hopeful project for the draining of Romney Marsh was under discussion.[14]   The usual plans of projectors for raising money for themselves or for the Crown were canvassed at Court, foremost of these, Sir William Courtine's new East India Company, a competitor which the London East India merchants viewed with indignation.   Sir Thomas Roe's West Indies Company, an enterprise which was still a vision of the future, caused some speculation and already gave its founder as much pleasure " as if by his industry the Indies were already conquered." [15]

The new ship, the *Sovereign of the Seas*, had been successfully launched at Deptford.   The Earl of Northumberland had thought of the name for this splendid giant of the ocean, two hundred and fifty-four feet long and armed with a hundred and forty-four guns.   The name, with its implied reference to his own sovereignty of the seas, delighted King Charles and, while Lennox was in Scotland, the whole court had gone to see the launch.   The occasion had been a disappointment, for the tide did not rise high enough and the *Sovereign* in the end slid into the water in the presence of a less distinguished company some weeks later.

From Ireland the King received, month by month, from his efficient Deputy, reports which showed that the royal authority and the royal revenues had never been in better state.   Wentworth had concluded a busy summer with a progress into the southern provinces where he intended to develop the country on a great scale.   Looking upon the land with the eyes of a practical, hard-working Yorkshireman, he saw that it was good. " The province of Munster is by much the best that I have yet seen amongst them," he reported to Cottington, " yet I dare confidently assure you if there were seven times as many people, there would be room sufficient for them all and make it a much better country for the dweller." The Irish were unworthy of their opportunities: here for instance was Limerick, "the bravest place for trade that ever I saw, seated in a rich country ... and the goodliest river doubtless in Christendom running under the walls." The water was so deep and the harbour so good that a ship of four hundred ton might "come with safety and lay her nose upon the quay." Yet owing to the miserable Irish sloth there was "not one ship of above a hundred ton belonging to the town." The pen in the Yorkshireman's hand quivered with indignation; it did not occur to him that the Irish themselves had any right to be consulted in the treatment of their neglected land. In his opinion they should have been glad to throw themselves on the King's mercy for their property. It was preferable to remaining, as they had for the past generation, a prey to the arbitrary seizures of unscrupulous English speculators, or to their own "petty but imperious" lords. Throughout the south he was received with a great show of enthusiasm and loyal addresses of welcome, "three at Kilkenny, two very deadly long ones at Clonmel, four not of the shortest here at Limerick." Limerick was gay with triumphal arches, including a tableau of "the seven planets in a very special and heavenly motion," with the sun in the midst of them squirting rose water on the Deputy out of an object which looked suspiciously like a doctor's syringe. [16]More remarkable than this joyous entry was the fact that in Ormonde, Clare and Limerick the local landowners, without further question, acknowledged the King's right to dispose of their land.

Wentworth had a plan for restoring Christ Church Cathedral, Dublin, not unlike Laud's plan for restoring St. Paul's. It would cost £30,000 but this could be extracted from the obedient Irish Parliament; the only obstacle was the behaviour of Archbishop Ussher who disapproved of vain expense on building, having as Wentworth complained, "a more domestic way of serving God Almighty than I like of, or David thought of when he purposed the building of a temple." [17]

While things went forward so favourably in Ireland, the King heard with equal satisfaction that the commission sent to investigate the illegal engrossing of forest land in Northamptonshire had imposed fines amounting to more than fifty thousand pounds, the Earl of Salisbury heading the list with the crippling liability of £20,000. The rich were not the only people to be disciplined for contravening the laws of the realm. An Elizabethan act had made it unlawful for any cottage to be built and occupied unless it had four acres of ground for cultivation and pasture. This regulation had often been ignored, usually by poor labourers and small yeomen's sons who could not find land but must needs have a roof to cover them. Fines now rained upon these people's heads, as well as on the richer landlords; but it was generally felt that the government should have something better to do than to " vex the poor people." [18]

Ship-money, on the contrary, seemed to be justifying itself, practically if not legally, for the coasts badly needed protection. The Barbary pirates that summer had made at least one successful raid in the south-west and carried away more than thirty captives, but in September an English squadron, which had sailed under Captain Rainborough to the west coast of Africa, dropped anchor in the Thames estuary and set on shore more than three hundred English men, women and children, released from Moorish thraldom. Rainborough also brought back with him an ambassador from the Moors, to discuss with the King of England the future prevention of piracy. When the Moorish envoy, a Portuguese eunuch with a very fine presence, rode in procession through the streets of London, with the released captives, all in white, following behind him, and four noble Barbary horses in glittering caparison to offer to the King, it seemed that the factious voices of Hampden and his friends had received an answer.[19] What did the legality of Ship-money matter, since it had proved its usefulness?

Worries and distractions interrupted the interests and pleasures of the Court. A scandal occurred in the autumn when Lady Newport, on her way home from the play in Drury Lane, slipped into the Queen's Chapel at Somerset House and was received into the Roman Catholic Church. Her husband protested; the Queen denied all participation in the matter, but Archbishop Laud declared that the priests who enjoyed her favour abused it to make conversions. The Queen retaliated by refusing to speak to the Archbishop for two months, but her favourites, Wat Montagu and Toby Mathew, thought it politic to vanish from Court for a while.[20] Charles himself, although distressed at Lady Newport's change of faith, spoke sternly to her husband for persecuting his wife for conscience' sake—a rebuke which may have had repercussions in the Puritan circles in which Newport moved.[21]

With so much else on his mind, the King had little time to spare for Scotland, although early in October he commanded his Scots council to take effective measures to disperse the multitudes of petitioners still in Edinburgh. The Council's half-hearted attempt to comply with this order provoked a riot in which the Bishop of Galloway was frightened out of his wits and Lord Traquair lost his hat and cloak in coming to his rescue; after that, the council made no further effort. " The Lord give this business a fair end for it has a fair beginning," wrote a Presbyterian lawyer, Archibald Johnston of Warriston, in his diary on the night of this savage tumult.[22]

The fair beginning was not essentially or exclusively the Lord's work; the King's supporters and the bishops were well aware that resistance was being encouraged and organised by a group of nobles, lawyers and ministers. The riots were frequently led by women, that breed of resolute harridans whose voices may still be heard uplifted in argument in the back streets of southern Scotland. Neither these women, nor the men and boys who joined them in bishop-baiting, would have acted so appositely had there been no guiding power to hold them together, keep their anger alive and unloose their rage at the proper moment, but the fanatic emotion which made them terrible was all their own. The religious and national feeling of the great majority in the lowlands of Scotland was guided by a sagacious and experienced few who saw how best to use it, but the feeling itself was deep, widespread and by no means irrational. As for the leaders of the party—nobles, ministers and men of law— they were not less sincere in their religion because they were also capable of political strategy and worldly calculation.

The nobleman who, ever since the beginning of the King's reign had been the foremost opponent of his Church policy for Scotland, was John Leslie, Earl of Rothes. The immediate and natural leader in the present crisis, he was a man approaching forty, tough, independent and well-experienced in politics. His lands were scattered, some in Fife, some in the region of Elgin, and his influence, though it was not to be compared with that of such great nobles and clan chiefs as Huntly or Argyll, was singularly widespread. He was a reasonably devout Presbyterian, but the political aspects of the cause had always been more important to him than the spiritual: as a Scot he resented and suspected the attempt to bring the Kirk into line with England, and as a nobleman whose ancestors had had their share of pillage at the Reformation he objected to the re-establishment of the bishops and the royal attempt to restore their ancient endowments.

With him were associated a number of other Scots lords mostly from the Lowlands—Balmerino, Lothian, Lindsay, Loudoun, Cassilis. It was not until the middle of October that a young man of stronger personality than any of these associated himself with the party and became, next after Rothes, the moving spirit of their actions. James Graham, Earl of Montrose, was twenty-five years old, newly returned from a tour of Europe, cultivated, witty and gallant. The news that he had signed the Supplication against the Prayer Book caused dismay among the bishops, for he was personally known to several of them and had always seemed friendly; it had been assumed, from his tastes, his friends, his travels—he had stayed long in Italy, studied in Padua, and visited Rome—that he would be a King's man. But Montrose, for all his European polish, was a believing Calvinist and had a fierce pride in the independence of his nation. These were the reasons which made him join his fortune with the opposition, not as some preferred to argue, his annoyance at the cold reception accorded him by the King when he had visited London.[23] He was a valuable recruit to the party because his easy grace and gay good looks made him an attractive leader.

A young man of a different social background, different gifts, and harshly different character was Montrose's contemporary, Archibald Johnston, Laird of Warriston. He came of a border family of small gentry, but his father had prospered in trade and Warriston inherited a shrewd business head. On the mother's side he had ancestors distinguished in the law and he himself had chosen that profession. Well under thirty, he was already one of the leading advocates at the Edinburgh bar. Warriston was not simply a religious fanatic; the spiritual diary which he kept reveals a man walking on the dizzy verge of madness. His exceptional gifts of logic, of memory, of concentration and calculation, were supported by no broadening wisdom and no human understanding. He could analyse a legal text or extract every particle of verbal meaning from a passage of Scripture, but he was lacking in ordinary powers of criticism; he was credulous to the point of silliness, intolerant from a rabid ignorance, unable fairly to examine his own heart or motives. For so narrow and hard a mind the long hours of prayer common to the Presbyterians meant a daily exercise in self-deception. "For the space of two or three hours I got an exceeding great liberty, freedom and familiarity with my God," he would write; and again, "the Lord all this time was powerfully, sensibly, speaking in me and to me, praying in me and answering to me." In a cold sweat of terror and devotion he learnt that "I was appointed for eternal salvation and my name written in the Book of Life" and was inexpressibly uplifted by the conviction that he would not only be glorified after death, which was "too little favour and common to all His saints and chosen, but He would even in this life glorify Himself visibly and sensibly in my life and death." He knew, no less, that unworthy as he was, he was God's chief instrument for the "welfare of His Church, Satan's overthrow, Antichrist's ruin, and comfort of the godly." The dazzling revelation of his mission made him reel "like a man drunken."[24] His intoxication lasted a melancholy and bitter lifetime.

Reflections such as these occupied the thoughts of Warriston in the intervals of applying his formidable intellect to the problems before the rebellious party in Scotland. He was at this time minutely studying the Confession of Faith of 1580, the document, deeply sworn, by which the Scots had once tried to stabilise the Church of Knox.

The principal leader of the clergy was Alexander Henderson, minister of Leuchars in Fife. He was an older man than the secular leaders, well on into his fifties, and with a patience and human understanding acquired during more than thirty years as the conscientious minister of a large parish. His abilities had long since marked him out for some more important charge, but his known opposition to the bishops had prevented his preferment to Edinburgh or Stirling. He had from the beginning of the present troubles taken a leading part in refusing the new Service Book and petitioning against it. Henderson stands out among his contemporaries for honesty and largeness of heart. He was firm in his devotion to the doctrine and worship of the Kirk, but he respected sincerity in others and was capable of tolerance, though not of yielding. He was a good diplomatist because he had the imagination to understand points of view other than his own and could meet them with argument rather than anger. A certain irascibility was occasionally apparent in his words, but it added to, rather than diminished, his authority.

These were the open leaders of the party. Two other men, who could not yet proclaim their sympathy, were already in private agreement with the rebels: Archibald Campbell, Lord Lorne, and Sir Thomas Hope, both members of the King's council.[25] Lord Lorne, eldest son to the Earl of Argyll, was already possessed of his father's lands and was, in effect, the head of a noble house and the chief of the largest clan in the Highlands.

The circumstances were unusual. His father, a treacherous old ruffian who had built up a formidable position in the Western Highlands by suppressing the disorderly clans whose territories abutted on those of his own people, had fled the country twenty years before on account of his creditors. Later, becoming a Roman Catholic in Flanders and entering the service of the King of Spain, he had forfeited his estates, and his son, at twenty-one, had become Earl of Argyll in all but name.

Lord Lorne, in the years during which he had controlled the great estates of his father, had restored order to the disordered finances of the house of Argyll. He had also suppressed the plundering MacGregors by land and the piratical Macdonalds by land and sea. He was an admirable organiser with a shrewd eye to advantage and, as he got the better of piracy, he had built up small fishing fleets and a petty coastal trade from the many villages on the indented seaboard of his land. By this time he was the wealthiest as well as the most powerful nobleman in Scotland.

He lacked nevertheless many of the personal characteristics useful to the chief of a clan and a great nobleman. He was small and unprepossessing, had neither a good presence nor a powerful voice, and his florid, rather undistinguished face was marred by a disfiguring cast in his pale blue eyes. With these physical drawbacks went a cautious and secretive manner; he had no charm. Yet his concentration of purpose and his profound gravity were impressive, and his exceptional intellectual powers were apparent to anyone who had any dealings with him. His colleagues held him in respect and his clan was greatly, and rightly, in awe of him.

Lorne was a convinced and devout Presbyterian, although as a member of the King's Council he had had to give official support to the royal policy. Sir Thomas Hope of Craighall, Lord Advocate of Scotland, was in the same embarrassing position. A scholar and practitioner of the law with more than forty years' experience at the bar, Hope was approaching his seventieth year and was generally acknowledged to be the finest legal mind of his time in Scotland. His mother, Jaqueline de Tott, came of a Dutch family, and Hope, a wealthy man with commercial interests both in Scotland and the Netherlands, stood foremost among those who kept the economic and religious interests of their country in close touch with the Amsterdam Exchange and the pulpits of Leyden and Dordrecht.

His judgment was exact, his intellect profound, his temper irritable, and his character cautious but firm; his honesty was strictly measured by what did, and what did not, hold good in law. The founder of a great fortune and prolific dynasty, he practised a certain shrewd self-interest, yet he could be obstinate in what he believed to be right, either by God's law or Scotland's, and, for all his worldly wisdom and commonsense, he had, at his prayers, heard the voice of the Lord offering him personal encouragement.[26]

As winter drew on, the crowds in Edinburgh gradually dispersed at the bidding of their leaders, but first they chose representatives of the three principal classes—nobles, ministers and burgesses—to remain in the city and act on their behalf. These small elected groups who, as time went on, were to wield extraordinary power, were familiarly known as the Tables.

The Tables, led by Rothes and Montrose, had audience with the council early in December when the Earl of Roxburgh, recently returned from London as the messenger of His Majesty's extreme displeasure, tried once more to hector them into obedience. They were so little impressed that Alexander Henderson took it upon himself to reprove the King's spokesman " for his oft swearing." [27] Deadlock had been reached: the rebels demanded that the King read and answer their Supplication, and the King, from the safe distance of London, resolutely refused to do so.

Throughout the winter the situation in Scotland grew steadily more dangerous. Some of the King's friends made attempts, neither well-sustained nor successful, to divide the ranks of the opposition by setting the citizens against the nobles and the gentry against the ministers. The manœuvre was too apparent, and the opposition only closed its ranks the more firmly. At least once in the darkness of the winter evenings, Lord Lorne came privily down from his eminence as a Councillor and consulted long and thoughtfully with the fanatic Warriston. He cancelled his usual winter visit to his castle at Inveraray and stayed through the drear season in the capital "to see the event of these matters" [28]—to see it from both sides.

The unhappy Council in Edinburgh sent off Lord Treasurer Traquair once again to London to face the royal displeasure and to try to explain the situation to the obstinate, incredulous King. Traquair was a lowland gentleman who had risen to a peerage and his present place in the Council by a small talent for intrigue and by courting the right people. He was shrewd enough to realise that, as the King's present policy could not succeed, unquestioning loyalty would pay him no dividend. With far less excuse, for his religion was negligible, he had also, like Lorne and Hope, entered into private communication with the rebels.

In England at the centre of the King's government, diplomatic relations with foreign powers were causing some anxiety. The King's neutrality in the European war was still the object of criticism at home and attack abroad. The King's nephews, Charles Louis and Rupert, on their return to The Hague where their mother lived in a house provided for her by the Prince of Orange, had taken service for the autumn in the Dutch armies engaged at that time in besieging the town of Breda, the frontier fortress which the Spaniards had captured twelve years before. The siege, long drawn out and full of incident, was the principal foreign news in England for several weeks. Many English volunteers fought in the Dutch forces, with the two Palatine princes, for the Protestant Cause against Spain. Several distinguished gentlemen were wounded; others behaved with conspicuous gallantry, and the Court at home hummed with their praises—wild Harry Wilmot dangerously wounded, gallant George Goring shot in the leg, brave Charles Lucas, first into the breach. The King thus faced increasing pressure to declare official war, and not leave it to individual Englishmen to redeem their nation's honour. The French ambassador, Bellièvre, who presented his credentials in the autumn, had come to complete the process by drawing England into offensive and defensive alliance with France and the Dutch against Spain. The French enjoyed the tacit support of the Vatican and the influence of Fr. George Con, the Papal agent at Court, would be exerted to help Bellièvre.

All this was watched with anxiety by Wentworth from Ireland, by Laud and Cottington in London. They knew the value of the King's agreement with Spain for the transport of bullion. Without the welcome silver from the Peruvian mines his finances would be hard to balance. Furthermore, peace alone could give his royal government the opportunities to establish itself beyond question. Wentworth was particularly anxious to avoid a war with Spain which would wreck his plans for the smooth and peaceful development of government in Ireland and at home. " God set us well over this brig o' dread," he wrote to the Archbishop. He meant the dread of a French alliance, not the dread of trouble in Scotland.

Lesser matters from time to time engaged the King's attention. He was perturbed at the wastefulness of his household; too many hangers-on, whole families of them, lived and ate free on the bounty of Whitehall. A Commission must be set up to inquire into this abuse. Then there were the Christmas masques in preparation; the one to be presented by the Queen and her ladies was to be exceptionally rich and beautiful. A large, temporary hall of fir-wood was being hastily erected to accommodate it; the King feared the smoke of candles for the new Rubens ceiling in the banqueting house.[29]

As to graver questions, the King was seriously distressed by the spread of Roman Catholicism and authorised the Archbishop to draft a proclamation forbidding his subjects to attend public mass at the chapels of foreign ambassadors. Partly as a result of Lady Newport's recent conversion, he set on foot a plan by which the eldest sons of Roman Catholic Lords were to be removed from their homes and educated under his eye at Court, thus preparing them for conversion to Anglican or, as he held, true Catholic doctrine. The scheme caused so much distress to many of his own and the Queen's friends that it was very soon abandoned. The Queen, indeed, regardless of caution or policy, arranged for her little flock of Court converts to take the sacrament together in her chapel at Christmas so that her friends could see how richly her efforts and her influence had worked.

The appearance at about this time of a book defending Anglican against Roman Catholic doctrine by a young Oxford scholar named Chillingworth, who had himself fallen at one time into the Roman error, gave great satisfaction to the King, who marked out its author for preferment.[30] Chillingworth's book, *The Religion of Protestants*, merited high favour for its serene and philosophic tolerance. On paper and in the minds of its best men the Anglican Church did indeed aim at a nobler and broader view of doctrine than that of any existing Church of the time, but broadness of doctrine which attacks the fanatic and narrow-minded with such zeal and relentlessness as that used by the King and the Archbishop is itself a tyranny. Chillingworth's noble words—" I seek not to offend any man, but for truth only "—sounded oddly against the background of silenced ministers, pilloried critics and resentful Scots.

The postponed Ship-money case was now before the Exchequer Court. Hampden and his friends had chosen their friend and colleague, the legal adviser of the Providence Company, Oliver St. John, to argue their case. St. John was a man of about forty who had been practising at the bar for a dozen years without attracting any particular notice. He had devoted much attention to constitutional law, and those who briefed him must have had occasion to admire his depth of knowledge in the political discussions which no doubt often followed the Company's meetings. The rest of the world was unprepared for the closely argued display of reason and erudition with which St. John opened his client's case. He developed two principal arguments, one general and one particular. The first was that if the King claimed the right to levy taxes on his subjects at will, the foundation of property itself was attacked and no man could possess anything but " at the goodness and mercy of the King " —a proposition evidently at variance with the accepted principles and practice of English law. His second argument referred back to the ruling of the judges that the King, in case of imminent peril to his subjects, could raise money without recourse to Parliament. But, as St. John with nice legal precision pointed out, there was no unusual peril when the Ship-money writ went out, and no pretence or excuse of it had been so much as hinted. " It appears not by anything in the writ that any war at all was proclaimed against any state." St. John's arguments, supported by whole batteries of precedents and quotations from statutes, lasted for two days. This might seem long enough, but Solicitor-General Littleton took four days to put the case for the Crown. Hampden's other lawyer, Holborne, then argued his client's case for six consecutive days. Attorney-General Bankes wound up for the King, taking three days to complete his arguments, in which he subtly combined his points of law with examples of the dangers already suffered and yet to be endured from the pirates who infested the seas. There could be grave dangers, he pointed out in answer to St. John's argument, without any such thing as a national war. This was true, but he did not explain why pirates, who were always a threat to English shipping, suddenly in 1636 had to be dealt with as an emergency.

The English passion for law enabled the audience to find these interminable arguments not only interesting but absorbing. Almost the whole of English history had been reviewed before the four of them had done; they cited statutes of all the Henries and Edwards, dredging up from the wreckage of the Hundred Years War, or the baronial struggles, this or that pearl of information about the levying of taxes; Bankes even cast back to the reign of King Egbert. There was very little in these arguments respecting broad principles, nothing whatever about right and wrong; no moral, no political indignation. The four honest, painful, learned men resembled for the greater part of the time nothing so much as a group of earnest archæologists, sieving with assiduity and without passion the dust of the past and selecting this or that recognisable fragment to prove their point. December was half spent before the arguments ended in the Exchequer Court. They continued with fervour in the eating houses of Westminster and the chambers and private dwellings of barristers and their friends. Politics apart, the Hampden case had raised a problem of fascinating complexity and interest. Certainly political passions were not silent; from Ireland the Lord Deputy Wentworth wrote in exasperation that he wished Hampden and his like could be " whipped home into their right senses." But political feeling about the case was at this time much more violent among the King's supporters than anywhere else. With the majority the Hampden case aroused not so much political indignation, as a vigorous concern about the proper interpretation of the law.

The four barons of the Exchequer, as the judges of that Court were called, were thoroughly perplexed. St. John and Holborne had produced precedents which troubled them—not morally, not politically, but legally. Whatever they felt on the broad principle of the King's rights, the technical aspects of the Ship-money writ, and of Hampden's case in particular, were far from clear. Littleton and Bankes had not been able to allay every doubt raised by Hampden's lawyers. This was a question that required consultation with all the judges. Judgment was postponed until the ensuing term; the case was transferred from the Exchequer to the special Court of Exchequer Chamber, and the judges of the King's Bench and the Common Pleas were required to consider and deliver their opinions upon it.

There may have been—probably was—a political motive in this decision. Lord Chief Baron Davenport, the principal Exchequer judge, was in an embarrassing position. He was a strong King's man and firmly believed in Charles's legal right to levy Ship-money. But the arguments for the defence had revealed to him a technical error in the writ directed to Hampden; he would therefore have felt compelled to pronounce in Hampden's favour. From discussions with his three colleagues he must have gathered that one of them, Denham, not only agreed on the technical question but was wavering altogether on the legality of Ship-money. The other two, Trevor and Weston, were strong King's men. This meant at best a division of the Exchequer judges two against two, with the Chief Baron giving judgment for Hampden—in effect a defeat for the Crown. It was very probably to avoid this that Davenport arranged for postponement and laid the Hampden case before all twelve judges.

Anxieties over this and other matters prevented the King from giving much attention that winter to the plan suggested to him by Captain Rainborough for ridding the Mediterranean entirely of pirates by using the English fleet to blockade Algiers. Rainborough's triumph on the Moroccan coasts in the summer was likely to remain a solitary success as the navy, in spite of recent expansion, was conspicuously failing to hold its own even in territorial waters. French and Spanish ships insulted English vessels at sea,[31] while Dutch shipmasters of Calvinist opinions successfully eluded the watch kept for them and unloaded parcels of forbidden religious literature on lonely parts of the Essex coast.[32] A Star Chamber decree prohibiting the printing and sale of unlicensed books made little difference to the dissemination of religious pamphlets. Some were secretly printed in England, more were printed in the Low Countries and smuggled over. A youth named John Lilburne, arrested on a charge of importing Bastwicke's pernicious book from Holland, was in prison awaiting his trial by the Star Chamber. He was the unlucky victim of whom an example was to be made, but he was only one of the many who had distributed forbidden books and were still doing so.

Newspapers from abroad had been prohibited early in the King's reign; no newspapers were authorised in England and the printing of news from Scotland was naturally forbidden. But the bolder Puritan booksellers circulated manuscript sheets containing the latest information about the Scottish dispute,[33] and sympathetic Londoners probably knew better what was going on in the north than did the King's English councillors, from whom he had so far concealed all details. Something more threatening to the King than the general sympathy of Puritan English for Calvinist Scots already existed. The dissident Scots had their agents and friends in England, while in the Low Countries exiled or visiting ministers, soldiers and merchants of both nations had for the last ten years drawn ever closer together, encouraged in this by the Dutch.

Only gradually did Charles come to admit that the Scottish business presented real difficulties in itself and was likely to become dangerously associated with the widespread Puritan opposition in England. In the circumstances, both the King and the Archbishop believed that severity alone would serve their purpose. The royal and episcopal authority must be exerted and examples must be made in both countries. The young Lilburne would be one; another whom Laud had in view was the headmaster of Westminster School, Dr. Lambert Osbaldeston, who had been indiscreet enough to correspond with the Bishop of Lincoln, the condemned and imprisoned Williams, and unlucky enough to have his letters found. In one of them he referred to "the little meddling hocus pocus," a person all too clearly identifiable as the Archbishop. Osbaldeston, on Christmas Eve, was still protesting that he could and would explain, but Laud was for making it a Star Chamber case and a serious one.[34]

In this atmosphere of righteous severity Lord Treasurer Traquair on his arrival with messages from the King's council in Scotland met with a cool reception. His clumsy efforts to blame the Scots bishops for provoking the crisis by hurrying matters too much greatly annoyed the King. So did the whole conduct of his council in Scotland. "We do no way approve the same," he wrote, "because your course herein hath been more derogatory to our authority than conducive to the true quiet of the country, for we can never conceive that the country is truly quiet when regal authority is infringed." He added to this reprimand a proclamation which the council was forthwith to issue. In this, the King declared that all those nobles who had dared to protest against the Service Book were worthy of his highest censure. If, however, they would immediately conform he would overlook their conduct, ascribing it rather to a " preposterous zeal " than to treasonable intent. But they must understand that in complete submission lay their only hope of mercy.[35]

The judges had begun at fortnightly intervals to give their opinions on the Hampden case; the first three spoke out strongly in the King's favour. Of these Robert Berkeley, on February 10th, 1638, was particularly eloquent. " The subjects of England," he declared, " are free men and not slaves "; but he went on to show that their freedom rested on the law, and that the law was, in its ultimate essence, the expression of the King's benevolent will. No conflict between King and law was imaginable. " Rex is lex," he said, " lex loquens, a living, a speaking, an acting law." [36] Seldom had the King's own view of his office been better expressed; he was the law, he was guardian and judge of his people's freedom. Berkeley's dictum matched well with the proclamation of mercy and the demand for unconditional surrender which the King had, in the same month, sent out to Scotland.

The King now dismissed his cares temporarily from his mind and went to Newmarket for a hunting holiday. He was displeased to find other people's dogs trespassing on his preserves, but an order for the destruction of all greyhounds or mongrels within ten miles of his Court set matters to rights. He had taken with him his giant, Muckle John, and his dwarf, Jeffrey Hudson, besides a large and cheerful retinue. After the days in the open air, the long evenings were passed pleasantly, with good food, good wine, chess and dice.[37]

These royal gaieties were unseasonable. For in Scotland, towards the latter end of that raw February of 1638 was celebrated " the great marriage day of the nation with God." To that wedding feast, so huge with consequences, King Charles was not invited.

Traquair's return to Scotland with the King's orders was the signal for which the opposition had been waiting. On February 20th, 1638, the council met, at Stirling, in miserable spirits, to issue the King's proclamation. Sir Thomas Hope dissociated himself from the action; Lord Lorne was conspicuously absent; nearly all the bishops sent excuses, fearing, not without cause, the angry crowds which had gathered in Stirling.[38]

In theory the contents of the proclamation and the council's intention to publish it at Stirling were kept secret to lessen the chance of an organised demonstration. But the opposition were well-informed, possibly by Traquair. Their leaders with about a thousand followers faced the King's herald at Stirling when he read out the proclamation and protested instantly. The council could think of no more dignified action than to send for the principal leaders, Rothes and Montrose, and implore them to disperse the crowd before a riot could break out. They could hardly have revealed more clearly their own weakness and the strength of their opponents.[39]

Rothes and Montrose, quietly triumphant, dispersed the demonstrators and transferred their attention from Stirling to Edinburgh where, forty-eight hours later, the farce of reading the King's proclamation was again enacted. This time the opposition lords had gathered an even larger crowd, and formal protests were accompanied by stirring speeches from the leaders. Montrose, to be seen and heard the better, climbed on top of an empty barrel. "Jamie," said Rothes, " ye will never be at rest till ye be lifted up there above the rest in three fathom of rope."[40]

In the troubled years since the Reformation the Scots had known many protests and popular demonstrations. Deeply imbued with tradition and by nature legal-minded, they did not act, in February 1638, without seeking for a precedent. They had found it—Warriston and others—in the year 1580. In that year the nobility and ministers had compelled the boy King

James VI to subscribe a Confession of Faith which ought to have established Calvinist worship and Calvinist organisation in Scotland for good. The cry in February 1638 was not for new things, but for a return to 1580.

Warriston had pondered the Confession for the past four months. He was joined in his deliberations by Alexander Henderson and another able minister, the narrow and arrogant David Dickson. These three seem to have been chiefly responsible for the document which became the manifesto and foundation of the party, the National Covenant. In effect it was a restatement of the Confession of 1580 buttressed by a protest against all that had since been done to alter true religion in Scotland. The closing paragraph was a defiant vow to maintain the faith.

" From the knowledge and conscience of our duty to God, to our King and country, without any worldly respect or inducement, we promise and swear by the great name of the Lord our God to continue in the profession and obedience of the aforesaid religion; that we shall defend the same and resist all those contrary errors and corruptions according to our vocation, and to the utmost of that power that God hath put into our hands, all the days of our life."

Six days after the scene at the Mercat Cross, on Wednesday, February 28th, 1638, the principal leaders of the revolt met in Greyfriars Kirk; Henderson preached a sermon, Warriston read out the lengthy document and the congregation of lords and gentlemen, led by the Earl of Sutherland, filed up to set their hands to it. On Thursday the gentry and the ministers were still signing; on Friday it was the turn of the Edinburgh citizens. They crowded in, overflowing the little church, gathering without in the churchyard.[41]

In the next weeks copies of the Covenant were carried over all Scotland, and in one kirk after another, in burgh and hamlet, through all the southern parts of the land, men set their hands to the sacred bond. " I have seen more than a thousand all at once lifting up their hands, and the tears falling down from their eyes," wrote a thankful minister.[42]   In Warriston's words, "this spiritual plague of Aegyptian darkness covering the light of the Gospel" had lifted at last and the Scots celebrated "the great marriage day of this nation with God."[43]

Archbishop Spottiswoode fled: "All that we have done these thirty years past is thrown down at once," the poor old man lamented as he journeyed to London and an exile's grave in Westminster Abbey.[44]   The council at Stirling, in a despatch so sulkily conceived as to be almost in itself a new revolt against the King, declared themselves powerless to mitigate the storm provoked by his ill-considered policy.[45]   "The fearful wrath of God" had come upon the land.

BOOK II CHAPTER I REFERENCES

1. Laud, *Works*, VI. i, 42.
2. *Harleian Miscellany*, IV, pp. 17–22; C.S.P.D. 1637, p.287
3. The almost indecipherable complexity of the case against Williams is well summarised in B. Dew Roberts: *Mitre and Musket*, London, 1938; for his condition in the Tower *see* Knowler, II, 167, and Hacket, *Scrinia Reserata*.
4. *Bankes MSS.*, 63/62, 63.
5. *C.S.P.D.*, 1637, p. 299.
6. *Register of the Privy Council of Scotland*, 1637, pp. 483, 484, 490.
7. *Ibid.*, p. 509.
8. Baillie, *Letters, Bannatyne Club*, Edinburgh, 1841, I, pp. 21, 41.
9. Laud, *Works*, III, p. 229; *C.S.P.D.*, 637, p. 355.
10. Rothes, *Affairs of the Kirk of Scotland, Bannatyne Club*, Edinburgh, 1830, pp. 8–9.
11. *Register P.C. Scot.*, 1637, pp. 529, 699.
12. *C.S.P.D.*, 1637, p. 420.
13. *Ibid.*, p. 301.
14. *H.M.C.*, XII, iv, p. 204.
15. *Strafford MSS.*, X, folio 251.
16. *Ibid.*, Vol. III, Wentworth to Cottington, August 28th, 1637; Vol. X, Wentworth to Cottington, August 21st; *C.S.P. Ireland*, 1633–47, p. 169.
17. *Strafford MSS.*, VII, Wentworth to Laud, October 18th, 1637.
18. Knowler, II, 117.
19. *H.M.C. Report, XII*, ii, p. 161; *Report, X*, iii, p. 166; *C.S.P.D.*, 1637, p. 431; Knowler, II, pp. 118, 129.
20. Knowler, II, 128.
21. *Gordon Albion*, p. 213.
22. *Register P.C. Scot.*, 1637, pp. 537 ff.; Rothes, p. 20; *Ancram and Lothian Letters*, ed.

Laing, Edinburgh, 1875, I, pp. 94–5; Gordon of Rothiemay, *History of Scottish Affairs, Spalding Club,* Aberdeen, 1841, p. 23; Warriston, *Diary, Scottish History Society,* Edinburgh, 1911, I, p. 271.

23. Guthry, p. 31; Wilson, p. 12; Burnet, *History,* p. 47; the *Scottish Historical Review* XXII. pp. 24 ff. gives the text of a protest to the Council dated October 18th 1637, and signed among others by Montrose. This is the first time that his name occurs and is a few weeks earlier than the date usually given for his joining the party.

24. Warriston. *Diary.* pp. 355, 357, 362.

25. Hope's *Diary,* and Warriston's *Diary* for these months make the opinions and sympathies of Lorne and Hope clear beyond doubt.

26. Hope, *Diary, Bannatyne Club,* Edinburgh, 1843, p. 89.

27. Rothes, p. 44.

28. Warriston, *Diary,* p. 289; *Breadalbane MSS., Letters,* 1636–9, Nos. 703, 706, 709.

29. *C.S.P.D.,* 1637; Knowler, II, pp. 130, 140–1; *C.S.P. Ven,* 1636–9, p. 374.

30. Knowler, II, pp. 133, 147.

31. *Strafford MSS.,* Vol XVII, Northumberland to Wentworth, January 26th, 1638.

32. *C.S.P.D.,* 1637–8, pp. 365–6.

33. *C.S.P.D.,* 1637–8, p. 27.

34. *Ibid.,* p. 377.

35. *Register P.C. Scot.,* 1638, pp. 4, 15, 16.

36. *State Trials,* ed. Cobbett, London, 1809, III, p. 1098.

37. *H.M.C.,* XII, ii, p. 176; *Portland MSS.,* III, p. 52.

38. Rothes, 65; *Register of P.C. Scot.,* 1638, pp. 3–4.

39. Rothes, *loc cit.;* Guthry, p. 33.

40. Rothes, 66–7; Gordon of Rothiemay, 33.

41. All contemporary accounts agree that the Covenant was signed inside the Church, but the venerable Edinburgh tradition that it was signed on a tombstone in the churchyard may perhaps derive from memories of the waiting crowds outside.

42. Livingstone, *Life,* ed. Tweedie, *Wodrow Society,* Edinburgh, 1845, p. 102.

43. Warriston, *Diary,* pp. 265, 322–3.

44. Guthry, p. 35.

45. *Register P.C. Scot.,* 1638, pp. 9–12.

CHAPTER TWO

SHIP-MONEY

March – June 1638

IN England, spring came early that year, bringing the hedge-rows out in a rush; tulips, even in northern gardens, were in flower before the end of March and " apricocks and plum trees . . . full of blossom." [1]   In this mild season the King became unwillingly aware of the disquieting turn that his fortunes had so suddenly taken.

The Covenanters—the name sprang into being within a few weeks of the Covenant—acted fast. The text of the Covenant, carried to London by an active young minister, was known to the King's opponents sooner than it was known to the King. Accounts of the Scots revolt spread rapidly to its many sympathisers. As for the Covenant, " the written copies are in all men's hands in London," complained Laud to Wentworth.[2] Even in the precincts of Whitehall there were those who sided with the rebels. The jester, Archie Armstrong, growing indiscreet in drink, called Archbishop Laud a " monk, rogue and traitor." He was packed off to gaol, and proceedings in the Star Chamber were contemplated, but abandoned at Laud's own request.[3]

The minuscule revolt of a tipsy jester was something that the King could suppress but he suspected that Archie had been encouraged by those of greater importance at Court or in London. Defiance of the royal authority was everywhere growing bolder. Petitions against the collection of Ship-money had reached the King from Lincolnshire, Northamptonshire

and the borders of Wales; the sheriffs reported that the difficulties of collecting the tax were almost insuperable in Somerset,
Hampshire, Surrey, Berkshire, Huntingdon, Norfolk, Worcester,
Derby, Nottingham, Northumberland, and in central Wales.
In Norfolk the resistance was exceptionally ingenious: when the
sheriff tried to distrain the cattle of those who would not pay,
their neighbours took the beasts into their own herds and made it
impossible for the sheriff's men to identify them. Even if the
sheriff's men managed to seize a few head of cattle they could
raise no money on them, for no one would buy property which
had been seized in this way.[4]

This obstinate and widespread defiance of the King's authority in England and Wales was as dangerous as anything that
had happened in Scotland. Rhymes and pasquinades against the
King and his policy and the most outspoken criticism were heard
everywhere in London. That the rebels of both nations were
likely to be in sympathy with each other was clear to any dispassionate observer; the King, the Venetian agent in London
reported home to his government, would never be able to put
down the revolt in Scotland with the help of his English subjects,
more than half of whom were themselves Calvinists.[5]

The directors of the Providence Company, using the half-
permission the King had given them to assert themselves against
Spanish attack, had been discussing the future of their depressed
and precarious settlements in the Caribbean. They had inter-
viewed a Scottish soldier of fortune, Lord Forbes, a rough
adventurer who had seen service by sea and land on the Baltic
shores with the Kings of Denmark and Sweden. But the
Providence Company had not at the moment the funds to employ
him about their business with Spain.[6]

Another Scottish soldier of fortune, Alexander Leslie, also
passed through London at this time. He was on his way home
from the German wars where he was a marshal in the armies of
the Queen of Sweden. An officer of so high a rank may well
have had friends and business in London on his way to Scotland.
Who and what they were is uncertain, but news of some kind he

brought with him from England when, at the end of March, he regained his native land. He saw much of the Covenanters, especially Rothes, who contemplated marrying his daughter to him. England and Scotland vibrated already with rumours of war.[7]

The feeling in the South and West of Scotland grew more violent with the advancing year. No one in those parts dared open his mouth to say a word in favour of the bishops or the King, for the people " possessed with a bloody devil," as one of their more temperate ministers put it, would set upon anyone who did so, and one Anglican clergyman, innocently travelling in Galloway, had all his clothes and baggage " torn in fritters " and barely escaped alive. Most of the bishops fled the country, not without cause; Sydserf, one of the most hated who was alleged to wear a crucifix round his neck, was three times stoned by an angry crowd. Known sympathisers were dogged in the streets of Edinburgh with angry mutterings and swords half drawn. The more extreme Covenanters were already clamouring for the expulsion from the Kingdom of all who refused to sign. There was to be no " banding, minching and carving by halves in God's cause."[8]

An indignant royalist who had seen the crowds signing the Covenant, copies of which were now in constant motion throughout the kingdom, declared that children of ten and beggarly rascals were allowed to set their hands to it; and certainly by this time many signed out of fear rather than conviction. Greater opposition existed in some men's hearts than appeared on the surface, but in general the tide of religious fervour ran strong and deep. With true gratitude hundreds attended Greyfriars' Kirk for the celebration of the Lord's Supper " purely", after twenty years during which the idolatrous habit of kneeling had been insisted on. The minister, though gravely hampered by a heavy cold, preached at great length on the text " When the Lord turned again the captivity of Sion." " Ye will find a very near parallel betwixt Israel and this Church," mused Warriston, " the only two sworn nations to the Lord."[9]

The King had sent for Traquair, Roxburgh and Lorne to report to him in England, but he confided in none save the Archbishop, and his interviews with these Scottish councillors were matters for speculation only. Lord Lorne, whose own tenants were said to be most " forward and hearty " for the Covenant, was believed to have expressed himself very freely to the King, who was evidently displeased with him.[10] Lorne's friends, kinsmen and clansmen, with touching faith in his influence and wisdom, cherished for some weeks the illusion that, by speaking plainly, their chief had made the King see that he could not with peace and safety compel the Scots to accept the Prayer Book and had induced him to change his policy. The truth was far otherwise; Charles had even considered placing Lorne under arrest. The old Earl of Argyll was credited with having told the King that unless his son were put under lock and key he would " wind him a pirn."

Lorne and his fellow councillors were allowed to go home. In England Charles had other troubles. Owing to his attempt to sell to Newcastle the monopoly in coal transport, a monopoly resisted by the London shipowners, the people of the South had had a chilly winter, short of their favourite fuel; the lifting of the monopoly in the warm spring did not at once mollify them.[12] Sectaries and fanatics or the merely demented continued to give trouble; a religious tailor in Hosier Lane denounced the King as guilty of blood and the bishops as false prophets and was led away protesting by a scandalised parish constable.[13]

In April eight ships carrying emigrants to New England were forbidden to sail; after a week's delay and discussion, the King withdrew his prohibition for this particular fleet but soon after gave out a proclamation that all further sailings were to be by special licence only. Sir Ferdinando Gorges, veteran survivor of the Elizabethan age and president of the New England Company, petitioned the King in eloquent protest; did not the Romans, Spanish and Dutch grow great by colonies, and should not England do the like? Lord Cottington, the Chancellor of the Exchequer, dismissed the petition in a contemptuous minute:

" Romans, Spanish and Dutch did and do conquer, not plant tobacco and Puritanism only, like fools." His opinion tersely summarised that of the King, who not long after was rating Lord Dorset because of rumours of Puritan practices among the settlements he had financed in Bermuda.[14]

Englishmen overseas and foreigners at home—both gave trouble, and the Walloon congregation in Norwich were again an object of attention that spring. Bishop Wren, in accordance with Laud's policy for the suppression of these communities, had turned them out of the episcopal chapel which they had used for many years. Sympathisers in Norwich had come to the rescue of the homeless congregation by giving them the use of a little church in the city. The Bishop now presented them with a bill, for alleged damage done to his chapel during their occupation, which their funds could hardly cover.[15] The small, persistent persecution went on.

The spring's most serious event for the King was the pronouncement in April of two more of the judges on the Hampden case; both gave judgment against the King. It cannot have been wholly unexpected, for these two, Sir George Croke and Sir Richard Hutton, had always doubted the legality of Ship-money, but the King and Court had probably not anticipated statements quite so decisive. The venerable Croke with great emphasis accepted the arguments put forward by Oliver St. John. " Royal power," he said, " is to be used in cases of necessity and imminent danger, when ordinary courses will not avail . . . but in a time of peace and no extreme necessity, legal courses must be used and not royal power." Hutton, elaborating the same arguments a fortnight later, asserted that, except in the emergency of war, subjects cannot by law be made to part with what is their own merely on a demand from the King.[16] This was as much as to say that *Rex* in Croke and Hutton's opinion was not *lex*, whatever Sir Robert Berkeley might have averred to the contrary.

Midway through April, before the pronouncement of Hutton but after that of Croke, while the Inns of Court laughed over someone's inevitable pun (" The King has Ship-money by hook but not by Croke "), the young Lilburne had been punished for distributing forbidden religious literature and had been the object of a new popular demonstration. He was a great deal younger than Prynne, Burton and Bastwicke, came of a respectable yeoman family in the North and had little or no learning. He had neat, unimpressive features, distinguished by fine eyes; was small, excitable, evidently delicate; talkative rather than eloquent. There was nothing gloomy about Lilburne's Puritan fanaticism; his manner was lively, and his clothes (within the limits of his humble purse) were trim and sparkish.

The Star Chamber imposed a savage sentence, and on April 18th, 1638, he was whipped from the Fleet to Westminster, where he was to stand in the pillory. The crowds which gathered round him during this painful procession were sympathetic, although some of those closest to him unreasonably asked him for a speech, a testimony of the Lord, as he staggered along. He told them with difficulty, for he was breathless and suffering greatly, that he would speak in the pillory. The promise, rumoured through the crowds, reached Westminster, where the Court of Star Chamber was in session, some minutes ahead of Lilburne himself. Judging by the size of the crowd in Palace Yard that another demonstration, like that for Prynne, Burton and Bastwicke, might take place, the councillors assembled in the Star Chamber took an unusual step. They sent a messenger to parley with Lilburne. A merciful convention allowed him a few minutes to recover before he was put in the pillory; during this interval while he sat, caked with dust and blood, trying to get his breath, a gentleman approached him from the Star Chamber telling him that he would be spared the pillory if he would humbly confess his fault. Lilburne by this time had got his breath again; he refused the offer, at some length.

The King's councillors, looking down on the scene in Palace Yard, saw with indignation that he not only addressed the people, but with acrobatic ingenuity distributed three copies of the offending book which he had secreted about his person.

They sent down to have him gagged but by that time the harm had been done.

When Lilburne reached the Fleet again he found that the Council had given orders that no one might have access to him. He was himself penniless; without the help of friends, he was deprived of medical care and forced to rely on the food which the gaoler provided. Bedding and fresh water had, of course, to be paid for and were therefore not for such as he. After a month of this, when hunger and discomfort were assumed to have lowered his spirits, he was sent for and questioned on the speech he had made. Attorney-General Bankes, who conducted the inquiry, was a humane man and did not bully or shout at the hungry, feverish, unshaven prisoner before him. Lilburne faced him—he would have faced anyone—with undiminished fire. The Lord, so far from deserting him, had marvellously comforted him in all his sufferings. He repeated the substance of his pillory speech with pride, refused to retract a word, and when the interrogation was handed to him to sign, he grasped the pen and, leaning heavily upon it, wrote—" This I will seal with my dearest blood by me John Lilburne." [17]

While Lilburne suffered and the Hampden judgments continued to be the talk of Westminster a remarkable event took place in Ireland. The King's Deputy in Dublin had the Lord Chancellor of Ireland arrested. Here was another conflict between *Rex* and *lex*, but Wentworth's friends felt that he might have waited until the Scottish storm had subsided before stirring up new trouble in Ireland. Lord Chancellor Loftus had powerful friends in England; why make more enemies for the King's government when its need was for friends, especially among lawyers? [18]

Wentworth saw the matter with different eyes. No time, he thought, was so right as the present for a demonstration of royal authority, attacked as it was both in Scotland and in England. Hutton's judgment in the Hampden case distressed him the more because the judge was a Yorkshireman and an old friend, to whose son Wentworth had given one of his sisters in marriage. He argued with him by letter, courteously but firmly. It was no part of a subject's duty, he said, to think out "curious questions" or brood on "vain flatteries of imaginary liberty." The King's ordinance, he said, outdoing even Sir Robert Berkeley's *Rex lex*, is "no other than the ordinance of God." [19] Something like this he must have had in mind when in April 1638, by his attack on the Lord Chancellor of Ireland, he set out to win a resounding victory for the King's prerogative and redeem in one of Charles's three kingdoms the losses it had sustained in the other two.

The Lord Chancellor, Adam Loftus, had in his own and his friends' interests, shamefully abused his position, for the last twenty years. He had at first been cautious with the keen-eyed Deputy, but had soon reverted to his earlier evil practices, such as trying cases in which he was personally concerned *in camera*, and evading the Deputy's and the King's authority whenever it suited him to do so. One of his victims, a farmer, John Fitzgerald, whom he had dispossessed and wrongfully imprisoned, appealed direct to the Deputy for justice. Wentworth, by taking his case over into the prerogative Court of Castle Chamber, of which he himself was President, precipitated a crisis which he had seen coming for a long time. Wentworth had two strong reasons for his act; the more important was the assertion of the King's right to override other courts, the less important was to get justice for Fitzgerald. Loftus also had two reasons for opposing Wentworth: as an experienced lawyer he believed it his duty to combat the encroachments of the prerogative courts; and, he did not want the facts about the Fitzgerald case brought to light.

When he was called upon to answer to Fitzgerald's accusation before the Court of Castle Chamber, Loftus tried to laugh it off. At a stormy meeting of the council Wentworth pressed the point, Loftus grew noisily rude and Wentworth ordered him out of the room. While he fumed in a neighbouring corridor, the council unanimously suspended him for contempt of court—an unusual offence with which to charge a Lord Chancellor. Wentworth, always too stubborn in small details, insisted that he should hear his sentence kneeling; "I will die first," said Loftus. Weeks of wrangling ensued during which the furious old gentleman held up the business of the realm by hiding the Great Seal, saying that he would give it up to no one but the King.[20]

Wentworth took no notice of one irrelevant but dangerous weapon which Loftus might use against him. The Chancellor cordially disliked his own son and had tried to defraud his daughter-in-law of her marriage settlement; this daughter-in-law, a beautiful and intelligent woman, enjoyed the Deputy's indiscreet but innocent admiration. It was, therefore, easy to start a scandal by hinting that the Lord Chancellor had been overthrown to please his wicked daughter-in-law and to serve the private ends of the adulterous Wentworth.

The tittle-tattlers at Whitehall preferred this version of the story and it was soon widely accepted. The King, while far from suspecting any such motive, was worried at the prospect of the duel between the Sovereign and the Chancellor to which Wentworth had committed him; although he supported his Deputy, it was with evident hesitation. He did, however, command Loftus to hand over the Great Seal to the Deputy and at the royal summons the Chancellor obeyed, formally, on his knees;[21] he had decided to abandon his defiant pose for that of a broken old man wrongfully oppressed by a ruthless tyrant.

Wentworth had triumphed in Dublin so effectively that he treated himself to one of his brief holidays and went off, that warm Whitsuntide, for a few days deer-hunting at his new park at Coshaw where he greatly enjoyed himself, although the midges were troublesome.[22]

The larger midges at Whitehall were also swarming and biting. The King's eldest son would be eight years old at the end of May and his father had decided to create him Prince of Wales and give him an establishment of his own. A place at Court was a coveted reward, and Charles intended that the little Prince's household should give honourable satisfaction to a number of the nobility and gentry. Unfortunately, the appointments were so widely canvassed for so long that in the end more hopes were dashed than gratified. The Scottish business had decided the King against any great expense, and the new household was planned in a disappointingly cautious manner. Charles showed his keen displeasure with the entire Scottish nation by appointing only Englishmen to attend his son. This hurt the feelings of the loyal Scots at Court and still left too few places to satisfy all the English claimants. Even the Earl of Newcastle, the Prince's new governor, was not content when he found that he had to share his kitchen and table with the Prince's tutor, the amiable but humbly born Bishop of Chichester, Dr. Brian Duppa.[23] The sallow, lively little Prince alone set a good example by accepting everything and everyone with the gayest good humour.

Other public and Court appointments caused envy or criticism. Lord Holland, who had absurdly hoped to be made Lord High Admiral, retired from Whitehall with a diplomatic illness to nurse his chagrin when the Earl of Northumberland was—very properly—preferred to him.[24] The valuable post of secretary to the Queen, eagerly coveted because of the indirect patronage its owner could wield, went unexpectedly to a man almost unknown at Court. Sir John Winter, nephew to the Earl of Worcester, was a Roman Catholic, which made him doubly welcome to the Queen, but caused inevitable criticism elsewhere. It did not escape public notice that he was of the same family as one of the principal conspirators in the Gunpowder Plot.[25]

The true reason for the appointment was not religious. Winter was one of the richest men in the country and had already made generous advances to the King. His lands in the Forest of Dean were rich in iron and coal, both well exploited. In bringing this powerful industrialist into the innermost circle of the Court the King was obliquely pursuing his policy of drawing the principal industries of the country into the orbit of the Crown.

Something of the same plan was in his mind when he embarked this summer in pursuit of one more mirage. For several years now, the Earl of Bedford and a company of shareholders had been attempting to reclaim the fens round Ely. The resentment of the fenlanders had found expression earlier in the year in petitions to the King, and in the summer rioting broke out. Untimely rain and the interference of the fenmen badly damaged the drainage works, and the whole scheme looked like coming to a standstill. The King who had long regretted the lease of the fen country to a private company, now stepped in and, as if in response to the outcry of the fenmen, took over the scheme himself. His intention was not to yield to the fenmen but to complete the profitable scheme. He was encouraged by the engineer Vermuyden to believe that soon there would be a fruitful plain where now were only reeds and waters, and in the midst of it a new town to be called Charlemont.[26]

This was the last of the King's happy dreams. Reality was fast catching up with him, although he did his best to shut it out by keeping the deplorable affairs of Scotland as secret as possible. He consulted with none of his council except Laud, and his discontented advisers went about the Court shrugging their shoulders in open annoyance at their exclusion and declaring that they washed their hands of the royal policy.[27] Although the Archbishop was at least admitted to the King's confidence, his advice was not taken, for when Charles decided to send a Commissioner into Scotland with powers to deal with the Covenanters, his choice fell on the Marquis of Hamilton, an appointment the wisdom of which the Archbishop gravely doubted.[28]

Hamilton was a bad choice but he was the only possible candidate for the task. No Englishman would have been able to handle the Scots at that time without increasing their antagonism. A Scotsman therefore had to be chosen, and one loyal to the King and possessed of enough prestige and power in his own right to impress his troublesome countrymen. Lord Lorne, the most powerful man on the Privy Council in Scotland, was ruled out because he had already shown his antagonism to the new Service Book; the only devoted loyalists on that dubious and divided body were lesser nobility who lacked the needful authority. The bare truth was that only three men could be considered: the Marquis of Huntly, the Duke of Lennox and the Marquis of Hamilton. Huntly, the greatest man in the north-east and the head of the Gordon clan, stood haughtily aloof from the Covenant and was in theory a devoted King's man. "You may take my head from my shoulders," he was to say a few months later, "but not my heart from my sovereign." He was good at a phrase. What else he was good at, no one well knew. He had spent much of his life in France as Captain of the French King's famous Scots Guard and had returned to Scotland only two years before on his father's death. His father had been a Roman Catholic; his mother, who was still alive, also practised that religion, as did many of his clan. He himself appears to have belonged to no very well-defined faith and, although his wife and children were Protestant, he gave countenance and protection to the old religion throughout his territories. His wife was a sister of Lorne, and Huntly had mortgaged a great part of his estates to his brother-in-law, without fully extricating himself from the quicksands of debt. Had he been appointed King's Commissioner it would have been difficult for him to set foot in Edinburgh where his creditors abounded. His embarrassments made him a figure of contempt in spite of his ancient name and handsome presence. "Three parts of his name is decayed," Rothes had sneered, "I would not give a salt citron for him." [29]

Next came young Lennox. The King trusted him and knew him well, and he had qualities which might have served better than Hamilton's, although his experience was small and his intellect unremarkable. But, like Huntly, he had too many ties with the Roman Catholics; one brother was a priest, another had just married a Roman Catholic bride, and rumour at this moment credited Lennox himself with being a secret convert. [30] That left only Hamilton; with a kind of accidental inevitability, this most disastrous of all King Charles's friends took up his position. This blundering, ambitious, complicated and stupid man was neither as bad nor as powerful as his contemporaries thought him. Opportunity made a fool and accident made a villain of him, as little by little in the next eleven years, he became, in popular opinion, the arch-traitor:

> He that three Kingdoms made one flame,
> Blasted their beauty, burnt their frame—
> Rather than he his ends would miss
> Betray'd his master with a kiss,
> And buried in one common fate
> The glory of our Church and State . . .[31]

The fierce indictments of contemporary opinion have long since lost their force. Bishop Burnet, in an accomplished apologia,[32] written many years later, covered the naked failure of Hamilton with a cloak of decency. Traditional history has, to a great extent, forgotten him. Other figures, in Scotland and England, tower above him—Argyll, Montrose, Strafford, Rupert, Hyde, the King himself. It is easy to forget and startling to rediscover in the voluble writings of contemporaries for how long, like a Colossus, Hamilton bestrode the political scene.

At this time he was in his early thirties, a rather fine-looking man, with a stately manner and ponderous way of speech which impressed and amused the King. He had been Charles's page as a boy, had been something of a favourite and had been married into the all-powerful Buckingham connection. He was restless and ambitious but with a native caution which held him back from dangerous ventures; he would have liked to play a heroic part and had once raised and led troops to assist the Protestant Cause in Germany, but he never got them to any scene of action, and his Swedish and German allies had complained of his incompetence so loudly that he had had to be withdrawn. Hamilton, undiscouraged, still believed himself to be an excellent soldier and the King shared his opinion, for

Charles was truly attached to him, with that rare, deep, tenacious friendship of his, blind to faults.

Hamilton not only believed himself a soldier; he believed himself a diplomatist. His mind had a purposeless subtlety; he concealed from his left hand what his right hand was doing, though there was usually no reason whatever why he should. The ingenuity and scope of his political schemes would have done credit to Machiavelli had any master-plan given them coherence. There was no plan; beyond his personal prejudices and his conviction of his own importance, he had neither guidance nor goal. Some negative and some positive virtues even his enemies allowed him. He was good-tempered, he was not cruel; his dependants thought him " one of the best masters to vassals and servants that our kingdoms afforded," [33] and he was consistently civil to his inferiors, an unusual virtue at that time. Hamilton was appointed on May 8th and on the same day both Charles and he sent letters into Scotland. The King wrote to his council there to meet at Dalkeith on June 8th to receive his Commissioner. Hamilton wrote to his friends and tenants in Scotland to meet him on June 5th at Haddington: he would show the Covenanting leaders that the King's Commissioner could command as large a following as they.[34]

Hamilton's preparations for his northern journey were interrupted by the sudden death of his wife. He had married her as a very young man much against his will, and the indifference with which the Court appears to have taken her death suggests that there was little pretence of love between them. Burnet asserts that he learnt to value her too late and was remorseful for his past neglect. It seems possible, for although several marriages were later proposed to him, he took no second wife. One other enigma presents itself in the study of this strange man. At the time of his wife's death he had three little sons, as well as two daughters. In the course of the next two years, and in the midst of Hamilton's political troubles, his three sons died, one after another. These deaths, like that of his wife, aroused little contemporary comment. What lies behind this reticence we do not know but if Hamilton can never be a tragic figure, he might be, on closer knowledge, a pathetic one.

When Hamilton was chosen to go to Scotland as Commissioner he had sense enough to feel dismayed and, with forethought for his own future, asked the King to give him his personal assurance that, whatever the outcome, he would not in any way suffer in his favour.[35] This point once settled, he spent a week in his master's company, discussing the policy to be pursued. The King's instructions were clear. Only one concession was to be made; Charles would permit the temporary suspension of his order to use the new Prayer Book, and he would receive petitions from his subjects about it, but in return he commanded that the Covenant be utterly repudiated and all copies surrendered at once. Hamilton had his authority to dismiss unsatisfactory or disloyal members of the council, to arrest any of the King's subjects who made public protestations, to bribe the Covenanters one against another if necessary, and to disperse the crowds by force. In the last resort he could proclaim the rebellious lords to be traitors. "You shall declare," so ran the King's instructions, "that if there be not sufficient strength within the Kingdom to force the refractory to obedience, power shall come from England, and that myself will come in person with them, being resolved to hazard my life rather than to suffer authority to be contemned." [36]

The threat of force could hardly, as things stood, be implemented, but as Hamilton travelled northward in the stormy wet weather which had succeeded the too early spring he summoned the sheriffs of the English counties and ordered them, to see that the local trained bands throughout the summer assembled for military exercises at least twice a week.[37] It was a first move to furnish the royal authority with essential force.

In London the law term drew to a close, not without events of some significance for the King. The ill-timed zeal of his supporters could be as troublesome to the King as the insolences of his opponents. A crack-brained clergyman, Thomas Harrison, marched into the Court of Common Pleas when Hutton was presiding and "suddenly and very abruptly said with a loud voice 'I accuse Mr. Justice Hutton of High Treason.'" The incident made something of a stir but it chiefly drew attention to Hutton's pronouncement against Ship-money which the King would rather have forgotten. Poor Mr. Harrison kept Whitsuntide in the Fleet to punish him for his indiscretion.[38]

Harrison's offence in accusing one of the judges was in effect an insult to the King's Majesty, and whatever Charles felt about Hutton's views on Ship-money, it was necessary to take action against Harrison. His case came up in the Star Chamber at the same time as that of a baronet, Sir Richard Wiseman, who had accused the Lord Keeper of bribery. The Star Chamber condemned Harrison to a fine of £5,000 and a public apology. Wiseman, whose offence was considerably more serious, received a much heavier sentence; he lost his baronet's title and was condemned to stand in the pillory and to pay a fine of £10,000.[39]

Both sentences, and especially Wiseman's, were intended to vindicate the reputation of the King's justice, but neither of them particularly interested the London populace or the Inns of Court. Harrison's views were not popular and Wiseman, who had presumably been driven a little crazy by unsuccessful litigation, had long been a familiar nuisance round the Courts, with his real or illusory troubles and wild accusations. The Lord Keeper, Coventry, who was the object of the slanders for which he suffered, was an old, quiet, respectable figure, who had risen under the late King James, had held office since the beginning of the reign, and had exercised on the whole a moderating influence on the King's policy.

One other Star Chamber sentence of some importance concluded the session. Christopher Pickering, a Roman Catholic, had boasted that the King was a secret convert, with other damaging allegations, which his unkindly neighbours had reported to higher authority. His follies, or rather the report of them, came at a timely moment, for they gave the Court of Star Chamber an opportunity to demonstrate that Puritans were not the only objects of its attentions. The hapless Pickering was condemned to suffer in his single person all the rigours that had been inflicted on Prynne and Lilburne separately; in this way Londoners were to have ocular demonstration that Roman Catholic subjects who libelled the King were no more spared than any others.[40] This piece of policy failed of its purpose. The illogical Londoners took very little notice of Pickering and what befell him, while the fate of Prynne and his fellows remained lodged in their biased memories.

Before the courts rose, the last of the judges gave their opinions on Ship-money. Nothing so effective as the pronouncements of Croke and Hutton was to be hoped or feared from the others. Denham was too ill to appear in court but sent a written opinion in favour of Hampden. Davenport and Bramston both made it clear that they upheld the legality of Ship-money but had to pronounce for Hampden in this particular case because the writ issued to him had a technical defect. Jones pronounced for the King and so, naturally, did Finch at tedious length.

The King had won by a majority of seven to five. The judgment pronounced by Davenport and Bramston showed that the majority for the legality of Ship-money itself—as distinct from the legality of the particular writ to Hampden—was nine to three. The Court might have regarded this as a victory but they were not quite so blind as to do so. The arguments of Oliver St. John on his client's behalf and the measured, emphatic pronouncements of two highly respected judges far outweighed the simple arithmetic of the King's majority. In June, Attorney-General Bankes announced the official result of Rex v. Hampden: the King had won, the legality of Ship-money was established. Bankes knew very well, as did every thinking lawyer of the King's party, that the supposed victory was a disastrous defeat.

How far the King himself recognised the truth of what had happened remains doubtful, but his customary calm was ruffled. He looked anxious and preoccupied, was hunting less often than usual and had almost entirely given up his other summer pastimes, tennis and pell-mell.[41]   But his royal spirit recoiled from any policy of conciliation and he resented pessimism in his advisers. His natural desire was to assert his authority the more emphatically, to challenge where he was challenged, and to overthrow. He had already decided on that course for Scotland. On June 11th, two days after Finch had made his pronouncement on Ship-money, Charles was writing to Hamilton in Scotland: " I expect not anything can reduce that people but only force . . . I give you leave to flatter them with what hopes you please . . . till I be ready to suppress them . . . I will rather die than yield to these impertinent and damnable demands." Ten days later his preparations had gone further; he informed Hamilton of forty cannon in readiness, and of an order he had placed in Holland for arms for two thousand horse and fourteen thousand foot, to make a timely end of " those traitors the Covenanters."[42]

He had not yet officially spoken to his English council of these bold plans, but he had sounded Cottington and Juxon on the state of the Exchequer and the Treasury, and had managed to understand from answers which must have been more tactful than truthful that he had at least two hundred thousand pounds at his disposal. A letter from Lord Deputy Wentworth in the same month, announcing an increase in the Irish revenues, may have further strengthened his belief that he had the means to reduce the Scots by war.[43]

On the last day of June he issued a proclamation to the lords lieutenants of the six northern counties to muster the trained bands, and on Sunday, July 1st, at a full meeting of his English council he gave them officially to know for the first time that a rebellion had occurred in Scotland which, in the event of further resistance, he intended to put down by force.

Of his English councillors, the Archbishop saw most clearly that the King's decisions did not match with reality. The royal authority was as much an article of faith with him as with the King but he did not believe that it could be held upright by faith alone. " My misgiving soul is deeply apprehensive of no small evils coming on," he wrote to Wentworth. "I can see no cure without a miracle and I fear that will not be showed." [44]

BOOK II CHAPTER II REFERENCES

1. *Strafford MSS.*, X, folio 192.
2. Livingstone, pp. 101–2; Laud, *Works*, VII, p. 427.
3. Knowler, II, 154; *Bankes MSS.*, 18/24, 42/30, 65/19.
4. *C.S.P.D.*, 1637–8, pp. 289, 293, 320 ff.
5. *C.S.P. Ven.* 1636–9, pp. 376–7, 387.
6. *C.S.P. Col.*, 1574–1600, pp. 263, 272.
7. *Breadalbane MSS.*, Letters, 1636–9, Nos. 718, 720; *C.S.P. Ven.*, 1636–9, p. 373.
8. *Breadalbane MSS.*, loc. cit.; Baillie, I, 16, 23, 51; *Strafford MSS.*, VII, Wentworth to Laud, July, 1638; Warriston, *Diary*, p. 340.
9. *Breadalbane MSS.*, loc. cit.; Warriston, 334–5, 344.
10. *Breadalbane MSS.*, Letters, 1636–9, No. 721.
11. *Ibid.*, No. 725; Baillie, I, 75–6.
12. *C.S.P.D.*, 1637–8, p. 295
13. *C.S.P.D.*, 1637–8, pp. 295, 259.
14. *C.S.P. Col.*, I, p. 276; *Acts of P.C. Col.*, I, pp. 228–9, 241–2.
15. *C.S.P.D.*, 1637–8, p. 356.
16. *State Trials*, III, pp. 1162, 1201.
17. Lilburne, *A Worke of the Beast*, London, 1641; *Bankes MSS.*, 13/12, 18/31. The weight with which Lilburne leaned on his pen is evident from the firmness and heaviness of his signature. *See also* M. A. Gibb, *John Lilburne*, London, 1947.
18. *Strafford MSS.*, X, Letters of May 1638 *passim*.
19. Knowler, II, 389.
20. *Strafford MSS.*, XI, folios 57–66.
21. *Ibid.*, XI, Wentworth to Croke, May 26, 1638
22. Knowler, II, p. 173.
23. *Ibid.*, 167.
24. *Ibid.*, 156.
25. *Ibid.*, 166.
26. *C.S.P.D.*, 1637–8, pp. 493–4, 503–6; 1638–9, pp. 301–2.
27. *C.S.P. Ven.* 1636–9, pp. 392–3.
28. *Strafford MSS.*, X, Laud to Wentworth, May 14th, 1638.
29. Rothes, pp. 62–3.
30. Baillie, I, 74.
31. Nedham, *Digitus Dei*, London, 1649.
32. Burnet, *Lives and Actions of the Dukes of Hamilton*, London, 1677.
33. Turner, *Memoirs, Bannatyne Club*, Edinburgh, 1829, p. 84.
34. *Register P.C. Scot.*, 1638, p. 19; Burnet, *Lives*, p. 43.
35. Burnet, *Lives*, p. 49.

36. *Ibid.*, pp. 50–1.
37. Baillie, I, 80.
38. Knowler, II, pp. 167, 170, 177.
39. *Ibid.*, p. 180.
40. *C.S.P.D.*, 1637–8, p. 474; Rushworth, *Appendix*, pp. 156–8.
41. *C.S.P. Ven.* 1636–9, p. 436.
42. Burnet, *op. cit.*, pp. 55–6, 59.
43. *Ibid.*, p. 59; Knowler, II, p. 175.
44. Laud, *Works*, VII, 456.

CHAPTER THREE

THE GLASGOW ASSEMBLY

June – December 1638

"NOT anything can reduce that people but only force," Charles wrote from Greenwich on June 11th, 1638. Before he received the letter Hamilton had evidence that this was true.

Thirty peers and gentlemen and six hundred ministers of the Covenanting party met him in Edinburgh, before a huge, attentive crowd. Mr. William Livingstone, "the strongest voice and the austerest in countenance" of all the preachers, appealed to him, in what was rather a sermon than a speech, to give peace to the land.[1]

No one expected peace: Hamilton's tenants had been unable to gather in Clydesdale in obedience to his commands, for fear of provoking armed resistance from the tenants and followers of Covenanting lords. Edinburgh castle was closely watched by Covenanting patrols lest Hamilton should try to strengthen it for the King. A new gunpowder plot to destroy the Covenanting leaders was rumoured, and they were already, like the King, buying arms in the Low Countries and north Germany against all eventualities.[2]

The eloquence of the ministers kept spiritual fervour at its height. "Not a man is known to fall from their number," wrote a spectator, "but daily coming in. There was never at any time such plenty of preaching and prayer as is now in Edinburgh. All the most able ministers are set a-work, preach every day in many places, and on the Lord's day three sermons in each church ordinarily, and so in all the halls and other great houses."[3]

In these circumstances Hamilton found all attempts to flatter Rothes into submission useless and was further embarrassed by the sulky and unhelpful behaviour of the Council. Sir Thomas Hope, from the depth of his legal knowledge, flatly contradicted him on several points of law and refused to admit that there was anything in the Covenant contrary to the laws of Scotland. "He is no fit man to serve you," wrote Hamilton helplessly to the King, " but the time is not proper for his removal."[4]

If the King's Advocate refused to condemn the document, Hamilton could not very well proclaim its signatories traitors, and the principal weapon with which the King had armed him fell to the ground. He went ahead, as best he could, with the first part of his plan and ordered the proclamation at the Mercat Cross of the royal pardon to all Covenanters who unconditionally submitted. This only gave the leaders a new occasion to justify themselves; Warriston answered the herald's words by reading out a Protestation which condemned the King's policy in unequivocal terms and demanded the calling of Parliament and of an Assembly of the Church. A few bold, anonymous royalists shouted " Rebels " from the windows of neighbouring houses, but their cries were soon drowned by the applause of the crowd. The Council that very afternoon dissociated themselves from Hamilton's action and insisted that their consent to it, which he had gained the day before, be erased from the minutes of the meeting.[5]

The motives of the King's councillors in undermining the royal policy are easily determined. A majority of them were either in sympathy with the Covenanters or afraid of them. Hamilton's motives for his next move are altogether obscure. He had been " stately and harsh " in his official interviews with the Covenanting leaders, but on the day of the Protestation he drew some of them privately aside and assured them " as a kindly Scotsman, if you go on with courage and resolution you will carry what you please; but if you faint or give ground in the least you are undone. A word is enough to wise men." [6] The incident remains unexplained. Hamilton alone in Scotland was in a position to know with absolute certainty that the King had no intention of yielding. He may conceivably have hoped to make a moral advantage for his master by advising the Covenanters to courses which would justify Charles in waging the war on which he had already decided.

By this time there was real as well as imaginary evidence of military preparation on both sides. Hamilton's own mother, a formidable dowager who seems to have thoroughly disapproved of her son, was alleged to have bought up in the Covenanting interest all the gunpowder in Edinburgh. General Leslie on his visit in the early spring had planned the organisation of a Covenanting army, before returning to Germany to offer the Covenant for signature to Scottish professional soldiers in the Protestant armies. From the beginning, some of the leading Covenanting lords had gone about with bodyguards of armed followers—a not uncommon habit in Scotland—and rumour soon credited the party with forty thousand men under arms. It was common report that the King was negotiating for the use of Spanish regiments from Flanders, and that the Archbishop and Lord Deputy Wentworth had a scheme for bringing over an Irish army to suppress the Covenant.[7]

Rumour deformed the truth, for the Deputy had no such plan, although such a plan was part of the King's policy. Already in the summer of 1638 the conflict between the King in England and the Calvinist majority in Scotland was linked to the confused and dangerous problems of Ireland.

The lowland Scots in Ulster were thrifty settlers, but their religious obstinacy and the behaviour of some of their ministers had already brought them into collision with the government and Church of Ireland and into contact with the Covenanters. Their womenfolk especially were " stark mad against the ceremonies of the Church," and as early as Easter 1638 the Bishop of Down reported that many of them were conspicuously absent when he administered the Sacrament. In the late summer copies of the Covenant reached them from Scotland and they began to sign it with pious enthusiasm, in spite of Wentworth's efforts to "crush that cockatrice in the egg." [8]

The lowland Scots were not the only inhabitants of Ulster. Besides several thousand English settlers in and around Derry an incalculable number of the native Irish, chiefly O'Neills and Macdonnells, worked and lived among the settlers or gathered on the lands of the remaining native chiefs and gentry. The Macdonnells were not confined to the Irish mainland; over long centuries they had flourished in the Western Isles and Western Highlands. Proud, prolific, warlike, they embraced, in an ancient, indissoluble tradition of loyalty and kinship, the whole of this coastal and island region, Scots or Irish, and made it unsafe by their disorders and marauding on sea and land. It was against them that Lorne, from his strategically placed lands in the south western Highlands, had waged successful war, building up at the same time greater security for trade and fishing and greater power for himself and his Campbells.

The Macdonnells were mostly of the old religion and had suffered, at the Reformation and after, both in Scotland and in Ireland. In Ulster they had been forced out of the better country by the licensed encroachment of the new Protestant settlers, and in Scotland they had been expelled from the best of their lands by the Protestant clan Campbell. The process of extinction might have continued but for an odd accident. The principal chief of the Irish clan, Randall Macdonnell, Earl of Antrim, had been taken away from Ireland as a child and carefully brought up under the eyes of the King and Court. He grew up frivolous, irresponsible and very good-looking; Archbishop Laud thought him delightful, so did the middle-aged widow of the great Duke of Buckingham. He married her and thereafter with teasing fondness called her "my old Duchess." They were in the heart of the Court circle, to which Antrim's feckless, voluble Irish charm was an unusual experience. Both the King and Queen found it irresistible. He was poor; his remaining lands were in confusion and his debts were enormous. To help him, the King granted him the Scottish peninsula of Kintire. It was one of the unwisest grants that Charles ever made, for Kintire, however just the Macdonnell right to it, had been taken over in the last thirty years by the Campbells.

Antrim pranced about the Court, boasting in his delightful brogue how he would land with a great host upon Kintire and make mince-meat of the Campbells. It was hardly surprising that Lorne complained of the matter privately to Hamilton, saying that if Antrim attacked him he would certainly defend himself. On this hint Hamilton merely wrote to the King advising him to make all the use he could of Antrim to harass Lorne. Antrim's wild boastings immediately flared up into extravagant projects. He appealed, both personally and with the support of the King, to the Lord Deputy of Ireland to help him to raise and arm the Macdonnells of Ulster for an attack on Scotland, and to establish an arsenal at Coleraine stocked from the stores in Dublin. Wentworth, unlike his English colleagues, had learnt in the last five years what value to attach to fluent Irish promises. He refused help to Antrim for three excellent reasons. In his opinion the Macdonnells were a race of smugglers and brigands, to be disarmed rather than armed. He had no intention of sending military stores to Coleraine, where the Ulster Scots were strong and "might chance to borrow those weapons for another purpose than his lordship would find cause to thank them for." Finally—and conclusively—he thought Antrim's offers absurd: as for leading thousands into Scotland, " he is as well able to do it as I to take upon me the Cross with so many for the Holy Land." [9]

The foolish business contained in little all the dangers that the shrewd Wentworth most feared. It gave gratuitous offence to Lorne whose doubtful loyalty should have been strengthened, not undermined; it encouraged the Catholic Irish whose endemic disorders needed, in Wentworth's view, to be kept under control; by favouring the Catholics it gave colour to the rumour that Charles was seeking help from the Spaniards and that they in response were about to send over the Irish regiments in their pay under the leadership of the long-exiled chief of the O'Neills; it gave the Scots settlers legitimate reason to arm themselves against possible attacks from the Macdonnells; and even had the scheme been wise, Antrim was wholly incompetent to execute it. There, in little, were the misjudgments and misapprehensions which at every turn weakened the King's policy. So much Wentworth could see. He could not see that Antrim's extravaganza was the beginning of the greatest single disaster in the King's reign: it was the first forewarning of the Irish Rebellion.

The King in his encouragement of Antrim showed clearly, for the first time, that mistaken and reckless cunning which, in the latter part of his reign, was to be so marked a feature of his policy. Like many hesitative and cautious men, he had moments of an abandoned rashness. This was becoming evident in his handling of the Scottish situation. His decision to make war was the outcome of an unjustified optimism about his prospects. He had great faith in his navy, which had already given chase to and seized several Scottish vessels laden with arms. He was planning to fortify the north of England, to seize Leith from the sea, and to blockade the Scots into submission, with, presumably, the additional compulsion of Antrim's invasion in the west. His warships were already patrolling the east coast of Scotland. He had recovered his spirits, and a general gaiety once again prevailed at Court where the troubles of Scotland " neither hinder seeing of plays or hunting." [10]

This cheerfulness was shared neither by the Archbishop nor by the Lord High Admiral, Northumberland. The latter declared, in a querulous letter to Wentworth, that the Exchequer was empty and the total expectation in revenue little more than £100,000. " The King's magazines are totally unfurnished of arms and all sorts of ammunition," he wrote, " and commanders we have none either for advice or execution; the people through all England are generally so discontented by reason of the multitude of projects daily imposed upon them, as I think there is reason to fear that a great part of them will be readier to join with the Scots than to draw their swords in the King's service." [11]

Northumberland was partly right in regarding the King's incessant interference with trade and manufacture as a chief source of annoyance, and Charles himself that summer, in a politic attempt to regain popularity, called in a number of patents. The principal grievance was, and remained, Ship-money. The King's defeated victory in the Hampden case had stimulated resistance throughout the country. In Northampton-shire the chief constable went about openly saying that the English, like the Scots, should rebel when their rights were infringed, and opinions of the same sort were uttered by respons-ible officials in Norfolk.[12] Ship-money and the religious question were now so freely and generally discussed that the university of Oxford put forward the legality of Ship-money and the new Scots liturgy as suitable themes for dialectical argument. The Archbishop, who was Chancellor of Oxford, instantly ordered these dangerous topics to be withdrawn.[13]

In the North, preparations for war had begun. The Earl of Arundel, Earl Marshal of the Kingdom, advised the re-arming of the fierce borderers on the English side with their traditional old-fashioned weapons, bows and spears, and sent for cannon and muskets for the projected garrisons at Berwick and Newcastle. Two professional soldiers, Jacob Astley and Will Legge, were reporting on the defences of Hull and Newcastle. But the mustering in the northern counties, ordered by Hamilton on his way through, was not progressing satisfactorily. Sir Edward Osborne, Vice-President of the Council of the North, found the local gentry obstructive and was troubled by the lack of profes-sional soldiers to train the levies and of any but the most anti-quated weapons with which to arm them.[14]

The King, while still confident of his ultimate victory, recognised that he would have to postpone the use of force until he had adequate force to use. The war could not take place before next summer, and the immediate problem, therefore, was to " play " the Scots rebels until he was ready to attack. This was the mood in which he received Hamilton who returned in late July to report his mission and to consult on further action.

Charles instructed him to yield to two of the Covenanters' demands. Let the Service Book be temporarily suspended (as it had been forcibly suspended anyway this made little difference) and let an Assembly of the Church be called, provided only that the bishops took their proper place in it.

When Hamilton again reached Edinburgh on August 10th he found that the situation had further deteriorated during his absence. The Covenanters, fearing trouble from the Roman Catholic and Episcopalian region round Aberdeen, where the influence of the Marquis of Huntly was predominant, had despatched the energetic Montrose to whip up support for the Covenant in the district. Great enthusiasm was not to be expected in this stronghold of Royalism, but Montrose, who had been granted the freedom of Aberdeen a few years before, was locally popular and had a most persuasive tongue. By inserting a mitigating clause in the Covenant to allay their doubts he obtained a larger number of signatures than the Aberdonian royalists were ever afterwards willing to admit. A total triumph it was not, but neither was it a rebuff and in the circumstances that amounted almost to victory.[15]

While the royalists of the north-east argued and wavered, the Covenanters were mustering and drilling their troops in all the country round Edinburgh. Lorne, understandably in view of the Antrim affair, was arming his people and had placed a competent soldier, Duncan Campbell of Auchinbreck, in charge of their training. Watching his movements from Ireland the Lord Deputy Wentworth reported that he was fortifying " those isles which are within three hours sail from the north of this kingdom. There are, as is reported, brought thither sixteen pieces of ordnance well provided and mounted in places of best advantage for the defence of his country, and the people taught the use of their weapons." The purpose of all this Lorne himself rather vaguely stated was " to do His Majesty service." [16]

In Edinburgh itself the people were active. They stormed and broke up Holyrood Chapel but the organ, unholy purveyor of Popish music, was saved intact and carried away by the

regrettably frivolous Montrose.[17]   More serious politically was
the signing of the Covenant during the summer by the leading
advocates in Scotland; the adoption of the Covenanting cause
and the desertion of the King by most of the Lords of Session
was as grave a blow to the prestige of the Crown in Scotland
as the division of the judges over Ship-money had been in
England.[18]

But the nine days' wonder was the solemn reconciliation
with the reformed religion, in Greyfriars Kirk, of the Jesuit
priest, Thomas Abernethy. The renegade marked his conversion
by supplying the names of nearly a score of Roman Catholic
priests who were secretly working in Scotland. He averred
with equal conviction, although he could not give their names,
that six thousand priests were active in England and upwards of
three hundred masses were read in London of a Sunday.   The
Pope of Rome, he concluded, had seen and approved the King's
new Service Book for Scotland.[19]

Hamilton, who perceived that events were now moving so
fast that the Covenanters themselves might resort to war before
the King was ready for them, stayed only a fortnight in Scotland,
made no immediate offer of an Assembly but cast about instead
for some means of weakening and dividing the Covenanters. He
consulted principally with Traquair, whose very considerable
ingenuity could be relied on, although his loyalty could not.
Between them they concocted a plan to checkmate the Covenanters. The Covenant was based on a Confession of Faith sworn
by King James VI in 1580; although he had sworn under compulsion, he had never in so many words repudiated the Confession. In spirit it was Calvinist but it was less explicit than the
new Covenant, and its wording could be reconciled with the
support of episcopacy; it said nothing specific to the contrary.
So at least Hamilton thought on examining the document.

The Covenanters themselves spoke freely of the Confession
of 1580 as the foundation of their faith. Should the King therefore re-issue the Confession of 1580 as his royal answer to the
Covenant and call on his friends to subscribe to it, the Coven-

anters would have difficulty in preventing the desertion of their own cause for another which looked almost exactly like it. If they objected to the Confession of 1580 after all that they had previously said about it, they would inevitably put themselves in the wrong.

Hamilton hurried back to England and spent a week at Oatlands with the King, persuading him of the wisdom of this action. Charles, who intensely disliked the Confession of 1580 and knew that his father had disliked it, was at first very unwilling to use it. He gave in because it was, after all, only a temporary pretext. He was shipping six cannon and nine hundred muskets to Newcastle that month, and Hull too was being armed.[20] By the following spring he would be in a position to enforce his will and until then he needed only to maintain his position and weaken that of the Covenanters. By re-issuing the Confession of 1580 he would cut the ground from under their feet at the same moment as he offered them the Assembly of the Church for which they had asked; in this way he might so divide their ranks as to prevent them from commanding a majority in the Assembly. It was to meet in Glasgow, in the heart of the country where Hamilton's influence was supreme, and that fact also might be turned to account.

Hamilton's return with this new offer took the Covenanters aback. Even their friends on the Council were momentarily defeated. Neither Sir Thomas Hope nor Lorne could think of any sufficient reason why the King should not revive the Confession of 1580 and call upon all loyal subjects to sign it in preference to the Covenant, but they saw very well that by doing so he would make fools of the Covenanters. Much against their wills, Lorne and Hope had to join with the rest of the Council in signing the renewed Confession. Immediately afterwards they consulted Warriston.[21]

Warriston perceived at once the cunning of the King's move and had at first no legal argument to oppose to it, although he bitterly upbraided Hope for having been so weak as to sign at Hamilton's bidding. He was enough of a respecter of persons not to upbraid Lorne. But in truth Hope's concession was far more serious than Lorne's, for his legal opinion on any subject carried more weight than that of anyone else in the kingdom. Warriston could expect to find no legal flaws where Hope had failed and he fell back on mere railing. The King's new move was, he said, "the devil taking the Lord's bow in his hand to outshoot him therein," and the revived Confession of 1580 was "the horriblest atheism, perjury and mockage of God." [22] If no legal flaw could be found in the King's offer, the Covenanters could only contest it by vilification, and at this they were already expert. When the King's herald, on Hamilton's command, at the Mercat Cross called on all loyal subjects to abandon the Covenant and re-affirm the Confession of 1580, the usual crowd had gathered and already knew what to do. "Away with any Covenant but our own!" they shouted, and when they grew quieter, Warriston in the by now familiar fashion read a formal protest. He was followed by Montrose, the most popular of the Covenanting leaders, who spoke with a genial eloquence which brought the signatories hurrying in—not to the King's Confession, but to the protest against it. [23]

The few moderate men left in southern Scotland were shocked at the out-of-hand rejection of the first conciliatory gesture which the King had made, [24] but in general it was assumed that the anti-Covenant, as it was offensively labelled, was a trick. The behaviour of the Covenanters was unreasonable but their suspicions were just. They received accidental confirmation from the sudden appearance in their midst of a prophetess. A minister's daughter, one Margaret Mitchelson, fell into trances, was powerfully moved of the Lord, spoke strangely of "Covenanting Jesus" and declared that the Covenant had been made in Heaven and that the King's document was damned. As she lay raving, the devout and curious thronged round her chamber door, and Warriston was so deeply impressed that he took her into his household. Here she frequently prophesied for many hours at a time before audiences which included such distinguished devotees as Rothes and Lorne. [25]

The King's Council, to crown all, found means to betray the royal policy. They refused to condemn the new Protestation of the Covenanters and, in sending out copies of the King's anti-Covenant to the various regions of Scotland for signature, they appointed the leading Covenanters to organise its acceptance. When Hamilton objected to this extraordinary conduct, they argued first that these men were the local great ones on whom public duties naturally fell—which was true—and secondly that they ought to be given a chance of showing their loyalty—which was absurd. Lorne, who of all the Council had the most lands and the greatest power, excused himself from pressing the signature of the 1580 Confession in his own country because, he said, it would confuse the people to offer new ideas to them so short a time before the Church Assembly was to meet.[26]

In the upshot the King's anti-Covenant was subscribed almost exclusively in the Gordon country and especially at Aberdeen. Huntly saw to this, indignant at the light-hearted incursion of Montrose earlier in the summer into what he regarded as his especial sphere of influence. He now made solemn entry into Aberdeen, flanked by his family of handsome sons, and required the citizens to show their loyalty by accepting the King's Confession of Faith. The Aberdonians for the most part obeyed, but Huntly was deeply mortified to find his summons rejected when he commanded the same obedience in Banff and Inverness. He achieved, all told, the respectable total of twelve thousand signatures among his friends, allies and dependants.[27]

Huntly's supporters notwithstanding, the King's anti-Covenant as a stroke of policy had failed. In spite of Sir Thomas Hope's initial acceptance of it, the majority of the Lords of Session withheld their support,[28] and after six weeks of cogitation Sir Thomas himself uttered an opinion which effectively killed the moribund document. He told Hamilton that on reconsidering the Confession of 1580 he had no doubt that it committed its signatories to an absolute repudiation of episcopacy.[29]

If this were true, and Hope's opinion was enough to make it so, the document was useless and dangerous to the King's cause and should never have been resuscitated. Hamilton abandoned it forthwith and devoted all his efforts to organising a majority for the King in the Assembly which was to meet in November at Glasgow.

He was both too late in starting this policy and too half-hearted in pursuing it. The Covenanters had begun to organise their supporters the moment the date was fixed, and they had settled the representation of the greater part of Scotland before Hamilton began to think about it. Their representatives were by no means always reputable and their methods of securing their election even less so. Blackmail and intimidation were by now common; the gangs of retainers who followed the Covenanting Lords kept all their opponents in dread of violence. Hamilton complained repeatedly that his life was in danger, and although his particular fears were exaggerated the entire episcopalian contingent from Aberdeen, who would have been the King's strongest supporters in the Assembly, were, justifiably, too frightened to venture on the journey.[30] But Samuel Rutherford, an eloquent minister who had been silenced some years before and exiled to Aberdeen, made the journey safely enough and prepared to take part in the Assembly. The hapless bishops who had dared to remain in Scotland were almost prisoners in Glasgow castle, living on the bounty and under the protection of Hamilton. Pending the Assembly they were targets for continual abuse. They were accused, naturally, of Popish leanings, of worldliness, arrogance and pride, but also of sabbath-breaking, gluttony, drunkenness and whoring. A loose woman who wandered up and down with a baby which she claimed to be the bastard of the Bishop of Brechin received a great deal of unseemly encouragement.[31]

The bishops would have preferred to abandon the attempt to hold an Assembly, being already certain that it could only do harm to their cause. Hamilton had another plan for them. He intended to challenge the legality of the Assembly unless the

Covenanters would allow the bishops to take their places. If this was refused he would dissolve the meeting as unconstitutional, and claim that the King's intention to convene a free Assembly of the Church had been wilfully obstructed by the Covenanters.[32]

The idea was good, but once again the Covenanters circumvented him. They organised a popular petition, to be placed before the Assembly, that the " pretended bishops " be tried for their manifold crimes. This move had a twofold purpose: as accused or suspected persons the bishops could legally be forbidden to take their seats in the Assembly until they had cleared themselves. The petition also served as propaganda, because it mainly consisted of a list of their supposed crimes. Hamilton heard—late on a Saturday night—that the petition was to be read from every pulpit in Edinburgh on the following morning. He hurriedly forbade this, but his action served only to show how low the authority of the Crown had fallen, for the indictment was generally read.[33]

The pretence of a desire for peace had by this time been almost altogether abandoned by both sides. General Leslie, who had slipped through the King's blockade in a small fishing boat, was again in Scotland, frequently in the company of Rothes, and openly organising an army. He was said to have boasted, when told that the King was fortifying Berwick and Newcastle, that Charles would do better to fortify the Cinque Ports lest the Protestant armies of Europe came to the help of their Scottish brethren by invading the King in his own country. The King at Whitehall had set up a Committee of the Privy Council to act as a Council of War, and had sent to Wentworth in Ireland to ship him over five hundred men under an able commander to garrison Carlisle. Meanwhile Hamilton had offered the constable of Edinburgh castle two thousand pounds sterling to hand it over to him.[34]

In this atmosphere of hostility and tension the Covenanting lords assembled at Glasgow, bringing with them, in defiance of the royal command " great bands and troops of men . . . with guns and pistols." Hamilton, whose power in the district was, or should have been, predominant, avoided open clashes by keeping his own people strictly on the defensive. But few religious conferences can have opened in a less religious atmosphere than did this on November 21st, 1638. The ceremony lacked something in solemnity because the crowds were so thick about the doors that the participants could only get to their seats with " such delay of time and thrumbling through as did grieve and offend us." When they were at last in their places nothing happened except an inaudible sermon; the preacher, a Dr. Bell, selected by Hamilton, was probably wise to make it so, for no sermon would have satisfied both the King's Commissioner and the Covenanting majority in the Assembly.[35]

On the next day the struggle between Hamilton and the Covenanters began in earnest. The Assembly did not consist only of ministers; these were a minority. Each presbytery was also represented by lay elders, and, in this peculiar character, almost every nobleman of the Covenanting party was present. As a result laymen outnumbered the clergy and far outweighed them in influence. The principle of admitting lay elders at all was open to question, and many of the elections had been shamelessly procured. On both these issues Hamilton intended to challenge the legality of the Assembly. Furthermore, when the bishops, as accused persons, had not been permitted to take their seats they had by letter denied the right of the Covenanters to bring charges against them and declared that the Assembly could not legally meet without them. This gave Hamilton another reason to pronounce the Assembly illegal at the outset. Unhappily for him, he could not rely on the support or co-operation of the King's Council. Hope was frankly and almost insolently, opposed to him and Lord Lorne, who had just by his father's death become Earl of Argyll, was deep, dark, and doubtful in his intentions.

Since the Aberdonians had not come and the bishops were excluded, the Commissioner was almost without any representative of the episcopalian party among the clergy. One man he had, Dr. Balcanquhall, who was fortunately tough, resolute and intelligent enough to be willing and able to defend the King's policy single-handed.

The first full day's work began with the frugal decision to have one session only each day, from ten in the morning to five in the afternoon. Participants, fortified by a good breakfast, would work through to an early supper and avoid the expense of mid-day dinner.[36] The rest of the day's debate was more controversial. Hamilton's attempt to challenge the legality of the Assembly failed because the majority voted that the election of a Moderator and a clerk should precede all other business, and the King's Commissioner had perforce to sit still while the principal minister of the Covenanters, Henderson, was elected into the chair, supported by the redoubtable Warriston as clerk. Warriston improved the occasion by uttering a short extempore prayer that the prerogative of King Jesus should triumph over all earthly prerogatives.[37] The two key positions had thus immediately been won by the Covenanters.

After this grave tactical defeat, Hamilton walked into an ambush. The Assemblies which, in the days of Knox, had been the architects of Calvinism in Scotland, had at a later date fallen under the sway of an organised King's party. It had been suggested that the old register books of these Assemblies be consulted for precedents as to how to proceed on the present occasion. Only those from 1590 had been officially kept, and these Hamilton now produced. He had hardly made the official announcement when Warriston rose to state that he had, during the last few months, succeeded in tracing the lost registers of the earlier Assemblies—the Assemblies which had not been under the King's influence. Hamilton immediately questioned their authenticity and for several sessions, on and off, there was heated argument and comparison of handwritings. But it was difficult to disprove their authenticity and impossible to shake the faith of the Covenanters in documents which Henderson had welcomed on the first day as the *Magna Carta* of the Kirk.

Hamilton made one last effort to outwit the hostile Assembly by requiring them to answer the official protest of the excluded bishops. The majority postponed the reading of the bishops' letter, not wishing to have any documents which impugned their legality put on record. The King's Commissioner had now only the faint remaining hope that he might be able to question the elections of some of the Covenanting elders when the returns were officially checked, and in this way get rid of a few of his more troublesome opponents. Even here he failed, for although heated argument broke out over a number of the elections, his questions were persistently overruled by the majority.

The end of the first week found Hamilton at his wits' end, with the Covenanters in full command of the situation and ready at any moment to proceed to the trial of the bishops. Nothing remained therefore but to dissolve the Assembly by any means before it could do more harm. On the morning of November 28th Hamilton called the King's Council and told them of his intention. Argyll asked if he was seeking their advice but Hamilton curtly replied that he had already decided on the dissolution and was asking only for the Council's support in his action.[38]

The rumour of a dissolution reached the Covenanters even before the matter was brought up in the Privy Council,[39] and they entered the hall prepared for a crisis. One of them took the precaution of locking the door and concealing the key. The question under debate was the Assembly's right to call the bishops to judgment. Dr. Balcanquhall, Hamilton's only effective spokesman among the clergy, delivered a formidable attack on the pretensions of the Assembly in spite of two or three snubbing interventions from the Moderator and the rumbling anger of his colleagues on the benches. His arguments were, naturally, of no avail against the determination of the majority, who as soon as he sat down voted the Assembly capable of proceeding to judgment on the bishops. Hamilton had waited only for this moment. In eloquent anger—and Hamilton could be impressively eloquent—he told them that they were unworthy of the great concessions that the King had made to them. " You have called for a free General Assembly; His Majesty hath granted you one, most free on his part . . . but as you have handled and marred the matter, let God and the World judge whether the least shadow or footstep of freedom can be discerned in this Assembly." [40]

Hamilton's accusation was just enough, but whatever the force and pressure used by the Covenanters to obtain their majority, Hamilton's right to object was corrupted at the source because he was acting in the name and on the instructions of a King who had never intended the Assembly to do other than pass the time until he should be ready to make war.

Alexander Henderson answered the attack with a dignified defence of the Assembly's procedure and its rights. He was far from questioning the King's rights, he said, " but let God by whom Kings reign have his own place and prerogative."

" Sir," said Hamilton, " ye have spoken as a good Christian and doubtful subject." He allowed Henderson sincerity of religion at least but now, to reveal the base intrigues of the Covenanting lords, he suddenly produced papers which he declared were the secret instructions issued by some of them showing the devious ways in which the elders had been elected. This was the strongest move Hamilton had yet made and was unexpected, for Rothes and Loudoun, two who had been busiest in the matter, sprang up to deny the authenticity of the documents with an alacrity that betrayed their alarm. Above the din of argument which ensued Hamilton's voice rose once more in denunciation. " By what law or practice," he demanded, " was it ever heard that young noblemen or gentlemen or others, should be rulers of the Church? " What kind of freedom was this which, in effect, delivered over the clergy to " the tyranny of lay elders who would . . . prove not only ruling, but over-ruling elders " unless timely checked? Let this Assembly disperse as a corrupt and illegal thing, and the King would then permit them to call another.

After the excitement of challenge and response a quietness seems to have fallen, for the voice of Argyll was now heard, speaking low and fast. Argyll had no right to speak, for he was not a member of the gathering, but his words carried weight because of his position on the King's council. "I have not striven to blow the bellows. But studied to keep matters in as soft a temper as I could, and now I desire to make it known to you that I take you all for members of a lawful Assembly and my honest countrymen."

Hamilton called on Henderson to dissolve the gathering. The Moderator, confused for a moment by the authority in his gesture, hesitated, but the Covenanting lords were all on their feet shouting to him to disregard the order. Hamilton had only one course left. He rose and made to withdraw, thus taking away the King's authority by which alone the Assembly sat. The dignity of his exit was marred by the unexpected discovery that the door was locked; he had to wait several minutes, in an attitude of righteous repudiation, while his servants forced it for him.[41] This awkward interim was filled by Henderson with extempore pulpit eloquence. Some, he said, were zealous to obey the commands of an earthly master: "Have we not also good reason to be zealous towards our Lord and to maintain the liberties and privileges of His Kingdom?" On his example, other ministers rose in their places to elaborate this noble theme, and the departing Hamilton left the room to the accompaniment of triumphant and sonorous preaching.

The councillors, all but Argyll, followed Hamilton out and reassembled with him that afternoon in Glasgow castle. His first care was to ask them to sign a statement declaring that "never servant did with more industry, care, judgment and patience go about the discharge of so great a trust, and albeit the success has not answered his desires . . . yet his deservings herein merit to be remembered to posterity." After securing this testimonial, he issued a proclamation declaring all members of the Assembly traitors should they continue longer in session. Both Argyll and Hope refused to sign this, and its publication had no terrors for the Covenanters.[42]

The Assembly sat on, and with it sat Argyll. "The Earl resolves not to wrong his conscience for any earthly respect," [43] wrote a loyal clansman, although others made question whether conscience alone dictated his behaviour. No lord in the Covenanting party had half the power of Argyll; from the moment he cast in his lot with them he was bound to be their leader.[44] He was so great indeed that his right to speak and sit in the Assembly was granted by common consent, although he had not been elected and had no official right to be there once the King's Council had withdrawn. No one even drew attention to the fact that he had not signed the Covenant and made no move to do so, although other late converts to the cause were daily setting their hands to it with tears and prayers.[45]

The Assembly sat on for a busy three weeks after Hamilton had proclaimed the dissolution. They abjured ceremonies and vestments; they abolished episcopacy; they deposed and excommunicated, individually, all the bishops in Scotland, and to maintain the purity of this new reformation they set up a permanent commission to examine into all reported abuses and to inflict penances, expulsions and excommunications on recalcitrant ministers or parishioners.

The powers of intimidation which this commission wielded were of a kind to impose political and religious agreement with the Covenanters on all but the boldest, both clergy and laity. Any ministers with episcopal sympathies would naturally be thrust out as " impure corbies " from God's ark and their places filled by those whom the Covenanters chose. Laymen, and especially the Covenanting lords, played a dominating part in this examination, rejection and replacement of ministers. The Glasgow Assembly brought into being a powerful instrument of secular policy and the mechanism by which something like a dictatorship could in due course be established.

On the day on which the Assembly abolished episcopacy in Glasgow, the King in London issued a massive proclamation annulling every act, made or to be made, by this gathering of traitors. He also repeated and enlarged his instructions to all the lords lieutenants of the northern and midland counties of England to look to the arming and drilling of the local trained bands of horse and foot, and to follow the advice of the experienced Colonel Astley whom he had sent on a tour of the north expressly to help them in their task.[46]

The situation which had arisen was, from the King's point of view, both confusing and grotesque. Not only had he no power to control or punish his enemies in Scotland but he had no power even to control his own Council. Argyll, now in everything but name the leader of the Covenanters, continued to exercise his rights and functions as a councillor. Sir Thomas Hope refused to speak to the Bishop of Brechin because he had been excommunicated by the Assembly; the Bishop protested that, as a Privy Councillor, Hope was bound to repudiate the Assembly,[47] but Hope, like Argyll, had his own opinions on the matter. The King's own councillors thus openly opposed the royal policy and disregarded the proclamation which the Council had been responsible for publishing.

In the midst of these confusions Hamilton, who had hitherto been merely incompetent, seems to have made the first of those deviations into half-treachery which marked his later career. Lord Deputy Wentworth, watching from Ireland, believed that he was fomenting trouble among the Ulster Scots with perhaps some idea of unsettling the country so as to procure a large grant of land there for himself.[48] Whatever his relations may have been with the troublesome Ulster Scots, Hamilton's conduct in Glasgow disappointed those of the King's followers who had hoped that he would disperse the Assembly by calling up his tenantry to drive them out. He was incomparably the most powerful landowner in that region, but he had a sound excuse for inaction; it would have been folly to risk beginning a war until the King himself was ready.

Hamilton's behaviour to Argyll was less explicable, for he conferred with him privately and parted from him with the greatest cordiality.[49] Hamilton may have had no more in mind than a legitimate desire to acquaint himself with Argyll's intentions, or to dissuade him from continuing in rebellion, but his conduct puzzled the King's loyal friends, and later, when the intimate alliance between Argyll and Hamilton became an accepted element in Scottish affairs, men remembered and speculated on their unaccountable *rapprochement* at the close of the Glasgow Assembly.

Conduct which puzzled the King's friends may have been less puzzling to the King. On the day on which he failed to dissolve the Assembly, Hamilton had written to the King a highly confidential and very strange dispatch. In this he had frankly blamed the stupidity and arrogance of the bishops for the disasters which had occurred and he had strongly advised the King to do all in his power to cultivate and win over Argyll of whom—almost alone of the Scots lords—he spoke with real respect. With one hand Hamilton was trying, clumsily, to act as a peacemaker while, with the other, he carried out the King's war policy. The King, who seems to have approved of the manœuvre was by no means always aware of how far Hamilton had carried it.[50]

By Christmas 1638 all hope of peace had gone. The actions of the Glasgow Assembly in repudiating the policy of Scotland's lawful sovereign and defying his Commissioner were tantamount to a declaration of war. Christmas festivities at Whitehall were curtailed under the excuse of Court mourning, because the Queen's brother-in-law, the Duke of Savoy, whom she had never met, had recently died. The talk was all of war; Arundel and Northumberland persistently offered advice on its conduct, while Colonel Astley and Captain Legge assisted the preparations in the north parts. Wentworth, from Ireland, urged the King to send for the three principal rebels to London—Argyll, Rothes, Montrose. If they came they were to be arrested; if they refused to come they were to be proclaimed traitors. In this way the King could demonstrate what punishment awaited those who further defied him and perhaps break up the Covenanting party by threats and fear.[51]

The Covenanters talked less and did more. The Lords, headed by Argyll, Rothes and Montrose, drew up minute instructions which were circulated throughout the country, allotting to each shire its quota of regiments and distributing the responsibility for raising, arming and training the men between the various presbyteries.[52]

The King's friends in Scotland, intimidated in the south and bewildered in the north, did nothing. Huntly contented himself with a religious demonstration: on the Sunday before Christmas, accompanied as usual by two tall sons, the Lords Gordon and Aboyne, he received the sacrament in Aberdeen cathedral from the hands of the Bishop whom the Assembly had excommunicated.[53]

Before leaving the country, Hamilton had the King's plate and tapestry removed from Holyrood and shipped to England. His own departure was held up by a brief illness, the result, Burnet asserts, of anxiety and overwork, although Archbishop Laud at the time described the indisposition scornfully as a bilious attack.[54] Early in the New Year of 1639 he returned to Whitehall whence he communicated the King's orders to the Privy Council of Scotland. His Majesty's intention was to be at his principal northern city and second capital, York, not later than Eastertide.[55] There he would expect his Scottish councillors to meet him and learn his will. It meant in effect that the King was coming with all his power against the rebels of Scotland.

BOOK II CHAPTER III REFERENCES

1. Rothes, p. 115; Baillie, I, p. 83; Balfour, II, p. 265.
2. Burnet, *Lives*, pp. 52–3; Baillie, I, 81.
3. *C.S.P.D.*, 1637–8, p. 529.
4. Burnet, *op. cit.*, p. 53; *Hamilton Papers, Camden Society*, 1880, p. 8.
5. Balfour, II, p. 276; Burnet, *op. cit.*, p. 64; Baillie, I, 91.
6. Guthry, p. 41.
7. Baillie, I, p. 81; *C.S.P.D.*, 1636–8, pp. 533–5; Rushworth, II, 811.
8. Knowler, II, p. 196; *Strafford MSS.*, VII, Wentworth to Laud, April 26th, 1638, and September 1638 *passim*.
9. Baillie, I, p. 93; Knowler, II, p. 187; *Strafford MSS.*, VII, Wentworth to Laud, August 7th, 1638; *Hamilton Papers*, pp. 12–13.
10. *Strafford MSS.*, X, Conway to Wentworth, August 3rd, 1638.
11. Knowler, II, 186.

12. *C.S.P.D.*, 1637–8, pp. 493–4, 503–4, 506.

13. *Ibid.*, pp. 560–1, 597.

14. *C.S.P.D.*, 1637–8, pp. 584, 590; *H.M.C. XII, App. II*, p. 189; Knowler, II, p. 218; *Strafford MSS.*, X, folio 199.

15. Spalding, *Memorials of the troubles, Spalding Club*, Aberdeen, 1850, I, pp. 92–3; Gordon of Rothiemay, pp. 82–6; Row, *History of the Kirk, Wodrow Society*, Edinburgh, 1842, pp. 494–5; Baillie, I, p. 97.

16. *C.S.P.D.*, 1637–8, pp. 595, 603; *Breadalbane MSS., Letters*, 1636–9, Nos. 736, 738; Knowler, II, 225–6.

17. Spalding, I, 97; Gordon of Rothiemay, II, p. 212.

18. *Breadalbane MSS., Letters*, 1636–9, No. 738.

19. Baillie, I, 108; Forbes-Leith, pp. 202–3.

20. Burnet, *op. cit.*, pp. 72–4, 79; Balfour, II, 286; *C.S.P.D.*, 1638–9, p. 18.

21. Warriston, *Diary*, pp. 391–3.

22. *Ibid.*, pp. 392–3.

23. Balfour, II, p. 293; Guthry, p. 43; *Large Declaration, concerning the late tumults in Scotland*, London, 1639, pp. 157–73.

24. Guthry, p. 44.

25. Burnet, *op. cit.*, p. 83; Warriston, *Diary*, pp. 393, 395, 397; *Large Declaration*, pp. 226–8.

26. Burnet, pp. 81, 87; *Register P.C. Scot.*, 1638, pp. 95–7.

27. Spalding, I, 112–14; Burnet, *op. cit.*, p. 86.

28. *Scottish Historical Review*, XIV, pp. 62–6.

29. Hope, *Diary*, p. 78.

30. Burnet, *Lives*, p. 84.

31. Baillie, I, p. 105.

32. Burnet, *op. cit.*, pp. 87–8; *Hamilton Papers*, pp. 46–9.

33. Burnet, p. 88; Balfour, II, 297–8.

34. Baillie, I, 111; *C.S.P.D.*, 1638–9, pp. 108, 120, 152; Knowler, II, pp. 228, 274; Burnet, *op. cit.*, pp. 88–90.

35. Baillie, I, 128; Warriston, *Diary*, p. 401.

36. Baillie, I, 128.

37. Warriston, *Diary*, p. 401.

38. Burnet, *op. cit.*, p. 101; *Hamilton Papers*, pp. 62–3.

39. Baillie, I, p. 138.

40. Burnet, *op. cit.*, p. 101.

41. *Large Declaration*, pp. 286–7; Gordon of Rothiemay, I, pp. 184–92; Peterkin, *Records of the Kirk of Scotland*, Edinburgh, 1843, pp. 129 ff.

42. *Register P.C. Scot.*, pp. 91–4; *Hamilton Papers* p. 63.

43. *Breadalbane MSS., Letters* 1636–9, Archibald Campbell to Glenorchy, December 7th, 1638.

44. Laud, VII, p. 517.

45. He apparently signed the Covenant for the first time in the ensuing April. *Breadalbane MSS., Letters*, 1636–9, No. 763.

46. *Register P.C. Scot.*, 1638–9, pp. 96–102; *C.S.P.D.*, 1638–9, p. 155.

47. Hope, *Diary*, p. 83.

48. *Strafford MSS*, VII, Wentworth to Laud, Nov.–Dec. 1638 *passim*.
49. Spalding, I, p. 120; *Breadalbane MSS., Letters*, 1636–9, Archibald Campbell to Glenorchy, December 31st, 1638.
50. *Hardwicke State Papers*, London, 1778, II, p. 113.
51. Knowler, II, 261.
52. *C.S.P.D.*, 1638–9, pp. 405–10.
53. Spalding, I, p. 126.
54. Spalding, I, p. 127; Burnet, *op. cit.*, p. 111; Knowler, II, p. 265.
55. Burnet, *op. cit.*, p. 112; *Register P.C. Scot.*, 1639, p. 106.

CHAPTER FOUR

THE FIRST SCOTS WAR

December 1638–July 1639

THE autumn in England had been marked by a number of public and private disasters. Widecombe Church was struck by lightning during evening service one Sunday and three of the congregation were killed; this was generally agreed to be a judgment, though whether on England's wickedness or Widecombe's remained in doubt.[1] A few days later an equally lamentable accident occurred at the other end of the kingdom; the chimney of the Lord President's house in York crashed through the roof and killed Sir Edward Osborne's eldest son. Osborne, Vice-President of the North and the King's most loyal and prominent servant in Yorkshire, was for some time prostrated with grief, to the hindrance of military preparations in those parts.[2]

The worst news came from Germany. The King's nephew, the Elector Palatine, who had been urged to fend for himself, had enlisted Dutch help to put a small army in the field. Marching to join the Swedes, he was cut off and routed by the imperial forces at Vlotho on the Weser; the Elector saved himself by precipitate flight, but his brother, Rupert, last seen charging to the rescue of a captured standard, was missing after the fight. Various rumours reached London, that he had been killed, or had died of wounds, before the truth emerged. He was alive and unhurt but prisoner in a remote Austrian fortress. The sad news provoked more Puritan criticism of the King's policy.

Instead of concentrating his interest and his energy on attacking their brethren of Scotland, he should have given more effective help to his Protestant nephews in their struggle for the Cause in Germany.

The Queen was the object of particular malice, for she had, it was argued, diverted her husband's attention from the forlorn plight of his sister. A recent arrival in England, the Duchesse de Chevreuse, added to the Queen's unpopularity; expelled from France for her incessant intrigues and believed to be in the pay of Spain, this beautiful, mischievous creature became the self-invited guest of the Court. " She spends as if our treasure were infinite," complained Laud.[3] But he could do nothing to stop her, for the Queen was attached to her and the King gave way. In the meantime she got the Court a bad name by flaunting her religion in the face of the Londoners and conducting an indiscreet love affair with the susceptible Lord Holland.

That same autumn of 1638 the King received another unwelcome visitor. His wife's factious and foolish mother, Marie de Medici, who, like Madame de Chevreuse, was well known to be in the pay of Spain, had fled from the Court of her son, Louis XIII, to take refuge in the Spanish Netherlands. She now invited herself to England. The arrival of this Italian, Roman Catholic princess, with a suite of six hundred attendants, could hardly have been worse timed, the more so that Marie de Medici had never been famed for tact. Her formal entry to London made a pleasing show for the populace and ensured her a temporary welcome, but soon her haughty behaviour to visitors, the extravagance of her household and the open establishment of yet another centre of Popish worship at her chapel, had made her cordially disliked not only by the censorious Londoners but by most of the Court as well.[4]

In the simplified popular version of political affairs, the Popish Queen's Popish mother living in state on English money was contrasted with the King's Protestant sister, the exiled Queen of Bohemia, living in poverty abroad, her eldest son defeated for lack of help and her second son a prisoner in Austrian hands.

The King, forgetful of his own flesh and blood, made ready for war against his Protestant subjects of Scotland instead of fighting his own and his sister's Popish foes. . . . So, in broad and displeasing outline, the picture presented itself to average Protestant Englishmen; it was not necessary to be far gone in Puritanism to see it in this way. The subtleties of European politics that were clear to a Laud or a Wentworth or to the King himself, eluded them completely, but in some ways they were not far wrong. The European intervention for which they yearned might not have been so much to their liking or their interest as they thought, but the Scots war on which the King was bent was to nobody's liking and nobody's interest at all.

Furthermore, the King's attempts to raise arms, money, and even troops in the Spanish Netherlands were unkindly taken by the Dutch, who suspected that his dubious neutrality was about to end in open alliance with Spain. The Protestant-Catholic animosities which had so long divided Europe seemed to them to be echoed in this new war in the British Isles. Indeed the whole course of events in Scotland bore, to them, a very striking resemblance to the course of their own revolt against Philip II seventy years before.[5] The same fear of a still closer Anglo-Spanish alliance also troubled the French and the Venetians, whose agents in London were instructed to inquire into the matter and keep a close watch on events. When informed European diplomatists entertained such suspicions, it was natural that the King's own subjects should do the same. In attacking the Calvinist Scots, Charles seemed to be taking up a definite position at last in the religious conflict of Europe, and to be taking it up on the wrong side.

The wildest stories circulated in London, coming sometimes from the lips of Scotsmen visiting friends in the South: for instance, that the Scots were about to proclaim an independent republic and could count on the help of the French, the Swedes and the Dutch.[6] Such rumours sprang from the belief that the King, after seeking Spanish help would enter the European war, on that side. In that event the Protestant powers and the enemies of Spain would defend their own interests by assisting the Scots, and the European turmoil would be extended to Great Britain.

The King's preparations went forward with a great show of seriousness. Sir Jacob Astley sent detailed reports of the fortifications of Hull, Newcastle and Berwick, with plans for projected gun-sites and trenches, lists of the arms in readiness and reports of what was needed and what most easily to be had. The King's Council of War at Whitehall placed large orders for arms in the Netherlands and worked out a plan of campaign which looked very convincing on paper.[7] Scotland was to be the object of a fourfold attack: the King, with the principal army, would cross the border while Hamilton and the fleet landed five thousand men at Aberdeen, Wentworth sent a contingent of the Irish army to Dumbarton, and Antrim with his Macdonnells invaded Kintire. The fleet, when not engaged in these landing operations, was to blockade the east coast of Scotland. The Lowlands, where the Covenanters were strongest, would thus be held between the King's army in the south and Hamilton's contingent, reinforced by Huntly and the loyal Gordons, in the north. Argyll would be fully occupied in defending himself from the Irish, and foreign help would be cut off by the vigilance of the fleet.

The plan belonged to the King's imaginary world of order and good organisation. He spoke in Council as though his projected army of six thousand cavalry and twenty-four thousand infantry was already in being; he answered no questions and gave no hint of knowing where the money was to be found to pay it. He had made a few personal economies, such as reducing the prices to be paid to Sir Anthony Van Dyck for a number of commissioned works, but he rejected any suggestion that Parliament should be called to vote him a subsidy, although Cottington, his chief financial expert, who in the last two years had increased the profits of the Court of Wards by another £20,000, suddenly declared that there was no money at all in the Exchequer.[8] Even the navy, object of so much care and forethought, was not large enough for the variety of tasks which the King's plan imposed upon it. Confident in the justice of his cause, the King relied on the support of his loyal subjects, a very few of whom justified his faith. The Earl of Worcester freely gave fifteen hundred pounds, and the Marquis of Winchester a thousand. It did not escape comment that both these generous givers were Roman Catholics. Lord Strange, eldest son to the Earl of Derby, and Lord Lieutenant of Lancashire, zealously performed his duties in raising the Lancashire levies and in equipping his own tenants. For the King's misfortune, Lancashire was a bitterly divided county and Lord Strange exceptionally unpopular with the Puritans.

The peers of England in general were called upon to perform their antique feudal duty to the King either by leading troops into the field at their own charge or by compounding for a sum of money to the Exchequer. A great number of them made excuses, announcing that they were too old, or—by the mouth of a guardian—too young, or too poor; the wealthy Lord Clare pleaded that he had seven daughters yet to marry and must save all for their dowries.[9] It was rumoured that the Lords Saye, Brooke and Mandeville might even refuse altogether. Mandeville was heir to pious old Lord Manchester, whose sons were a constant source of anxiety to him. First his younger boy Wat Montague, became a Roman Catholic and got into disgrace for making conversions at Court, and now his eldest was a notorious Puritan. Manchester, to conceal the shortcomings of his family, busied himself vigorously to put his own quota of men into as smart a shape as possible for the King's service.[10]

In the Court circle at least, especially among the younger men, a number offered to raise and equip small bodies of cavalry —Lord Carnarvon, Lord Goring's eldest son George, and Lord Wilmot's son Harry, who had both newly returned from the Low Countries, carrying honourable scars from the siege of Breda. Cottington put up the money for fifty horse, and Secretary Windebanke's eldest boy, a popular young spark known to his friends as " Signior Tomaso," was prominent among the courtiers who assumed the insignia and duties of cavalry officers. Most noticeable was Sir John Suckling, the gamester and poet, who poured what remained of his credit and all his effervescent energy into equipping a troop that should outshine all others. The unkind said that he had supplied his men with cockades and then his means had given out. This was not true; his men were complete with plumes, swords, armour, battle-axes and fringed scarves—everything except training.[11]

A few gifts of money came from prominent lawyers and rich citizens, but the Inns of Court refused to make any joint offering,[12] and the City of London, when approached for a loan or a gift, was equally obdurate. Sir Paul Pindar, jeweller and Turkey merchant, on whose riches the King had drawn before to pay for works of art, generously advanced a hundred thousand pounds [13] and placed the King's affairs on a more solid footing. How long they would remain so was more doubtful. The Lord Deputy of Ireland complained that some of the King's servants —he mentioned Arundel, Holland and Hamilton—thought themselves privileged " to take out by handfuls and scatter abroad at their pleasure." [14] In the circumstances it seemed unlikely that Astley's efficient schemes for strengthening Hull and Newcastle would be put into practice. The two cities had been instructed to proceed with them at once at their own expense, an order which was altogether too heavy a strain on their purses and their loyalty.[15]

In January the King decided on the principal army appointments. So great were the jealousies at Court that no decision could have given general content, and Charles had to balance the claims of ancient lineage against military skill. Arundel, whose knowledge of war was as antique as his hereditary title of Earl-Marshal, was nominally appointed commander-in-chief. Next under him was a competent professional soldier, the Earl of Essex; this choice was made with an eye on the Protestant critics of the Court,[16] for Essex was friend and close kin to the dissident peers, had fought for the Dutch abroad and was respected by the Puritans. This was a good appointment but the

King spoilt its effect by yielding to his wife's plea on behalf of one of her favourites.

The Queen, always precious to him, became more so when on January 20th she all but died in giving birth to her seventh child. Princess Katherine lived only to receive her name at the font.

> " Ah, wert thou born for this, only to call
>   The King and Queen guests to your burial?
>   To bid good-night, your day not yet begun,
>   And show us a setting, ere a rising sun?"

wrote Richard Lovelace, and fifty more lines to the same effect.

Under the shadow of the Queen's pain and their joint loss, the King would give her anything and she begged the generalship of the cavalry for the Earl of Holland.[17] This appointment was equally insulting to Arundel and Essex because to command an army without commanding the cavalry was to have only the semblance of authority. The cavalry consisted chiefly of troops raised, equipped and officered by the principal nobility and courtiers in answer to the King's feudal appeal; these felt no great enthusiasm for serving under the notoriously frivolous, haughty and incompetent Holland. The appointment caused annoyance to the King's friends and aroused the derision of his opponents; Leslie contemptuously commented that he would make " my Lord of Holland rise without his periwig." [18]

The King completed his list by placing Hamilton in command of the fleet. It was reasonable to entrust the principal venture by sea—that of making a landing at Aberdeen—to a Scot, but Hamilton himself protested that he knew nothing about the management of ships,[19] and bitter offence was caused to the Earl of Northumberland who was Lord High Admiral of the fleet and saw no reason why his experience and knowledge should be set on one side.

Confusion reigned in other spheres. The King had prohibited all armourers from working except at his direct command.

This prohibition made it impossible for lords and gentlemen, who had undertaken to arm their own companies, to get what they wanted or to get it in time.[20] The arms ordered in the Low Countries proved on arrival to be very bad. Of two thousand pikes none were good, and nearly three hundred were downright useless; more than a third of the swords were defective; the belts and hangers were of poor quality or used leather, and some of the bandoliers were found to be made of brown paper.[21] The troops which gradually came together from the counties were indifferent and ill-equipped. Desertion was very common, mutiny less so, although it occurred. Some Herefordshire men set upon and wounded an officer before dispersing home again to their villages. Most of them grumbled bitterly when they found how far from home they were to march, and made up for the inconveniences to which they were subjected by plundering the strange and, to them, foreign parts of England through which they passed.[22]

From the north, Sir Jacob Astley reported that the borderers were tough, broad-shouldered men, used to fighting, who would do well in plundering expeditions against the Scots, but they must be armed with muskets; the bows and arrows with which Arundel had diligently supplied them in the previous year hardly answered to the needs of modern war. He asked also for artillery and suggested that the Durham pit-ponies be commandeered for drawing cannon. The armour hitherto supplied for the use of the northern troops was inadequate and a whole consignment of pikes had been too short for practical use. He reported disquieting tales of the mustering of the Scots in large numbers on the farther side of the border.[23]

In Yorkshire, the Vice-President of the North, the gentle Sir Edward Osborne, still grief-stricken over the accident which had cost him his son, had failed to bring the obstructive gentry under control; some complained of the cost of equipping the men; others went to the Netherlands for a time to avoid their duties. The decision to organise heavy-armed cavalry had to be reversed because the horses available were suitable for light cavalry only; all arrangements had to be altered and the equipment cancelled and changed. The man-power of Yorkshire was considerable, but too few professional soldiers could be found to train the recruits, and the shortage of armourers or gunsmiths in the north was frustrating. The most forward recruits were unfortunately the tenants of the Roman Catholic gentry, and these, who had long been prohibited the use of arms by law, came to the rendezvous with hardly a sword or pike between them.[24] The King's growing doubt of the strength he could raise in England was reflected in the direct negotiations which he opened with the Spanish government in Brussels to release troops for his use in Scotland.[25]

The hostile muttering of public opinion made an uncomfortable accompaniment to the King's preparations. To demonstrate that Archbishop Laud had no sympathy with the Papists, the famous dialogue in which he had long ago confuted Fisher, the Jesuit, was republished, but trenchant as were Laud's theological arguments against the Roman doctrine, they did not divert the attention of the Puritans from the continued stream of prosecutions in the Courts of High Commission and Star Chamber. A Lincolnshire curate, who refused to wear a surplice, was imprisoned and fined £1,000 for having preached a sermon against sabbath-breaking and the King's publication of the Book of Sports. No doubt his behaviour had been uncanonical; he had assaulted a wandering piper who had played on the village green for his parishioners to dance on a Sunday afternoon.[26] Bishop Williams, still obstinate, was now answering to another libel charge, together with the headmaster of Westminster School, Lambert Osbaldeston, for their outspoken exchange of letters about " the little meddling hocus pocus." Osbaldeston was sentenced to the loss of his ears and to stand in the pillory in front of his own school. With characteristic inefficiency, the officers of the court did not notice him slipping quietly away while sentence was being pronounced. The hue and cry raised for him revealed nothing, save some charred papers in his study and a derisive note left on his desk, " If the Archbishop inquire after me, tell him I am gone beyond Canterbury." Literal-minded, his pursuers sought him at the Kentish ports, but he was well hidden in London, beyond the clutches of the Arch-bishop.[27]

A new headmaster had to be found for Westminster School, and Laud, seeking for a divine of unimpeachable views, sent for Dr. Richard Busby from Oxford, thus in the midst of his gathering troubles, making the wisest and most beneficial appointment of his career.

Lesser voices all over the country were raised against the Archbishop. Conventicles in London, in Shropshire, in North-amptonshire, on the borders, were discovered and broken up, but Astley, the practical soldier, implored the King to leave the Puritans alone, at least while he was trying to raise troops. In February the Scots had issued an appeal to the people of England, for religion's sake, and this document, in print and in manu-script, ran from hand to hand all over the country. A chapman whose cloak-bag was crammed with copies was seized at Penrith; another was reported to be distributing them in the region of Manchester, and a clergyman in Bedfordshire was put in the pillory for handing out a manuscript version.[28] Daring rhyme-sters dropped abusive doggerel in market places, pinned it on doors, even threw it down within the precincts of the King's palaces. "Desiring Your Highness to pardon my pen," con-cluded one of these anonymous critics, to the King—" carry Laud to the Scots, and hang up Bishop Wren." [29] Whenever two or three are gathered together, went the common tale, two of them will be exclaiming against the government; the health of the gallant Scots with destruction to Laud " the Pope of Lambeth " was proposed by those whom drink made bold in alehouses.[30]

A raid on the Postmaster's office, carried out on Secretary Windebanke's instructions, proved only what was already suspected, that the Scots were in friendly correspondence with some of the most influential men in England. Lord Brooke, a leader among the Puritan nobility, was seriously incriminated, but the King, in a rare access of caution, decided to leave him unmolested for fear of revealing too broadly the strength of the opposition.[31]

As spring came on, the streets of London were disturbed by the Puritan prophetess Lady Eleanor Davies, wild-eyed and loud-voiced, foretelling the total destruction of the city before Easter.[32]

The Archbishop was harassed with misgivings which pursued him even into his sleep. He dreamed that the King desired to marry a minister's widow and asked him to perform the ceremony, but he looked in vain through his Prayer Book without being able to find the Order for Marriage.[33] Waking, he could at least turn from the espousals of King Charles and the Scottish Kirk to less distressing topics. He continued his campaign against the Walloon congregation in Canterbury [34] whose resistance, though dogged, gave him no such cause for anxiety as did that of the Scots.

Other happier interests still from time to time cheered him. He had been corresponding with Edward Pocock, the Oxford Professor of Arabic, whom he had sent to Constantinople in quest of Greek manuscripts and whom he advised to visit Mount Athos. Disposing of the treasures in his own possession he presented this year to the university of Oxford five hundred and seventy-six volumes in Hebrew, Arabic and Persian. In his home town of Reading he was busy endowing a fund for the relief of the deserving poor.[35]

The King in his natural optimism still believed that a silent majority in Scotland were in his favour and "only wanted a head and arms" to rise against the Covenanters.[36] This belief was not quite groundless. Some of those who had been indifferent at first had been provoked by the aggression of the Covenanters into belated resistance; unexpected trouble broke out even in the Campbell country, and Glenorchy who, after Argyll, was the principal Campbell chieftain, found difficulty in getting the Covenant subscribed in his lands; at one point a mutiny against the Covenant seemed likely to break out even in Argyll's own forces in the Western Highlands. The resistance was speedily crushed and the Covenant enforced under threats of dire punishment.[37]

Eastwards from the Campbell country, along the fringe of the highlands, lay Lord Ogilvy's lands. He and his people were staunch Royalists, but they were neither strong enough nor in a strategic position good enough to effect anything. The most important Royalist in Scotland was the Marquis of Huntly with his Gordons, representing a fighting force of at least two thousand men. Furthermore, the highlanders in general did not love the lowlanders and might prove dangerous. But to most of these Gaelic-speaking, hunting, fighting, cattle-herding people, the King's policy mattered far less than the ancient enmities or friendships of their chiefs. Many of them had, out of rivalry or dislike of the Gordons, subscribed the Covenant. A leader had not yet arisen who could inspire them to make common cause; and the Covenanters rightly trusted in their bitter divisions.[38] They held an equally contemptuous view of the Irish troops which the Lord Deputy was to send to the King's help; Rothes had confidently threatened to " dight their doublets." [39]

Alexander Leslie, the Covenanting commander-in-chief, was not an outstanding military genius but he was an experienced organiser. The Scots army had no troops so glorious as the plumed cavalry on which Sir John Suckling had lavished his money and his taste, but officers and men had the cause at heart and those who could not fight helped to the best of their ability. " I furnished to half a dozen of good fellows muskets and pickets, and to my boy a broad sword," recorded Dr. Baillie, the earnest and kindly minister who was, until the wars came, professor of philosophy at Glasgow, but who now found himself the chaplain of a regiment.[40] The problems of inadequate pikes, brown-paper bandoliers, infantry without arms, and cavalry without horses did not afflict the Scots. Professional soldiers, who had come home from Germany in great numbers to assist in the Holy War at home, were distributed throughout the country to teach the young men how to handle pike and musket. The patriarchal system of society made recruiting easier than in England. Apart from Argyll, no major highland chief with a clan at his call was a Covenanter, but over all the lowlands ties of kindred and traditional obedience brought the soldiers in as soon as the heads of families gave the word. The traditional and professional experience of a people with whom war, until the last generation, had been endemic served the Scots well. Equipment, commissariat and transport were smoothly organised; the building of wagons, the casting of bullets were planned well in advance; it was known how much powder and match each musketeer should have, what arms were to be issued, in default of muskets, what was essential, and what could be dispensed with.[41]

The principal difficulty was money to bring the men together from the remoter parts and to keep them in the necessities of life. "Our soldiers were all lusty and full of courage," wrote Baillie, "most of them stout young ploughmen: the only difficulty was to get them dollars for their voyage from home ... for among our yeomen money at any time, let be then, uses to be very scarce; but once having entered on the common pay, their sixpence a day, they were galliard." The citizens of Edinburgh contributed generously because their ministers in fervid sermons "moved them to shake out their purses." Supplies of wheat for the army were built up by the simple process of raiding the garners of those who had not signed the Covenant.[42] But the enthusiasm for the Covenanting cause in Edinburgh and round about was for the most part unfeigned, and travellers out of Scotland reported that the women of Edinburgh and Leith helped the men to fortify the cities, carrying earth for the ramparts in baskets and aprons.[43]

Argyll, who was principally engaged in defending the west against invasion from Ireland, commanded his tenants and friends on the long, vulnerable coast to build boats for patrolling the seas. He had fairly ousted Rothes as the foremost man in the party, and was gradually assuming a new grandeur. In future he planned to have twelve or sixteen young gentlemen of his kin to attend always upon his person as a guard of honour.[44]

The young Montrose, who had some academic knowledge of warfare learnt at a military school in France, was acquiring practical knowledge from Leslie with astonishing speed. The first, bloodless, action of the war was his. In the second week of February 1639 he heard, at Perth, that Huntly had called a gathering of his clan at Turriff in the heart of the Gordon country. Montrose, with a picked band of musketeers, marched swiftly through the Grampian passes and occupied Turriff at daybreak, an hour or two before Huntly and his clansmen arrived. Huntly lacking instructions from England and uncertain what consequences might follow should he begin the war, looked askance at the intruders in his country but thought it wiser not to challenge them. He sent his clansmen home again.[45]

While the King's Scottish champion withdrew, baffled, the offers of his Irish champion resounded through Dublin. The Earl of Antrim, after contemptuously refusing a passage on the regular packet boat and demanding the use of the royal frigate *Swallow*, had landed in Dublin and proclaimed to all that he would raise ten thousand foot and three hundred horse, and transport them all to Scotland in a fleet of his own building. Wentworth, who knew that Antrim could not raise a loan of £300 from any merchant in Dublin, so poor was his credit, paid no serious attention to these " vast, vain, and child-like propositions." The young man vapoured, complained, outlined his plans with energy to the Deputy's council, asked for supplies of powder and shot from the royal arsenal, hurried to his country estate and began assiduously felling trees for the ships, discovered that his workmen could not make masts, sent measurements to the Deputy for some from the King's shipyards (the measurements were wrong: the masts did not fit), reappeared in Dublin with a boon companion who was to assist in the conquest of Scotland and asked the Deputy to knight them both for the great services soon to be rendered. That, at least, seemed a harmless vanity and Wentworth, having " much ado to forbear smiling," bestowed the accolade on the two sillies. Antrim's companion had an unusual, Irish name, Phelim O'Neill.[46]

Anxiety underlay Wentworth's laughter. Contrary winds delayed the dispatches from London to Dublin, and his information was scarce and worrying: the Queen was interfering in the army appointments, the Puritans were rebellious, the King's preparations were inadequate. He put together a gloomy, accurate picture from the many hints. For his own part he had sent over a garrison of five hundred men to strengthen Carlisle; he wished he could believe the King's other garrisons were as good. Ireland stirred uneasily; the O'Byrnes were suddenly on the move, raiding and burning in the Wicklow hills. Other raiders broke out in Donegal; the Scots in Ulster grew insolent and he compelled them to take an oath of loyalty to the King. Since the removal of nearly all the King's fleet from the Irish coasts to blockade the east coast of Scotland and prevent trade with the Continent, the fishing boats and merchant vessels of the Ulstermen defied the customs officers and communicated with the Covenanters. A pirate from Dunkirk entered Dublin harbour in broad daylight and towed away a Dutch merchantman. This kind of thing brought the royal authority into contempt. Wentworth saw very well, but saw too late, that his master was taking too great a risk. On March 21st he wrote imploring the King to reconsider his plan and postpone the war by any means.[47]

The letter cannot have reached Whitehall before the King himself had left. After distributing Easter gifts of venison to the Lord Mayor and all the ambassadors resident in his capital, he began his journey to York to join his army on March 27th, 1639. Hamilton at the same time proceeded to Yarmouth to embark the troops for Aberdeen. The Earl of Northumberland, to console him for being passed over as Admiral and General, was left behind to look after the King's most precious possession. He was made responsible for the safety of the Queen: " She is my jewel," said Charles.[48]

On March 30th when the King reached York the war was already lost. In the previous fortnight the Covenanters in a series of swift, concerted moves had consolidated their position.

On March 20th the only important Royalist on the Scottish side of the border, the Earl of Douglas, fled, allowing his castle and his pregnant wife to fall into the hands of the Covenanters.[49] A Roman Catholic by conversion, he had been wholly unable to hold his Protestant tenants in check.

On March 21st, between four and five in the afternoon, Alexander Leslie with some "choice companies" of musketeers rushed Edinburgh Castle. "In half an hour that strong place is won without a stroke," marvelled Dr. Robert Baillie, but it was no great marvel, for the garrison was almost without arms.[50] Immediately after, a band of Covenanters under Rothes appeared before the castle of Dalkeith, the King's chief arsenal, where the Crown Jewels of Scotland were kept and Traquair was in command. He refused the keys but hinted that experienced soldiers might effect an entry by other ways. The Covenanters scrambled in by the unguarded windows, and Traquair stood by while they carried away the arms, the powder, and the Crown Jewels in triumph to Edinburgh.[51]

On Sunday, March 23rd, at Dumbarton—the seaport on the south-west coast where the King's Irish troops were to land—the provost with forty armed men met the Royalist governor of the castle with his lady as he came out of kirk and asked him home to dine. When the governor refused, he was forced into the provost's house and compelled to give up the keys. The Covenanters occupied the castle, of which the garrison, to a man, came over to their side. What had possessed the King to leave in Dumbarton a garrison rotten with disaffection—lamented the Lord Deputy of Ireland—when it could easily have been garrisoned effectively from Ireland had the King but given leave? Now it was gone and with it all hope of landing Irish troops in Scotland.[52]

Huntly all this time was busy about Aberdeen, but he had been strictly charged not to begin the war until Hamilton and the fleet arrived—the fleet which was still in Yarmouth roads waiting for the troops to embark. Huntly, who had gathered together about three thousand followers, did what he thought best: he sent a flattering embassy to Montrose, who was mustering his troops within his own territory, suggesting a gentleman's agreement that neither should enter the other's country. The messengers found Montrose busy issuing his troops with lengths of blue ribbon to make themselves cockades (" one of Montrose's whimsies " said his critics sourly), and he showed little interest in Huntly's offer. He was, he said, the servant of the Covenant and had orders to occupy Aberdeen, which, with or without Huntly's permission, he intended to do in as orderly and peaceable a manner as possible. Huntly's messengers went disconsolately home again, noticing the evil omen of an angry sunset as they went—the sky seemed as if fresh blood had been " poured into a bright silver basin." [53]

Three days later in high, windy, brilliant, weather Leslie and Montrose marched on Aberdeen, with horse and foot, drums and trumpets, and banners flaunting to the sun the legend, " For God, Covenant and Country." Huntly had already withdrawn, and the port and stronghold, on which the King had built his highest hopes, received the conquerors in helpless dismay.[54]

On March 30th in the afternoon the King made his official entry into York, driving in a coach, with Lennox and Holland in attendance. The Yorkshire trained bands lined the way, and Arundel, accompanied by the mayor of York, came out to meet him. At about the same hour the Covenanters were entering Aberdeen, but he did not know of this until five days later. It was the worst news out of Scotland since he started on his journey.[55]

He was still convinced of his ultimate victory, and although he sent to instruct Hamilton to blockade Leith and abandon the project for Aberdeen, he gave more time to considering the punishments to be inflicted on the rebels when they were conquered than to the means of conquering them. The proclamation with which he intended to enter Scotland, at the head of his army, promised his loyal subjects peace and a Parliament, but added a long list of traitors exempted from pardon either of life or estates. It included the names of Argyll, Rothes, Montrose and Warriston. The double-faced Traquair, who had presented himself at York with specious excuses for his conduct at Dalkeith, was already under arrest.[56] For once, however, he had followed the advice often given by Laud and Wentworth, and bestowed rewards on the loyal. At York he raised the loyalist Lord Ogilvy to the dignity of Earl of Airlie and created another faithful Scot, Robert Dalzell, a soldier of some reputation, Earl of Carnwath.

The first military necessity seemed to be the security of Berwick, and the King began to denude his other garrisons in order to strengthen it. There was big talk, rather late in the day, of improving its fortifications; Astley, always practical, was for a dry ditch—like that at Bergen-op-Zoom—rather than the complicated engineering of a moat. The King's mind wandered to a happier future. When the war was over Berwick must be suitably rewarded; it was dreadfully poor, something must be done to restore its dwindling trade. Even the best church in the place—the King spoke with shocked recollection of a previous visit—was so dilapidated that he would have been loth to stable a horse in it.[57]

York provided plentiful entertainment for the King and his followers. Charles and his chief officers lodged at the King's House, the magnificent residence enlarged by Wentworth as the seat of the Lord President of the North. Sir Arthur Ingram's noble mansion, with its famous Italian garden, served for other members of his suite. Officers and gentry in general found good but expensive accommodation at the *Talbot* and the *Dragon*, and cheaper lodging at the *Bell*.[58] In the friendly atmosphere of the city confidence rose again, and Charles was disposed to disregard the gloomy letter which the Lord Deputy of Ireland had sent urging him to postpone the invasion of Scotland for another year or at least until his prospects of success were greater. Charles responded by ordering Wentworth to give full support to the Earl of Antrim in his proposed attack on Kintire by himself leading the Irish army in person against Argyll. How this was to be done when the navy was wholly occupied elsewhere and the principal port in western Scotland had already been lost, he did not explain.[59]

Charles meanwhile watched his " cavaliers on their brave horses" perform before him in the " ings," the meadows by the city, a sight as merry as " the recreations in Hyde Park." A day or two later he reviewed the rest of his cavalry, including Sir John Suckling's resplendent troop, at Selby. Afterwards he visited the Abbey and admired its fine East window.[60]

Soon after his return to York an astonishing rumour reached him that Huntly had not only abandoned Aberdeen but had signed the Covenant. To his indignation he found that some of his own following dared to defend the document. To stop this creeping rot he tendered to the lords gathered at York a new oath of loyalty and obedience in the coming war. Lord Saye and Lord Brooke both refused it, Lord Saye asserting that, since the union of the crowns, he could not hold it lawful to kill a Scot. Charles lost his temper: " My Lord," he cried, " there be as good men as you that will not refuse to take it, but I find you averse to all my proceedings." Saye continued in his refusal and Charles placed him and Lord Brooke under arrest.[61]

Five days later with a gesture of generosity he released them, but Saye left York immediately, taking his entire contingent of troops with him, because, he argued, they were his personal attendants, not the King's soldiers.[62] The sly. peer was well nicknamed " Old Subtility," for his last statement was a pointed criticism of the King. If Charles revived the obsolete feudal practice of calling on his lords for military duties, why should not they, in their turn, revive other obsolete feudal practices, such as maintaining a personal armed retinue as in the Wars of the Roses?

Essex, the King's General of the Infantry, had meanwhile received an appeal from the Covenanting leaders to use his best endeavours to prevent a war. With scrupulous correctness he at once handed the letter to the King, a fact which did not prevent Lord Holland, his associate in command of the army, from

informing some of his particular friends that in his opinion
Essex was a traitor. This disagreement between the respective
generals of the King's cavalry and the King's infantry was speedily
reflected in brawls and disorders among their men.[63]

The news from the south was not of the best. Hamilton
had had difficulty in embarking the levies raised in East Anglia;
they were very unwilling to fight the Scots.[64] In London, the
players of the Fortune Theatre had been reprimanded by the
council for making a mock of Laudian ritual on the stage to the
high delight of the vulgar audience. Trade in London was
almost at a standstill because of the interruption of the war and
doubt of its results; the utterly irrepressible Lilburne, from his
prison, managed to issue a paper calling on the apprentices to rise
against the government.

To alleviate this dangerous situation, Charles, from York,
suddenly sent word that licences, projects and restrictions touching twenty-seven different commodities, from hatbands to
seaweed, from iron to red herrings, were to be withdrawn.
The idea was good, but it came too late and its sole effect for
that summer was to flood his inadequate secretariat in London
with extra work. Secretary Windebanke's office, manned
largely by his relations, already felt itself to be overworked with
the occasional raiding of suspect Puritan households and the
examination of their tedious papers. Robert Reade, the Secretary's nephew and right-hand man, wrote peevishly to his cousin
" Signior Tomaso " that he scarcely had time to undertake the
wooing by proxy of the latter's bride; a charge which had been
entrusted to him when Tomaso marched north with the King.[65]

More energy was displayed by the Queen and her friends.
She set on foot a collection for the expenses of the war from the
ladies of her attendance; each was asked to forego some desired
finery and offer to His Majesty's cause a suitable proportion of
her dress allowance. Far larger sums, it was thought, could be
raised from the King's Roman Catholic subjects, grateful for the
reliefs he had given them. This second collection was organised
by the Papal agent, George Con. He was helped by an active

committee of prominent Catholics, the Queen's secretary Sir John Winter, Wat Montagu of course, Sir Basil Brooke and Sir Kenelm Digby. But the comings and goings between the committee and the Queen gave rise to rumour of a Popish Plot.[66]

The suspicions which his policy aroused were again brought home to the King by the Earl of Leicester, his ambassador to Paris, who reported to him at York in the course of April. He made it more than ever clear to Charles that the rebel Scots had considerable hope of assistance from France, or indeed from any European power opposed to the Spanish interest. A few weeks later when the King's negotiations for troops in Brussels began to ripen, and a contingent of four thousand men was offered to him by the Cardinal Infante, governor of the Spanish Netherlands, Charles had come to the conclusion that it would not be safe for him to accept. Too many of those English lords and gentry who had obeyed his summons to bring troops against the Scots were now openly criticising his policy. Here were two armies, English and Scots, about to fight one another when either or both would far more gladly put their arms at the service of the King's nephew, the Elector Palatine, and the Protestant Cause in Europe. So ran the dangerous, irrepressible current of criticism.[67]

All the while the King's financial position deteriorated. The Hampden trial had virtually ended his hopes of raising any substantial sums by extra-Parliamentary taxation. His monopoly policy had been deliberately abandoned in the vain attempt to regain popularity, and all the expected revenues of the Crown had been pledged for the next five years.[68]

In the shadow of these anxieties the King marched to Durham. On the way the Comptroller of his Household Sir Harry Vane, who was becoming ever more favoured as a confidential adviser, splendidly entertained him at his country seat, Raby Castle. On Sunday, May 5th, the Bishop, preaching before him in Durham Cathedral, recently so much restored and beautified by John Cosin, expounded the duties of obedience to the King, taking the text: "Let every soul be subject unto the higher powers." The King later ordered this excellent homily to be printed and distributed. The citizens of Durham notwithstanding continued to receive and entertain travellers from Scotland and some of them got into trouble for drinking a health to the Covenant.[69]

At Newcastle the King was received on May 6th with ringing of bells and firing of cannon. Again he reviewed his troops and again listened to rumours, delusive or dismaying, from Scotland: reliable news was harder to come by, although Scots came and went at will in the town, in spite of the sentries, sat and drank in the taverns and freely talked sedition to the inhabitants. A Scots courtier, Lord Roxburgh's son, suddenly deserted to the Covenanters, whereupon the King arrested his father. The only result was another desertion, that of the hitherto loyal Lord Southesk who was, justifiably, afraid lest he should suffer Roxburgh's fate because his eldest and youngest daughters were married respectively to Traquair and Montrose.[70]

The principal excitement was the arrival of the fugitive Lord Aboyne, Huntly's second and favourite son, a spirited boy of eighteen, who gave the King the first clear account of what had happened in the north. After the fall of Aberdeen Montrose had sought out Huntly and persuaded him to sign a modified version of the Covenant. A few days later, acting apparently in the belief that Montrose had guaranteed his safety, Huntly entered Aberdeen with his two sons, where, on Easter eve he was to his great indignation, compelled to go to Edinburgh virtually as a prisoner. Since one breach of faith justified another, he got permission for his younger and favourite son, Aboyne, to return home on parole to fetch him money and necessaries. Parole was granted and Aboyne, on his father's instructions, escaped to join the King.[71]

Aboyne believed, rightly, that the Gordons would rise to avenge the capture of their chief. While he was with the King at Newcastle they had already, in a sudden onrush, broken through Montrose's outpost at Turriff, and driven the Covenanters out of Aberdeen although only for a few days. Aboyne now asked the King for ships and men to assist his clansmen from the sea, and Charles dispatched him with a commendation to Hamilton.

He found Hamilton out of humour with the war. He had sailed from Yarmouth with eight warships and about thirty Newcastle colliers used as transports. He had aboard five thousand men, supposedly infantry, although barely two hundred understood the use of a musket. As he approached the Firth of Forth beacons flared up on every hill; the fisherfolk were watchful against him all along the coast; his landing parties in search of water were repelled. He had to fetch all his supplies from the nearest friendly base, which was Holy Island. Small-pox broke out among his troops. To crown all, his mother, emerging from her widow's retirement to fight the battles of the Covenant, announced that she would shoot him with her own hand if he tried to land his army.

This was the first great venture of the King's Ship-money fleet, the warships which were to have been his glory and pride. Cruising ineffectively between the Firth of Forth and Holy Island, it cut a lamentable figure. The polished cannon on the decks fired only once and that was in error. Hamilton had with some difficulty managed to convey ashore the King's proclamation of pardon to those who laid down their arms; he believed that it would be obediently read at the Mercat Cross of Edinburgh and timed a full salute of his guns to mark the moment. The salute was fired, but the proclamation was not read then, or at any time in Edinburgh.

Hamilton himself at first refused, then agreed, to parley with the Covenanting lords. His conduct aroused suspicion and it was widely said that he had conferred for two hours in secret with them at night in a deserted part of the links of Barnbougall. Probably he was the victim of slander and an accident; he had gone prospecting for water with a landing party, the boat had run aground and he had been for a time stranded among the dunes.

To Hamilton, in this baffled state, suddenly appeared the

zealous Aboyne with the King's letter of recommendation. Hamilton was usually jealous of young noblemen who had gained the King's attention and he at once disliked and disapproved of Aboyne.[72] An admiral less sour might have felt the same, for Aboyne was only eighteen and he asked for a couple of warships. Grudgingly Hamilton yielded in part to the King's command, supplied Aboyne with a ship, men and guns and let him go his way. He sailed north, came close inshore at Aberdeen and trained his guns on the town.

Montrose, who had been patrolling the restive Gordon country, hurried back to Aberdeen. Leslie and the bulk of the army had long since gone southward taking the artillery with them, and he saw that he would have difficulty in holding the town against an attack from the sea and a rising of the countryside, especially as the citizens would probably welcome the invaders. He decided to evacuate the town, gather reinforcements and guns at his Perth headquarters, and retake it; better a retreat and return than a rash and possibly disastrous defence. Aboyne, therefore, was able to make an undisputed entry into Aberdeen in the first week of June.

The King meanwhile had left Newcastle after knighting the Mayor, reviewing his troops and ordering the removal of the unsightly wooden galleries which defaced the principal churches of the town.[73]

The weather, which had been unseasonably cold, wet and windy, had suddenly turned to a sweltering heat, darkened and made oppressive by an ominous eclipse of the sun. The heavily dressed infantry slogged their way from Newcastle to Alnwick, mutinously realising, as the thirsty, shadeless march continued, that no adequate arrangements had been made for food, drink or shelter. The lack of water was the worst. At night they slept where they could, the officers disputing for places in the mud-floored rooms of wretched alehouses, and buying up all the poultry they could find, the men grumbling over the dryness of the bread ration as they pitched their tents. Alnwick Castle, through long disuse, was so dilapidated that no decent lodging for the King could be found there; he slept in the adjoining abbey.[74]

Discomfort and disorder increased as they advanced to Berwick where they were joined by some of the men from Hamilton's ships, a reinforcement which only temporarily raised their spirits. The border town, sullenly in sympathy with the Covenanters, was too small to lodge the whole of the King's army. They camped outside, south of the Tweed, in the open ground called the Birks. Charles lived under canvas with his men, in his well-appointed royal tent, round which the formal order of the Court was maintained. Windebanke's son "Signior Tomaso" complained (but not, of course, to the King) that he found his duties of mounting guard tedious and exacting, but Charles, busied as always with letters and proclamations to be considered and revised, imposed heavier burdens on his secretaries than on his soldiers; it was, as one of them grumbled, to " play Pyramus and Thisbe and the Lion too," before all was done.[75]

Astley had rightly complained that the King's lines of communication were too long drawn out, and indeed the centre of the army organisation was still partly in London. The royal secretariat there was responsible for much that had gone wrong; it had planned wagons for transport and portable ovens in great numbers for the baking of bread, but while the secretaries in London proclaimed the excellence of their arrangements, those in the north received nothing they wanted. " It is not as you and your colleagues conclude in your committee, but as we find and feel," [76] they grumbled.

The King did not spare himself. While the camp was being organised he tired out two horses, riding from one part to another, inspecting and encouraging. His conscientiousness could not make up for his lack of military experience, but the troops although wet, hungry and discontented, were momentarily impressed by his activity and received him with ephemeral enthusiasm, which he took for a sign that their hearts were in the war. It was not so: the rising tide of discontent was now swelled by an undercurrent of fear. Rumours of Scottish strength were ever more persistent and a sinister silence on the far side of the border added to the growing uneasiness.[77]

On June 1st Lord Arundel, with the splendid attendance and caparison of the Earl Marshal of England, crossed the Tweed into the rebel kingdom of Scotland. In the first village he read out King Charles's proclamation, calling his subjects back to their obedience, to an audience of barefoot women and gaping children. There was hardly a man to be seen. When the ceremony was over the women offered their eggs and milk for sale, and Arundel's men after buying some of the eggs marched home again.[78]

Next day, Whit Sunday, Charles heard a sermon in his tent. Towards evening news came that the Scots forces under Leslie were a day's march off at Kelso. The time for action had come. A thousand of the splendid cavalry, under Lord Holland, set out towards Kelso at first light on the following morning. Their marching order had been the occasion of an angry scene between the Earls of Holland and Newcastle. Newcastle, as governor of the Prince of Wales, rode at the head of the so-called Prince's troop, who had the honour to carry his arms on their colours. Holland assigned them a place in the rear; Newcastle claimed a place in the van. Holland insisted, whereupon Newcastle had the Prince's colours furled rather than see them so dishonoured. In this order they left Berwick, Newcastle pondering on the challenge which he would send to Holland as soon as the fighting was over.[79]

The cavalry were accompanied at the start by three thousand infantry, but as Holland made no allowance for the different pace of their marching, they were out of sight, reach and hearing by the time he approached Kelso. This was unfortunate, for late in the summer afternoon, out of the deceptively peaceful landscape whose rolling hills and leafy copses gave abundant cover, Holland perceived a huge body of Scottish infantry—eight thousand, he reckoned—closing in upon his column in a well-ordered half-moon. He halted his men. The Scots also halted.

They eyed each other suspiciously in the blazing sun. The Scots had only a handful of cavalry but the highly professional appearance of their infantry was as intimidating as their number. Holland sent a trumpeter to request them to withdraw. The trumpeter came back with a counter-request from Leslie that Holland should withdraw. Holland having no other suggestion to put forward, accepted the hint. His cavalry wheeled about and fled, pursued by derisive shouts from the Scots.

The news of their discomfiture spread fast over the country-side. Two of the King's officers, leaning over the parapet of Berwick bridge that evening and speculating on the fortunes of the cavalry, were rudely interrupted by a passing Scotsman with news of Holland's flight. The account was speedily confirmed by the arrival of Lord Holland himself and all his men. To cover their ignominy, the cavalry started a rumour that the scoutmaster who had permitted them to ride straight into the jaws of the Scots was alone to blame. He was a local man, appointed by the Earl of Arundel, and as ill-fortune would have it, a Roman Catholic. It was not very logical to suspect a Roman Catholic of betraying them to the Covenanters, but the King's cavalry were in no mood for logic. Arundel indignantly defended the scoutmaster on the grounds that he had done good work against the Scots in the time of Queen Elizabeth.[80]

The King meanwhile had received a personal message from the Lord Deputy of Ireland. Wentworth, increasingly worried by all that he heard of the conduct of affairs, was anxious that his master should avoid anything so fatal as a military defeat at the hands of rebel subjects. He sent an active and highly intelligent Scotsman, John Leslie, Bishop of Raphoe in Ulster; this energetic, devoted and trustworthy cleric frankly implored the King to put off all idea of invading Scotland that summer.[81] Charles was still hesitant when the Covenanters' army appeared in force on the opposite bank of the Tweed. With speed and efficiency they made themselves a camp partly of tents and partly of turf and wood huts. The King carefully examined their activities through a perspective glass, and refused to be perturbed either by their nearness or their numbers.

Although the local farmers yielded to the temptation of selling their produce only to the English who were paying scarcity prices, the commissariat of the Scots had been too well organised for this to be of any great consequence. Alexander Leslie managed all with an authority astonishing in that little, gnarled, misshapen body; his manner, homely, friendly yet firm, worked well with the notoriously difficult Scots lords, of whom he had a dozen or more as colonels under him. The remarkable unity and good order of the Scots camp were largely his doing, but he owed something also to the ministers, mostly chosen from the younger men, who not only preached and prayed with fervour but carried arms like the soldiers and worked beside them on trenches and fortifications.[82]

Every company had its standard, stamped in letters of gold, " For Christ's Crown and Covenant," and most also had a piper or a fiddler to keep up their spirits. A tougher race than the English, used to exposure in toil and sport, following the plough or following the deer, they hardly noticed the weather which alternated between heavy thunderstorms and steamy heat and was a constant trial to the English forces. " None of our gentlemen," boasted Dr. Baillie, " was anything worse of lying some weeks together in their cloak and boots on the ground, or standing all night in arms in the greatest storm." [83]

In spite of the dross that the Covenanting party had collected to itself during eighteen months of triumphant progress, the inspiration which moved them to war was still profoundly religious. Even Sir Thomas Hope, the shrewd, calculating, ambitious lawyer, fancied that he caught a whisper from the Lord in answer to his prayers: *I will preserve and save my people.* Simpler men, with no stake in the matter but their consciences, believed in all sincerity that the Lord was with them. Night and morning in the Scots camp, psalms were sung, Scriptures expounded, loud and vehement extempore prayers raised to Heaven. The honest admitted that brawling and swearing also occurred but with so many thousands it was hardly to be avoided.[84]

In the King's quarters a different atmosphere reigned. In the King's mind, when he was at prayer, quietly, in his tent, the war seemed a war for religion and for the authority which was a part of that religion. But it was not a war of religion for the Lords Holland and Newcastle, venomously preparing to fight a duel in the fashionable French manner, three a side; nor for Windebanke's son, sulkily regretting the expensive pleasures of London; nor for Sir Edmund Verney, the King's standard-bearer, who had always thought the war unnecessary; nor for the hedgers and ditchers, the herdsmen and farm-hands who from Herefordshire and Suffolk, Lincoln and Lancashire, had been marched against their will to the border and who were wondering how their families fared, or what stay-at-homes made love to their girls in the June hayfields. Unlike the Scots, they had no ministers to inspire and instruct them. Only the most deplorable off-scourings of the Anglican Church had been routed out to play the part of chaplains. The better of them assumed fastidious airs which annoyed the troops, and the worse chewed tobacco and drank with the men in a way most unfitting to their cloth.[85]

In a camp demoralised with doubt and irritation, Charles called a council to his tent. Although the hostile Lords Brooke and Saye had left him at York, a spirit of obstruction persisted among many of the lords who remained. Lord Bristol, who had never been in the King's favour and had nothing to lose, spoke for several others when he flatly told the King that he must call Parliament before proceeding any further in the religious policy which had driven the Scots to revolt. The disheartened King, unwilling to discuss his policy further in public, gave Bristol a private audience which lasted for nearly two hours.[86] Charles did not agree with him, but he saw clearly from the discussion that he could not, in the face of so much opposition, successfully complete his war on the Scots that summer. In the course of the next few days, after a last vain appeal to London for a loan, he decided to abandon the campaign. He deliberately postponed the achievement of his plans, but he did not change his policy. He would enforce his will on the Scots when he had power to do so; until that time he would put them off with temporary concessions and promises.

Peace negotiations opened, in the English camp, on June 11th and were concluded a week later. The chief spokesmen for the Covenanters were Rothes, Henderson and Warriston with others in attendance. The King's manner, haughty at first, softened later, and he made on some of them—notably on Henderson and Baillie—a very agreeable impression. The King had much of the argumentative and legal-minded Scot in him and his attitude was not unattractive to his fellow Scotsmen; they respected and understood the depth of his religious feelings, while they disagreed with his doctrines. The King was feeling his way, not without subtlety and intelligence, with these men whom he intended in the final event to divide and outwit. It amused him to compel them into embarrassing admissions. When they spoke of the powers of excommunication which they claimed for the Assembly, Charles asked Rothes whether it had power to excommunicate him, the King of Scots. Rothes side-stepped: " Sir," he said, " you are so good a King as you will not deserve; but if I were King and should offend, I think the Church of Scotland might excommunicate me." [87] The King did not appear unduly displeased by this answer.

A few days later when the Earl of Argyll made his appearance, Charles gave him a long audience and permitted him to kiss his hand.[88] Not two months ago, he had wished to proclaim Argyll and Rothes traitors, exempt from all pardon. If in their hearts they did not fully trust his new graciousness, they were not to blame. But they preserved the conventions that the King himself laid down for them, and replied with courtesy when courtesy was offered. Not so Warriston; his trenchant language embarrassed his colleagues, especially Henderson, who was shocked to hear him openly express his distrust of the King's offers. When Charles promised the Scots another Assembly and Parliament to discuss the future of their Church, Warriston declared his belief that the King was playing for time, with the intention of ultimately overruling by force whatever the Assembly might decide. Charles turned on him in royal wrath; "The Devil himself," he declared, "could not make a more uncharitable construction." [89] The King's indignation was genuine because in his anger at such insolence he had probably forgotten that this devilish interpretation of his actions was unquestionably correct.

Warriston spoke out what others only thought. Rothes and Argyll were not deceived, although Henderson and some of the milder ministers—the warm-hearted, voluble Baillie of course—were convinced that the war was over, the King their friend and the Kirk safe. The Covenanters had little to lose by the postponement of the struggle and possibly much to gain. In that, the calculations of their ablest men were wiser than the King's. They were gaining sympathy every day in England, and they had friends abroad. Charles's attempts to borrow troops from the Cardinal Infante to use against Scotland were known and abhorred in Holland, which had suffered much from the King's intervention in their war; a Dutch warship in English territorial waters had recently held up an English merchantman transporting fifteen hundred Spanish soldiers to the Netherlands. This kind of thing made the Dutch sympathetic to any and all opponents of King Charles.[90] France, deeply involved in a war with Spain, might be drawn into sympathy with Scotland on the same pretext. In the meantime an Assembly and a Parliament in Scotland could only build up more strongly the constitutional position of the Covenanters.

With such mental reservations on both sides the Pacification of Berwick was signed in Lord Arundel's tent on June 19th, 1639. Both armies were to disband. The King undertook to come in person to Scotland for the meeting of Parliament and for the Assembly of the Kirk to be called in the early autumn. On the following day many of the English lords were entertained by Leslie at dinner and conducted round the Scottish camp, where the soldiers received them with friendly enthusiasm and the pious wish " God bless His Majesty and the Devil confound the Bishops." [91]

On the border, temporary peace had come. But on the same day, outside Aberdeen, the first battle of the long civil wars was being fought out between Aboyne's Gordons and Montrose's Covenanters. They had not heard of the Treaty.

Montrose had returned with reinforcements and some cannon, the latter in charge of two artillery officers from the German wars, Middleton and Henderson. The first attempt to assault the town on its western side was repelled by the counter-attack of the Gordons, but towards evening a second attack was mounted from the south, across the narrow approach known as Brig o' Dee. On the early morning of the second day, June 19th, Montrose had his batteries moved close against the bridge and, in a day-long continuous cannonade, battered down part of the city gates and the morale of the defenders. The Gordons withdrew leaving the citizens to surrender and Montrose for the third time entered Aberdeen as a conqueror, and for the third time resisted the pleas of some of his officers and of the more vindictive ministers for a general sack of the town.

The fame of the great cannonade re-echoed through Scotland, carrying the names of Montrose's two artillery officers into ballad fame.

> His name was Major Middleton,
> That manned the Brig o' Dee;
> His name was Colonel Henderson;
> That let the cannons flee.[92]

It was on June 24th that Hamilton, still in his character of King's Commissioner, had peace officially proclaimed at Edinburgh and received the keys of the Castle for the King. Already, between the signing and the proclamation, doubt and suspicion had grown, for Charles had publicly announced that the calling of a new Parliament and Assembly must be held to annul the acts of the "pretended" General Assembly of Glasgow. This the Covenanters declared was contrary to the spirit of the Treaty, and Hamilton, making his solemn entry to Edinburgh, was accordingly greeted with cries of "Traitor" or pious exhortations to "Stand by Jesus Christ." [93] The King's use of that insulting phrase—the "pretended" Assembly—added to the mounting unrest and when, on the evening of July 1st, the new Assembly was officially proclaimed by the luckless Traquair, and the bishops were summoned to sit in it, Edinburgh broke into riot. Traquair was rescued from the rabble only by the intervention of some of the better-behaved Covenanting gentlemen who gave him their protection.[94] He hurried back to Berwick to consult with the King.

He found that the King's mood had already hardened. No sooner had the Scots army disbanded than the wilder sparks among the King's officers began to boast that they could have eaten them alive had the King but risked a battle. Huntly, newly released from Edinburgh Castle, had reached Berwick to fall on his knees before his royal master in a blaze of indignation, frustrated loyalty and fatherly pride in the exploits of his favourite son, Aboyne. The King bestowed a number of knighthoods on his gallant officers to console them for not having been able to show their mettle. He also wrote to Attorney-General Bankes and Solicitor-General Littleton to inform him by what means they could compel obstructive sheriffs to collect Ship-money.[95] While they, far off in London, considered the best means of prosecuting these offenders, the King, assisted by Hamilton (who slept nightly in his room),[96] worked out his further policy against the men with whom, a fortnight before, he had signed a treaty of peace.

Traquair now slyly advised the King that no act passed by an incomplete Parliament, one for instance from which the clergy were absent, would be good in law. He therefore advised Charles not to summon the bishops either to the new Assembly or the new Parliament because he would the more easily be able to annul the proceedings of an incomplete Parliament.[97] Charles agreed to this disingenuous plan, and Traquair returned to Edinburgh, with full powers as the King's Commissioner, in succession to Hamilton, to call and conduct the coming Parliament.

For Hamilton himself the King had other plans and he had been freed of the difficult responsibility of acting officially for the King in order that he might act, unofficially, with greater freedom. On July 17th the King issued to him a secret warrant to approach at his own discretion any members of the Covenanting party he chose and to pretend sympathy for their point of view if by that means he could better serve the King. Half spy, half conciliator, and wholly confused, Hamilton was by his dubious, but authorised, machinations to bring only fresh trouble on his master.[98]

The unreality of the peace settlement was already clear. When Charles summoned the Covenanting Lords to wait on him at Berwick several of them, but principally Argyll, failed to appear. The King received those who had come, led by Rothes and Montrose, with a coldness markedly different from his manner at the signing of the Treaty. He objected strongly to what he described as breaches of the agreement on their side—the Edinburgh riots, the continuation of inflammatory preaching, the persecution of those who had remained loyal to him. He declared himself above all unsatisfied with so small a deputation from their party and commanded them to go back and fetch Argyll, Henderson and the provosts of Edinburgh and Stirling.

The lords withdrew, well aware of a rumour raised all round the Court that the King intended to seize Argyll, and very probably the rest of the deputation, as soon as they came back.[99] Had such a stroke seriously been intended and had it succeeded, it would have crippled their party; it was not surprising, therefore, that none of them returned to Berwick. A week later three others appeared bearing their excuses and those of Argyll and hinting that they feared to fall into a trap. The message gave the King the excuse he needed to end all pretences. He curtly informed the messengers that if the Covenanters trusted him so little, he trusted them even less; he would not come to

Edinburgh for their Parliament but would return to London forthwith.

Before he left Berwick, the King sent for Wentworth's emissary the Bishop of Raphoe. He spoke fully and privately to this discreet messenger on the evening of July 27th, saying all that he wished the Lord Deputy of Ireland to know but would not trust to paper. What he wrote was the brief and significant request to Wentworth: " Come when you will, you shall be welcome——" [100]

A year too late, the King was turning for help to the ablest of all his councillors. The Lord Deputy of Ireland was to come home at last.

BOOK II CHAPTER IV REFERENCES

1. *C.S.P.D.*, 1638–9, p. 97; *Harleian Miscellany*, III, 211.
2. Knowler, II, pp. 232–3.
3. Laud, *Works*, VII, p. 425.
4. *C.S.P.D.*, 1636–9, p. 471.
5. The resemblance between the events of the Low Countries in the 1560's and those of Scotland in the 1630's is so close that it is surprising that it should so long have escaped comment. The part played by the nobles (for Rothes read Brederode, for Argyll read William of Orange) is very similar, and the means chosen is the same. Supplications were presented to the government, the mob was encouraged to demonstrate, etc. Much of the similarity was natural, the same causes producing the same effects. But some of it may perhaps have been imitative. There is room for a thorough study of Dutch-Scottish relations during the century of the Reformation.
6. *Bankes MSS.*, 62/28b.
7. *C.S.P.D.*, 1638–9, January 1639 *passim.*
8. *H.M.C. Buccleuch MSS.*, Vol. I, pp. 278, 282–3; *C.S.P.D.*, 1638–9, p. 196; Knowler, II, 246.
9. *C.S.P.D.*, 1638–9.
10. *H.M.C. Buccleuch MSS.*, I, pp. 278, 282–3.
11. *Ibid.*, p. 278; Knowler, II, 287.
12. *Buccleuch MSS.*, I, p. 277.
13. *C.S.P.D.*, 1639, p. 3.
14. *Strafford MSS.*, VII, Wentworth to Laud, February 7th, 1639.
15. *C.S.P.D.*, 1638–9, p. 372.
16. *C.S.P. Ven.*, 1636–9, p. 497.
17. *C.S.P.D.*, 1638–9, pp. 362, 378.

18. *C.S.P.D.*, 1639, p. 234.
19. Burnet, *Lives*, p. 113.
20. *Buccleuch MSS.*, I, p. 282.
21. *C.S.P.D.*, 1638–9, p. 184.
22. *C.S.P.D.*, 1639, pp. 19–20, 49–50, 59, 95.
23. *C.S.P.D.*, 1638–9, pp. 357, 385–6, 437, 505, 564.
24. *Strafford MSS.*, X, Osborne to Wentworth, *circa* Dec. 1638; *C.S.P.D.*, 1638–9, pp. 291–2, 311, 328, 445.
25. *Clarendon State Papers*, II, pp. 19–24.
26. *C.S.P.D.*, 1638–9, p. 362.
27. Rushworth, II, pp. 803–17.
28. *Ibid.*, pp. 512, 555; *H.M.C.*, XII, App. II, p. 216–17; *C.S.P.D.*, 1638–9, pp. 417, 437, 588.
29. *C.S.P.D.*, 1638–9, p. 633.
30. *Ibid.*, p. 90; 1639, p. 300; *Bankes MSS.*, 42/78.
31. *C.S.P.D.*, 1638–9, p. 518.
32. *Ibid.*, p. 620.
33. Laud, *Works*, III, p. 231.
34. Bulteel, *Relation of the Troubles of the Foreign Churches*, London, 1645, pp. 48–51.
35. Laud, *Works*, VI, ii, p. 521; V, i, p. 177; III, p. 233.
36. *Strafford MSS*, X, folio 312.
37. *Breadalbane MSS.*, *Letters*, 1636–9, Nos. 759, 761.
38. Baillie, I, pp. 82–3.
39. Knowler, II, 272.
40. Baillie, I, p. 211.
41. Numerous letters in *Breadalbane MSS.*, *Letters*, 1639–59, refer to the organisation and raising of this army.
42. Baillie, I, p. 213.
43. *H.M.C.*, XII, App. IV, p. 503.
44. *Breadalbane MSS.*, *Letters*, 1639–59, Argyll to Glenorchy, April 6th, 1639.
45. Gordon of Rothiemay, II, 212; Spalding, I, 93–4.
46. *Strafford MSS.*, VII, April 10th, 1639; X, Dec. 10th, 1638, Feb. 10th and 26th, April 19th, June 3rd, 1639; Knowler, II, 300–7, 318 ff.
47. *Strafford MSS.*, X, May 30th, 1639; XI, October 30th, 1638, June 20th, 1639.
48. *C.S.P.D.*, 1638–9, pp. 506, 607, 622.
49. *C.S.P.D.*, 1639, p. 4; Balfour, II, p. 323; Burnet, p. 115.
50. Baillie, I, 195; Row, p. 511; Balfour, II, p. 301.
51. *C.S.P.D.*, 1639, p. 198.
52. Balfour, II, p. 323; Baillie, I, 195–6; *Strafford MSS*, X, Wentworth to Northumberland, 19th April, 1639.
53. Gordon of Rothiemay, II, 220–4.
54. *Ibid.*, 226–7; Spalding, I, p. 108.
55. *H.M.C.*, XII, *Appendix* IV, p. 504.
56. *C.S.P.D.*, 1639, pp. 41, 80–1.
57. *H.M.C.*, XII, *Appendix* IV, pp. 504–5.
58. Aston, *Diary, Surtees Society*, Durham, 1910, pp. 4–5.

59. Knowler, II, 313, 318.
60. *Ibid.*, p. 507; Aston, *Diary*, p. 5.
61. *C.S.P.D.*, 1639, pp. 59, 139; *H.M.C., XII*, App. IV, pp. 507 f.
62. *Ibid.*, p. 509.
63. *H.M.C., XII*, App. IV, p. 508; Aston, p. 6.
64. *C.S.P.D.*, 1639, p. 74; Rushworth, II, ii, p. 1327.
65. Knowler, II, p. 351; *C.S.P.D.*, 1639, pp. 96, 140; Rushworth, II, ii, p. 916.
66. *C.S.P.D.*, 1639, p. 74; Rushworth, II, ii, p. 1327.
67. *C.S.P. Ven.*, 1636–9, p. 545; *C.S.P.D.*, 1639, p. 180.
68. *C.S.P. Ven.*, 1636–9, p. 545.
69. Rushworth, II, ii, 923; Aston, *Diary*, p. 8.
70. Aston, *Diary*, pp. 9–10; *C.S.P.D.*, 1639, pp. 144–5, 155, 167, 173.
71. Spalding, I, pp. 160, 165, 169–71.
72. *C.S.P.D.*, 1639, pp. 126, 127, 146, 331; Guthry, 56–7; Burnet, *Lives*, pp. 121–2, 124, 137–9.
73. *Archaeologia Aeliana*, N.S. XXI, p. 101.
74. Aston, *Diary*, pp. 12–13; *C.S.P.D.*, 1639, p. 368.
75. *Ibid.*, pp. 267, 272; Aston, *Diary*, p. 21.
76. *C.S.P.D.*, 1638–9, pp. 566, 593–4; 1639, p. 270.
77. Aston, *Diary*, p. 14; *C.S.P.D.*, 1639, p. 243.
78. *Ibid.*, p. 272.
79. *Ibid*, p. 267, 283; *H.M.C.* XII, Appendix IV, p. 517.
80. *C.S.P.D.*, 1639, pp. 272, 281–3; Rushworth, II, ii, pp. 937–8.
81. *C.S.P.D.*, 1639, p. 273.
82. Baillie, I, pp. 210–14.
83. *Loc. cit.*
84. *Loc. cit.*; Hope, *Diary*, p. 89.
85. *Correspondence of Jane, Lady Cornwallis*, London, 1842, p. 292; *C.S.P.D.*, 1639, pp. 294, 330.
86. *Ibid.*, p. 294.
87. *Ibid.*, p. 319.
88. *Breadalbane MSS., Letters*, 1639–59, Letter of June 22nd, 1639.
89. Warriston, *Diary*, p. 8.
90. *C.S.P.D.*, June 1639, *passim*.
91. Rushworth, II, ii, p. 960 f; *H.M.C., XII, App.* IV, p. 514.
92. Maidment, *Ballads*, Edinburgh 1871, I, p. 290; Gordon of Rothiemay, II, pp. 276–7.
93. Burnet, *op. cit.*, p. 144; *C.S.P.D.*, 1639, p. 355.
94. *C.S.P.D.*, 1639, p. 370.
95. *Ibid.*, pp. 341–2, 348; *Bankes MSS.*, 5/40 and 41.
96. C.S.P.D.,1639, p. 409.
97. Burnet, *op. cit.*, p. 149.
98. *Hardwicke State Papers*, II, pp. 141–2.
99. *C.S.P.D.*, 1639, p. 407.
100. Knowler, II, p. 374.

BOOK THREE

AN ARMY IN IRELAND
August 1639 - November 1641

CHAPTER ONE

THE RETURN OF THE LORD DEPUTY

August–December 1639

THE Bishop of Raphoe made the journey from the Scottish border to Ireland in nine days, and on August 5th, 1639, put the King's letter into the hands of Wentworth at his hunting-box in the green wooded country near the Naas. Here for some years past the Deputy had been building a stately red brick mansion as a country residence for future governors of Ireland. He studied the architectural maxims of Vitruvius and superintended the design with critical care. The strongly vaulted cellars for supplies of wine and grain were already completed and the walls with their straight, symmetrical, handsome windows had risen as high as the second storey; when the house was ready he hoped to have the honour of entertaining the King there. The urbane and solid structure among the pastures and deer forests was a manifestation of the new Ireland which he had been striving for the last six years to create and of which he had often spoken, with enthusiasm and honest self-praise, to the Archbishop and the King.

Although he had watched the events of the last year with irritation and anxiety, he faced the future without misgiving, for he was accustomed to succeeding in what he himself undertook and did not doubt his ability to solve the English and the Scottish problems as he had solved the Irish. He was confident that he could redeem the past errors of the King's policy and rebuild his shaken authority on a firm foundation. He believed that the motives of the Covenanters and of the English Puritans were political, not religious. They aimed not at bishops and ceremonies, but at monarchy itself " which they would have circumscribed and brought under the government of their narrow and shrivelled-up hearts." [1]   He was right in perceiving that their religious views had significant political consequences, but he was wrong in believing them to be for that reason hypocritical and contemptible. For him it stood out, simple and clear, that the " strait bond of allegiance " was man's first earthly duty and that his heavenly duty was a purely private matter. In his own active and devoted career he was sustained by profound belief, but he was—strangely for so vehement a spirit—of a contemplative mind. He found peace in private meditation and regarded the ceremonies and organisation of the Church as things to be obediently endured because authority imposed them; he lacked the imagination to understand that for others the problem was not so simple, and, when he did not understand, Wentworth's dictatorial temperament led him to condemn.[2]

He received, a few days after the summons from the King, a letter of welcome from his old friend Northumberland, who had with relief and joy heard the news of his impending return. This quiet, proud, efficient nobleman was still unshaken in his loyalty to the King, although the appointment of Hamilton to command the fleet and of Holland to command the army had been a double disappointment to him. The summoning of Wentworth heralded, he hoped, a thorough reform in Charles's executive policy.

Northumberland had been the confidant of Wentworth's personal views on the Scots revolt some months earlier. Nothing would serve in Scotland, Wentworth had then said, but a downright demonstration of the King's power and justice—such a demonstration as his own firm government had given in Ireland. The Scots must first be defeated in war, which would not be difficult if the King's forces were efficiently used; next the King must appoint a strong governor to crush the pretensions of the nobility and reorganise the revenues of the country for the benefit of the Crown. The governor of conquered Scotland must be an Englishman.[3] Wentworth may have meant no more by this emphasis than that he did not wish to see Hamilton appointed, but he had confidence in his own powers, and he may have hoped for the opportunity to prove them in Scotland as he had done in Ireland.

It remained for him now only to settle his public and private affairs in Ireland before rejoining the King in London. Lord Chancellor Loftus, after a long wrangling year spent under arrest in his house in Dublin, was permitted to leave for England to answer before the Star Chamber for some of his misdemeanours. With his fall, the more dishonest speculators at the Council Table in Dublin had been reduced to obsequious silence. The composition of the Council was far from perfect, in Wentworth's opinion, while any of them remained on it, but at least they were balanced by the men of his own choosing or training—more especially his three devoted supporters, Christopher Wandesford, George Radcliffe and Philip Mainwaring, whom he had brought from England with him six years before. Of those with longer experience of Ireland, the most important was the young Earl of Ormonde, of a Norman-Irish family, whom Wentworth had encouraged and put forward, seeing in him an unusual mixture of conscience, ability and traditional knowledge. Before leaving for England, Wentworth initiated in the Court of Castle Chamber a series of prosecutions designed to quell any further rebellion from the Ulster Scots and to profit the Crown. Scottish landowners who had signed the Covenant were brought before the Court on charges of treason and sentenced to the forfeiture of all their lands.[4]

Answering the King's letter, Wentworth assured him of the loyalty and peace of Ireland but urged him to fortify Berwick and Carlisle before withdrawing his troops from the north. " The higher these incendiaries cast their smoke and flame, the higher duties may your Majesty justly call from us your faithful and obedient servants, to the performance whereof I shall cheerfully pass along through all the periods of this life, it being a very narrow and contemptible prospect for me to look upon myself, or anything that is mine, where your Majesty's honour and Crown are so deeply and so importantly concerned." [5]

He arranged for his two little daughters to spend the winter in England with their grandmother. "Nan, they tell me, danceth prettily," he wrote, but he believed that Arabella's French accent was not good. Both girls, he assured her, were well provided for and dowries of ten thousand pounds a-piece would be paid on their marriages. So, from his writing-desk, looking out on the serene summer landscape, with his only son sitting beside him, he set his affairs in order.[6] Neither then, nor for some months afterwards, did he feel any real anxiety as to his master's future or his own.

The same false optimism reigned at Court where the events of the past months were freely misinterpreted. The Scots, with infinitely superior forces, had not fought: therefore the Scots, though stubborn and rebellious, were not strong. The achievement of the eighteen-year-old Aboyne in taking Aberdeen was cried up to prove the power of the King's friends in Scotland. The humiliation of the royal army at Berwick was forgotten, then transformed, until defeat became triumph in disguise, and the poet Cowley could welcome the King with lyrical delight:

> Others by war their conquests gain,
> You, like a God, your ends obtain,
> Who, when rude chaos for His help did call,
> Spoke but the word and sweetly ordered all.[7]

The idea that the King had "sweetly ordered all" was not confined to poets and the Court; for a very short time and for different reasons it was shared by some of the English Puritans and by the Londoners, who received the King on his journey southwards with unusual enthusiasm in the belief that his behaviour to the Scots meant that he had changed his religious policy. The same illusion cheered the King's sister, the Queen of Bohemia, who from her exile in The Hague had followed the course of his policy with increasing anxiety; his renewed friendship with the Spaniards, his unwillingness to help her eldest son to regain his lands and his inability to secure the release of her younger son from captivity in Austria had given her infinite distress. But with sisterly loyalty she attributed his actions to the evil advice of others, fixing her especial animosity on Archbishop Laud. The news of the Pacification of Berwick gave the Queen her first real happiness in many years. She believed that her brother had truly given the hand of friendship to his fellow Scotsmen and might even authorise General Leslie and some of the Covenanting forces to fight for her son in Germany. " My dear brother did all himself," she wrote of the peace which had been made, " in spite of papists and clergy who did all they could to disturb it. Leslie doth offer to go with his troops to the Prince Elector." [8]

In the same month occurred another event to raise her own and her son's hopes. Bernard of Saxe-Weimar, the greatest soldier of fortune then fighting in the European conflict, died suddenly at Breisach on the Rhine. Bernard, in alliance with France and in French pay, had seized Breisach from the Spaniards some months earlier, thereby blocking the vital line of communication from the Habsburg dominions in South Germany to the Spanish Netherlands. The French had assumed that Bernard would obediently place Breisach under their authority. Bernard, aware of the immense power that this fortress gave him in the strategy and politics of Europe, made no haste to do so. Its future was still undecided when he died. He left his army, by testament, to his second in command, the capable Swiss mercenary Erlach, who was thus enabled to offer his services (and with them the immediate possession of Breisach) to the highest bidder.

If money alone counted, the French would evidently gain Erlach and all that he possessed. But a wild hope entered into the usually cautious mind of the Elector Palatine: the army was largely a German army, Breisach was a German town. As a Rhinelander himself and a German, gravely wronged by the House of Austria, he believed he could make an appeal to the heart and honour of these German soldiers, who were known to be restive in the service of the French. If he could put himself at the head of this army, if with its help he could reconquer his own lands on the Rhine, he would become within a few months a prince to be reckoned with in European politics. The prospect was dazzling, and his chances of success were the greater now that his uncle, King Charles, had made peace with the Scots, and might support his enterprise with the promise of an army from Scotland.

The Elector lost no time. Hardly waiting to assemble his formal suite or charter suitable shipping, he put himself on the first boat he could find and hurried to join his uncle at Berwick to procure his consent to the hopeful plan. He missed Charles at Berwick but caught up with him at Durham and accompanied him to London, divulging his scheme as he went. On the journey, all the hopes that he and his mother had built on the recent peace with the Scots were laid in dismal ruin. Everything pointed to the continuance and intensification of his uncle's policy in the old direction.

The Spaniards, unable since the fall of Breisach to send troops to the Netherlands by the overland way of the Rhine, had, with the King's permission, secured the use of neutral English shipping for men as well as money, and while Charles was treaty-making at Berwick the Dutch stopped three English ships in the Channel on suspicion of carrying men from Spain to Flanders. The challenge was justified for there were fifteen hundred soldiers on board, of whom the Dutch took off the greater number, although one ship escaped and put into Portsmouth. Hence the Spanish officers, leaving their men in billets, made their way to London where they strolled between the Spanish embassy and Whitehall, haughtily complaining of the cowardice and perfidy of the English captains for yielding to the Dutch in their own waters. In due course they were allowed to march their men across England, by way of London, to Dover, where shipping was officially supplied to them for the Spanish Netherlands.[9]

Charles, on returning to London, immediately gave orders for the account of the Berwick negotiations which the Covenanters had published to be formally burnt by the common hangman, as unauthorised and seditious.[10] Two days later he assured the Scottish bishops that they need fear nothing from the forthcoming Assembly which he had called in Scotland: " though perhaps we may give way for the present to that which will be prejudicial both to the Church and our own government, yet we shall not leave thinking in time how to remedy both." [11]

Archbishop Laud, perturbed at the way in which the Scots revolt had encouraged the English Puritans, was considering stronger action against their excesses. An unusually large number of conventicles had been detected in various parts of the country during the past year. The worst case was that of a Dover stonemason named Trendall; he could not read, but on Sundays he would expound the Scriptures from seven in the morning until six at night with only an hour's interval for dinner. He declared that the Anglican hierarchy was unpleasing to God, and his audience of cobblers, fishermen and shipwrights with their wives and daughters found great comfort in all that he said.

The examples of Prynne, Burton, Bastwicke and Lilburne had evidently not been effective and Laud cogitated more terrible punishments. As a young man he had assisted with advice at the trial of Edward Wightman, the last English heretic to be burnt alive. Seeing some parallel between Wightman's aberrations and those of Trendall, he wrote to the aged Archbishop of York, Richard Neile, who had presided at the trial, for confirmation of certain details. Neile, a frail, kindly old man who disapproved of flogging in schools felt quite differently about heresy and obediently supplied the details.[12] Happily for Trendall, more pressing problems were to divert attention from him before the horrible precedent could be applied.

Before the end of August the Queen formally received a new emissary from the Pope, an attractive young Florentine nobleman, Count Rossetti. Although Rossetti, like Con before him, had no official standing at Court, being merely a private envoy to the Queen, the King was present when he had his first audience with Henrietta Maria, a circumstance which greatly stimulated the usual hostile rumours. The departing Con was, moreover, given an official escort from the royal navy as far as the French coast.[13]

While honour and consideration were accorded to the Spaniards and the Pope, the Elector Palatine can hardly have failed to observe the suspicion with which his uncle treated those who had fought for the Protestant cause. A group of Scottish officers who had served in the previous year in his own ill-fated army had come back from Germany in the course of the summer. They arrived at Newcastle after the war was over and asserted, on being questioned, that they had come to volunteer for the King. Charles suspected that they had intended to join the Covenanters and, in spite of their past record in his nephew's service, threw them all into prison where they remained for several months.[14]

In Scotland, meanwhile, on August 12th, Lord Traquair had opened a new Assembly of the Kirk in the King's name. On Traquair's right hand walked the King's principal supporter, the Marquis of Huntly, but such lustre as his splendid person shed upon the royal cause was tarnished for those who knew that he was able to appear in public in Edinburgh only because he had been granted special immunity from arrest by his creditors.[15] The episcopal party was badly served at the outset by George Graham, Bishop of Orkney, who, on the day of the Assembly's opening, publicly repudiated both his office and the erroneous belief in episcopacy which had led him to accept it.[16]

The Assembly next proceeded to repeat all that had been done at Glasgow in the previous autumn. Their actions showed that they were pursuing a constitutional as well as a religious reform. The King, by placing churchmen in positions of trust, had curtailed or evaded the influence of the nobles. In Scotland the old medieval struggle, never fully resolved, between the

King and the barons, had taken on a new form shaped by the ideas of the seventeenth century. By making the cause of Kirk and conscience their own, the Scots lords had found the surest way of weakening the power of the Crown by attacking the Crown's instruments, the bishops and the episcopal clergy. In the confusion of religious fervour and political calculation which characterised the Covenanting movement, politics had gained the upper hand. The acts of the Edinburgh Assembly made this very clear. They asserted a right to hold annual Assemblies, which would exercise a regular scrutiny over the King's religious policy. They not only abolished Episcopacy and declared that no churchman might hold any place of civil power, but declared that the appointment of bishops had always been wrong and contrary to God's law. Thus they ensured their own position for the future by retrospectively condemning the entire royal policy for the past forty years.

The King, hearing of this procedure, fully realised the distinction between a reversal of his religious policy and a total repudiation of it. He had been willing to yield to the abolition of episcopacy, having every intention of reimposing it afterwards. It was another matter to agree that it should be proclaimed, from all time, illegal and contrary to God. That he could not allow, and he wrote peremptorily to Traquair to refuse to accept any such resolution.[17]

He wrote too late. Traquair was unable to quell the pretensions of the Assembly who were now planning to impose the political and religious tenets of their party on all Scotland by forcing the entire adult male population to subscribe the Covenant. To make it possible for the King's supporters to do so, the additional clause which Montrose had added for Huntly's benefit earlier in the summer was incorporated in the Covenant, but this merely consisted of a reaffirmation in very general terms of loyalty to the Crown and meant as much or as little as circumstances dictated.

Traquair, faced by a deputation from the Assembly, led as usual by Rothes and Montrose, flanked by Henderson and

Warriston, was either too frightened or too stupid to comply with the King's latest commands, but after a little protest and hesitation accepted the Assembly's resolutions in the King's name.[18] It only remained for the Scottish Parliament, which he opened, also in the King's name, on August 31st, to give to the resolutions of the Assembly the force of laws.

Parliament in Scotland was more commonly called, in the European fashion, " the Estates," namely: nobility, clergy, barons (smaller gentry) and burghers. Neither· in its structure nor in its procedure did it at all closely resemble the Parliament of England with its simpler division into Lords and Commons. In practice and tradition the King had used the bishops to control the nobles. The Reformation, by destroying the power of the bishops, had shattered a principal weapon in the King's hand. For this reason James VI had fought and won the struggle to bring back the bishops; for this reason he had coined his catch phrase " No Bishop, no King." Because of this the King, Wentworth and Laud, as well as the King's friends in Scotland, believed that the cause of the present rebellion was not the religious fervour of the people but the political ambitions of the nobility.

The superficial ingenuity which had inspired Traquair to argue at Berwick that the King could the more easily disallow the action of Parliament if it met in an incomplete form, without the bishops, was misapplied. The absence of the bishops in the Parliament of 1639 gave the Covenanting lords the opportunity for which they had been waiting to gain control of the government of Scotland. Once they had established themselves in power, all the King's horses and all the King's men would never again dislodge them.

The Scottish Parliament was in the habit of choosing a small committee known as the Lords of the Articles. This body was the intermediary between the Council, or the King, and Parliament. It acted as a committee on all proposed legislation, and the recommendations which it made to Parliament were usually accepted as tantamount to commands; on occasion the voting rights of the Estates were delegated to it. It was difficult to keep a full Parliament in session for more than a few weeks at a time in a country as sparsely populated as Scotland; the country's day-to-day affairs could hardly be carried on with all its principal citizens away from home. Parliament was therefore adjourned, often for very long periods. During the adjournments, the Lords of the Articles exercised the authority of the whole body. To control this committee was therefore to control Parliament, and successive Kings had, with greater or lesser effect, striven to do so. The Lords of the Articles were selected from each of the Estates, and the manner of their election had varied greatly over the centuries. Of late years the nobles and clergy had come to have the chief say in the matter, and the King had relied on the clergy to see that his own supporters were well represented.

In the Parliament of 1639, with no clergy, the question immediately arose: how were the Lords of the Articles to be chosen? The nobility asserted their right to decide on the new procedure and debated the matter behind closed doors for nearly five hours.

In this lengthy debate Argyll and the Covenanters had the best of it and nominated a majority of their own men for all three Estates. But it was evident to the far-sighted Argyll that he might not always be able to count on a victory of this kind if the nomination of the Lords became the exclusive concern of the nobles. He suggested therefore that in future each Estate should make its own nominations. This apparently democratic suggestion was based on the knowledge that the Covenanters could make and control a majority in the lesser Estates, the barons and burgesses, and this would stand them in good stead if the King were to create for himself a faction among the nobles.[19]

The Covenanters now controlled this particular Parliament and this Parliament might easily come to control the future destinies of Scotland. Once it had made the acts of the Assembly into laws, confirmed the abolition of Episcopacy and the exclusion of the clergy from secular office, the Lords of the Articles could arrange for the best positions in the King's government, forcibly vacated by his episcopal councillors, to fall into their own hands. With the Lords of the Articles well entrenched, with two of the King's own council—Argyll and Hope—working wholly in the interests of the Covenanters, the King's government in Scotland by the early autumn of 1639 was no more than a beleaguered fortress of which the Covenanters had blocked every strategic outlet and seduced a number of the garrison. Such was the consequence of the King's concessions at Berwick and the misplaced ingenuity of Traquair.

The naked emergence of the political motives of the Covenanters and the increasing influence of Argyll caused anxiety to some members of their own party, foremost among them the young Montrose. He was the hero of the war, he alone had had to face effective armed opposition and he alone had come to Edinburgh fresh from military victory at Brig o' Dee. He alone of the Covenanting nobles—the matter was worthy of notice—had the manners and appearance of a popular leader. His value to the party was therefore considerable and his influence important. He had naturally been appointed one of the Lords of the Articles; but he did not stand with Argyll and Rothes in striving to retain the choice within the control of their party. On the contrary he supported the Royalist Marquis of Huntly in asking that the King be given the right and the opportunity of confirming the appointment of the Lords of the Articles.[20]

This was the first clash between Argyll and Montrose. Their rivalry, which was later to be a dominating element in Scottish politics, arose from differences of character and tradition. Argyll was a Highland chief, born to lead and to govern, nurtured in the knowledge that he would one day exercise powers of life and death over thousands of clansmen, and that his first duty was to protect the land and lives of his people and destroy or subdue their enemies. Intense, concentrated and sincere religious feelings enabled him to accept these inherited traditions as sacred duties which God authorised for him anew every day at his prayers. He was not a small man, reaching for political power

—like Rothes, like Traquair; he was a man naturally born to greatness whose sense of religious mission, whose duties and responsibilities, impelled him to make full use of his abilities. His abilities, at least in organisation and the management of men and affairs, were incomparably greater than those of any other man in Scotland. The extension of his power was therefore, to him, natural, just and God-directed. At times, the Lord greatly blessed his endeavours, which proved to Argyll that they were pleasing in His sight.

The tradition of Montrose was different. He was not a Highlander and although he and some of his forebears occasionally styled themselves, or allowed themselves to be styled, chiefs, they enjoyed in practice no more rights over their fellow Grahams than were commonly exercised by the heads of families in southern Scotland. Their authority was respected by their kin, but it was not, as Argyll's and Huntly's was, the only effective law in a great region of land. Montrose and his ancestors belonged to a small, important group of noblemen whose lands lay along the foothills of the Highlands and whose traditional task had been alternately to defend the low-lying country from Highland raiders and to conciliate and tranquillise the land. The royal policy of successive Scots Kings had made these men by tradition respecters of the law and servants of the Crown. While Argyll's heritage was one of leadership and command, Montrose had been bred to an ideal of service and devotion. He had also travelled widely, had studied both in France and in Italy, had been on easy terms with men of many faiths and nations. He wore his Calvinism with a difference, did not confuse the personal wishes of the Almighty with his own, nor believe that every man who opposed Kirk or Covenant was necessarily damned.

Differences of tradition were accentuated by differences of character. Montrose was of a frank, impetuous character with the unsuspecting nature and cheerful over-confidence of one who had from childhood easily inspired affection and commanded admiration. Argyll, of a more secretive and complex temperament, whose youth had been crossed by family quarrels and jealousies, lacked that generosity of spirit which, in Montrose, made up for many faults. He had no great faith in the goodness of the world or of his fellow men and was vindictive and suspicious.

Both Montrose and Argyll had qualities of mind which raised them above such men as Traquair, Rothes, Huntly or Hamilton. Both men had vision; both worked for something greater than the mere winning of the next trick. Each in his different fashion sought the general good: for Argyll this meant the patriarchal government of Scotland by himself and his friends with the co-operation of the Kirk; for Montrose it meant the maintenance of the King's authority against the sectional ambitions of the few, together with the establishment of such checks on that authority as would guarantee the purity and independence of the Kirk. Of the two, Argyll's idea was to prove the easier of achievement.

In the autumn of 1639 time had not fully revealed these differences. But Montrose's defence of the King's rights was inconvenient: the Covenanters' seizure of political power had been bold enough to provoke criticism. It was essential therefore to maintain unity in their ranks and to stimulate the uncritical support of the people until they were abundantly sure of victory. If the King marched against Scotland again, as they well knew that he would, their chances of defeating him depended on their unanimity.

For this reason an inspired rumour about Montrose was at once circulated in Edinburgh. It was succinctly summarised in a tag fixed to the door of his lodging: *Invictus armis, verbis vincitur.* " Unconquered in arms, he was conquered by words." The tale went round that the fearless champion of the Covenant had been talked over by the King in private at Berwick and was no longer to be trusted.[21]

The arguments between the Covenanters and the King's friends in the Scottish Parliament were accompanied by disquieting rumours from England. The stream of Spanish troops and money continued to pass through the country; five more shiploads had been disembarked at Plymouth, to pass overland to Dover and thence get the advantage of the shorter passage to the Low Countries. The King remained deaf to the protests of the Dutch ambassador.[22]

An Armada of seventy-five vessels, with an army intended for the Netherlands, sailed up the Channel in mid-September. A Dutch fleet, less than half the size, attacked it, but the Spanish commander, relying on the neutrality, and hoping for the assistance, of the English Government, took refuge in the Downs. The Dutch admiral, Maerten Tromp, who was reinforced within a few days by supplies of ammunition from France, blockaded him. Week after week the two great armaments rode at anchor under the English coast while a third fleet, the King's Ship-money fleet, with the famous *Sovereign of the Seas* among them, watched from a safe distance. The situation was grave enough to embarrass even the King, for the Spanish Admiral instantly invoked the treaty of alliance and asked him to order the Dutch away. Charles, who knew that the Dutch would not relinquish their prey so easily, did not intend to involve himself, or his cherished fleet, in a clash with their navy. He attempted to pacify the Spanish ambassador by selling the Spanish fleet gunpowder at a very high price and assisting a few smaller vessels to run the blockade. Then he went to Windsor and postponed further action while the more indiscreet Roman Catholics, at Court and in the country, declared that the English fleet would certainly be ordered to the help of the Spaniards in the event of a fight. Among the King's Protestant subjects, from the Kentish coast to the Scottish lowlands, ugly rumours multiplied. The King's recent negotiations for help from the Spanish Netherlands against the Scots caused a general belief that the army on board the Spanish fleet had never been intended for the Netherlands but had come to assist the King against his rebellious subjects. Charles unintentionally encouraged these damaging speculations by making arrangements for billeting Spanish troops at Dover and Deal in case bad weather or the hostile Dutch should force the Spanish ships inshore.[23]

At about the same time he sent a party of courtier soldiers to inspect the fortifications of the Isle of Wight. They did little good, for with the cheerful assistance of the governor of Cowes Castle they shot off all the powder in the place firing salutes " in a frolic, at drinking of healths." Later one of their number, the high-spirited George Goring, delighted his companions by scrambling up the ladder to the public gibbet in the main square of Newport, pushing his head realistically through the dangling noose, and calling upon all who heard him to take warning from his untimely end and shun bad company.[24] The royal inspection of the kingdom's southern defences, however ineffective, only added to the general suspicion. Clearly the King was not himself fortifying these places against attack: was he therefore arranging to receive foreign troops to man them, and if foreign, presumably Spanish?

The King had no such intentions. While the Dutch fleet watched the Spanish in the Downs, and the English fleet watched both, the King, receiving representations from the Spanish and the Dutch envoys, pondered on the financial advantages to be gained from both or either. The deadlock was unbroken when the Elector Palatine took his leave, still meaning to place himself at the head of Bernard of Saxe-Weimar's troops, even though he had abandoned the hope of any help from his uncle for this enterprise. As his ship put out to cross the Channel all three fleets, competing in an empty courtesy to the King's nephew, saluted him with a salvo of guns.[25]

A week after the Elector's departure, Admiral Tromp, tired of waiting, opened fire on the Spaniards. What resulted was not so much a sea battle as the massacre of the helpless Armada. Under the onslaught of Dutch artillery and fire-ships, more than twenty Spanish ships ran ashore between Walmer and Deal: fourteen surrendered; several were burnt to the waterline. About a dozen escaped. The Spanish disaster was watched by crowds of joyful spectators from the English cliffs and beaches.

Sir John Pennington, the English admiral, had orders to prevent the fighting, which meant, if it meant anything, that he must command the Dutch to cease fire and close with them if they refused. He knew that to order his men to protect the Spaniards was to invite mutiny and, thanking God for a slight fog and a contrary breeze which excused his inaction, he spent the day in his cabin writing dispatches. When Admiral Tromp had completed the destruction of the Spanish fleet in English territorial waters, he courteously acknowledged King Charles's sovereignty over the seas by striking sail and firing a salute of nineteen guns.

From the south coast to the Scottish lowlands a sigh of relief and joy went up from the King's subjects; in Edinburgh they praised the wonderful mercies of the Lord which had delivered them from the greatest danger of the time; in London and along the south and eastern coasts they thanked God for deliverance from a second Armada; the Walloon pastor of Canterbury, heartened in his losing struggle with Archbishop Laud, composed a lengthy hymn in French to mark the great deliverance:

> Près de Folkestone, Hythe, Dovre et Diel
> Ce combat a esté cruel,
> Horrible et redoubtable. . . .

Spanish soldiers and mariners seeking shelter in the billets which had been ordered for them, were received, if at all, with angry looks and unwilling hands. Their wrecked ships, though the King's Council fulminated from a distance, were plundered by the Kentish fishermen.[26] In spite of this demonstration of popular feeling, some Roman Catholics at Court were indiscreet enough to complain of Sir John Pennington's culpable neglect in abandoning the Spaniards to their fate. At one moment it was even rumoured that proceedings would be taken against him.[27]

Charles was still battling with the aftermath of the great fight in the Downs when he received news—soon after known throughout the country—that his nephew, the Elector Palatine, was a prisoner. Cardinal Richelieu had almost brought negotiations for control of Breisach and the Saxe-Weimar troops to a happy conclusion for France and had no intention of permitting any last-minute attempt by the Elector to disturb his plans. He had him seized and shut up in a royal prison. While the mortified Prince fumed behind bolts and bars at Vincennes, his uncle of England, through his ambassador in Paris, lodged a dignified and useless protest.

In tavern and dinner-table talk among the King's Protestant subjects, the fate of the Elector Palatine provided more grounds for criticism. His two eldest nephews were now both prisoners, the younger, Rupert, in Austria, the elder in France; this was a fine way for the King of Great Britain to look after his sister and her orphan children!

To do him justice King Charles sincerely strove to relieve his nephews, and negotiations were almost continuously on foot for the release of both. But he was mistaken in dismissing the persistent misinterpretation and attack on his policy as groundless and insignificant because the first essential, if he wished to reduce the Covenanters and silence his critics in England, was to regain public confidence.

Lord Deputy Wentworth, who had arrived from Ireland in the midst of these events, made the same error. Convinced that firmness and a strong hand would be enough, he failed to realise that in a country where administration depended in the last resort on the goodwill and co-operation of the gentry, the King could be strong only if he had their support.

Wentworth, in spite of his ability and energy, brought with him indeed the burden of his own unpopularity to increase the dislike and suspicion of the royal policy. He was already known to the foreign ambassadors resident in London, and was soon known to the public, as wholly devoted to the Spanish interest in foreign policy. His conduct in Ireland had made him enemies in England: the City of London detested him for the part he had played in rejecting their offers for the renewal of their grant of lands in Derry. Lord Chancellor Loftus (now in England) and his friends had made his name odious in legal circles by emphasising the high-handed way in which he had used the prerogative to overrule the other Irish courts. Astonishing stories of his arrogance and cruelty were current in London, many of them groundless or greatly exaggerated. Earlier that year, a number of people had been before the Star Chamber on a charge of slandering him, by saying that he had caused the death of a poor prisoner in Dublin Castle by striking him with his cane. They were found guilty of deliberately inventing and spreading this libel,[28] but the case did Wentworth only harm. All London now knew the story and there were many who distrusted the Star Chamber verdict and pitied the slanderers as victims of Wentworth's wrath.

Wentworth's reputation was bad, not only in London; he had provoked the antagonism of all those in the north of England and especially in his native Yorkshire who had, for whatever motives, opposed the patriarchal despotism which he exercised as Lord President of the North. It was the King's singular ill-fortune that his ablest, strongest and most devoted servant had a facility for making enemies and for giving an ugly outward appearance to almost all innocent actions.

The immediate outcome of his arrival was a stiffening of policy towards the Scots. Traquair had been too weak to obey the King's orders to withstand the demands of the Assembly, but now, in the midst of his troubles with the Scottish Parliament, he received renewed instructions from the King couched in much more emphatic terms. Charles told him to refuse altogether to allow Parliament to abolish Episcopacy as " unlawful ": that word was on no account to be tolerated. The King declared himself perfectly willing to quarrel altogether with his Scottish Parliament provided that the quarrel could be made on a political, and not a religious question.

Traquair, thus encouraged, decided to gain time by an adjournment. Two of the Covenanting lords, without his permission, immediately went to London to protest against this interference with the session. Charles, advised it was thought by Wentworth, refused to see them and commanded them to leave London within six hours. This was on November 7th, 1639. On the following day the King dispatched to Traquair an order to prorogue Parliament until the following summer. Traquair did so with little success on November 14th, for the Lords of the Articles claimed the right to remain in session, thus maintaining in Edinburgh a body which exercised a great number of the powers of Parliament, and which continued to protest vigorously against the high-handed closing of the session before any legislation could be passed.[29] Traquair, knowing how ill he had advised the King, hurried to London and in a lengthy exculpation before the King's inner council—Hamilton, Wentworth and Laud—denounced the wickedness of the Covenanters and urged the King to make a second war.

Later, this weathercock politician was accused of having fatally influenced the King's decision. But Traquair only confirmed Charles in an opinion that he had not ceased to hold since he left Berwick. His preparations for next summer's campaign had begun several weeks before Traquair reached Whitehall and he had already sent out, for the fourth year in succession, demands for full payment of that famous temporary emergency tax, Ship-money. Orders for arms had been placed at Hamburg and the English arsenals were hard at work at the King's command; the fortification of Berwick, Carlisle, Hull and the Tower of London went on apace. To the great relief of the King, the party favourable to him in the divided city of London had got their candidate, Alderman Henry Garraway, chosen as Lord Mayor. With Wentworth's efficiency, with money from the City—a loan of £100,000 was hoped for—the King was confident he could subdue the rebel Scots.

Laud, Hamilton and Wentworth united to urge upon him one more measure to ensure success. Wentworth owed his success in Ireland partly to the dexterity with which he had over-persuaded and controlled the Irish Parliament. He believed that, with reasonable planning, the same thing could be done in England. His voice was therefore the strongest in urging Charles to abandon his stubborn resentment of Parliaments and summon in England a Parliament which could be organised into voting him adequate subsidies to quell the outrageous Scots. In the interim he called upon the King's councillors to show their devotion to their royal master by freely lending to him. Wentworth knew very well, after ten years in the service of King Charles, that almost all the men round the Council table —and he himself not least—had made huge profits through the King's direct grants or the exploitation of his financial schemes. The moment had come for them to make some repayment. They could, he argued, easily raise three hundred thousand pounds between them, and he himself put down twenty thousand pounds for a beginning.[10]

BOOK III CHAPTER I REFERENCES

1. Knowler, II, pp. 372, 382; *Strafford MSS.*, X, Wentworth to Charles Price, Dec. 8th, 1638.

2. In a MS. account of his life among the Strafford MSS. possibly written by his tutor and chaplain Charles Greenwood, occurs the following: " He was bred up in Calvin's opinions wherein he was afterwards more moderate preferring piety before contention, labouring to be well grounded in fundamental truths rather than to trouble himself with disputes, and he chose rather to be devout than to make show of it . . . for many of his last years in his devotions he used Gerard's *Meditations and Exercitium Cotidianum*." As a young man he bought *Le Jardin Sacré de l'Ame Solitaire* by Antoine de Nervèze, in which he wrote the inscription *Qui nimis notus omnibus ignotus moritur sibi*. The picture built up by these and other hints is of an essentially meditative and private type of religious belief, not very usual among his contemporaries in the political world. It casts an interesting light on his tragic career and flawed yet noble mind.

3. *Strafford MSS.*, X, Wentworth to Northumberland, August 28th, 1638.

4. *Ibid.*, Wentworth to the Council, July 18th, 1639; *C.S.P. Ireland*, 1633–47, pp. 223, 251.

5. Knowler, II, 376–7.

6. Knowler, II, 376, 378–9.

7. Cowley, *Poems*, Cambridge, 1905, p. 22.

8. *C.S.P. Ven.*, 1636–9, p. 551; *The Letters of Elizabeth Queen of Bohemia*, transcribed by L. M. Baker, London, 1953, p. 133.

9. *C.S.P.D.*, 1639, June, *passim*; *C.S.P. Ven.*, 1636–9, pp. 553, 555, 560.

10. Rushworth, II, ii, pp. 965–6.

11. Burnet, *Lives*, p. 154.

12. *C.S.P.D.*, 1639, p. 421; 1639–40, pp. 80–5.

13. *C.S.P. Ven.*, 1636–9, p. 570; *C.S.P.D.*, 1639, p. 463.

14. *C.S.P.D.*, 1639–40, pp. 263–6.
15. *Register P.C. Scot.*, 1639, p. 122.
16. Rushworth, II, ii, p. 957.
17. Burnet, *op. cit.*, pp. 156–7.
18. *Register P.C. Scot.*, 1639, pp. 131–2.
19. *Breadalbane MSS, Letters*, 1636–9, Letter 786; *Acts of Parliament of Scotland.* v. pp.252–5
20. *Ibid.*, Letter, 789.
21. Guthry, p. 65.
22. *C.S.P. Ven.*, 1636–9, p. 574.
23. *C.S.P.D.*, 1639–40, pp. 18, 22–3, 41; *Breadalbane MSS, Letters*, 1639–59, Letters of September 25th and 30th, 1639; *C.S.P. Ven.*, 1636–9, pp. 573, 575, 577.
24. Rushworth, II, ii, p. 969; Oglander, p. 98–9.
25. *C.S.P.D.*, 1639–40, pp. 22, 24–7, 32–40.
26. *C.S.P.D.*, 1639–40, pp. 33, 35, 45; 1640–1, p. 19; *Breadalbane MSS, Letters*, 1639–59, Letter of October 18th, 1639; Cross, *History of the Walloon Church*, London, 1898, pp. 97–8; *Clarendon State Papers*, II, pp. 72–9.
27. *C.S.P.D.*, 1639–40, p. 37. For this great sea battle see also C. R. Boxer's article on Tromp in *The Mariner's Mirror*, XL, (1954) and his edition of Tromp's journal for 1639.
28. *C.S.P. Ireland*, 1633–47, p. 113; *C.S.P. Ven.*, 1636–9, p. 595.
29. *Register P.C. Scot.*, 1639, p. 142; Burnet, *op. cit*, p. 160.
30. *C.S.P.D.*, 1639–40, pp. 149, 158; Laud, *Works*, III, p. 233.

CHAPTER TWO

THE SHORT PARLIAMENT

December 1639–May 1640

THE explanation of Wentworth's confident belief that he could manage a Parliament was to be found in his own experience. Not only had he managed an Irish Parliament, he had very nearly managed the last English Parliament. In those days he had been one of the principal Parliamentary leaders in opposition to the Crown but his aim had been to achieve an understanding with the King in the interests of Parliament. He had failed to do so because the King and Court had blankly refused to co-operate; owing to their intransigence the leadership of the House had been taken out of Wentworth's hands by the more extreme Sir John Eliot.

Eliot was now dead and Wentworth knew, or thought he knew, from his own past experience the calibre of the surviving Parliamentary leaders—John Pym, William Strode, John Hampden, Denzil Holles. He knew that managing a Parliament depended on the intelligent co-operation of the King (or his Deputy as in Ireland) with those in the Commons who understood Parliamentary strategy and were working in the King's interest. He believed that it would be possible to organise a vocal Court party in the House which, if it could count on an intelligent response from the King's council, would be able to outmanœuvre the old opposition. With his own intimate knowledge of the moods and reactions of the House of Commons, he did not doubt his ability to supply that co-operation. In this confidence he awaited the assembling of the English Parliament in April. With the King's permission he also summoned the Irish Parliament for March so that its obedient behaviour, on which he could count, would provide an example to England. In the meantime all his efforts were bent on making effective preparations for war on the Scots.

A small Council of War was appointed to decide on the necessary measures and this time the King seemed willing to employ those who had the most knowledge of military and naval matters. Northumberland was appointed General of the future army and Secretary Windebanke had the delicate task of telling the last commander-in-chief Lord Arundel that he was not merely superseded but excluded from the Council of War.[1]

Windebanke seems to have acquitted himself tolerably of this duty. The little man's hands were, that winter, inordinately full of business, for the King had dismissed the other Secretary of State, Sir John Coke. Coke was seventy-five years old and had always been slow, old-fashioned in his ideas and rather obstinate. He was suspected, perhaps unjustly, of taking bribes from the Dutch, as Cottington probably did from the Spaniards and Windebanke from everyone, but his going left a valuable appointment vacant and stirred up a chatter of intrigue.

Windebanke was too busy to act as secretary to the Council of War and, before a new Secretary of State was chosen, it was essential to put at least some competent clerk into this post. The place was one of trust rather than of profit, and choice fell on Edward Nicholas, an unassuming man who had already spent half a lifetime serving the Court in various secretarial capacities. One of the King's few happy chances in that evil time made him decide on this honest, painstaking, faithful servant, who was to become the unrewarded, unreproachful general factotum of the Royalist cause through twenty disastrous years.

The Council of War, with Wentworth dominating and Nicholas taking notes, met regularly three times a week throughout the winter, the King himself being frequently present. On paper, the Council did well. The defences of the Tower were set in order, and those of Berwick made rapid progress. Hull was to be garrisoned with troops from Ireland. In spite of a stormy winter, with destructive gales, heavy snow and floods in Essex and the fens, preparations at these strong points seemed to be satisfactory. In the very heart of the Covenanting country, the King held Edinburgh Castle, the only remaining fruit of the Pacification of Berwick. His garrison there was commanded by the tough old soldier Patrick Ruthven. Before the supposed peace with his Scots subjects broke down he had managed to send men and supplies to stand a six months' siege if necessary, and more ammunition was from time to time smuggled in, disguised as barrels of beer.

Plans were made for the manufacture of swords in England at the rate of 1,000 a month, and for a corresponding supply of muskets, light cannon, powder and shot; others were to be bought abroad, the whole to serve an army of 35,000 foot and 3,000 horse. Portable bread ovens and flour mills were arranged for, and the usual inventors who put forward ingenious plans, such as that by which a single man could fire two hundred muskets simultaneously, were briskly dealt with. Measures were also taken to prevent the exploitation of so-called "dead pays" by officers who made false musters. For this offence the death penalty was decreed, but in order to remove the temptation the pay of the officers was to be exceptionally liberal and—of course—prompt.[2] The lack of good officers having been a principal weakness of his army in the previous summer, Charles was full of gifts and promises to distinguished Scottish and English soldiers serving abroad, some of whom accepted his offers. He was also in treaty with the government of the Spanish Netherlands for arms and men, and a little later he opened similar hopeful negotiations with the King of Denmark. His diplomatic soundings were not exclusively military. His daughters, Mary and Elizabeth, were nine and five years old, and he appears, in the course of the winter, to have made tentative and very secret offers of the elder to the King of Spain for the Infante Don Balthasar Carlos and of the younger to the Prince of Orange for his son.'

The winter was thus on the whole profitably occupied, although the Court did not unlearn its habits of frivolity and intrigue. Wentworth, had he more carefully considered the men and motives which he despised, would have been aware that to work a thorough reform in the royal administration he needed more than his own and the Archbishop's energy, Northumberland's solid ability and the honest care of Edward Nicholas.

From November onwards the King was daily rehearsing the masque which was to be given at the Christmas revels; this, one of the most elaborate ever to be mounted, may have served a lesser purpose in keeping some idle hands out of mischief. Although the King and—rather surprisingly—the Master of the Ordnance, Lord Newport, found time to take part in it, the performers were mostly drawn from the smaller fry of Whitehall. Davenant had supplied the words, Inigo Jones the decor, and the subject was yet another variation on the King's favourite theme: it represented the furies of disorder and rebellion stilled by " the great and wise Philogenes "—the King who loved his people.

Two fashionable marriages varied the Court's routine, the King giving away the brides in person and the Queen helping in the ceremony of putting them to bed. These successive events, and a third which was intended to follow, represented policy as well as pleasure. The bridegrooms were the sons of the Earl of Cork, the most successful of all the entrepeneurs in Ireland and still so rich, even after a brush or two with Wentworth, that the King thought it wise to flatter him in hopes of a loan. Giving three well-born and well-dowered girls to three of his sons was an act of royal forethought, but the bridegrooms were very young and the second bride babbled so indignantly to her girl friends of her disappointment on the wedding night that the third intended bride drew back and even appeared in public on the arm of a previous admirer. The third intended bridegroom, a formidable young tough, who took after his father, instantly challenged the rival to a duel. All this pleasingly diverted the Court from more serious business, but did not, in the end, much profit the King. The Earl of Cork had kept the careful habits of his humble origin; he made the same pair of expensive shoes serve each bridegroom in turn, and, when the weddings were over, he packed his pretty daughters-in-law into a hired coach and drove to Court with them to tell the King that he could not, with so many family responsibilities, spare any money for a loan.[4]

There was frequent speculation at Court on the appointment of a new Secretary of State to replace Coke. Wentworth was in favour of the Earl of Leicester for the post; he was brother-in-law to Northumberland and represented the same moderate and intelligent point of view. The King, however, was entirely averse to this choice, and Hamilton, later supported by the Queen, strongly urged the claims of the pushful Sir Harry Vane, the Comptroller of the Household. A professional courtier, and a man of the world, Vane, for all his ambition, did not think himself ideal for the post; he wrote slowly and lacked method, two embarrassing drawbacks since he would be expected to take full notes at council meetings.

Wentworth neither liked nor trusted Vane and, with that harsh indifference to other men's feelings which was his greatest failing, chose this moment to offend him by an act of astonishing tactlessness. The King had decided to gratify Wentworth's own yearning for worldly greatness by raising him from a Viscounty to an Earldom. Wentworth chose for title the name of the region in Yorkshire where his lands were chiefly situated, Strafford. But he wished also to have a courtesy title for his only son. At some remote period of the Wentworth family history they had been associated with Raby Castle, the present seat of Sir Harry Vane. The new Earl of Strafford asked the King to make his son Viscount Raby. Vane was justifiably indignant and his indignation was fully shared by all his friends and by all Strafford's enemies. For a few weeks, while the outrage was news, the Court was tacitly divided into two camps on the rights and wrongs of Vane and Strafford.[5] It was unfortunate that Strafford should have exercised his talent for making enemies at a time when he most needed friends, but an error which might have been trivial in its consequences became serious when, on February 3rd, 1640, the Queen and Hamilton got their way and Vane, much to his surprise, was appointed Secretary of State.

This was not the only new appointment that winter. The old Earl of Stirling, the unpopular and ineffective Secretary of State for Scotland, conveniently died. The broad hints of Traquair, who had long had his eye on the place, were disregarded by the King, who appointed instead Hamilton's brother, the twenty-four-year-old Earl of Lanark, a reserved, melancholic young man, obedient to his brother's commands.

The most important change was caused by the death of Lord Keeper Coventry. This distinguished, traditional and moderate man was an old friend of Strafford's. Although he had steadfastly supported the King's policy from the beginning of his reign and had upheld the legality of Ship-money, he was a respected and respectable figure. Within ten days of his death the King appointed as his successor the truculent and highly unpopular Finch, who took over his new honours and responsibilities with " such a clatter " of self-importance as to irritate and annoy his subordinates and his fellow councillors.[6] Instead therefore of having the co-operation of men whom he trusted, Strafford had seen no fewer than three posts of influence in the State and at Court fall into what he could only regard as the wrong hands.

An air of confident gaiety prevailed at Court. The Queen was pregnant, always a cause for congratulation and rejoicing, and the King was in the highest good humour. He sat late at cards while Windebanke's assistants waited impatiently to all hours of the night with letters for his signature.[7] From Mortlake he ordered new sets of tapestries which, before spring came, were " all ready finished upon the looms." [8] The masque, assiduously rehearsed for nearly three months, was pronounced with complacency by Inigo Jones to be the finest he had ever staged. The Queen's mother, the royal children and a distinguished throng of courtiers and ambassadors were edified by the sight of the King, in silvery blue, and the Queen, attired as an Amazon, descending from the clouds to vanquish the furies of rebellion.[9]

Some days after this performance another delegation from the Covenanters reached the Court, on February 20th, 1640. It was again led by Lord Loudoun, a dour, intelligent lawyer who had risen to prominence in the party during the last year as a principal henchman of his cousin Argyll. This time the King agreed to see them, though without any intention of granting or even receiving their requests. They still obstinately demanded, " on the knees of their hearts " as they rather oddly put it, that he should accept the legislation put forward by the Scottish Parliament as well as the new method of choosing the Lords of the Articles.[10]

The Scots, on the way to London, had distributed copies of their own account of the Pacification of Berwick, the account which the King had had burnt in the previous August. In open conversation they had compared the King to a truant schoolboy who had promised them everything when his schoolmaster Laud was not by, and had taken it all back again when the Archbishop resumed his sway.[11]

In the circumstances the King received them with asperity [12] and rejected their demands. They had expected some help from his Council, especially Pembroke and Salisbury, both of whom were suspected with some justice of having assisted in the distribution of Covenanting propaganda. But in this the Scots were disappointed, for when Pembroke was confronted, in the King's presence, with a letter which Rothes had sent asking for his good offices on behalf of the Scots, he thought it wiser to reject it with indignation.[13] The time had not come for him to show his hand.

While the King coldly argued with Loudoun and his fellows,

he wrote privately to the Royalist commander of Edinburgh Castle, instructing him to be in readiness to fire on the town as soon as he should think it necessary.[14]   Charles had no intention of coming to any peaceful agreement with the Scots, but he held their commissioners in England with delays, questions and arguments for another reason.   Some time during the winter Traquair had sought to regain his favour by placing in his hands a copy of a letter which the leading Covenanters had written to the King of France.   This rhetorical composition implored Louis XIII to show his ancient friendship for Scotland by mediating for them with his brother of England.   They had nothing to conceal, the Covenanters declared, and were willing that all their acts should be illuminated as with a ray of sunlight.   The malicious asserted that there had been some trouble about this phrase between Montrose, whose poetic inspiration it was, and Maitland who had asserted that the word " rai " meant not a sunbeam but a vulgar kind of fish.[15]

This letter, in the King's opinion, was evidence enough to put all its signatories at the mercy of the law.   They were the best known of the leaders—among others, Rothes, Montrose, and Loudoun himself;   Argyll had as usual avoided incrimination. If it could be released at the moment when Parliament met, the King thought it would demonstrate that the Covenanters were shameless traitors seeking the intervention of a foreign power in the affairs of Great Britain.   It might well be the means of rallying the English against the Scots, and if one of the traitors, Loudoun, could be confronted in person with his crime and arrested for it, the dramatic effect of the revelation on Parliament assembled at Westminster would be all the stronger.

Charles's natural faith in his own government contributed as much as the possession of this letter to the confidence with which he awaited the assembling of Parliament.   Manifestations of popular discontent continued without materially disturbing his optimism.   He believed, and the over-confident Strafford ministered to that belief, that all opposition, whether secular or religious, was the work of a minority.

The vicar and people of the suburban parish of St. Giles'-in-the-Fields urgently complained to the Privy Council of three Catholic priests who were openly conducting missionary work. They had already twenty-one conversions to their credit so that—the vicar palpably exaggerated—there would soon be no Protestant parishioners left.[16] The Council took no action in response to the complaint. Meanwhile, quarrels between the Laudian clergy and their parishioners continued. One or two obstinate men, lamented the vicar of St. Ives in Huntingdon, could disturb a whole parish: his entire flock, once amenable, had refused to come to the altar rails to receive the sacrament, because two recalcitrant Puritans had set a bad example. The significant thing, overlooked by the vicar of St. Ives and the King of England, was not that *two* began the trouble, but that all the rest joined in.[17]

Puritanism mingled with local resentments to cause scenes of violence. The mayor of Sudbury insolently shut up a government official in a cage used for criminals, where the people pelted him with mud and stones in spite of the joint efforts of the vicar and parish constable to rescue him. In Herefordshire one of the bishop's secretaries who attempted to establish the episcopal right to some common land was killed by a rabble of poor folk. More significant were the proceedings at Lewes Quarter Sessions when a group of Sussex justices, led by Anthony Stapley, registered a formal protest against the alterations and innovations recently made in some of the neighbouring churches. These things, they proclaimed, were contrary to the will, and insulting to the glory, of God.[18] In Northumberland, and more especially at Newcastle, the Puritans gave trouble of a more instantly dangerous kind. Scots known to be Covenanters were freely entertained and allowed to roam about the borders, spying out the King's military preparations. The mayor of Newcastle, accused of having allowed two of them to make a thorough inspection of the city walls, replied coolly that he had taken them for merchants travelling on business. The northern churches meanwhile were said to be half-empty while Puritan meetings were so full and so frequent as to defy all attempts at suppression.[19] In London at the Middle Temple Edward Bagshaw, an influential and popular reader, announced a course for the coming term to show that by an ancient law—25 Edward III Cap. 7—the clergy were not entitled to any say in Parliament either in civil or religious matters. Lord Keeper Finch ordered him instantly to alter his subject. Bagshaw, feigning the astonishment of innocence, argued that the subject was a most interesting one in law. Finch conceded that it was, but at the present time " unseasonable," and Bagshaw capitulated.[20]

Resistance to the collection of Ship-money was by this time almost nation-wide; even the county of Devon with its powerful seafaring tradition was as sullen as inland Bedfordshire. The Sheriff of Yorkshire encouraged the gentry to refuse to pay, and the Sheriff of Northamptonshire reported that he could not assess the county because the Grand Jury, going flatly against the majority decision in the Hampden case, had declared Ship-money illegal.[21] Finch roundly told the judges before they rode on circuit, to insist on the legality of Ship-money and the duty of paying it. " I know not how it comes about," he complained, " that there is not alacrity and cheerfulness given to the obedience of His Majesty's writs for Ship-money."

In London the Royalist Lord Mayor Garraway and the aldermen whose interests in Spanish trade bound them to the King were in a minority against their discontented colleagues. Apart from the Londonderry business, still bitterly resented, an ill-timed quarrel broke out between the powerful Merchant Adventurers and the Duke of Lennox. Charles had recently granted to his young cousin the exclusive rights of levying the dues on the shipment of raw wool from London. In theory these dues were intended to curtail the export of material which could be worked up in England. The profitable trade of the Merchant Adventurers Company was at the cost of the English weavers and knitters, and the King's attempt to check a process which was altering the structure of English economy and causing widespread distress had been prompted in the first place by anxiety at the growth of unemployment in the wool-working districts. The idea behind the intervention was benevolent but its implementation was, as usual, defective. The inspectors and collectors employed by Lennox had no responsibility except to bring in enough money to satisfy the Duke's stewards and to help themselves to a few pickings by the way. The inevitable trouble between the Duke's men and the merchants reached a peak during the spring of 1640 when Lennox, asserting his rights with the co-operation of the King's navy, impounded all ships with cargoes of wool in ports throughout the kingdom.[23]

The King and his friends accidentally stimulated the opposition while their deliberate efforts to placate their critics were few and misconceived. The recalling in the previous year of more than twenty different monopolies, patents and other forms of interference with trade and manufacture had not been wholly successful and the King found it necessary to abolish a number of the same monopolies over again,[24] which suggests that the previous ordinance had been disregarded.

To show his goodwill he ordered the release from prison of two members of the 1629 Parliament who, partly owing to their own obstinacy, had remained under constraint for the whole of the intervening eleven years. William Strode and Benjamin Valentine might, at any time, have bought their way out by paying the fines imposed on them for their opposition to the King's will in the House of Commons, but as they denied the justice of their condemnation they had preferred to stay in prison. Neither of them on his release showed any gratitude to the King and each went down into the country to organise his own re-election to the coming Parliament.

The election cast its shadow far before it. Lord Keeper Finch, when he instructed the judges in their special duties before they rode on circuit, had touched on other questions beside Ship-money. "There are some," he said, "that affect popularity, diving into the people's hearts with kisses, offerings and fawnings." The judges were to keep a sharp watch for any signs of this reprehensible behaviour among sheriffs and magistrates and were to prevent the neglect of justice, law and order which might arise from it.[25]

This "diving into the people's hearts" was suspect because those who did it had ulterior motives, and although Finch may have had habitual corruptions or deflections of justice in mind, it is more likely that he was thinking of the forthcoming Parliament. "Kisses, offerings and fawnings" by local great ones within two months of a projected Parliament would be mainly directed to securing the suffrage of the freeholders for candidates of their own choosing.

In theory Members of Parliament were elected in the county by freeholders and in the towns by burgesses of a certain standing. In practice, elections frequently degenerated into contests between rival landowners or rival families to get their friends and dependants chosen. Sometimes, to make certain of a seat, the same man would be a candidate in more than one borough. Should he be elected for both, he could make his choice between them afterwards. At other times a bewildered sheriff or mayor, caught between rival factions and anxious to offend no one, would make a double return and leave it to the House of Commons themselves to decide at Westminster which candidate had been truly elected. Bribery, intimidation, flattering promises or dishonest counting of votes were common. But in spite of this disorder something like a representation of local and national interests was obtained. The promises made, and sometimes implemented, were truly related to local needs; the men returned to Parliament were rarely professional politicians—a breed unknown outside the close circle of the Court and government—and they almost always bore some relation to the places they represented, having interests or lands or kinsfolk in the neighbourhood. A great number were lawyers, some were local squires, some the sons, and some the secretaries or stewards, of noblemen.

Party organisation as such hardly yet existed, although the Court, for the past hundred years, had been in the habit of securing seats in Parliament for the principal advisers and officials of the Crown. This was an accepted procedure, but when the critics of the Crown showed signs of attempting the same thing so as to ensure coherent representation in the Commons, the Court looked upon it as an outrageous conspiracy. In 1640 the critics of the King had what they had never had before: in the directors of the Providence Company, that largely Puritan group of influential men, they had an executive body which could to some extent unite and organise the efforts of their friends.

The King's Council on the one hand and the Providence Company on the other may be said faintly to foreshadow, in their relation to the forthcoming election, the executive committees of the party in power and of the opposition party. But in this peculiar and somewhat fortuitous political development the heads had come into existence without bodies. Neither the Council nor the lords and gentlemen of the Providence Company could count on the support of anything that resembled a political party. For the last seventy years a " Court " party and a " Country " party had been vaguely spoken of, but the terms meant nothing definite. No programme and no defined principles held these " parties " together. The greater number of the Commons were governed by family loyalties, by personal obligations and by the local interests of their boroughs, and might be swayed now one way, now another.

When it came to an election, the Court had to depend in the last resort not on those who supported its policy and principles but on the intelligence and zeal with which courtiers could exploit local rivalries and influence to get their friends returned to Parliament. The same was true of the opponents of the Court, whose leaders were now, almost for the first time, acting as a co-ordinated group.

There was in truth little to choose between the methods employed by the Court and by its opponents in striving for the upper hand in counties and boroughs. Lord Saye busily organising the return of his two sons to swell the opposition was neither more nor less reprehensible than the royalist lords who mobilised their families and dependants in the interests of the

Court. The courtiers, finding local sympathies aroused and marshalled against them in more regions than usual, cried out indignantly on all this " bandying for places." Their own clergy were encouraged to preach political sermons on obedience, but when Puritan preachers were found to be preaching political sermons too, that was a monstrous interference with the election. Both sides, of course, behaved with primitive dishonesty and each was shocked at the behaviour of the other. When Edward Nicholas, the Court candidate, failed to be returned for Sandwich because of a lying tale circulated in the town that he was a Papist, the King's supporters had legitimate reason to complain. But so had the opposition, when the royalist mayor of Hastings, overruling the will of the majority, returned the Court nominee, Windebanke's nephew.[26]

Early in March, while the elections in England were still incomplete, Strafford left for Ireland carrying the King's authority to raise the Irish army to nine thousand men and to obtain subsidies from the Irish Parliament. Not doubting his success, the Court already counted with confidence on this fiery and loyal force to destroy the Scots.[27] Strafford himself, more realist and less light of heart, punctuated his journey to Chester, where he was to take shipping, with the dispatch of salutary advice. He was irritated to hear that the Yorkshire gentry were making trouble about Ship-money, and urged that they be firmly reprimanded, but he did not doubt that one single, resounding victory, such as that which Charles would shortly win against the Scots, would establish his authority for good.[28] An untimely attack of gout delayed his crossing to Ireland: " that God should give me so good a heart only to take my legs from me in such a conjuncture of His Majesty's affairs as this is," he lamented, between mockery and earnest, to Laud, and when he managed to reach the sea, the winds were contrary. Parliament had been in session for two days before he reached Dublin and formally communicated to it the King's commands.

The Irish, Lords and Commons alike, received him with deferential enthusiasm. Publicly thanking the King for having bestowed on them " so just, wise, vigilant and profitable a governor," they voted the necessary subsidies and cheerfully agreed to enlarge the army, during the next two months, to a total of eight thousand foot and a thousand horse. Pending the collection of the subsidies, Strafford wrote to Cottington to hold up all the rents of the Londoners' forfeited estates in Derry to pay the Irish troops. At the same time the episcopal clergy of Ireland, gathered in Convocation, added their contribution to the moneys already voted in Parliament. In little more than a week Strafford had achieved all that was necessary in Dublin and could set sail for England again in a ship well named the *Confidence*. The English Parliament had but to follow the example of Ireland, he wrote triumphantly, " and His Majesty will have the Earl of Argyll and the rest of them very good cheap." [29]

The Court, in the quiet interlude between the elections and the meeting of Parliament, prepared for Easter. In Holy Week, Laud had the pleasure of presenting to the King young Nicholas Ferrar, a shy but welcome visitor from the Anglican retreat at Little Gidding. He had come to present to the Prince of Wales a sumptuous illustrated Bible that the ladies of the Ferrar household had arranged and bound for him. The King had time for a long interview with the devout young man and a long, admiring contemplation of his beautiful books, about the arrangement and composition of which he asked many questions. He sympathised with Master Ferrar's misfortune in being afflicted with a stammer, and discussed its cure. Singing, he said, was a help; it was also important to form every sentence complete in the head before uttering it. Determination alone was not enough and pebbles in the mouth were quite useless; he knew, for he had tried.

After his audience at Court, Ferrar carried the book to the Prince at Richmond in time for Easter. Young Charles unfastened the satin ribbons that secured the bright volume with exclamations of joy—" Here's a gallant outside ! " Opening it, and finding it was the Bible—" Better and better ! " cried the tactful child as he eagerly turned the pages, while the little Duke of York asked if the ladies of the Ferrar family would make him, too, a Bible the equal of his brother's.[30]

All this while, from the four points of the compass, several hundred gentlemen were travelling to London for the opening of Parliament. It took place on April 13th, 1640. The King, whose impediment prevented him from making a long speech, left it to Lord Keeper Finch to make his policy known. Finch was well known to all as the subservient Lord Chief Justice who had supported all the King's measures both on the bench and in the Star Chamber; he was remembered, too, for his unscrupulous enforcement of the forest laws in Essex, and as Speaker of the last Parliament, he had been manhandled by some of the Commons for serving the interests of the King and not of the House. He was for all these reasons the last man to persuade a suspicious House of Commons to support the King, and he also lacked the gift of handling a delicate situation. Ten years of uninterrupted authority, during which his every petty ambition had been gratified, had swelled his self-conceit. His speech to Parliament was patronising and arrogant; he made no attempt to persuade, to conciliate or to disarm potential critics.

Never, proclaimed Finch, had a country been blessed with so good a King, so virtuous a Queen, so hopeful a band of royal progeny. The Scots, out of unspeakable wickedness, had rebelled. It therefore behoved the English to grant generous subsidies that the rebels might speedily be crushed. This done, the King would graciously listen to any grievances that they wished to make known. He added that they must repair the insolencies of previous Parliaments by immediately passing a retroactive Bill, prepared for them by the royal councillors, granting the King Tonnage and Poundage for the whole reign: they were in fact to confirm the customs duties which Charles had levied on his own authority for the past ten years at the increased rates to which he had recently raised them. As Finch concluded his address, Charles dramatically handed to him the Covenanters' letter to the King of France. But this revelation of treason, which was expected to rally all loyal Englishmen against the Scots, failed of its effect. The contents of the letter neither convinced nor interested the Commons, while the tone of Finch's speech irritated them considerably.

In the first week of the session petitions complaining of Ship-money and the King's church policy came in from six different counties, and the attempts of the King's supporters to keep the Scots' treasonous letter before the House were frustrated by John Pym, the member for Tavistock. The secretary of the Providence Company had served in six previous Parliaments and was able to apply his practical organiser's mind to his knowledge of Parliamentary procedure. He was tacitly accepted as their leader by the King's opponents whose opinions he summarised in a long, clear analytical attack on the royal policy. His friends followed him up and neither Speaker Glanville, nor the two Secretaries of State, nor the various Court nominees and supporters, could force the debate back into the narrow channel mapped out for it in the King's interest by Lord Keeper Finch. The arrest of Lord Loudoun as a traitor for his participation in the Scottish letter to France and Windebanke's report of his preliminary examination before the Privy Council were treated by the Commons with as much indifference as if they were events in the moon.

On the sixth day of the session, the King's critics passed from complaint to action. They moved the re-investigation of the Hampden case; they called for an inquiry into the imprisonment of Strode, Valentine, Holles, and the late Sir John Eliot after the conclusion of the last Parliament; and they accused Finch of having committed a breach of privilege ten years before when, as their Speaker, he had tried to break up the session against their will. They thus implied that the King's judges had broken the law, and that the man he had appointed Chancellor was himself a delinquent.

This was the situation at the end of the first week, when Strafford, who had been delayed at Chester by another untimely attack of gout, at length arrived in London. The second week was spent in the concentrated efforts of the King's party to regain the initiative in the Commons. Convocation, which had met at the same time as Parliament, had virtuously voted a subsidy to the King, but it proved useless to hold up Convocation as an example to the Commons. On April 23rd, St. George's Day, Secretary Windebanke in a flight of eloquence appealed for a glorious gift to honour the glorious day, but the Commons, unmoved, continued to ask for redress of grievances before they voted supplies. The list of these was formidable—Ship-money, the exaction of coat-and-conduct money for the troops of the previous summer, monopolies and the whole variety of economic nuisances, intermission of Parliaments, breach of privilege and, of course, religion.

Strafford, still hopeful, saw in the intransigence of the Commons a strong possibility that they would give offence to the Lords and hoped that, by winning the Upper House, Charles could coerce the Lower House. In pursuance of this new strategy the King in person appealed to the Lords, offering to intermit the raising of Ship-money if they would vote supplies. Strafford, with great eloquence and a more compelling personality than Windebanke, secured a majority in the Upper House to condemn the resolution of the Commons to take grievances before supply. Following up this advantage, Finch, at a general meeting of both Houses, solemnly announced that while they delayed the war had already begun. The rebel Scots had fired on the King's garrison in Edinburgh.

So ended the second week. On Monday, April 27th, as soon as they met again, the Commons declared that the conduct of the Lords in discussing supply was a breach of their privileges and demanded a consultation between both Houses. Strafford believed that an open quarrel between the two Houses was now at hand, but he was thinking of the old assertive leadership of the Commons in the past. John Pym was determined that there should be no quarrel and he had several friends in the House of Lords—Warwick, Saye and Brooke—who were as resolute as he to prevent a breach. The fire that Strafford had tried to kindle was stamped out in two hours' talking. Further news from Edinburgh reached London in the course of the week: not the Scots, it seemed, but the King's garrison had fired the opening shot of the war.

In the Westminster taverns there was wild talk that the populace would burn Lambeth Palace over the Archbishop's head rather than let him make his unholy Bishops' War on Protestant Scotland. Strafford still obstinately believed that, with moderation and dexterity, the King could get his way with the Commons. The effective opposition was the work of a handful of members; the King's spokesmen—Vane, Windebanke and a dozen more—with help from Speaker Glanville could surely wrest the initiative from Pym. He suggested that the Secretaries of State be instructed to reduce the King's demands, to ask for six subsidies only, not twelve as heretofore, and to offer in return, and only after the subsidies had been voted, the grace which had already been offered in the House of Lords— the discontinuation of the present levy of Ship-money.

But the King would not sink his demands lower than eight subsidies, Secretary Vane handled the matter ineptly in the House, and Speaker Glanville, in an effort to conciliate the Commons, hinted at a doubt as to the legality of Ship-money. This, from a notorious King's man, greatly heartened the opposition, and an impertinent message was sent to Whitehall, that the Commons wished to hear Counsel's opinion on Ship-money before they further considered the propositions which had been laid before them.

Vane, whether on his own initiative or not, suddenly tried to break the deadlock. He told the House of Commons that if they would raise the subsidies to twelve and vote them instantly, Ship-money would be abolished. Pym and his friends took this, rightly, as the index of the King's distress. So far from accepting the bribe, they redoubled their demands that grievances, *all* grievances, be settled first.

Strafford believed that something might yet be done to control, cajole or compel this intractable Parliament, but the majority of the King's advisers were against him. The King himself was both angered and agitated by the business-like way in which Pym and his friends had appointed special committees to collect and examine popular complaints against the royal policy. Graver still, it was rumoured that the opposition leaders were in touch with the Scots and intended to bring up the religious grievances of Scotland as well as their own in the House, thus completely reversing the purpose for which Parliament had been called and exposing the King to a fundamental attack on his policy. Faced with this threat the Council met early in the morning on May 5th; Strafford, who came late owing to some mistake about the time, found himself unable to stand out against the majority who, with the King, were strongly for a dissolution. At eleven o'clock that day the King, in a speech of reproof and disappointment, dissolved the fourth unmanageable Parliament of his reign, and the last that he was ever able to dissolve.[31]

BOOK III CHAPTER II REFERENCES

1. *C.S.P.D.*, 1636–40, pp. 193–4.
2. *Ibid.*, pp. 224, 228, 296, 327–40, 398–9, 455, 468; Balfour, II, p. 373; *H.M.C.*, X, i, p. 48.
3. *C.S.P.D.*, 1639–40, pp. 109–11, 368, 420, 434; *C.S.P. Ven.*, 1640–2, p. 62; *Clarendon State Papers*, II, p. 83; Groen van Prinsterer, *Archives de la Maison d'Orange-Nassau*, 2nd Series, The Hague, 1858, III, pp. 159, 169.
4. *Ibid.*, pp. 297, 365; *Lismore Papers, First Series*, V, pp. 112, 118, 119, 148.
5. *C.S.P.D.*, 1639–40, January, *passim*.
6. *Ibid.*, p. 436.
7. *Ibid.*, p. 474.
8. *H.M.C.*, XV, II, p. 296.
9. *Ibid.*, p. 365; the text of the masque *Salmacida Spolia* is to be found in Davenant's *Works* and some designs for the dresses, drop scenes and effects have survived among the drawings of Inigo Jones.
10. *C.S.P.D.*, 1639–40, p. 472.
11. *Ibid.*, pp. 446–7, 557.
12. *C.S.P. Ven.*, 1640–2, p. 23.
13. Rushworth, II, ii, p. 984; Burnet, *Lives*, p. 165.
14. *C.S.P.D.*, 1639–40, p. 558.
15. Rushworth, II, ii, p. 956; Burnet, *op. cit.*, p. 161. In defence of Montrose's French as well as Maitland's it is fitting to record that Cotgrave's *Dictionary* gives " rai "

as another form of " rayon " for ray or sunbeam; he also gives the fish now commonly called " raie," as " rai."

16. *Commons Journals*, p. 41.
17. *C.S.P.D.*, 1639–40, pp. 444–5, 456.
18. *Ibid.*, pp. 260–1, 386; Brilliana Harley, *Letters, Camden Society*, London, 1854, p. 67.
19. *C.S.P.D.*, 1639–40, pp. 321–2, 345, 346, 401, 429, 469, 515 f.
20. *Ibid.*, pp. 522–4; Rushworth, II, ii, p. 990.
21. Rushworth, II, ii, p. 991.
22. *Ibid.*, 987.
23. *C.S.P.D.*, 1639–40, January–March, *passim*.
24. Rushworth, II, ii, p. 1203.
25. Rushworth, II, ii, p. 987.
26. *C.S.P.D.*, 1639–40, pp. 561, 564–5, 580–3, 587.
27. *C.S.P. Ven.*, 1640–2, p. 21.
28. Knowler, II, 393–4.
29. *Ibid.*, 394–403; *C.S.P. Ireland*, 1633–47, p. 239.
30. *Nicholas Ferrar: Two Lives*, ed. J. E. B. Mayor, Cambridge, 1855, pp. 126–37.
31. *Lords & Commons Journals*; Rushworth, II, ii, pp. 1114–20, 1131–7, 1154–5; *C.S.P.D.*, 1640, pp. 33, 39, 61, 64, 76–9, 108–10, 144–5; Whitaker, *Life of Sir George Radcliffe*, London, 1810, pp. 233–5.

CHAPTER THREE

THE SECOND SCOTS WAR

May–November 1640

THE dissolution of Parliament left the King no choice but to proceed with a firm hand. Strafford, in whose strength he trusted, still believed that resolution and efficient management could prevail. At the Council meeting on the day of the dissolution, he brushed aside the doubts of the realist Northumberland, and stirred his more cheerful and more irresponsible colleagues to some measure of activity.

Ireland—he asserted—was the King's to command, and in Ireland an army of 8,000 would be ready in a few weeks to be landed in the Western Highlands, or wherever else seemed best. If the English were slow to help their sovereign to subdue the rebel Scots " You have an army in Ireland you may employ here to reduce this kingdom." That phrase, or something like it, fell from his lips and was scribbled by Secretary Vane into his remarkably incoherent notes.[1] Whether Hamilton made any comments on this project, does not appear from Vane's notes. But Hamilton must have known that of all actions likely to inflame the Scots, and especially the lowland Scots and the Campbells, against the King, this of bringing Irish forces to fight them would be the worst. It could only appear to them as though the King had given the royal authority and arms to the savage forces which for centuries they had tried to check.

After the strenuous Council meeting of the morning, Strafford spent the afternoon of May 5th at his own house in a long session with the Spanish ambassadors. Three envoys to the

Court of King Charles, two from Spain and one from the Spanish Netherlands, now represented the Habsburg interest in England. Since the Spanish fleet had been shattered and the Rhine valley barred by the French occupation of Breisach, the co-operation of King Charles was more than ever essential for the transportation of the necessary troops from Spain to the battlefront in Flanders. The traffic had been quietly increasing for the last year and transports containing three thousand Spanish soldiers had been convoyed from the Downs to the Flemish coast while Parliament was still sitting. But the Spanish and Flemish governments needed a regular, reliable arrangement and were prepared, in their present straits, to pay handsomely for it.

The propositions discussed at Strafford's house on the afternoon of May 5th were dazzling: the Spaniards offered four million ducats in return for a permanent guard of thirty-five English warships to convoy their transports through the Channel.[2] Four million ducats would make King Charles master in his own house again, if he could fulfil his side of the bargain, but the Spaniards would want something more than mere promises before they paid over the money. The King had a fleet fully capable of performing the task if he could find enough sea captains to carry out his orders but, as the Spaniards had discovered during the disastrous battle in the Downs of the previous autumn, the King's power to command his navy was less than his will to do so. In spite of this the Spaniards were still prepared to give the King the benefit of the doubt; they still believed —partly because they wished to believe—that he could and would help them. The King of Spain had even indicated that he would be willing to discuss the possibility of a marriage alliance between his only son and Charles's eldest daughter.

With four million ducats in prospect the King felt strong enough to assert his authority with vigour against those who had opposed and embarrassed him in the last Parliament. Within twenty-four hours of the dissolution three leading men in the Lords and three in the Commons were arrested and their lodgings ransacked for evidence of correspondence with the Scots. They were the Earl of Warwick, Lord Brooke, Lord Saye, John Pym, John Hampden and Sir Walter Earle. The next day, four more members of the House of Commons had to answer before the Council for having questioned in Parliament the King's right to exact money for the equipment and transport of the levies. Another member of the House, John Crew, was peremptorily required to hand over his notes of the complaints reported to him as chairman of the committee chosen to inquire into religious grievances. Crew refused, on the grounds that the information was confidential and privileged; he followed the seven others to prison.[3]

Garraway the Royalist Lord Mayor, was summoned and told that the King must now double his previous demand for a loan of £100,000 from the City; he was requested to submit a list of citizens capable of advancing sufficient sums by Sunday at latest or the demand would be raised to £300,000 and be fully enforced. Garraway did his best, but on Sunday four of the aldermen who should have supplied the names of the richest citizens refused to give any information; for this offence they were at once arrested, but they remained stubborn.[4]

The rumbling discontent of London, the great, angry, Protestant seaport, suddenly burst into a roar of rage. Apprentices, effervescent with May Day humour joined the mariners and dock hands, a whole angry, young, vehement population, indignant that their merchant ships were held up, their trade hampered, their once glorious fleet an object of scorn, their favourite preachers imprisoned, Papists and Spaniards encouraged everywhere, Parliament turned out of doors because it had complained of their grievances, and the old sea-dog Warwick, whom the mariners loved, shut up in the Tower.

They came together on the south bank, from Southwark and Blackfriars: someone beat a drum to attract more. In their hundreds they poured westward, making for Laud's palace at Lambeth. Laud fled and his servants stood on their guard while the rabble surged round the walls and a young seaman tried to break in the door with a crowbar. The ringleaders were arrested but the apprentices smashed into the gaol and let them out. "God bless them all, God speed them all!" cried an excited Londoner as he fought back the constables who were trying to recapture the prisoners; later when he was informed against and questioned for these exuberant exclamations he declared that he had been praying for the King and his Council, not for the rioters at all. New crowds began to assemble at Southwark and Blackheath; Charles ordered the Lord Mayor to call out the trained bands against them when, with the suddenness of a summer storm, they dispersed.[5]

Charles, still unable to believe that anything in his government could have provoked such a demonstration, was sure that his ill-wishers had set the people on. Using the royal prerogative for the purpose for the second time in his reign, he had the man who had beaten the drum put to the torture, but the victim said nothing, having nothing to say. The seaman who had wielded a crowbar against the Archbishop's door was charged with high treason, the law being somewhat stretched for the purpose. He was hanged and quartered and his head spiked on London Bridge. His name was Thomas Bensted and he was only nineteen years old; for some time afterwards he was remembered on the London quaysides as a martyr whose innocent blood was on the guilty hands of Archbishop Laud.[6]

The May Day riots of London were echoed later that month by Whitsuntide riots at Colchester. A fantastic rumour went round among the ignorant poor of this Puritan district that Laud and the hated Matthew Wren, Bishop of Ely, were plotting mischief together at the house of a prominent Roman Catholic in the neighbourhood, which was said to be stuffed with arms. Gunpowder plots always found ready believers, and the mayor of Colchester, who was a sensible man, was confronted with angry crowds asserting that their town was in danger. Some of them claimed to have seen two villainous Irishmen slinking about the walls evidently intent on starting a fire. In order to quiet them the mayor had to call out the trained bands.[7]

While such grotesque suspicions went about, Convocation was still in session at Westminster, protected by an armed guard against the hostility of the populace. The legal position was doubtful as Convocation usually met only when Parliament was sitting and the King's critics were not slow to complain that the Anglican clergy continued undisturbed in their debates while the King's lay advisers, the Parliament of England, were silenced.[8]

The Archbishop agreed with Strafford that the best hope for the future lay in dauntless resolution: no concessions and no retreat. Convocation in May 1640 proclaimed the official triumph of the Laudian reforms in a series of new Canons. These set forth in unequivocal terms the doctrine of the Divine Right of Kings and decreed that it should be expounded by the clergy to their parishioners at least once a quarter. Twice a year they were to preach sermons on the importance of conformity to established doctrine. The hierarchy of the Church was confirmed and the placing of the Communion table in the East was made compulsory. Following the example set by Strafford in Ireland in the previous year, Convocation imposed an oath on all members of learned professions. They were to swear never wittingly to subvert " the government of this Church by Archbishops, Bishops, deans and archdeacons, &c. as it stands now established." Of all these defiant Canons, this provoked the loudest outcry. Were men to endanger their immortal souls, asked the Puritans, by swearing loyalty to an *etcetera*, a cipher, a monster, a mask which might conceal the Mass, the Pope, the Church of Rome?[9]

The Etcetera Oath—it soon had no other name—was the instant target of all abuse. " &c " to the Puritans became " the curl'd lock of Antichrist."[10] Insolent and jeering opposition broke out, showing how little reverence was felt for the King's or the bishops' authority. When the Bishop of London's Chancellor, with a huge mace borne before him, entered one church to exact the oath, the verger barred his way crying, " I care nothing for you, nor for your artichoke," and the jeering congregation took up his mockery.

An additional complication shadowed the passing of these unfortunate Canons. The Bishop of Gloucester, Godfrey Goodman, had warned Laud beforehand that he could not subscribe them. This woolly-minded, kind-hearted old scholar, once chaplain to the King's mother, had been elevated to a bishopric early in King Charles's reign and had been an exasperation to Laud ever since. He was an unabashed pluralist—like many of his colleagues—and his financial confusion and his debts were as openly criticised as was his ritualism in his Puritan-ridden diocese. In religion he was one of those who hoped that the unity of Catholic Christendom might yet be restored, and a means of reconciliation with Rome be found. The Canons of 1640 were too secular for him; by attaching the Anglican Church firmly to the King and the State they seemed to him to deepen and perpetuate the cruel gash in the spiritual unity of the Church made at the Reformation. He was neither a Roman Catholic nor an English Catholic; he believed, with the Creed, in one Holy Catholic Church and, as he pathetically told Laud, he would sooner be torn in pieces by wild horses than agree to Canons which appeared to accept and confirm the separation of Christendom.[11]

When it came to the point, Goodman tried to evade the issue by refusing to subscribe the Canons on the ground that they ought not to be passed unless Parliament was sitting. That a man whose opposition was based on Catholic principles should at the last minute take refuge behind a Puritan argument was too much for Laud. He suspended him from his bishopric and confined him in the Gatehouse.[12]

While the problem of Bishop Goodman was yet unsolved, a new Ship-money case, not brought by the Crown, had come before the courts. A London citizen, who had had his goods distrained because he refused to pay, brought an action against the sheriff for unlawful seizure. His case provided a public platform on which Ship-money was again discussed with no advantage to the Crown.[13]

These incidental troubles would have mattered little had

Strafford achieved the Spanish alliance with its promise of four million ducats. But Strafford, within a week of the dissolution of Parliament, fell gravely ill and during the interval of nearly a month when he could not attend to business, the French and the Dutch between them prevented the implementation of an Anglo-Spanish treaty. Cardinal Richelieu, perceiving that the King was no longer master in his own country, saw no purpose in wasting an ambassador on him. Accordingly, he withdrew the French envoy and left no one except a secretary—Montreuil, a very good observer—to attend to French interests in England.

At about the same time, and with almost equal contempt, Richelieu released the King's nephew the Elector Palatine. The young man wished to come to England but was prevented by an agitated letter from Secretary Vane, telling him that his uncle could not receive him at present.[14] The arrival of his dispossessed Protestant nephew would be calculated to agitate the Puritan opposition and would moreover be extremely inconvenient when the King was wooing the Spaniards.

The Spaniards in England no doubt drew conclusions unflattering to King Charles from the contemptuous indifference of Richelieu. The behaviour of the Dutch envoy, the Baron de Heenvliet, caused the breakdown of the negotiations altogether. For France, a great power, English assistance to Spain would have been hampering and inconvenient; but to the Dutch it might be a matter of life and death. Heenvliet therefore spared no pains to prevent the agreement. He made it clear that if English ships assisted Spaniards in the transportation of their troops, the Dutch would no longer treat them as neutrals; in fact, that Charles could not become the ally of Spain on the terms at present offered without involving himself in a war with Holland. At the same time he sought out the leading merchants of the East India Company whose ships, more frequently than any others, were hired for the Spanish traffic. The East India Company had no love for the Dutch, their principal rivals in the trade with Asia, and for that reason they had willingly lent themselves to the unpopular transport of men and money to help in the war against them. But the East India merchants were Protestant, none the less; their ships were each provided with Foxe's *Book of Martyrs* as well as the Bible for the leisure reading of the crew.[15] Heenvliet played on the religious question while at the same time offering substantial concessions from the Dutch East India Company. Within a very few weeks, he had thrown difficulties in the way of the Spanish treaty which would, at the very least, take months to resolve, if indeed they could be resolved at all.[16] Strafford's vision of rebuilding royal authority on a foundation of Spanish gold faded into a remote future. Meanwhile the Scots war had to be fought.

In his desperate need for money the King permitted the Queen to sound the Pope's emissary, Count Rossetti, on the possibility of a loan from the Vatican. The Privy Council having for the most part subscribed handsomely to his funds (Hamilton gave £8,000) the King assessed all the Court officials and mulcted them in suitable forced gifts. Reviving his monopoly policy, he sold to another group of courtiers, among whom were his favourite attendant Endymion Porter and several of Windebanke's relations, the sole right to manufacture white writing-paper for the next fifty-seven years.[17]

On a sudden inspiration, late one Saturday afternoon, he seized the bullion deposited in the mint by London merchants and confronted them on the following Monday with an offer of 8 per cent interest on this unintentional loan to the Crown. The loyal Garraway, who was striving hard as Lord Mayor to raise loans and troops in the City, was startled by this unforeseen action and shocked still more when the King announced his intention of debasing the value of all coins below a shilling. The City revolted at this, imploring the King not to resort to measures so harmful to trade; rather than run the risk of any more royal experiments in finance, they agreed to advance the £200,000 he had asked of them some weeks before.[18] Having bought him off with this promise, they did not in fact keep it.

While the King and his Council wrestled with the money problem—Strafford grimly resolute, Cottington cheerfully fatalistic and Northumberland in glum despondency—the problem of raising the local levies troubled the nation at large.

English administration, and therefore the responsibility for bringing the troops together, rested on the gentry and the King had now reached the limit of his unpopularity with them. The breakdown in contact and understanding between the Crown and the men whose duty it was to execute its policy was almost total. After ten years in which they had submitted to persistent interference, to the irritation of knighthood fines, of petty prosecutions for enclosure, of prohibitions, licences and regulations affecting their closest interests, they saw themselves faced with the heavy trouble and not inconsiderable expense of making the largest levy of troops within the memory of man. And for what? For a war on their Protestant neighbours and fellow-subjects, provoked by the Archbishop.

So few were the gentry who fully supported the King in this dismal season that when his ministers had arranged for the return to Parliament of those favourable to his policy, they had done so at the expense of local administration. Sir Edward Osborne, the devoted Vice-President of the North, wrote despairingly to Strafford that every loyal gentleman in Yorkshire had been required in Parliament and, during their absence, the obstructionists had hindered all levying of troops and preparation for war.[19] This experience was not peculiar to the North. From the Home Counties, the Midlands, the Welsh marches, and the West came news of truculent and mutinous levies, and gentry either unwilling or unable to set them in better order. The long tradition of a decent obedience to the Crown made the gentry go through the business of getting the troops together but they were slack and dilatory and very bitterly resented the heavy charge for coat-and-conduct money, for clothing and transporting the men, which had to come out of their own pockets. A single vocal obstructionist could easily persuade his indifferent and unwilling colleagues to neglect a task that none of them liked. Examples of hindrance, even of downright refusal, sometimes came from the highest; sheriffs and deputy sheriffs, Lords Lieutenant and their deputies hesitated to send out the necessary warrants, argued and protested. The King's Council reprimanded some, summoned a few to London, even placed some under arrest: useless demonstrations in the face of hostility so deep and wide.

This evil brought another in its train. The King seemed doomed to involve himself ever more deeply in misunderstandings, for the only group in the country which strongly supported him were the old Roman Catholic gentry. They could not help him to raise the troops because they were excluded from the administration, but they provided the officers of the army as it came into being. This was inevitable. While the sons of the Protestant squires were mostly unwilling to go, the sons of the recusant gentry were eager to serve a King who had been generous to them. Many of them were, in any case, trained soldiers. The wars abroad had for two generations provided one of the few careers open to the younger sons of Catholic landowners, excluded by their religion from the professions. Far more professional soldiers therefore were to be found among English Catholics than among English Protestants. Although English Protestant adventurers fought in the armies of the Dutch and Swedes, by far the larger number of English soldiers serving abroad were Roman Catholic volunteers in the Spanish and Austrian forces. Many of these young men, feeling a genuine gratitude to a King who had protected their religion, and a genuine distaste for the opinions of the rebel Scots, had thrown up their foreign commissions and come home to help in the religious war.

The number of Roman Catholic officers in the army was therefore relatively high, although not as high as rumour made it. Nothing that the King did could stifle the continuous whispering of the old story that he was in some way selling England to Spain. In Scotland, for instance, it was stated that " His Majesty has absolutely taken the King of Spain by the hand " and in return for men and money had ceded him the Cinque Ports and a part of Ireland.[20] These tales were partly the echo of the alliance which had not materialised, and partly the outcome of the shocking situation on the English coasts. The Ship-money fleet, languishing for lack of funds, was involved in preparations for the Scots war, and the Channel guard was consequently so weakened that the Barbary pirates were again active and had recently carried off sixty men and women in the neighbourhood of Penzance. A fleet of twenty-four Dunkirkers —privateers who operated in unofficial alliance with Spain— were systematically landing and pillaging the Kent and Sussex shores, the navy being forbidden to meddle with them for fear of extinguishing for ever the King's hope of an alliance with Spain. As a result the Dunkirkers boldly spread to the Irish Sea and before the end of the summer had established a useful base on Islay where they co-operated with wilder Gaelic sea rovers from Ulster and the Hebrides.[21]

All these things naturally added to the discontent and anxiety of the King's subjects, the majority of whom made their living by the sea, and gave ground for the rumours which spread dangerously among the newly levied troops. Among those who were being assembled at the ports to be taken to Scotland by sea wholesale desertion began because they had heard—and believed—a story that they were to be carried off to Barbados for slaves.[22]

In other parts of the country the discontented levies broke into disorder and set themselves to levelling all unpopular enclosures. The Deputy Lieutenants of Staffordshire, having got the recalcitrant levies together and marched them into Uttoxeter, were called up from the supper table by the dismaying news that the men had left their billets and were throwing down and burning the fences round some newly enclosed forest land. In Derbyshire the troops tore down Sir John Coke's palings and set fire to his mill; later they killed the deer in Lord Huntingdon's park and released the prisoners from the county gaol. Riot, mutiny, robbery and violence were reported from Leominster, Hereford, Marlborough, Warwick, Oxford and Cambridge. The prisoners in the house of correction at Wakefield were set free by passing troops. In the fens, where the dismally wet spring had made the floods worse than usual, the perpetual outcry against the drainage project found expression in new riots. Since the King had officially taken over the scheme the fenlanders' resentment became easily fused with bitter feelings against his Church and his war. On a rumour that Laud's most efficient henchman, Matthew Wren, was at a meeting in Wisbech Church, a gang of angry soldiers battered on doors and windows shouting, " Give us the damned Bishop of Ely." All over the eastern counties, recruits burst into the churches, tore out and made bonfires of the Communion rails, usually with the approval of the inhabitants.[23]

If the men suspected an officer of Popery they sometimes refused obedience until they were satisfied that he would take the sacrament with them. Secretary Windebanke's second son, following in the footsteps of his elder brother " Signior Tomaso " as a wag and a character, nonplussed his men by affecting a fanatic Protestantism, kneeling down, praying loudly, and quoting the Scriptures on all occasions. Wisely, he also distributed free drinks and tobacco.[24]

The situation was less often a jesting matter. The Somerset levies murdered a Catholic officer before deserting homewards. The Dorset levies, who had marched very unwillingly as far as Faringdon in Berkshire, flared into violence at the supposed injustice of a martinet lieutenant, he too a Catholic. They stormed his lodging, and when the wretched man tried to save himself by scrambling out of the window along the iron strut which supported the inn sign, they pelted him down with stones, and later dragged him through the streets and clamped his lifeless body in the pillory.[25]

The disorders of the troops, violent and dangerous as they often were, menaced the royal government less than the open and secret protests of the professional classes. A dozen law students of Lincoln's Inn displayed their sympathies at the Three Cranes Tavern one evening by holding under the pump a hanger-on of the Court until he agreed to drink confusion to

Archbishop Laud. More sober and more serious were meetings like that which took place at Kettering during the summer when twenty-seven clergymen and some local worthies, including a justice of the peace, solemnly approved the cause of the Scots and pledged themselves in no circumstances to take the monstrous " Etcetera oath." [26]

While disaster approached, the King, who had replenished his stables at some expense in the spring, was hunting at Oatlands, from time to time riding in to Whitehall to see what progress his plans were making. At his pretty country palace early in July the Queen gave birth, with less difficulty than usual, to her eighth child, a healthy boy. To celebrate the occasion Charles ordered the release of all Catholic priests. A fortnight later the Archbishop came out from Lambeth to christen Prince Henry, who was carried to the font by a procession of brothers and sisters. His father created him Duke of Gloucester, but in the old medieval way he came to be known by the place of his birth and to the family he was always " Henry of Oatlands." Sometime in early childhood, in the palace gardens, he planted a cedar. The great tree is to-day the only surviving memorial of the once happy, gay and graceful Court brought there summer after summer by King Charles and his Queen.[27]

The birth of his youngest son and certain illusory hopes from Scotland greatly cheered the King. He believed that his enemies were ill-provided and quarrelling among themselves. He was wrong on the first point. The army of the Covenanters was incomparably better than his own. Parishes loyally provided their quota of men and arms, and the many professional soldiers still in Scotland, with others who had come home too late for last year's campaign, saw to their training. France had sent no help after all, but regular shiploads of arms came in from Holland, and the King's navy showed itself quite incompetent to check this traffic. The good wives of Edinburgh sacrificed three thousand pairs of sheets to make tents for the men. A gloomy informant of the King's in Edinburgh reported that three times as many men were in arms as in the previous year, better equipped, with more artillery. Charles preferred to trust in the cheerful reports of Lord Conway, his general at Newcastle, who persistently assured him that the Scots had no army worth speaking of and that all their talk of great forces was an empty vaunt.[28]

The King hoped with more reason that the Covenanting party was itself disintegrating. Montrose had been restive since the autumn and had exchanged letters with the King and with friends at Court. Uninformed as to the King's true intentions, puzzled and wounded by the reckless proceedings of some of his colleagues, he tried to be at one and the same time loyal to the Covenant and to the Crown. When the Scottish Estates met again in June, with no Royal Commissioner in the chair, and defied the King's order that they should immediately prorogue their meeting, Montrose protested against this flouting of the King's authority. He was overruled. The Estates confirmed the legislation of the previous autumn and resolved on November for their next meeting, all without the agreement of the King or of his representative. They had thus set up a precedent for meeting, legislating, and organising their future sessions without the help or consent of the Crown: a silent and profound altera- tion[29] which made the effective government of Scotland inde- pendent of the King.

A few weeks later occurred the first open quarrel between Montrose and Argyll. The Stewarts of Atholl and their neigh- bours the Ogilvys were rumoured to be stirring on the King's behalf. Late in June, Argyll, armed with a commission from the Estates, led a picked body of Campbells into the braes of Atholl to disarm the Stewarts. When their principal men came to his tent under a safe conduct, he arrested them and, deprived of leadership, the royalist movement in Atholl collapsed. Argyll improved the occasion by explaining the constitutional position to the misguided gentry of Atholl; some of them understood him to say that the conduct of the King in bringing an army against Scotland rendered him liable to deposition. Certainly from the time of that campaign in Atholl rumours began to circulate in Scotland that Argyll was for dethroning the King.[30]

The Atholl campaign at an end, Argyll transferred his attention from the Stewarts to the Ogilvys. Their chief's principal seat, Airlie Castle, had been occupied by an officer under Montrose's orders several weeks earlier. The occupation had been conducted with courtesy and restraint because Lord Airlie was next neighbour and first cousin to Montrose. Argyll trusted neither Montrose nor the measures he had taken. Disregarding his assertion that the Ogilvys had been rendered harmless, he marched on Airlie Castle with his clansmen, ordered Montrose's small garrison out, plundered and set fire to the place. The Earl of Airlie and his son were both in London with the King; in the castle was only the young Lady Ogilvy who was shortly expecting to lie in. Whatever military justification Argyll might plead, his harsh behaviour to a defenceless woman has remained from that day to this embedded in the ballad history of Scotland.

> Lady Ogilvy looks o'er her bower window,
> And O but she looks warely!
> And there she spied the great Argyll,
> Come to plunder the bonnie house of Airlie. . . .

When Argyll's men had taken all they wanted, the Ogilvys had not left in all their land so much as "a cock to crow day." There were those among the Covenanters, Montrose the chief of them, who bitterly blamed Argyll for this unnecessary violence. These quarrels echoed across the Border and news of them reached England in an exaggerated form; some said Montrose and Argyll had had a personal quarrel, and Argyll had accused Montrose of conniving at the escape of Lady Ogilvy and her unborn child.[31]

While the Campbells dealt with the Stewarts and Ogilvys, another detachment of Covenanters under Robert Monro, a professional trained in Germany, had attacked the Gordons, laid waste the regions of Banff and Strathbogie and carried off hostages from Aberdeen.[32]

The violence of these proceedings as well as the conduct of the Estates caused anxiety to others beside Montrose. They feared that their country was to become, as it had been in the past, a prey to the violence and ambition of those who exploited the political situation for their own ends. Their fears were confirmed when an extraordinary proposition was laid before the leaders of the Covenanting forces. It was suggested that in the present emergency Scotland should be divided into two regions—north of the Forth and south of the Forth—each to be under the military command of a single great lord. Argyll was to be in charge of the north, Hamilton of the south. Opposition to this scheme among the officers of the Covenanting army caused it to be abandoned almost at once; it is indeed hard to understand why Argyll thought that it had any chance of acceptance. For what were the soldiers to make of it? Hamilton, to whom overriding power was offered on the south side of Forth was the *King's* commander. The implication was that some private understanding existed between him and Argyll. The ordinary straightforward man could only assume that one or other of them was playing false. Montrose was not alone in assuming that both these great lords, whose private relations with each other had been the subject of speculation since the Glasgow Assembly, were concerned to gain some high advantage for themselves rather than to serve either King or Covenant.

The scheme was allowed to drop, but it was not surprising that Montrose and a party of friends gathered together soon after at the house of one of his kinsmen at Cumbernauld and there, at Montrose's instigation, drew up a secret agreement directed against Argyll, known as the Cumbernauld Bond. It was a statement of loyalty both to the Covenant and to the Crown, to which they added a joint undertaking to defend its true principles against " the particular and indirect practising of a few." [33]

Montrose no doubt saw a double purpose in creating this inner alliance of like-minded men within the ranks of the Covenanters. He intended to prevent the peculiar machinations of Argyll and Hamilton, whatever they were, and at the same time to reaffirm what he believed to be the honest intentions of true Covenanters towards the Crown.

He remained wholly sincere in his attachment to what he believed to be the original and authentic purpose of the Covenant —the freedom of the Scots Kirk. His doubts of Argyll notwithstanding, he was ready to take his place in the field against the forces which the King was preparing in England. Within a few days of signing the Cumbernauld Bond he brought his regiments, well equipped and in good order, to the rendezvous of the Covenanting army near Coldstream.

While the Scots forces gathered together in strength, Lord Conway at Newcastle, still astonishingly ill-informed, declared that they had not the power to invade. A week later, perturbed at evidence of their increasing numbers, he reported that they must either invade or disband: their army was too large to remain for long in that poor country. He seemed to think the latter course the more probable. But the Scots army among the border hills continued to grow. Suddenly, on August 16th, the King's Council in London, who had been fed all that summer with contemptuous and confident dispatches from Lord Conway, received the shocking announcement that he expected the Scots to cross the border in force at any moment and that, in the face of the odds, he could not hold Newcastle.[34]

In a crisis the King's natural courage gave him resolution. He immediately announced that he would go north to place himself at the head of his threatened and invaded people. The dissuasions of his advisers, who doubted the effect his presence would have, retarded him for a few days only and on Thursday, August 20th, he left for York.[35]

Early in the following week Strafford followed him. He had, until a few days before, intended to return to Dublin to embark the Irish army for which hitherto Hamilton had sent no shipping. An unforeseen disaster prevented him. Northumberland, the commander-in-chief, had fallen ill. Some said his illness was diplomatic. The kinder modern word is psycho-somatic; Northumberland tended to succumb to illness when he could no longer face his responsibilities. Once the admirer of Strafford, Northumberland had, all this year, failed to respond to the over-confident energy of his friend. Since the early spring he had predicted that the King would not be able to raise money enough to wage a successful war, and his reiteration of this comment at the council table, with a kind of gloomy relish, had long been his chief contribution to discussions of royal policy.[36] Northumberland, unlike Strafford, did not look upon an impossible task as a challenge to be taken up with defiant energy. He thought it foolish to attempt the impossible and no part of his duty to encourage the King in such a policy. His bad health, neither for the first nor the last time, was remarkably convenient.

Strafford's ill-health was his misfortune; at forty-seven he was already worn out with pain, knotted with gout and tormented by the stone. But he did not shirk the task before him. Taking up the burden cast down by Northumberland, he hurried northward to command the unruly rabble which had by this time come together from all parts of the kingdom in his native Yorkshire. Sir Jacob Astley was doing his best to equip them: " I am to receive all the arch-knaves of this Kingdom and arm them at Selby," he said, with an old soldier's humorous resignation.[37]

Strafford's confidence seemed unshaken. He had soundly rated Conway for his cowardly dispatch, refusing to believe that the situation could be so desperate and urging him to behave with more soldierly resolution.[38] In Huntingdon, at dusk, at the end of his first day's journey, he received news that the Scots were over the Border. Even in this he claimed to see cause for rejoicing: the English would surely not endure to let their ancient enemy triumph on their own soil and would rise in wrath to defend it.[39] Cheered by this illusion, he continued his painful journey northward.

On August 20th the Scots at Coldstream crossed the Tweed

into England. After the wet summer, the river was very full, and Montrose, to encourage his men, waded through on foot, the first of the whole army. Some attributed the act to the young man's desire for public notice and his wish to contradict the growing suspicion " that in his heart he was turned royalist."[40] But Montrose was a man of action, without so much guile; a natural leader in the field, he had done what time and the hour demanded.

While the Scots advanced without opposition from the Tweed to the Tyne, the King reached York. The discontented gentry of the county had petitioned him a fortnight earlier against the expense of raising troops, complaining that the disturbed summer had injured both trade and the harvest, and asking insistently for a new Parliament. In a long interview with these petitioners, Charles enlarged persuasively on the danger which now threatened their native county, and won so much upon them that they agreed to raise more forces which, with their King in person to command them, would hold the Tees, as a second line of defence against the invaders.[41]

The King, like Strafford, still believed that he could rally support for his war and was considering a new means of doing so, by calling the nobility of the realm to an emergency council at York.[42] He had not forgotten his intention of placing himself as soon as possible in the front line of his people's defences, and on August 27th he led an army out of York for the relief of Newcastle; he had got as far as Northallerton before he realised that he was already too late.[43]

The Scots had advanced in business-like fashion across the Northumbrian hills, sometimes encouraged by the music of the pipes and sometimes by the singing of psalms. The people made no move against them, although a woman shouted at Leslie, " Will Jesus Christ not come to England without twenty thousand men at his back?"[44] At Wooler they easily brushed off a skirmishing party sent against them from Berwick. Lord Conway at Newcastle, among the unfinished fortifications, declared that the Tyne must be held at all costs and added, " but there goes more to it than to bid it to be done." [45] He placed four cannon, two thousand foot and a thousand horse, the best part of his forces, at the most vulnerable place, the ford of Newburn, a few miles west of Newcastle. They were still hurriedly throwing up a breastwork when the Scots army appeared in the village on the farther bank. The English forces opened fire but with little effect. Leslie dismantled one of his light cannon and had it carried to the top of Newburn Church tower; from this dominating position the cannon balls that he sent "bowling in among the English" caused considerable alarm.

Under cover of the bombardment, he started the crossing. The honour of leading the way fell to the volunteers from the Edinburgh bar, led by a younger son of Lord Advocate Hope. This intellectual contingent meeting with stiff resistance from the English musketeers, a second party plunged into the water to their help and, supported by firing from the batteries, advanced on the English position. At this the English foot soldiers, who were mostly pressed men, abandoned the breastwork. The first line of the English defences being down, the Scots poured across the ford to take possession of the undefended river bank. Harry Wilmot, an intelligent young professional, in command of the English cavalry, tried to charge them as they landed; but their discipline was too good; their musketeers had instantly taken command of the ground, and against their steady firing the raw English cavalry was helpless. They fled in panic, trampling down and scattering what was left of their own infantry. The personal courage of a few cavalry officers and, it was said, of one artillery officer named George Monck, alone redeemed the honour of England at that "infamous, irreparable rout of Newburn." [46]

The Scots had begun to cross at four in the afternoon. At half-past five the incoming tide made the ford impassable for the rest of the daylight, so that the invading army passed the night divided by the river. No English were left to take advantage of their dislocation. The fleeing troops had meanwhile reached Newcastle with the news that the Scots were over the Tyne.[47]

All that summer forethought and energy had been spent on the fortification of Berwick, and not until the last few days had it entered Lord Conway's mind that the Scots would be so astute as to outflank Berwick, which was ready for them, and come in upon Newcastle, which was not. The town was fairly well-provided: cheese and biscuit were plentiful; good store of powder and muskets had been laid in and some heavy artillery; cannon balls and bullets had unaccountably been overlooked. But the true reason why neither Conway nor any experienced soldier contemplated holding the city was that its outer defences had been neglected. It was not defensible against siege and could not be held once the Tyne had been crossed. Conway evacuated the major part of the troops and the heavy artillery by road to Durham; he had the powder-barrels loaded on shipboard and hurried away on that same tide which was even then hampering the Scots crossing at Newburn.[48]

On the following day when the advancing Scots reached Gateshead they were astounded to learn that Newcastle had been abandoned. On Sunday, August 30th, Leslie entered the city at the head of his army. "Never so many ran from so few," lamented the stunned English, and Leslie, incredulous of so immediate a success and suspecting a more deadly line of defence farther back, made himself strong at Newcastle and sent to Edinburgh for more troops.[49]

The King fell back to York while Strafford, who had joined him, exchanged angry messages with Conway. Anger kindled hope and neither the King nor his chief minister accepted the first defeat as final. Strafford's formidable presence intimidated the disaffected gentry and put fresh heart into the loyal. The troops were drilled and disciplined; laxity and disorder were severely punished. The rabble began to assume the outward semblance of an army,[50] and again the King's delusive expectations rose. In theory the fleet, under Hamilton, would soon land forces from Ireland in the West of Scotland and make an effective diversion in Leslie's rear. Meanwhile the first rumours of Newburn were contradicted by others: the battle, it was alleged, had cost the Scots very heavy losses, and several people claimed to have slain the Earl of Montrose in person. Some grains of encouraging truth were mixed with the chaff of consoling lies; an explosion in the powder magazine at Dunglass, behind the Scots lines, killed several of their chief officers, destroyed important stores, and started new rumours of treachery in their own ranks. The Scots forces in Newcastle, at first welcomed as liberators, soon annoyed the inhabitants by glorying in the discomfiture of the English. This arrogance and the disorders which inevitably went with a military occupation would, the King believed, arouse the long-delayed surge of national feeling against the invaders.[51]

His Queen and his councillors in the South were far less cheerful. The Scots had issued a printed manifesto justifying their action, and this, in spite of all prohibitions, was popular reading in London. The temper of the Londoners and the machinations of the King's principal opponents were alike to be feared. Released from the Tower, Warwick, Brooke, Saye, Pym and Hampden had remained in London and were known to meet frequently for consultation. The Earls of Bedford and Essex joined them. Their excuses for the consultations were the affairs of Providence Island and the New England colonies but, as the Court well knew, they spent more time discussing the affairs of their native land. That Pym was on friendly terms with Secretary Vane's eldest son was a detail the significance of which seems to have eluded the Court, at least for the moment.

After the outburst of May, London was restless and full of rumours; Cottington, who had been made Lieutenant of the Tower, had orders to keep the city quiet by whatever means seemed best. But there was nothing tangible to attack, only an atmosphere of hostility and suspicion, and occasional placards and scrawled papers calling on the apprentices to defend the reformed religion. At the time of the May riots, the King had found, and shattered with his own hand, a scratched message on a window-pane: "God save the King, confound the Queen and her children and send the Palsgrave to reign over us." Hatred of Popery, hatred of the Queen and her friends, vague murmurings for a Protestant succession continued. A woman named Anne Hussey declared that she knew of an Irish-Popish plot to overwhelm the country. She may have been encouraged by those anxious to provoke a crisis—the secretly-consulting peers and commoners at Lord Warwick's house. Nothing can be proved. It is as likely that her hysterical intervention was spontaneous, since it was common knowledge that Spanish troops and bullion had been conveyed through England.

All that summer the Court had openly bragged of the strength of Strafford's Irish army which was to deal with the Scots, and all the previous summer Lord Antrim had broadcast his intention of sending his wild Macdonalds into Scotland to eat the Covenanters alive; such things gave fuel enough to the underground fires of rumour about Irish-Popish-Spanish enterprises. Now the flames flickered everywhere. Ships and mariners going to and coming from the Netherlands discharged and brought back, with other cargo, the international political speculations of the quaysides. At one moment the Dutch were regaled with a story that King Charles had been deposed and his sister, the exiled Elizabeth of Bohemia, proclaimed the new Protestant Sovereign amid wild scenes of rejoicing. Not to be outdone, the Dutch themselves generated a story of a gigantic plot, contrived between the rebel Scots and the King's Popish subjects to destroy the Church and murder the King. The English consul in Holland thought it better to communicate this fantastic tale to Archbishop Laud, who passed it on to the King in the North, but neither of them appears to have known what to make of it. The King's Council in London at least took the precaution of preventing public demonstrations by closing all playhouses, bear-gardens and places of common resort.

Harassed by doubts and rumours the Queen would have liked the King to come home, having a wifely but unjustified confidence in his ability to deal with the trouble. She sent to him the one piece of information distilled from these doubts: Warwick and his friends were planning to present him with a remonstrance for which they were gathering the signatures of many other peers.[52] The King was not wholly unprepared for this development which may even have been welcome to him. He seems to have thought it possible that he could outwit the opposition peers by rallying to his support the rest of his lords, if he could make them see that their position and authority, logically dependent on his own, were threatened when his were threatened. Strafford's skill had almost created a breach between the Commons and the Lords when the peers had thought their rights infringed during the last Parliament. The Short Parliament had eluded his control for two reasons—because Pym had been clever enough to close the gap between Lords and Commons, and because the Protestant and irritable atmosphere of London had encouraged the King's critics and discouraged his friends. A half-Parliament, a Parliament of peers alone, called at York, far from the pressure of London's angry mariners and bold apprentices, might be won to the King's support. The support of the peers of the realm might—indeed could—save the situation. Their influence, direct and indirect, over county administration was very large; their financial interests in trade and industry were extensive. Much of the wealth and power of the Kingdom was concentrated in their hands. By calling a Council of Peers at York the King hoped to form against his critics a party large enough to serve him in the present and, if it should be essential to call Parliament again, powerful enough to divide and weaken the Commons.

The King therefore received with equanimity the remonstrance drawn up by the cabal of his critics in London. It had been drafted by John Pym with the help of Oliver St. John. The Providence Company peers—Warwick, Saye and Brooke—had brought a number of others to set their hands to it: Essex and his brother-in-law Hertford, the austerely pious Lord Mandeville, Lord Howard of Escrick who was powerful in the North. The grievances stated were those which the Short Parliament had raised: innovations in religion, favour to Roman Catholics, monopolies, Ship-money. Another more specific protest was added: the peers implored the King not to transport any troops out of Ireland.[53] The fear that the wild Irish—this formidable, alien, Popish people, this ancient and hostile force—might be unleashed against them by the King, or by Strafford in the King's name, came increasingly to overshadow the minds of the English.

Charles answered this remonstrance by sending out writs calling his peers to a Great Council, to meet at York on September 24th. The writs were signed on September 7th; on the 10th the King reviewed his army. The two thousand horse and sixteen thousand foot, smartened up by Sir Jacob Astley's drilling and Strafford's discipline, looked very well to the unpractised eyes of civilian observers. Secretary Vane ventured the opinion that Gustavus Adolphus had never had better. With these, and Strafford's boasted army from Ireland, the Scots were as good as dead men. At Court, the plan was still to play for time in which to rouse the English against the invaders, to win the support of the peers, to raise money with their help, to land the Irish in Galloway or on the west coast, and to smother with a show of force and a new enthusiasm for the war the factious criticism of opponents.[54]

These hopes were founded on a series of misapprehensions. The Scots army was in good heart, had suffered no serious loss at Newburn and had quickly recovered from the accident at Dunglass. The English, even in the north, grumbled a little but showed no sign of rising to expel the invaders. The Irish army remained in Ulster for lack of shipping. Hamilton, in charge of the fleet, had provided none, acting out of a kind of crafty loyalty: he did not believe that the King could win the war, and knowing the fanatic anger and suspicion aroused among the Covenanters by the mere idea of an Irish army, he thought it better that no Irish army should set foot on the Scottish mainland. Admittedly, since Dumbarton had once more been seized by the Covenanters, a landing could now only be made from the Solway Firth where Carlaverock Castle was loyally held for the King by the Catholic Lord Nithsdale. But if Hamilton intended not even to attempt to bring the Irish over, he would have done better to say so instead of allowing the plan to be agreed on, but failing in his own part in it.

The King's optimism continued for some days longer. To demonstrate that his calling of a Great Council betokened no change of policy, he showed every mark of open favour to Strafford and on September 13th bestowed upon him the Order of the Garter. The ceremony was splendidly performed and the new Knight was formally escorted to the steps of the throne by the Marquis of Hamilton and the Earl of Holland. Strafford disliked, despised and distrusted them both; his elevation to the noblest and most coveted honour in the Kingdom, at such a time and with such support, was as substantial in meaning and permanence as a Court masque.

He no longer shared the optimism of the King but understood very clearly the strength of the Scots, the feebleness of the English army, the disaffection of the countryside, and the delays and dishonesties of his fellow ministers. While he maintained an outward air of hectoring confidence, all his hopes had perished. He admitted the truth to his old friend George Radcliffe: "Never came man to so lost a business." [55]

The King's hopes, on the other hand, still continued to rise. On September 18th a party of marauding Scots crossed the Tees. This incursion was reported to a young professional soldier, Captain John Smith, who was stationed not far off with a troop of horse. Descending rapidly on the careless raiders, he beat them back, helter-skelter, to their own lines. It was the first—and the last—successful action by an English officer in the war. Charles, who mistook this solitary action for the dawn of a new spirit in his army, was uplifted. When he heard, at about the same time, that the citizens of London were preparing a petition for a new Parliament, he resolved to place the petitioners under arrest as soon as they arrived in York. As for calling another Parliament, he was wholly opposed to it. [56]

Four days later he changed his mind. Ruthven, the governor of Edinburgh Castle who had defied the Covenanters since the spring, capitulated on September 15th. For the past nine weeks, since a cannon shot from the town rendered their well unusable, the garrison had had no fresh water; many had died, all were ill, Ruthven himself had lost most of his teeth, gone very deaf and was horribly afflicted with scurvy.[57] Carlaverock Castle fell at the same time. As for the new spirit of the army at York, there was no such thing. A few honest professionals applauded Captain Smith, but the rank and file were unmoved or resentful, and civilians who obstinately regarded the Scots as liberators condemned John Smith as a bloody-minded incendiary. He was—like most of the King's best officers—a Roman Catholic.

Even Charles was now aware that he could hope for no spontaneous change in the temper of his people, and that he stood to gain most by conciliation. As in the previous summer at Berwick, so now at York, he played for time. When the deputation from London appeared on September 22nd with their petition for Parliament, he received them without resentment, and he allowed it to be rumoured, before the Council of Peers was opened, that he was willing to call a Parliament.[58]

When the Great Council met on September 24th the King's strategy was not what had first been planned. He did not try to win support from the peers for the present war but sought instead to conciliate them so that he might have them on his side in the coming Parliament. He permitted, even encouraged, plain speaking, and listened with patience to the attack on his policy eloquently put forward by the Earl of Bristol. He promised a Parliament: he agreed to the appointment of Commissioners to treat with the Scots and allowed a group of lords to be chosen, among whom scarcely one was favourable to his policy. These concessions made, he sent a deputation of peers to London to ask for a new loan.[59]

All this looked like a change of policy and was meant so to look. The King who, a fortnight before, had elevated Strafford to the highest honour in the realm, now exposed him to attack without coming to his defence, and allowed him to be harried and questioned about his part in advocating the war. Not only in the Great Council, but in private also, the King sustained this pretence of having abandoned his chief minister. Lord Clanricarde, an Irish peer, who had long disputed with Strafford over a grant of land, argued his point before the King, who compelled Strafford to yield. Clanricarde, on the father's side, was Norman-Irish, and in religion a Catholic; but he gained his point for a different reason. On his mother's side he was half-brother to one of the principal opposition peers, the Earl of Essex.[60] By supporting him against Strafford, the King was only extending into private matters the policy of conciliating his opponents before Parliament met.

The subsequent course of events has made the Great Council at York appear as the natural forerunner of the Long Parliament and the first in the long series of political defeats which the King sustained at the hands of his enemies. It fits more truly into the sequence of meaningless concessions which had marked his policy towards Scotland over the last eighteen months. He now extended that policy to England and once again conceded everything to win time in order that he might divide his opponents, make a party for himself and regain all.

When the Council broke up in the last week of October an armistice had been signed with the Scots, writs had gone out for a new Parliament, and the City of London had offered a loan. The Covenanting forces were to occupy the six northern counties and to be paid the sum of £860 a day until peace was concluded. The Commissioners of both parties, who had hitherto assembled at Ripon, were to transfer their discussions to London, so that Parliament could be consulted as to the final terms of the peace treaty.[61] This transference of the treaty to London was an astute stroke on the part of the King's opponents, for it enabled them to work in the closest possible co-operation with the Calvinist Scots and thus to have the weight of both nations behind the Parliamentary attack on the King.

The King's second war against the Scots, in which victory had been essential, if his authority was to survive, had come to dismal defeat. But it had not ended. The armistice might lead on to a firm peace and the victory of the Covenanters—as the King's opponents in both countries believed; but it might equally break down into a renewed war, with the King's party strengthened in England and the Covenanters divided in Scotland. Much depended on the events of the next months, and Charles was not without hope.

His friends were working hard to place as many supporters as possible in the new Parliament. Even before the end of September Lord Northampton, a simple, devoted loyalist, had written from York to his wife in Warwickshire to busy herself in finding suitable people for the various boroughs where his family was powerful; he had also peremptorily summoned home from an educational tour on the Continent his eldest son, whom he hoped to make one of the knights of the shire.[62]

The internal divisions of the Covenanting party, temporarily closed at the moment of invasion, had opened again. Montrose at Newcastle had criticised Argyll in the most indiscreet manner and early in October he and some of his friends raised an angry complaint that all the affairs of Scotland were " contrived and carried on by a few." The young man and his growing party were effectively stifled by the damaging revelation, made within the next few days, that he had entered into private correspondence with the King. Montrose, with the ingenuousness of a spoilt child, who had always done as he liked without question, protested that he saw nothing wrong in his action. But it made a bad impression and for the moment discredited him as a possible leader of a moderate or middle party. The Covenanting ranks, momentarily weakened, closed again.[63]

Montrose was not the King's only hope in Scotland. Indeed, he rather distrusted the young man on account of his previous record as an active rebel. Hamilton had with the King's knowledge been in private correspondence with the Covenanters ever since the Glasgow Assembly. He still believed that he

could best serve the King by working out some kind of agreement or co-operation with Argyll. His behaviour was clumsy
and disingenuous; it was not wholly bad. As a lowland Scot,
he was far more acutely aware than any of the King's other
advisers of the harm that had been done by the Antrim project
in the first Scots war and the more serious Irish project of the
second. He believed that he could do better for the King
secretly than he could openly, at least as long as Strafford, the
author of the Irish scheme, was still the chief minister.[64]

While plans for managing Parliament and dividing the
Scots occupied the King's mind, he was not neglecting possibilities of foreign aid. He had been disappointed in help from
his uncle the King of Denmark, whose envoys had paid a brief
visit to him at York but had not been sufficiently impressed by
his prospects to entertain talk of a treaty. The Spanish alliance
had broken down and the King of Spain, who now had a
Portuguese and a Catalan revolt simultaneously on his hands,
was unable to spare money for Charles's assistance. Charles
therefore turned for help from Spain to Spain's enemies. Very
privately he renewed the offer of his younger daughter, Princess
Elizabeth, to the only son of the Prince of Orange. The Prince
of Orange was among the richest noblemen of Europe and by
election the effective ruler of the Netherlands, so that the alliance
promised to be of the greatest financial profit. The King was
extremely anxious that his sister, the Queen of Bohemia—who
lived in The Hague within a stone's throw of the Prince of
Orange—should not come to hear of the matter; he knew that
she had hopes of his daughters as brides for her sons and he
wished to confront her, therefore, with a *fait accompli* lest she
should attempt to stop the betrothal.[65]

Three promising projects were thus before King Charles; at
the best, the winter of 1640 might see a Parliament controlled
and managed, the Scots rebels divided, and the House of Orange
ready to pour the much-needed money into his coffers. The
further presence of Strafford, generally detested as he was, was
not necessary and might be harmful to the King's cause. Charles

had allowed him to face the attack on the royal policy almost unaided throughout the Council of Peers, and when the Council rose, Hamilton, who may well have had the royal warrant for what he did, urged Strafford to leave the country. Hamilton, most of all, must have wanted him to go, because, while he stayed, the King's intentions for the Irish army must remain ever present to men's minds.

The minister's immense personal unpopularity, as well as the Irish complication, were dangerous to the King his master, and had he gone it is possible that Charles would have faced Parliament in a clearer atmosphere. But everything depended on the ability of the King and his Council to manipulate the coming Parliament, and, with Strafford away, there would be no minister at Charles's command who could undertake so difficult a task. Strafford's continued help and advice was therefore of the first importance. In a sense also the violent hatred that he aroused might be turned to account. He might, at the worst, be made a scapegoat as he already had been from time to time during the Great Council. Either as adviser, or as a chosen victim, or as both at once, he could still be useful. All these things were evident both to him and to the King, but Charles rightly felt that he must give his faithful servant the chance of escaping, if he wished to do so. Strafford preferred to stay. Before the King left York for London he had a long private consultation with him: what was said, but for one detail, rests on conjecture only. The King knew that Strafford would be in danger both from the populace and from the House of Commons, and that his removal stood high among the demands of the Covenanters. But he still believed that this new Parliament would be better managed than the last, and the outward sign of his confidence was the promise that he gave to Strafford: on the word of a King, he said, he should not suffer in life or fortune, whatever turn events might take in London.

Strafford, who for the last thirteen months had seen every hopeful project of the King's or his own wrecked by misjudgment in the execution, set little store on this promise. But he could not abandon the work for which he had unceasingly striven. His hopes and beliefs were alike bound up with the monarchy as was also a great part of his personal fortune. For his master's and for his own sake he must try to save the King's government. Therefore he obeyed the King's command, only taking the precaution to visit his house in Yorkshire and set some order in his private affairs before taking horse for London. Weighing the hopes and dangers in his clear and resolute mind he did not quite despair. " I am to-morrow to London," he wrote to Sir George Radcliffe, a friend from whom he concealed nothing, " with more danger beset, I believe, than ever man went with out of Yorkshire; yet my heart is good and I find nothing cold within me. . . . All will be well, and every hour gives more hope than other."[66]

BOOK III CHAPTER III REFERENCES

1. *C.S.P.D.*, 1640, pp. 112–13.
2. *C.S.P. Ven.*, 1640–2, pp. 44–5.
3. *C.S.P.D.*, 1640, p. 156.
4. *Ibid.*, pp. 154–6.
5. *Ibid.*, pp. 167, 221–2.
6. *Canterburie's Amazement*, London, 1641.
7. *C.S.P.D.*, 1640, pp. 342–3.
8. *Portland MSS.*, III, p. 63.
9. Cardwell, I, pp. 389 ff.
10. Cleveland, *Poems*, London, 1642, p. 26; Bray, *Anatomy of Etcetera*, London, 1641.
11. See Soden *Godfrey Goodman* Chapter XXVI for a careful account of this rather complicated incident.
12. Laud, *Works*, III, p. 287 f.
13. *C.S.P.D.*, 1640, pp. 307–8.
14. *Ibid.*, p. 162.
15. Louis B. Wright, *Religion and Empire*, Chapel Hill, 1943, p. 71.
16. *C.S.P. Ven.*, 1640–2, pp. 50, 53.
17. *C.S.P. Ven.*, 1640–2, pp. 26, 52; *C.S.P.D.*, 1640, p. 226; *C.S.P.D.*, 1639–40, pp. 493, 525, 546; Burnet, *Lives*, p. 166.
18. *C.S.P.D.*, 1640, pp. 451, 491, 500, 521–2; *C.S.P. Ven.*, 1640–2, p. 59.
19. *Ibid.*, p. 10.
20. *Breadalbane MSS., Letters*, 1639–59, Glencarradale to Glenorchy, June 2nd, 1640.
21. *C.S.P.D.*, 1640, pp. 124–5, 450; *C.S.P. Ven.*, 1640–2, p. 55.
22. *Ibid.*, p. 509.
23. For the attitude of the gentry and the various mutinies of the troops, see *C.S.P.D.*, 1640, May–July, *passim*; see also Rushworth, II, ii, pp. 1191–4; *H.M.C.*, *XII*, iv,

pp. 520-2; *William Salt Society Collections*, XV, p. 205, *Yorkshire Archaeological Society, Record Series*, LIV, p. 230.

24. *C.S.P.D.*, 1640, p. 492.

25. *Ibid.*, pp. 316, 333.

26. *Ibid.*, pp. 487, 636-7.

27. Albion, p. 339; Laud, *Works*, III, p. 236; *C.S.P.D.*, 1640, p. 495; *C.S.P. Ven.*, 1640-2 p. 62; the tree, known by long tradition as Prince Henry's, flourishes at the time of writing (1953) in the beautiful garden of the Oatlands Court Hotel Weybridge.

28. *C.S.P.D.*, 1639-40, pp. 382-3; 1640, pp. 99-100, 215-16; Warriston, *Diary*, p. 97.

29. Balfour, II, pp. 373-9; Rushworth, II, ii, p. 1044.

30. *Breadalbane MSS., Letters*, 1639-59, Glencarradale to Glenorchy, May 25th; Napier, *Memorials of Montrose*, Edinburgh, 1848, I, pp. 258, 259, 266-7.

31. Napier, I, pp. 264-5; *C.S.P.D.*, 1640-1, p. 53.

32. Balfour, II, p. 381; *C.S.P.D.*, 1640-1, p. 53.

33. Napier, I, 154-5.

34. *C.S.P.D.*, 1640, pp. 516, 563, 571, 587-8.

35. *Ibid.*, pp. 590-1, 609; *Hardwicke State Papers*, II, p. 147.

36. Knowler, II, p. 401; *C.S.P.D.*, 1640, pp. 112-13, 179, 514, 591.

37. *Ibid.*, p. 462.

38. *Ibid.*, p. 600.

39. *Ibid.*, p. 627.

40. Guthry, p. 32.

41. *C.S.P.D.*, 1640, pp. 595-7, 625, 630.

42. *Ibid.*, p. 640.

43. *Ibid.*, p. 645.

44. Livingstone, p. 106.

45. *C.S.P.D.*, 1640, pp. 616, 626, 632-3.

46. Maidment, *Analecta Scotica*, Edinburgh 1834, I, pp. 383-5; *Breadalbane MSS., Letters*, 1640-69, 813; Gumble, *Life of General Monck*, London, 1671, p. 10.

47. *H.M.C. Various*, II, pp. 256-8.

48. *Loc. cit.*; *C.S.P.D.*, 1640, p. 658; 1641, pp. 38-9; Balfour, II, p. 388.

49. *H.M.C., XII, App. IV*, p. 523; Balfour, II, pp. 388, 390.

50. *H.M.C. Egmont MSS*, I, I, p. 120.

51. *C.S.P.D.*, 1640-1, pp. 23-4, 28-9.

52. *Ibid.*, p. 652; 1640-1, pp. 46, 53; *C.S.P. Ven.*, 1640-2, pp. 74, 76-7; Rushworth, II, ii, pp. 1310-3, 1321, 1266-7.

53. *C.S.P.D.*, 1640-1, p. 23.

54. *Ibid.*, pp. 47, 63.

55. Whitaker, p. 203.

56. Walsingham, *Brittanicae virtutis imago*, Oxford, 1644; *C.S.P.D.*, 1640-1, pp. 74, 84.

57. Balfour, II, p. 403; *C.S.P.D.*, 1640-1, p. 111.

58. *Ibid.*, p. 84-5.

59. *H.M.C. XII, App. IV*, p. 524; *C.S.P.D.*, 1640-1, pp. 92-7; Rushworth, II, ii, pp. 1275 ff.

60. *C.S.P.D.*, 1640-1, p. 197; his mother was Frances Walsingham, wife first of Sir

Philip Sydney, then of Elizabeth's favourite Essex. After the execution of Essex she married the Irish Catholic peer, Ulic Burke, Earl of Clanricarde.

61. Rushworth, II, II, pp. 1295–6, 1302–4.
62. C.S.P.D., 1640–1, p. 113.
63. Napier, I, pp. 302–5; Guthry, p. 87; Burnet, *op. cit.*, p. 179; *Breadalbane MSS.*. *Letters* 1639–59, Glencarradale to Glenorchy, October 6th, 1640.
64. Clarendon, Book II; Burnet, *op. cit.*, pp. 179 ff.
65. C.S.P.D., 1640–1, pp. 278–9.
66. Whitaker, pp. 214 ff.

CHAPTER FOUR

PARLIAMENT AND THE CROWN

November 1640–March 1641

THE King reached Westminster to find his prospects for controlling Parliament sadly clouded. The High Commission Court, in session in St. Paul's Cathedral, had been broken up a week before by a rabble shouting "No Bishop." A few days later, Archbishop Laud, going into his study to examine a further batch of rare manuscripts which he was presenting to Oxford, stopped short on the threshold: flat on its face on the floor lay the great portrait which Van Dyck had painted of him. "I am not superstitious," Laud would boldly write in his diary as he recorded every dream that disturbed his rest. He was not superstitious about the fall of a picture but—"God grant this be no omen."[1]

In the City of London the King's friends lost ground. All the efforts of the Lord Mayor, Sir Henry Garraway, of Alderman Abel of the Vintners' Company, of Reynardson of the Merchant Taylors, of Alderman Gurney and other loyal supporters, failed to secure the election of a King's man for the next Lord Mayor. The effective control of the City passed for the time being to the opposite party, who immediately postponed the payment to the King of the promised loan until such time as Parliament should meet; they had no intention of making the King financially independent of the Commons. At the Parliamentary election meanwhile they had rejected their own recorder, the Royalist Sir Thomas Gardiner, and chosen four notorious opponents of the Court, one of whom, Samuel Vassell, had been in prison for several years for refusing to pay the King's unparliamentary taxes.

The failure of the King's friends to secure Gardiner's election was serious, because Charles had counted on him for Speaker, and it was not easy to think of another man who would be at once acceptable to the Commons and not hostile to the Crown. After anxious consultation with his friends, the King decided on William Lenthall, a respectable lawyer, in whom he thought he saw the makings of a good servant. His choice was unfortunate for his own party; Lenthall was a timid man, prone to follow the majority, and it was not Charles whom he served during his many years in the Speaker's chair.

With misplaced economy the King decided to eliminate the solemn procession which was usually a feature of the opening of Parliament. This disappointed the populace, who always resented the curtailment of any public display, and left an impression of doubt and foreboding, at a time when a show of boldness was needed.[2] The truncated ceremony took place on the afternoon of Tuesday, November 3rd, 1640; this time the King himself made the opening speech and although his manner seemed nervous because of his difficulties of utterance, his matter was bold enough. Twice over he referred to the Scots as rebels and told Parliament that their first duty was to provide money to keep the English army in being.

The King's speech was coolly received and the Commons proceeded to their own chamber to pursue a policy independent of it: a policy inspired and directed by John Pym. John Pym had had his rehearsal as leader of the House in the spring; all the summer he had been in the inner councils of the opposition peers. His abilities marked him out as the principal man of the Commons, whilst his relations with the Lords Warwick, Saye, Brooke, Mandeville and the rest linked him to the King's critics in the Upper House. The secretary of the Providence Company, by virtue of his business training and his business associates, occupied a stronger position than any political leader in the

Commons had done before. He had the necessary connections with the City, the navy and the peerage, and he had the clear mind, the cool judgment, the comprehensive grasp of an administrator of genius. Other men in the House of Commons, among his friends and associates, could supply the qualities he lacked: John Hampden diplomacy and charm, Oliver St. John expert legal knowledge, William Strode and Denzil Holles fiery eloquence, Arthur Haslerig and young Harry Vane (the Secretary's Puritan son) the reckless drive of fanaticism. But these things were brought together, organised, directed, almost, in the theatrical sense, *produced* by the skill of John Pym.

John Pym was the principal architect of the constitutional revolution of the next eighteen months, and therefore one of the most significant single figures and one of the most remarkable intellects in the constitutional history of England. A West country man, born in 1584, he was a child of the Elizabethan age, reared in hatred of Spain, in strong Protestant beliefs, and in the faith that God intended the English to establish his Gospel by sea-power and settlement over the face of the earth. Like most prosperous country gentlemen, he had been educated at the University and the Inns of Court—Pembroke College, Oxford, and the Middle Temple. At one time he had held a post in the Exchequer Office but he had gained the greater part of his experience in business as the secretary of the Providence Company and in the management of overseas enterprises. A regular member of Parliament, at first for Calne in Wiltshire and later for Tavistock, he had a high reputation among the King's opponents as a forceful and well-informed speaker, but he had never—like the fiercer Strode and Holles—acted with violence or on impulse. He was a man of clear perceptions and patient resolution whose eloquence consisted in the application of his well-arranged knowledge to enforce his point of view. In his youth he had been married, but had long been a widower; his immediate family consisted of two grown-up sons of whom little is known. He was one of those men to whom personal and emotional ties are of no great strength and it was natural to him to live for and in his work. Sober in his habits and strenuous in his duty, he was capable of rising at three in the morning and working steadily—but for an hour or so for his devotions—until the following midnight. The only surviving likeness of him taken in his lifetime shows him as a broad-browed heavy-jowled man, with small alert eyes, a straight nose, and a full-lipped mouth framed by the typical curled moustache and pointed beard of the epoch. He wears his hair brushed straight back from the forehead and long enough to conceal his ears. His dress is the respectable black of a professional man, set off by a plain linen collar.

The first task of the House of Commons was to disentangle the confusions of a singularly troublesome election. The strenuous efforts of the Court and its opponents to get their friends and dependants into Parliament had many of them continued beyond the contest at the polls. Three or four members claimed to have been duly returned for boroughs which had a right to only two; half a dozen such cases were not unusual in an average House of Commons. In November 1640 there were nearly thirty of them, the House would in the next weeks hear a great deal about how many votes had been procured by canvassing in alehouses, and how " fourteen pounds was laid out on beer and tobacco " by the candidate's friends.[3]

The Committee of Privileges, for settling disputed elections, was selected on the first day. It was always a large Committee, with a maximum of forty members. This time, by some mis-counting, forty-seven members were elected to it, but nothing was done to alter the error for fear that the Court party should be left in a majority. Of the forty-seven, half at least were within the orbit and influence of Pym and his friends. For the next week or two they expeditiously solved the problem of the disputed returns by declaring the men they wanted to be truly elected and disallowing the elections of their rivals. It can only be said, in extenuation of this conduct, that had the Court party been in control of the Committee of Privileges—as it had hitherto usually contrived to be—it would have acted in the same way.

The Court party, in spite of all efforts, was more poorly represented than in April. Neither Edward Nicholas nor Windebanke's nephew and right-hand man, Robert Read, had managed to secure a seat. The irritation and distrust which had shown itself throughout the summer in the obstructive conduct of the gentry had only to be voiced by a few in the House of Commons for the overwhelming majority to join in. Those whose feelings varied from irritation to anger at the King's taxes, monopolies and wars, and from a vague disquiet to real distress at his neglect of the Protestant Cause and favour to his Catholic subjects, were not for the most part bent on reforms either in religion or the constitution. They spoke and thought in the old-fashioned way of grievances and abuses; their concern was to make life, and possibly their consciences, more easy. They wished to stop the unceasing demands for Ship-money, for coat-and-conduct money, for unwanted knighthoods, the petty fines for petty enclosure offences, the small blackmailing requests for subscriptions to the rebuilding of St. Paul's Cathedral. They wished to prevent the interruption of honest labour and the lawful occupations of town and country for a third year in succession by an expensive and unnecessary levy of troops. Almost every member of the House of Commons, in that autumn of 1640, excepting only the King's servants and courtiers, thought that the King's policy was wrong and his government bad. They were concerned to get rid of the ministers responsible—Archbishop Laud who had oppressed the Protestants and made the Scots revolt, and Strafford who had thrust the second war upon them and supported the alliance with Spain.

So far this attitude was traditional. But Bedford, Saye, Brooke and others among the Lords, Pym, Hampden, St. John and their like among the Commons, were thinking of changes more far-reaching than the removal of the King's " evil counsellors." That phrase was time-honoured, medieval; critics, parties, factions of one kind and another had been attacking and removing the King's " evil counsellors " since the days of

King John. What they wanted was something more: the transference of effective power from the King's hands into that of the High Court of Parliament. Therein lay the only permanent safeguard against the increase of royal power at the expense of their own. They believed themselves to be preserving the ancient balance of the constitution but the plain truth was that the law, as they practised and understood it, and the local administration of England, had made the ordinary life of the country depend at every point upon them, and hardly at all upon the Crown. The entire machine—law-courts, parishes, poor law, city and country—could run very well without the King; but it could not run without the gentry. In other words, the gentry were essential to the power of the King, but he was not essential to theirs. Neither Bedford, Pym nor any of them harboured a thought so shocking as the removal of the King; but they did envisage of a policy by which his theoretical power and his actual power should be brought into line with each other and properly defined. Otherwise they might risk the continuance of the present intolerable situation in which the King directed policy without power to execute it, and they, with power to prevent and obstruct policy, had none to direct it. It was a natural outcome of all this, so natural that few people at first noticed or commented upon it, that the House of Commons within a few weeks of its assembling, assumed the practice of sending out its own orders and instructions on public affairs to justices of the peace throughout the realm.[4]

Early in the session the Scottish Commissioners had arrived in London to consider, with the English Parliament, the terms of the treaty which was to end the war. The Committee of Estates in Edinburgh had given them instructions, some of which reflected precisely the same constitutional policy which inspired Pym and his associates; for instance, they suggested that the forthcoming treaty should provide for the calling of Parliaments in both countries at regular intervals of from two to three years.

The Scots were well received in London and were given Saint Antholin's Church, always a well-known Puritan centre, for their services. Here their preachers, principally the impressive Henderson, commanded congregations so large that late-comers thought no shame to haul themselves up to the windows and catch what they could from the outside. Thirty years of derisive jokes at the broad speech of " our brethren of Scotland " stopped overnight; all was now friendship and admiration.[5]

The King therefore faced from the beginning a formidable and intelligent alliance between his critics in Parliament and the Scots. In the circumstances it was unfortunate that Lord Keeper Finch, on the first day of the session, had tried to justify the summer's war by declaring that the King had undertaken it not at the advice of one or two ministers only, but at that of his entire council. By this speech he put all the King's servants under the same cloud and so prevented the King from making use in Parliament even of those who enjoyed some personal popularity.

Strafford, enjoying the last tranquillity he was ever to know in his own home in Yorkshire, condemned the folly of what Finch had said.[6] The condemnation is interesting because it reveals something of what was going on in his mind. He had a clear idea of Pym's ability and less sanguine expectations of the present Parliament than the King. His disapproval of what Finch had said shows that he sincerely hoped to draw the anger of the King's critics as much as possible upon himself. The Archbishop would hardly escape it, but Strafford had been the more prominent of the two during the last year, and it was his belief that the Commons would almost certainly impeach him first. He had seen in his youth three Parliaments in turn waste their fury in attacks on the King's favourite Buckingham; the same situation was now about to arise in his own case. But the outcome would be different. The King had never allowed Buckingham to be put on trial, so that the favourite's guilt had been left in permanent doubt. But if this Parliament were allowed to impeach and try Strafford they would have to abandon general vilification for sober charges which could be sustained in law, and would have to prove them to the satisfaction of the House of Lords. It was one thing to call a man "the source of all evils," as they had Buckingham, or "Black Tom Tyrant", as they now called Strafford. It was another to prove treason against him, article by article, more especially as he had committed none.

This then was Strafford's intention and his hope. He would stand out as the man frankly responsible for the King's policy, and face whatever charges John Pym and the Commons brought against him: *and he would refute them.* He knew the law of England as well as any lawyer in the land and better than John Pym; he knew by past experience the temper and complexity of Parliaments and he knew that a good half of those discontented, disturbed and angry gentlemen, whose resentments were now fixed upon him as the author of their evils, would be perturbed and shaken when they saw the weakness of the legal case and heard the arguments that he himself could so eloquently urge. In all Pym's calculations he knew that there could be no room for an impeachment that failed. Once let impeachment be tried and fail, and the Commons would be divided from the Lords and divided among themselves. Then let the King use well and quickly their moment of weakness; he could redeem much, perhaps all. This idea, or something like it, must have been in Strafford's mind when he set out from Yorkshire, feeling, as he had said, "nothing cold within me."

In plain truth he did not much miscalculate, and the match he was to play with John Pym was a close one. Had he been as intelligently supported by King and Court as Pym was in Parliament, he might have succeeded; more than once between the dark November of 1640 when the contest opened and the bright May of 1641 when it ended, it seemed almost as though he had won.

John Pym was wary from the start. He avoided the traps. Parliament opened on November 3rd and, to the surprise of many, not a word was said about Strafford for more than a week. For the first days every other kind of complaint was aired and encouraged: this was good strategy, for it established so many different complaints and grievances against the King's government that Pym could later choose which to press and which to abandon, as the mood of the House shifted.

In the Short Parliament the King's critics had contrived to organise half a dozen petitions from the counties complaining of their grievances. In the first week of the Long Parliament about twenty petitions had already come in, mostly from counties and towns, some from individuals; these were directed against Ship-money, innovations in religion, Star Chamber sentences, monopolies and exactions. Mrs. Burton and Mrs. Bastwicke petitioned for the release of their husbands, a servant of Prynne brought a petition from his master, and Oliver Cromwell, the member for Cambridge, raised the case of Lilburne. The petitions were inspired by the more active critics of the King, who had bestirred themselves to get them drawn up and signed. Popular feeling does not manifest itself spontaneously in writing; it manifests itself in argument in alehouses and church porches, in parlours and studies, in the market place or hunting field. But the petitions, in this autumn of a disturbed and unhappy year, were a very fair representation, only a little heightened and organised, of what a great number of the King's subjects were thinking.

Pym wove them together with his habitual skill into a cogent speech against the government at the end of Parliament's first week. Their grievances were, he said, of three kinds. The ancient privileges of Parliament had been attacked by long intermission of the assembly and by the arrest of members merely for speaking their minds; true religion had been persecuted while such clergy only were preferred who "pretended Divine Authority and Absolute Power in the King to do what he will with us"; the liberty of the subject had been invaded by illegal taxes, the revival of obsolete laws and the advantages granted to projectors and monopolists. The Star Chamber, once the defence of the poor against oppression, had become merely "an instrument of erecting and defending monopolies, to set a face of public good on things pernicious." The King's subjects had even been threatened with invasion by foreign and Irish troops. Modestly, after this deep and wide attack, he claimed for Parliament no more than the right and duty of " declaring the law where it is doubtful and providing for the execution of the law where it is clear." [7]

On November 10th George Digby, presenting the complaints from Dorset, showed himself to be a speaker of persuasive fervour and charm. He was eldest son to the Earl of Bristol and son-in-law to the Earl of Bedford and belonged to the group of discontented nobility who shunned the Court. He himself, a talented and attractive young man, and a dilettante of the sciences, had wished to shine at Court but had been reprimanded by the King for a high-spirited quarrel and had retired in mortification. This new recruit to Pym's forces distinguished himself by the suggestion that the House draw up a Remonstrance against the ministers responsible for the King's policy. The idea was well received and a committee was at once appointed to collect the necessary material.[8]

Other speakers, on this and the succeeding day, took up and enlarged the grievances outlined by Pym. Sir John Colepeper, presenting a petition from Kent, denounced Ship-money, monopolies and the expensive levying of troops. Sir Edward Dering, scholar and antiquary, who represented the county of Kent along with John Colepeper, was smarting from a recent interview with the Archbishop, who had curtly refused his plea on behalf of a Puritan minister. He was the first to name Laud in person. " Our manifold griefs do fill a mighty and vast circumference," he eloquently proclaimed, " yet so that from every point our lines of sorrow do lead unto him and point at him, the centre from whence our miseries do flow."[9] Few voices were raised in defence of the royal government and when William Widderington, recently sheriff of Northumberland and now its representative in Parliament, spoke, like a loyal Borderer, of the invading Scots as rebels, Denzil Holles, the hot-tempered member for Dorchester, compelled him to withdraw the offensive phrase.[10]

On Wednesday, November 11th, the attention of the

Commons was divided between the misdeeds of monopolists and the suspicious behaviour of Secretary Windebanke (who had been returned to Parliament for Corfe, a constituency controlled by Attorney-General Bankes). Windebanke, it seemed, had slightingly dismissed the hysterical Mrs. Hussey when she had come to him earlier that summer with her tale of seven thousand Irish Papists hidden about London and only waiting to cut all good Protestant throats.[11] This ridiculous affair was being hotly pursued, when at about eleven in the morning, Sir John Clotworthy, the member for Maldon, acting presumably on a hint from Pym, made a violent and incoherent speech against Strafford. This was the opening move in the well-planned attack that Pym had been holding back until the time was ripe.

His decision to open the attack this day and hour was the outcome of news which he seems at that moment to have received. Strafford, who had reached London the previous night, had just taken his seat in the House of Lords. Pym respected the skill of his adversary too highly to give him so much as a day's grace to plan a counter-stroke; as soon as he knew that Strafford was at Westminster he could risk no more delay. He was, of course, ready with a roughly drafted general accusation, and the feeling against Strafford was so strong that, to command enthusiastic support from all quarters of the House, he had only to rise and outline the case for his impeachment. George Digby in a high flight of eloquence denounced Strafford, whom he hardly knew, as " that grand Apostate to the Commonwealth," and only Lord Falkland, who sat next to his friend Edward Hyde, and represented Newport in the Isle of Wight, raised a philosopher's gentle voice to warn the House against the danger of proceeding too fast on undigested evidence. The danger of proceeding too slowly was, in Pym's opinion, far greater. By the close of an extended morning session he was able to carry up the accusation to the House of Lords.[12]

Strafford was no longer present. Knowing what was afoot in the Commons—for one of the Court members must surely have got word to him—he had slipped away to Whitehall for a last-minute consultation with the King. What, if anything, was decided at that interview, is unknown, but Strafford miscalculated the speed of Pym's action and mistimed his return. When he reached the portals of the House of Lords, Pym with a delegation from the Commons had already laid the impeachment before them. He was compelled to withdraw, and was taken that afternoon to honourable confinement in the house of Maxwell, Gentleman Usher of the Black Rod. He bore all with an air of haughty unconcern, although some of his fellow peers openly rejoiced in his discomfiture. The mighty had indeed fallen, and Dr. Baillie, who with the Scots Commissioners saw it all, recorded gravely in his diary that the evil man had been taken away " all gazing, no man capping to him, before whom that morning the greatest of England would have stood discovered." [13]

Returned to the House of Commons, Pym, still maintaining the attack on all fronts, switched the attention of his colleagues back to the reprehensible behaviour of Secretary Windebanke, and they were upon this fruitful subject when a messenger from the Upper House informed them that their lordships had sequestered the Earl of Strafford and placed him in custody. For this the Commons returned suitable thanks.[14]

During the next weeks the committee appointed to draw up the charges against Strafford worked hard, fetched witnesses out of Ireland and the North, sifted and examined innumerable allegations. From time to time the committee reported and the charges were discussed in the House. Lest the impeachment should fail for lack of strict legal proof, Pym also investigated the possibility of having a Bill of Attainder introduced to dispatch Strafford. A Bill of Attainder—a Parliamentary Bill which simply *decreed* a man guilty of treason—did not need to rest on precise points of law: a general presumption of guilt, or more crudely a general hatred of the victim, was enough. This ruthless form of action had been evolved in the Wars of the Roses, but discontinued since.

The preparations went forward for Strafford's trial, but they did not occupy the House of Commons to the exclusion of all other matters. Pym deliberately prevented the impeachment of Strafford from becoming at this stage the " Great Business," the only business which could fill and inspire the House, and the days of the Commons were fully occupied with grievances of other kinds. Religion was the foremost. The attack on the King's religious policy was directed against favours to Roman Catholics, and the Romanising tendencies of the Archbishop. The Commons had refused to take the Communion at St. Margaret's, Westminster, until the altar rails had been removed and the Table brought down into the nave. But no one had yet spoken against the organisation of the Church or said anything against bishops in general. Sympathy for the Scots did not necessarily argue a slavish desire to copy their conduct in all things, and although a minority in the House of Commons was opposed to episcopacy itself, Pym knew them to be a minority and did not at this stage encourage them lest their inconsiderate fervour should provoke a breach among his supporters.

Laud's cleverest opponent within the Church itself, John Williams, Bishop of Lincoln, took his seat in the House of Lords amid considerable popular rejoicing, on November 16th. He had been in the Tower for over three years, except for a few weeks when he had offered bail that he might attend the Short Parliament but had been prevented from doing so. Williams, the moderate churchman, who had always feared the consequences of Laud's emphasis on ritual, enjoyed at the moment the popularity of a martyr, and was well aware of the strength of his position. His friends in both Houses were, in the main, Pym's friends: Bedford, Saye, Hampden. He was clever, diplomatic, with Welsh vitality and charm; he was also ambitious and, after his long eclipse, saw himself as the new architect and statesman of the Church who would redeem the fatal errors of Archbishop Laud, find for the Church a middle way, and rebuild a Protestant Episcopate on the love of the people and the support of the lords and gentry.

Larger crowds than those that had cheered Bishop Williams

on his progress from the Tower to the House of Lords lined the streets of London a fortnight afterwards for the triumphal entry of Prynne and Burton on November 28th and of Bastwicke a few days later. Their more distinguished sympathisers followed them in coaches and rode behind, wearing sprigs of rosemary [15] —rosemary for remembrance, rosemary, the grey-green sea-colour which was to become in the next ten years the insignia of the extremists, of those who thought all men free and equal before God—grey-green for liberty and the reign of King Jesus.

Animosity against Roman Catholics had re-doubled. Count Rossetti, the papal envoy, was rudely knocked up at one in the morning by some city magistrates with an angry crowd at their back demanding to search his house. Imperturbably dignified and amiable, he asked the justices in and courteously showed them his pictures and works of art. They retired, apologetic and embarrassed. A few weeks later, none the less, Rossetti yielded to the Queen's entreaty, gave up his house and agreed to live under guard in the house allotted to the Queen's mother.[16]

The King, late in the day, tried to disarm criticism by dismissing all Roman Catholics from Court except the Queen's personal servants. Little old Toby Mathew's brief summer was at an end; he slipped away to pursue philosophic speculation and make his cups of chocolate among the friendly people of Ghent. Wat Montagu held out longer, relying on the protection of his father, the aged and pious Earl of Manchester, and his brother Lord Mandeville, one of the most eminent Puritans in the House of Lords.

Of those who had helped the King in protecting the Catholic minority in England, the first to be sacrificed was Secretary Windebanke. Windebanke's own religion was unobtrusive; his interest in life had been in acquiring and retaining a position at Court, building up a fortune the foundation of which had been laid by his father and grandfather, also servants of the Crown. As to taking money from Spain, issuing licences to exempt recusants from paying fines and prohibiting the prosecution of Roman Catholic priests, these things were part of his work; he was a little man who obeyed orders and enriched himself, within reason, on the side. Suddenly, in the heartless cold of an early winter, he found that he was a solitary hare running for dear life before the whole pack of Commons. John Glynne, an able barrister of strongly Calvinist views, reported from the committee on religion that sixty-four priests had been released from prison in the last year on Windebanke's order, that more than seventy letters of grace signed by him had been issued to Papists throughout the Kingdom; finally—most damning of all—that the total sum in recusants' fines collected by him in the last thirteen years was only just over four thousand pounds. Recusants were supposed to pay a shilling a Sunday to the poor. A simple calculation showed that if Windebanke's figures were right only about a hundred and forty-six Catholics in the whole of England could have been mulcted.[17] Windebanke, hearing of these accusations, hurried home and hid under the bedclothes. Messengers from the Commons, sent to seek him, were told by his servants that he had been up late the previous night and must have his sleep out. In the House his nephew and right-hand man, Robert Read, vainly attempted to justify his uncle, then rejoined him and under cover of darkness rode to the coast. The weather was foggy and the wind sluggish, but they bribed a man to put them across the Channel in a rowing boat.[18] When the Commons sent for Windebanke again he was out of reach in France. He was safe but was never to be happy again; the French Court were good to him and he was not in want. He was invited to fashionable masques and to the wedding of Richelieu's niece. But he remained inconsolable, asking, always in vain, why his master the King did not exonerate him before Parliament by declaring the simple truth that he had only obeyed orders. Windebanke was not born to carry the dangerous responsibilities of office or to sacrifice himself with uncomplaining loyalty, and he remained to the end a querulous, reproachful victim.[19]

But he respected his master's confidence, however unfair he felt his punishment to be. His colleague, Secretary Vane, was less scrupulous; he also had a son, young Harry, to whom he seems to have been genuinely attached, who followed with deep conviction the most extravagant religious sects and held extremist views on God and politics. Old Vane was indiscreet and self-important and he hated Strafford. Possibly, indeed probably, he had hinted and babbled at home of things said and done at the council table. Probably Windebanke did the same with his wife and family—but none of them were Puritans, still less fanatics. Old Vane, moreover, if his son was to be believed, left his notes of council meetings scattered about among his private papers. Here young Vane, searching with his father's permission for a family document, had in the course of the previous summer come upon and read the notes of the meeting held on May 5th, 1640; from these he had learnt that Strafford had suggested bringing over the Irish army to reduce " this Kingdom." Young Vane smelt the importance of the document and, after a brief tussle between filial loyalty and his sense of public duty, copied it for Pym. John Pym, to spare young Vane's feelings as far as possible, copied it again himself so that the source of the betrayal would be less apparent.[20]

It was common knowledge that Strafford had planned to bring over the Irish army to attack the Scots in the rear. But this conduct, however bitter the resentment it had aroused, could not easily be construed as treason because at the time the Scots had been in arms, and Strafford as the King's minister was bound to consider the means to put them down. His peers, however much they might condemn his policy against the Scots, could hardly in logic say that it was treasonous.

But the note taken at the council meeting and now in Pym's hands was capable of a far more dangerous interpretation. " An army in Ireland you may employ here to reduce this kingdom ..." Which kingdom? The notes gave no indication. Had Strafford, in anger at the behaviour of the Short Parliament and impatience at English resistance to the royal policy, meant not Scotland but England? Had he suggested bringing over Irish troops to subdue not the rebel Scots who were in arms but the recalcitrant English who were not?

The sentence could bear that interpretation. It is possible that John Pym sincerely believed that it did. The known ruthlessness of Strafford's methods, no less than the widespread belief that the King had negotiated for military help from the Spanish Netherlands, made this interpretation perfectly credible. If it was indeed a possible and a credible interpretation of the words, then Strafford had committed an act from whose treasonous implications there was no escape: he had advised the King to make war on his own peaceful subjects and had offered the means to do it.

This was the awful value of the evidence which young Vane had produced. But how could it be used? Young Vane was not very willing that his intrusions into his father's private papers should be revealed; it would be better if old Vane himself could be inveigled into incriminating Strafford. The House of Commons accordingly sent a message to the King for permission to examine Privy Councillors on oath on what had passed in council. The request put the King in a quandary; a more outrageous intrusion into the inner sanctum of government could hardly be thought of, but if the King refused to allow it, his refusal would imply that he doubted Strafford's innocence or had something to hide. Of two evils he may have chosen the lesser when, on December 4th, he gave the House permission to question his own councillors. The Venetian ambassador, wise in the cunning statecraft of the Republic, recorded this demand of the Commons as the most serious attack yet made on the sovereignty of the King and his yielding to it as infinitely unwise. Certainly this decision, coming as it did on top of the tacit repudiation of Windebanke, made the King's remaining councillors very unwilling to put their loyalty to their master before their own interests or to give him any advice which might possibly be quoted later to their disadvantage.[21]

With the flight of Secretary Windebanke the King lost his most important representative in the Commons. An order that no monopolist might occupy a seat in the House excluded several more. When, on December 7th, the Commons proclaimed

Ship-money an illegal tax, it was evident that any members who injudiciously supported the King might be expelled or suspended on the grounds that, in one way or another, they had been concerned in collecting Ship-money; most loyal gentlemen had at one time or another in the past few years, been involved in assessing their neighbours or assisting the sheriff in the pursuance of his duties. The chief offenders in the Ship-money business were the King's own judges, and Lord Falkland, in words of unusual forcefulness now directed the batteries of the House of Commons against the judicial Bench and the Lord Keeper himself.

The judges, by their monstrous dictum, said Falkland, had " allowed to the King the sole power in necessity, the sole judgment of necessity, and by that enabled him to take from us what he would, when he would, and how he would." He hinted at corruption. "I doubt not," he went on, "we shall find when we examine them, with what hopes they have been tempted, by what fears they have been essay'd, and by what and by whose importunity they have been pursued before they consented to what they did." Among them all none was more culpable or more worthy to be removed than Lord Keeper Finch; "he who hath prostituted his own conscience hath the keeping of the King's." After so powerful an accusation the impeachment of Finch was only a matter of time.[22]

A diversion postponed the formal accusation of Finch for some days yet. On December 11th one of the members for London, Alderman Isaac Pennington, presented a petition with fifteen hundred signatures for the abolition of the ungodly institution of bishops, " root and branch." This move by Pennington and the fiercer Puritan spirits in London was not from Pym's point of view happily timed, because any action that might be taken on the Root and Branch petition was likely to divide the House. Pym managed to have it referred to the committee for religion, and to satisfy the Londoners, while disregarding their petition, he managed to direct the main force of the religious attack on to Laud's Canons and Laud himself.

The principal spokesmen were Sir Walter Strickland and Sir Edward Dering. Dering had already planted some good phrases in debate by declaring that if Laud did not aim to be Pope of Rome, he certainly aimed to be Patriarch of Lambeth, and complaining that wicked Popish books were licensed while good sound doctrine was prohibited " by the supercilious pen of my Lord's young chaplain." Now he proceeded in an impressively learned oration to condemn the Laudian Canons passed by Convocation in the spring.[23] From this it was a short step to the impeachment of Laud and his principal lieutenant Matthew Wren on December 18th. Wren was allowed to remain at liberty on giving bail of £10,000, but Laud, on whom the Scots Commissioners had demanded justice as a principal incendiary in the late war, was to be secluded immediately in the house of the serjeant-at-arms. He asked leave of the Lords to go home to Lambeth to fetch some necessaries and a few books; this, with a movement of mercy towards the broken old man, they granted him. He spent the short day collecting his papers at Lambeth, and was permitted, for the last time, to attend evensong with his household in his own chapel. It was December 18th, Friday, a week before Christmas, and he found marvellous comfort in the lesson, the fiftieth Chapter of Isaiah, and the psalms for the day.

The floods are risen, O Lord, the floods have lift up their voice. . . . Blessed is the man whom thou chastenest, O Lord . . . that thou mayest give him patience in time of adversity: until the pit be digged up for the ungodly. . . . They gather them together against the soul of the righteous: and condemn the innocent blood.
But the Lord is my refuge. . . .

He had asked that he might make his departure from Lambeth after dark " to avoid the gazing of the people." But a kindly surprise awaited him; as he passed down to the river to his barge " hundreds of my poor neighbours stood there, and prayed for my safety and return to my house. For which I bless God and them." [24]

The attack on the institution of episcopacy had been for the moment diverted into a personal attack on Laud and Wren, and it was possible for Pym to turn the attention of the House again to the less controversial question of Lord Keeper Finch. On December 21st, three days after the Archbishop had been removed to prison, the man whose office it was to sit in black and gold robes on the Woolsack and preside over the sessions of the peers, appeared before the Commons, bare-headed, to answer the accusations unanimously made against him: not one voice had been raised in protest. He was not, like Strafford and Laud, hated with violence and venom, but he was perhaps more universally disliked than any man in England. In this, his last public appearance as Lord Keeper, he behaved with unexpected restraint and dignity, calmly repudiated Falkland's suggestion that he had been bribed to pronounce Ship-money legal and affirmed his conviction that he had interpreted the law faithfully as he understood it. He had, however, made his preparations and before the House reassembled on the morning of December 22nd he had got himself aboard a ship in the cold and dark and was on his way to the Netherlands. [25] Windebanke at Paris, Toby Mathew at Ghent, Finch in The Hague—they were only the first of the flock of English refugees who in the next twenty years were to become a familiar, pathetic and finally boring spectacle in the little towns of the Netherlands, Paris and the French provinces, even in Venice, Madrid and Rome; keeping up their English customs and their conventions of gentility in reduced circumstances, talking of a past which grew in retrospect ever more rich and glorious, and believing in a future when they and the King would enjoy their own again. Finch was one of the fortunate: he survived. At the age of seventy-six he would totter triumphantly back to a seat in the House of Lords.

The Commons continued with the impeachment of Finch even after his flight, for it was essential to prove, beyond question, the abuses of the law which had been permitted under the King's authority by the men of his own appointment. As Falkland, who continued to direct this impeachment, very aptly put it: "He used the law against itself, making it, as I may say, *Felo de se*."[26] This kind of argument sustained the claim of the House of Commons made in Pym's opening speech to do no more than "declare the law where it was doubtful and provide for the execution of the law where it was clear." Falkland, of all those who in these months supported Pym's policy, had the deepest views on political theory; he was more philosopher and theorist than practical man, or he might have seen more clearly that an onslaught on the Chancellor and the judges, with whatever justice and moderation it was conducted, was bound to have a revolutionary rather than a steadying and restorative effect on the legal structure of the state.

His friend, Edward Hyde, a working barrister and a more practical man of affairs, came in the end to see very clearly that the tendencies of the dominating group in the House of Commons had been revolutionary from the beginning. But in the winter of 1640-41 he was as eloquent and as forward as Falkland for the destruction of the powers which the King had tried to gather to himself. While the subservient Bench was Falkland's target, Hyde was the principal speaker against the prerogative courts, the abolition of which the House now began most insistently to demand.

Before the close of the year it had become clear that the demands and behaviour of this Parliament were different from those of its predecessors. They had attacked the King's policy; this Parliament was attacking the King's position. Even a document like the Petition of Right, forced through by the 1628 Parliament, had been an attempt only to stop the enforcement by the King of an unpopular policy; it prevented him from exploiting his powers of raising and billeting troops in such a way as to punish or control those who objected to his policy. It had not fundamentally altered his position or curtailed his sovereignty in any crucial point.

But the Long Parliament (as it came to be called) attacked the roots of sovereignty. This was not done by pompous statements of political theory; it was done in a direct, business-like, Pym-like manner, by fastening systematically in turn upon every vital place. By asserting their right to inquire into the levying of Ship-money and of coat-and-conduct money for the troops, the Commons had tacitly implied that all the administrative officers of the Kingdom were answerable, not to the King, but to Parliament. It was an extension of this principle to assert, tentatively and in one single instance at first, Parliament's right to know what went on in the King's inmost councils and to question those who advised him on how and why they spoke. If the King's lesser officials were answerable to Parliament, why not his ministers? Why not the King? By accusing the judges, Parliament implied that it alone could decide the validity of laws: that Parliament, and not the King, was the fountain of justice. It followed logically from this that the prerogative courts must go; if the King was not, in his proper person, the fountain of justice, no court could function by his authority alone. The High Court of Parliament remained; it could indeed prosecute and try men—as it would shortly do Strafford—because it embodied the King's justice. King-in-Parliament was the source of law, not the King alone.

Two pillars supporting the monarchy remained: the revenues and the armed forces. Before the end of the year the House, pursuing the question of monopolies, tax-farming and other alleged abuses, had asked to examine the officers responsible for collecting the royal revenue and their books. The King conceded the request, again for fear of seeming to conceal anything upon which a dangerous construction could be put. The outcome was an order of the House of Commons soon after Christmas that the officers of the customs were to pay no more money into the royal coffers except for the daily expenses of the household.[27] To this unprecedented impertinence the King had no choice but to submit. The sums of money which had to be officially paid to the Scots pending the conclusion of a treaty, together with such other expenses as paying the remnant of the

English army, now passed through Parliament only. Parliament not the King, had taken over and renewed the loan made by the City.

The question of the army remained in abeyance. The local levies had gone home, but the cavalry and some of the infantry which had been raised by the King's supporters remained in being; with the six northern counties occupied by the Scots forces and the treaty not yet signed, it was only reasonable to keep some kind of an English army in existence, although notoriously Roman Catholic officers—the gallant John Smith among them—had been asked to resign. With Strafford's impeachment the chief command fell vacant, and the King had bestowed it once more on the Earl of Essex, who was trusted by Parliament, very well liked of the men, and not openly hostile to the King. There, in a kind of neutrality, the matter rested.

Parliament, under Pym's guidance, had taken order for everything except the control of the army and their own future. The King could still dissolve Parliament when he chose and was not bound to call it except when he pleased. To curtail this latter right, the Parliamentary lawyers had dug up an old, never implemented, Bill of the time of Edward III for the annual holding of Parliaments. This, in a modernised form, was debated in the House before the end of December. In two months, therefore, the beginnings of a constitutional revolution had been made at every vital place and there was as yet no sign of the King taking any counter-measures. Even if Strafford achieved what he—and the King—hoped, and triumphantly disproved the accusations made by the Commons, the Commons had made themselves so strong in other ways that it would be hard to force them back from the position they had gained.

In the circumstances gloom and depression should have prevailed at Court, but the Venetian envoy reported with faint disapproval in December that the King and his friends were cheerful. The loss of a daughter, the four-year-old Princess Anne, early in the month, probably went nearer to the Queen than it did to the King; her health responded all too quickly to anxiety and strain, and during these crucial months she lost weight and sleep, became excitable to the point of hysteria, and gave way to tears at the least frustration. The King was physically and emotionally of different stuff. His nerves were good and his health excellent. The regularity and order of his personal life continued, he prayed, ate and slept regularly, and was sustained by his unalterable conviction that God might chasten him for a time but would not desert a righteous King. He did not doubt that he would in the end overthrow his enemies.

His hopes in the winter of 1640–41 were fixed on the help of the House of Orange. The Baron de Heenvliet, the diplomatic Dutch nobleman who in the previous summer had undermined the King's Spanish alliance, had busied himself to some purpose, though very secretly, with this new project. By the middle of December it was generally known at Court that the only son of the Prince of Orange was to marry one of the King's daughters. The Prince of Orange, a rich and powerful nobleman in his own right, was by election the commander-in-chief and the virtual head of the government of the Protestant Netherlands. The position of the House of Orange in relation to the Dutch was unique; three princes of that house, William the Silent and his two sons, Maurice and Frederick Henry, had with ability and devotion guided the politics of the northern Netherlands during the seventy years of their war of liberation from Spain. The government of the Dutch provinces was republican and, inevitably, as the danger of Spanish victory faded, good republicans in Holland grew suspicious of the quasi-hereditary power of the House of Orange. The position of Frederick Henry was however still nearly as secure as that of a ruling sovereign—far more so than that of King Charles—and the private resources of the family were unquestionable.

The Prince of Orange, while careful not to offend Dutch susceptibilities, was very willing to establish his family on an equality with the reigning houses of Europe; late in life he had married the beautiful Amalia von Solms, maid-of-honour to Elizabeth of Bohemia, and his wife's ambition for their only son helped in persuading this otherwise sage statesman to involve himself with the difficult fortunes of the Stewart dynasty. He offered to advance £100,000 to King Charles immediately and asked that the princess who was to be his son's bride should be sent to Holland to complete her education. In the earlier stages of the negotiation he had looked no higher than the King's second daughter, the five-year-old Princess Elizabeth, and things had gone far enough with this little girl for her intended bridegroom to send her a jewel worth a thousand pounds.[28] The match was almost made before the Princess of Orange took it upon herself to confide in the Queen of Bohemia from whom the matter had hitherto been carefully concealed. The poor Queen expressed outward pleasure at this piece of family news, but was deeply mortified at her brother's secretive behaviour. She justly suspected, from the embarrassment of her former maid-of-honour, that something else was being kept back, and guessed, with anguish, what that something was. For years she had trusted in a tacit understanding with her brother that he would give his eldest daughter to her eldest son. She wrote at once to a faithful friend at the English Court, imploring him to use all his influence to prevent the ambitious Prince and Princess of Orange from stealing her son's bride.[29] Her suspicions were correct: as it became clear to Heenvliet that King Charles was desperate for the alliance and the immediate financial relief that it would bring, he shifted the demand from the younger to the elder daughter, and by the middle of January 1641 had secured Princess Mary, nine years old and very pretty, for the twelve-year-old Prince William.

With this foreign alliance and financial help secured, the King's confidence grew. He began to marshal such forces as he had for the counter-attack. The flight of Finch, leaving the Woolsack vacant, had opened the way for new appointments. The King made Sir Edward Littleton Lord Keeper in his room, moved Sir John Bankes, hitherto Attorney-General, to Littleton's place as Chief Justice of the Common Pleas, and promoted Sir Edward Herbert to Attorney-General instead of Bankes.

All these men were strongly loyal to the Crown and had supported Ship-money, but as if to cover these appointments with an act of conciliation, the King gave to Oliver St. John, who had conducted Hampden's defence, the lucrative post of Solicitor-General. The massing and arrangement of his legal strength was of great importance, because the conflict between him and Parliament was essentially an argument over the interpretation of the law. In theory neither side admitted to making or desiring the least innovation: the King claimed that his view of the laws —interpreted by Finch, by Strafford, by Bankes, by the late ingenious Noy—was the correct one. Pym and his friends —supported by barristers of weight and learning like Maynard, Selden, Hyde, and by the writings and dicta of the late Sir Edward Coke—contended that the interpretations of the King's advisers were subversive and their own correct. Neither denied that the law, in some absolute sense and meaning, already existed; it needed only to be restored and made manifest in action.

In this theory of law subverted or law interpreted the coming impeachment of Strafford played an important part. If he could shake the legal contentions of his prosecutors as to the manner in which he had exercised his office as the King's Deputy, he would go far to undermine the widespread belief among the law-conscious English, from barristers to country justices, that the King had, in his personal role, acted against the law. Once this belief, the outcome of the last years' inconveniences and interferences, began to weaken, it might be possible for the King to show that impeachment had a double edge, and that his Attorney-General could bring charges against his opponents quite as effectively as they could bring charges against his ministers. This policy would need patience and the right men in the right places at the right time. The King's choice of men for preferment in the legal offices of the Kingdom during his personal rule had, unfortunately, given him no very great reserves on which to draw. The lawyers of brilliance, daring and strength were nearly all on the opposing side. Finch had already shown

387

himself unequal to the crisis, and his departure removed a man who was by this time a liability to the King's cause. Littleton and Herbert, both good, solid, helpful, honest men and the best appointments that could be made in the circumstances, lacked the courage and vision essential for the task before them.

These appointments revealed something of the King's intended policy. He sought to win over his less violent critics among the peers, those whose opposition was not so much fundamental as incidental—men who objected to the mismanagement of the Scots war but whose traditions and past relations with the Court made them essentially the servants of the Crown rather than its opponents: men who, although Protestant in feeling, were neither Puritan nor Presbyterian in their religious sympathies. The King had already gone far to win Lord Bristol, who had been the spokesman of the opposition peers at York. He aimed also at Bedford and at the moderate Hertford, believing rightly that these men could be detached from intransigents like the troublesome Saye and Brooke, the dark and dangerous Warwick. The same process, if well begun in the Lords, could be extended to the Commons. The fears of those who had been disturbed by what appeared new and overbearing in the King's last years of government were to be systematically allayed by the moderation of his present conduct, while their suspicions of the extremists among his critics were gradually aroused. The majority in Lords, Commons and the country at large were conventional: they feared any kind of " overturning "—the word was frequently on their tongues. They had disliked Ship-money, patents, monopolies, licences, because these things overturned or threatened to overturn conventional ideas about property rights. But the attitude of some of Pym's more extreme followers, especially in religion, threatened to " overturn " other things equally important to them: the relation of Church and State or the social hierarchy itself. It could only be a matter of time and forbearance on the King's part before the feelings, so strong against his government at the end of the year 1640, should begin to rise against the opposing party.

This was the dominant theme in King Charles's policy during the next months, but it was not the only theme. He felt the necessity—and the Queen felt it still more acutely—to have more deadly alternatives in reserve in case his long-term policy did not work fast enough. He still controlled the army, and although he had made the Earl of Essex commander-in-chief he knew that a number of army officers drawn from the Court circle were devoted either to him or to the Queen, or, at any rate, much opposed to John Pym, Puritans and Covenanters. Many of the Roman Catholic officers had had to withdraw, but the King kept in touch with the best of them: to Captain John Smith he offered a baronetcy gratis which the sensible young soldier refused on the grounds that his fortune was too slender to support so high a rank.[30] He was naturally on good terms with the young noblemen who officered his personal guards and who, all that winter, lent a decorative martial air to his Court: Harry Jermyn, the Queen's Master of the Horse, George Goring, governor of Portsmouth and son of Lord Goring a principal courtier and favourite with the Queen, Harry Percy, brother of Northumberland, John Suckling and William Davenant, poets and courtiers turned soldiers, Hugh Pollard, John Berkeley, John Ashburnham, more soldiers than courtiers, and Harry Wilmot who had distinguished himself, if anyone could be said to have done so, at Newburn. There was also an Irish officer, Daniel O'Neill. Protestant by conversion and well known at Court, he was by birth the nephew of the Red O'Neill, the exiled Earl of Tyrone and the tacitly acknowledged leader of Catholic Ireland.

These men and others were much about the Court in the early months of 1641; several of them combined their unexacting military tasks with Parliamentary duties, being among the small number of King's men who had successfully procured seats in the Commons. They formed a group, or several groups, who moved in and out of each other's lodgings of an evening to take sack and tobacco, met in the Westminster taverns, and attended —some of them—the Queen's drawing-room. Their business in politics and at Court had nothing to do with the King's policy of moderation and patient waiting. They represented the beginnings of a new striking force, a new extremism of which the Queen was the moving spirit.

Pym, who took care to be well-informed, was not unaware of the growth of the military *junto* about the Queen, but he was, rightly, more anxious in the opening weeks of 1641 to prevent any split in the House of Commons which could assist the King in forming a body of moderate-minded supporters. For the first eight weeks of Parliament the Commons had been so carried away with the questions they had to debate that they had not even noticed the physical discomfort of their meeting-place. In the long intermission, many windows had been broken; this had not mattered greatly in the Short Parliament of the spring, but in an exceptionally cold and wet December, icy rain whistled through broken panes while they debated the affairs of the nation. Not until January 4th did they take action to have the windows reglazed.[31]

This attention to their personal comfort indicated a slackening in tension which might have been dangerous to Pym, especially as the Puritans, both in the House of Commons and the City, encouraged by the Scots, were becoming very hard to control. In Pym's judgment this was not the moment to listen to the clamour for the removal of bishops, an " overturning " of accepted institutions which was bound to dismay the majority of moderate men. He strove, with patient skill, to confine Puritan enthusiasm within safer channels. Let them attack Roman Catholics, let them complain of inefficient clergy, of whom there were plenty; let there by all means be an inquiry into the number of English livings recently bestowed on the episcopal Scottish clergy who had had to flee from their own country; let there be an inquiry into the number of idolatrous images to be found in English churches, and let Dr. Cosin who had introduced some at Durham be impeached. Let a vote of censure be passed against the clergy who had preached against the Scots or the behaviour of the Short Parliament; let the Vice-

Chancellor of Oxford, Dr. Christopher Potter, Provost of Queen's College and chaplain to the King, be compelled to ask the House's pardon on his knees because he had suspended Dr. Henry Wilkinson of Magdalen Hall for preaching a godly sermon.[32] But in spite of the London Root and Branch petition and in spite of a Kentish petition which came in to support it in January—Pym would not allow the question of the bishops to be taken up yet.

With the bishops, the Prayer Book was also protected from the full blast of Puritan rigour. Both Houses still officially advocated its general use throughout England, and conventicles were, in theory at least, discouraged. The Prayer Book, and compulsory attendance at the parish church on Sunday, had been confirmed by Act of Parliament under Queen Elizabeth; since the Commons insisted that they were preserving the law, they were not at this stage prepared to overrule an Elizabethan Act to please a minority, however clamourous.[33]

The situation was not easy for Pym. While the Scots pressed hotly for the reform of the English Church, he was urging on the Commons the importance of placing before the King as soon as possible the Bill for the frequent calling of Parliaments. An interval of three years, instead of the one year of the old Bill of Edward III's time, was now the longest to which they would consent. The proposed measure, commonly referred to as the Triennial Bill, had its third reading on January 20th, 1641. It had barely passed from the Commons to the Lords for their consent when the agitation against the bishops began again, this time in the form of a petition from numerous godly ministers asking for a thorough reform of the Church and complaining in particular of the secular offices which bishops now so frequently occupied.

The King himself at this juncture caused a diversion. At the last assizes in London one of the priests, who had long officiated in and about the City, had been tried under the law of Elizabeth which made it a felony for a priest of the Church of Rome to enter the country. His name was John Goodman and he was a kinsman of the unfortunate Bishop of Gloucester, although not, as was commonly reported at the time, a brother.[34] Father Goodman had been trained at Douai for the English mission and was steeled to martyrdom if it should come. He was the first to be tried under this law for many years and he hoped, reasonably enough, that a saving hand would be extended to him from the King's majesty. He did not hope in vain. Charles, at the request of the Queen reprieved Goodman on January 22nd. The instant outcry in London for a time diverted attention from other matters and the City refused to pay any further instalments of the promised loan until Goodman went to the gallows. So far all instalments of the City loan had gone to satisfy the Scottish army of occupation; the next payment was intended to cover some of the arrears due to the English army, and although the money would go through Parliament to the forces, the King was none the less anxious that the troops should get it because of the hopes he was beginning to build on the army's loyalty.

For the next ten days the life of Father Goodman brought the King and the Houses of Parliament together in a series of unsatisfactory interviews in the banqueting house at Whitehall. The King, deprived of almost all the councillors on whose eloquence he had relied, conducted these interviews himself with dignified tenacity. The first was chiefly devoted to the Church question; here Charles said with firmness that he would permit reform but not alteration, and desired that everything might be as it had been under Queen Elizabeth. He did well to cite Queen Elizabeth, the accepted norm for the laws of the realm. More than half the members would, in the long run, want nothing more in the Church than the abandonment of controversial ceremonies, the retirement of the bishops from secular power and an end to visitations and inquisitions. Pym, who knew this very well, but knew also the uncontrollable zeal of the extremists, cannot have been happy about this evident appeal of the King to the moderate men of both Houses. For him it was fortunate when the excitement about Goodman communicated itself to the Houses, who once again waited upon the King in person, this time with a general remonstrance about papists, and a particular request that the law might take its course. Charles, still admirably patient, conceded to both Houses of Parliament the right to make the final decision on Goodman, but reminded them that if a priest were hanged in England they might justly fear reprisals on English merchants and mariners in the dominions of Catholic sovereigns.[35] They went away to think this over, returning five days later with a new remonstrance against the continued presence of Roman Catholics at Court, and more especially that of Rossetti whom they took to be a Papal nuncio. The King, still exercising patience, informed them that Count Rossetti was not in any sense a nuncio but came on a private mission to the Queen, who was permitted by her marriage treaty to receive a personal envoy from the Vatican. He reminded them that he had himself expelled Roman Catholics from the Court, had enforced the penal laws during the previous year and had on numerous occasions put it beyond doubt that he was utterly opposed to the Church of Rome.[36] On the following day he sent to the House of Lords a petition which he had just received from Father Goodman; in this the devoted priest declared that he would far sooner die than be a cause of ill-feeling between the King and his people. With this moving document before them, the Lords revolted against the vindictive Commons. Goodman's death was indefinitely postponed.

In the midst of the agitation over the fate of Father Goodman, and the repeated audiences of the two Houses at Whitehall, during the short January days of the least brilliant winter King Charles's Court had yet seen, one gay social evening became memorable. It happened at " a house with stairs," as Sir John Suckling casually describes it, near Haymarket: the house was that of the younger brother of the Duke of Lennox, the dashing Lord d'Aubigny who had made a runaway match not long before with the high-spirited beauty Lady Catherine Howard. She it was who now provided the marriage feast for her sister's wedding to Lord Broghill, one of the numerous sons of Lord

Cork—he a nineteen-year-old gallant with a duel or two to his credit, she one of the prettiest brides in English poetry:

> Her feet beneath her petticoat,
> Like little mice, stole in and out,
>   As if they feared the light:
> But O she dances such a way
> No sun upon an Easter day
>   Is half so fine a sight.

The cates were plentiful, the company good, the usual jests were made, the usual healths drunk—

> On the sudden up they rise and dance
> Then sit again and sigh, and glance:
>   Then dance again and kiss:
> Thus several ways the time did pass,
> Whilst ev'ry woman wished her place,
>   And ev'ry man wished his.

So the time passed for those who were young and happy on Wednesday evening, January 27th, 1641, while Strafford lay in the Tower and Father Goodman at Newgate, and the King at Whitehall wondered what next to do, and the Queen wept over her frustrated hopes, and the Londoners muttered about Papists and Bishops.

> Such sights again cannot be found
> In any place on English ground. . . .

So John Suckling wrote in his " Ballad upon a Wedding " to Richard Lovelace who had missed it. Within two years the handsome bridegroom would be fighting a savage war in Munster, Lord d'Aubigny killed on the slope of Edgehill, his widow planning, not a wedding party. but a *coup d'état*, and the poet himself dead in exile.

On January 30th the Commons had at last completed the case against Strafford and he was brought from the Tower to the House of Lords to hear the accusation. The charge, containing nine general accusations of subverting the laws, and twenty-eight individual cases of alleged injustice, took a considerable time to read. When he had heard them he asked for some days to prepare an answer, and with that was escorted back to the Tower. He wrote tenderly to his wife that night, and in a more business-like manner to the Earl of Ormonde, a trusted friend in Ireland. In both letters he used the same phrase: there was, he thanked God, " nothing capital " in the charges against him. The Commons, in his opinion, had failed to make out their case for high treason and he saw the way towards acquittal opening out before him.[37]

While Strafford optimistically examined the articles of his impeachment in the Tower, Pym was still with difficulty holding back the attack on the bishops for which the extremists in the Commons were spoiling. In a debate on Church government, arising out of the recent petitions, George Digby proved helpful; he strongly argued that the Triennial Bill, which was even then awaiting the King's signature, would, by ensuring frequent Parliaments, prevent the growth of abuses in the Church.[38] The question of the Church was accordingly referred to a committee where the extremists could inveigh against the bishops without causing further difficulty in the House. To satisfy the Scots and maintain their friendship while postponing the alterations in the Church for which they hoped, a further sum of £300,000 was voted towards the expenses of their army. In the course of the debate on this question the member for Grimsby, Gervase Holles, whose political opinions were the opposite of those of his cousin Denzil, spoke sharply of the Scots' rebellion, words for which Speaker Lenthall suspended him until the end of the session.[39] Another Royalist had been conveniently silenced, and the alliance of the Scots and the House of Commons effectively confirmed.

By this time Edward Hyde and his committee had prepared

the accusations against the judges who had supported Ship-money, and on February 12th the first of five impeachments was launched. Sir Robert Berkeley, while presiding in the Court of King's Bench, was peremptorily summoned to appear before the House of Commons; he had no choice but to obey. Four days later the King, perceiving that no money would be voted for the English army unless he gave in to the Commons over the Triennial Bill, consented to this measure. Both Houses discussed the propriety of ringing bells and lighting bonfires to mark their triumph, but the King in a well-phrased speech reminded them that in three months they had taken his government to pieces like a watch that needed repairs. He suggested that the time had come when the watch should be put together again and made to go.[40] City loans, generously passed on to the Scots, were well enough, but what of his revenues, what of the legitimate needs of the state?

With this reminder he left them, but all was now moving rapidly towards the trial of Strafford. At the end of the month he appeared once again in the House of Lords to make a formal answer to the charges. The King had intimated that he wished to be present but he did more than merely attend on this occasion; he came down to the House of Lords before Strafford was brought in, and had some minutes of private conversation with him before the hearing began. During the subsequent proceedings the King, so far from maintaining a judicially dispassionate air, honoured the prisoner at the bar with friendly salutations. All this must have been deliberate, possibly even pre-arranged with Strafford. He intended to show, and thought it safe to show, that he was satisfied with the way in which the minister had refuted the charges brought against him. Since this was a mere preliminary to the trial itself, the open demonstration by the King that he had pre-judged the issue was very ill-received by Parliament.[41] But it was not a mistaken action in itself, because it was evidently a matter of some importance in the presentation of Strafford's defence that the King, whom he had served, should not seem to doubt his capacity to justify all that he had done.

So far Pym had done no more than organise the preliminary strategy of the struggle. Much was claimed, much attempted, much begun. The destruction of royal power, the abolition of the prerogative courts, the impeachment of the judges: the attack had been mounted but it had not yet been carried through. The King had given his consent, so far, only to the Triennial Bill, and the other projected constitutional changes might never come to fulfilment. The whole widespread attack depended on Pym's ability to retain public confidence and the support of the House, and on the King's inability to win back either. If Strafford out-argued and defeated his accusers, he would go far to reverse the situation in Charles's favour, and his hopes that he would do so were well founded. Pym's principal anxiety was still the maintenance of good relations between the Commons and the Covenanters. If the attack on Strafford was to be successful, it was essential that the Scots War should appear unprovoked and unjustified. It was therefore unfortunate that a memorandum privately drawn up by Henderson, on the reform of the English Church, should by an accident become public at this moment. The Covenanters now appeared as aggressors, determined to force their form of worship on England and the storm which Pym had long dreaded broke over the House of Commons. Honest churchmen and patriotic Englishmen fiercely attacked the Scots; and Pym only with great difficulty managed to get the matter talked out and so, once again, temporarily shelved.[42]

The King meanwhile had publicly announced the betrothal of his daughter to the Prince of Orange's son, diplomatically representing it as a change of foreign policy. The principal object of this treaty, he declared to the House of Lords, was to help his dear sister the Queen of Bohemia and her orphan children. The new alliance was certainly a Protestant one, and as such an improvement on the Spanish friendship of the past, but the King was not to be successful in the pretence that it was intended for his sister's benefit because his nephew, the Elector Palatine, refused to enter into the deception. Disregarding a message from the King forbidding his journey, he arrived in

England on March 2nd, received a hollow, embarrassed welcome from his uncle and aunt, and, with calculated indiscretion, let it be known that he had come to claim his promised bride, the Princess Mary, and to appeal to Parliament for the help his uncle had never given him.[43]

The romantic popularity of his mother inspired the Londoners with sympathetic feelings for the young German prince, but he had not himself the qualities which inspire devotion; otherwise he would have been not merely an exasperation but a danger to his uncle. As it was, he did little, after making his dramatic arrival, except press in vain for a clause in the marriage treaty promising him—in return for relinquishing his own claim on the bride—financial help and possession of a fortress in Holland.[44] Failing to get this, he remained as a sulky, uninvited and expensive guest at the palace of Whitehall, for he was not above taking free board and lodging when he got the chance.

Three weeks after the Elector's arrival the trial of Strafford opened on March 22nd, 1641, in Westminster Hall.

BOOK III CHAPTER IV REFERENCES

1. Laud, *Works*, III, pp. 237–8; *H.M.C.*, XII, II, p. 262.
2. *C.S.P. Ven.*, 1640–2, p. 93; Clarendon, III, I.
3. Verney, *Notes on the Long Parliament, Camden Society*, 1854, pp. 2–3.
4. Twysden, *Journal, Transactions of the Kent Archaeological Society*, I, 1858, pp. 188–9.
5. *C.S.P.D.*, 1640–1, pp. 244–6; Rushworth, III, i, pp. 12–16.
6. Whitaker, p. 220.
7. Rushworth, III, i, pp. 21–4; D'Ewes, *Journal*, ed. Notestein, Yale, 1923, pp. 7–11.
8. Rushworth, III, i, pp. 30–5, 37; D'Ewes, ed. Notestein, p. 20 n.
9. Rushworth, III, i, pp. 39–40; Dering, *Speeches*, London, 1641.
10. *Commons Journals*; Balfour, II, p. 425; D'Ewes, ed. Notestein, p. 20.
11. See Book III, chapter iii, p. 350.
12. Clarendon, III, 3–4; D'Ewes, ed. Notestein, pp. 25–9.
13. *Lords Journals*; Baillie, I, pp. 271 f.
14. *Commons Journals*.
15. Lady Brilliana Harley, *Letters*, p. 104.
16. Albion, pp. 341, 347.
17. *Commons Journals*.
18. *H.M.C.*, II, I, p. 267.

19. *C.S.P.D.*, 1640–1, pp. 297–9, 314–15, 437. Robert Read's letters to Windebanke's sons, written from Paris and scattered through the State Papers Domestic for many months give a very clear idea of the Secretary's last days.

20. *Commons Journals*, II, p. 118; Verney, p. 37; Clarendon, III, 135–7.

21. *C.S.P. Ven.*, 1640–2, p. 105.

22. Rushworth, III, I, pp. 86–7.

23. *Ibid.*, pp. 55, 101–4; D'Ewes, ed. Notestein, pp. 146–9.

24. Laud, *Works*, III, p. 239.

25. *Commons* and *Lords Journals*; Rushworth, III, i, pp. 124–8.

26. *Ibid.*, IV, i, p. 140.

27. *Commons Journals*.

28. *C.S.P.D.*, 1640–1, pp. 278–9, 291.

29. *C.S.P. Ven.*, 1640–2, pp. 113, 117.

30. *Brittanicae Virtutis Imago*.

31. *Commons Journals*, 63.

32. *Commons Journals*, 64, 72; Rushworth, III, ii, p. 1327.

33. *Lords Journals*; Rushworth, III, i, p. 144.

34. Soden, *Godfrey Goodman*, pp. 311–2.

35. Rushworth, II, ii, p. 1334; III, i, pp. 158–60.

36. *Ibid.*, pp. 165–6.

37. Knowler, II, p. 415; Carte, *Ormonde*, Oxford, 1851, V, p. 245.

38. Rushworth, III, i, pp. 170–4; D'Ewes, ed. Notestein, p. 263.

39. *Commons Journals*.

40. *C.S.P.D.*, 1640–1, pp. 460–1.

41. *C.S.P. Ven.*, 1640–2, p. 128.

42. Baillie, I, p. 306; D'Ewes, ed. Notestein, p. 417.

43. *C.S.P. Ven.*, 1640–2, pp. 130, 133.

44. *C.S.P.D.*, 1640–1, pp. 493–4.

CHAPTER FIVE

THE END OF STRAFFORD

March–May 1641

THE destruction of Strafford was the key to the political strategy of John Pym. The success of his attack on the King's position and the permanence of his achievement depended on victory in this crucial conflict over the guilt and the life of the Lord Lieutenant of Ireland. Therefore the whole of Strafford's Irish policy became for Pym no more than the material for his impeachment; the politics and personalities of Ireland had no significance for him except as they contributed to this end.

But the politics of the three kingdoms—England, Ireland, Scotland—could not cease to act upon each other merely because it had become a political necessity in England to destroy the work of Strafford in Ireland. While John Pym understood very well what he was doing at Westminster and what effect Strafford's fall would have on the power of Parliament and the government of the country, he did not understand what he was doing to Ireland, what the effect would be or what the ultimate consequences to all three kingdoms.

Sixteen of the twenty-eight articles of the impeachment were directed at Strafford's Irish policy. He was attacked principally for two things—for increasing the direct power of the King through the judicial use of the Court of Castle Chamber, and for interfering with Irish manufacture, produce and customs duties. These two things—the use of the prerogative courts and the interference with trade—were the elements in the King's policy most unpopular in England; to prosecute Strafford for his use of them in Ireland was to cast by implication an even blacker shadow on Charles's proceedings in England. In English politics and in Pym's policy the whole picture fitted together.

But in Irish politics Strafford's actions had a different face, and in attacking him on these two issues Pym was in effect taking the part of the most unscrupulous of the recent settlers in Ireland, whose tactics of exploitation Strafford had consistently fought.

These men were well represented in the English Parliament and several had seats in person; others had sons, sons-in-law, cousins, friends or dependents who were willing to act for them. In the Irish Parliament, still in session at Dublin, this same group of people, quiescent in the previous session while Strafford's influence was dominant, became active as soon as his fall appeared imminent and his influence waned. Strafford had left as his deputy in Ireland, when the King called him to England, his close friend and right-hand man, Christopher Wandesford, but Wandesford, a conscientious second-in-command, was of too mild a nature to deal strongly with an opposition which had been held in check only by fear of Strafford himself.

For different reasons the majority of the Irish Parliament had now turned against Strafford and, with few exceptions, Protestant settlers and Catholic Irish united to repudiate their past obedience. The blockading of the Scottish ports during the war had damaged Irish trade and almost all the Protestant settlers of northern Ireland, whether Englishmen or Scots, sympathised with the Covenanters and resented Strafford's past enforcement of an oath of loyalty to the King. The Irish army, kept expensively in being by money voted in their Parliament, was not liked by the majority of the settlers, who feared and suspected Strafford for thus arming and training the warlike native population. The repressive measures taken against those of Covenanting sympathies in Ulster by the Bishops of Down and Derry aroused bitter feelings against the Church.

While the more recent settlers and all the more vehement Protestants hated him, the Catholic Irish gentry had supported him only so long as they felt confidence in his strength. They had been driven to accept his plan for the redistribution of land in the belief that his final settlement would make an end of the uncertainty and constant fear of expropriation in which they had lived for the past generation. With Strafford impeached in England and the land question broken off before the re-organisation of tenure was completed, their state was worse than before. No love was lost on the man who, by making promises for the future which he was now in no position to perform, had compelled them to put their estates at the mercy of the King. The suspicions of the Irish gentry were increased by the last important appointment that Strafford made in Ireland. He had replaced Chancellor Loftus by Sir Richard Bolton, chief baron of the Irish Exchequer, a man of unspotted reputation who had spent half his lifetime of seventy years in the Irish courts and had published legal works which established him as the principal authority on Irish law: an upright man, a man whose knowledge of the laws was un-surpassed—but an extreme and austere Protestant. No doubt his religion was a private matter for him, as it was for Strafford himself. His political affiliations were not with the restive Protes-tant settlers and his loyalty to the Crown was sincere and strong. But the Catholic Irish only saw in his appointment another reason to doubt Strafford's good faith with them.

The unfortunate Wandesford was powerless to control the angry outbreak against Strafford from almost all quarters of the assembly when the Irish Parliament met for its second session. Both sides of the House were ready to add their accusations to those which were being made in England against the minister. Sir George Radcliffe, Strafford's chief personal adviser and friend, was shouted down when he suggested that they ought to in-vestigate the wild charges now being flung against the Lord Lieutenant before they believed them. He was himself impeached a few days later. So, in turn, were all Strafford's friends and assistants, the Bishop of Derry who had carried out the Laudian policy in the north, and the blameless Chancellor Bolton.[1]

In the midst of disaster the Lord Deputy Wandesford lay down and died. He was only forty-eight and there does not seem to have been much wrong with him except a winter chill and anxiety too great for him to bear. Ireland was now without any deputy of the King in Dublin. Strafford, from his imprisonment, suggested to Charles two men to fill the gap—Lord Dillon who was almost instantly rejected by the King on account of his Roman Catholic connections, and the Earl of Ormonde.

James Butler, twelfth Earl of Ormonde, was the most distinguished and powerful of the Norman-Irish lords. Brought up in England, he was a Protestant and an Episcopalian. His background, his education, above all his energetic and intelligent mind, had secured him friends and connections in every party in Ireland. Probably no man was more widely liked and trusted, as far as any man in Ireland could be trusted. He was now thirty years old, a tall vigorous handsome young man, with a certain nobility of thought and action and a singular grace of manner.

His relations with Strafford had begun seven years earlier in a young man's quarrel about his right to wear a sword in Parliament. Soon, however, Ormonde had recognised Strafford's quality as Strafford had recognised his. Since then he had been one of those to whom Strafford principally looked to carry out his plans for the better government of Ireland.

Ormonde had shown both loyalty and political skill when the Irish Parliament turned on Strafford. With great dexterity he had held off the attack in the House of Lords for several days by dragging the red herring of a point of privilege across the trail.[2]

Had the King dared to take Strafford's advice and put Ormonde into the Deputy's place left vacant by Wandesford, the collapse of Strafford's policy in Ireland might have been averted. But Charles was still convinced of the wisdom of playing for time and conciliating the most dangerous forces of the opposition, and he felt that the appointment of a Norman-Irish peer and a known friend of Strafford to the post of Lord

Deputy would alienate the dangerous faction of powerful settlers led by the Earl of Cork. For the time being he left the Deputy's place vacant and appointed two Lords Justices to carry on the government of Ireland in his name. The men on whom he fixed, Sir John Borlase and Sir William Parsons, were between sixty and seventy years old, strongly Protestant and in the main devoted to the settlers' interests.

Strafford himself, while he was anxiously aware of the consequences which his fall might entail for Ireland, was, still principally concerned to redeem his position, and with it the King's policy, at the forthcoming trial before the peers at Westminster. He saw with relief, on examining the charges, that he could disprove most and shake all of them. But he underestimated the effect that the mere making of such charges might have on the minds of his peers or the state of feeling in London. Pym was indeed relying on the effect made by the reiteration of Strafford's crimes to build up a resistance to any evidence that might be brought to disprove them. Three weeks before the trial the Commons, following the example set them by the industrious propaganda made by the Covenanters through the printed word, published the charge against Strafford, which was thus, by the time the trial opened, as familiar to all as the latest horrid murder on a broadsheet.

The Lords took exception to this impermissible act on the part of the Commons against one of their number but Strafford's enemies in the Upper House managed to prevent a breach. Two more events in the House of Lords darkened his prospects; Littleton, the new Lord Keeper, a personal friend, fell ill, so that he could not preside at the trial, and Lord Arundel, as Earl Marshal, became therefore in some sort the arbiter of the trial's progress and arrangement. Arundel, a haughty conservative under suspicion of Catholic sympathies, ought to have been the King's loyal servant, but his pride had been deeply wounded by his loss of the military command in the previous year on—he presumed—Strafford's advice. Throughout the trial he was markedly hostile to the prisoner.

One great hope of acquittal lay with the Bishops. It was to be expected that all their votes in the House of Lords would be exercised in Strafford's favour, and Pym, knowing how far this would endanger the success of the impeachment, had encouraged in the House of Commons a Bill against the exercise of temporal or judicial power by bishops or clergy, this being held incompatible with their spiritual function. The effect of the Bill was forestalled by the dexterous action of Bishop Williams in the House of Lords. He suavely suggested that the impeachment of their noble colleague the Earl of Strafford, being a matter of life and death and therefore a *causa sanguinis*, was not fit to be meddled with by men of their cloth; the bishops, he said, might therefore, of their own choice, waive their undoubted right to speak and vote on the case.[3] Most of them, in a legitimate anxiety to preserve the Church and therefore not to give any cause of anger to the Commons or the people, were thankful to accept this means of escape.

The trial opened in Westminster Hall on March 22nd. From then, for seven weeks, the affairs of the nation were at a stand: everything waited upon the outcome of this central event. No other business engaged the law courts; no other talk or news filled London and Westminster. Great crowds assembled outside the Hall and all who could contrive to get themselves a seat on the public benches did so. They came early, prepared to sit it out, however long the sessions, bringing bread and cheese and onions and bottles of ale against the pangs of hunger. Other needs they also relieved without moving from their places. The ladies and gentlemen in the galleries reserved for the Court thought this behaviour ill-mannered and lacking in reverence to the King.

Strafford himself was not the dread figure that many of them had expected to see. Weakened by anxiety and illness, crippled by recurring attacks of gout, he no longer looked like the overbearing tyrant who had declared—according to the indictment—that he would make " the little finger of the King heavier than the loins of the law." Instead of an upright, dominating vigorous man, the crowds in Westminster Hall saw a stooping grey-beard, his head sunk between his shoulders, well wrapped in a warm cloak, and wearing—by permission of his peers—a close-fitting fur-lined cap to shield him against the draughts. The appearance of Strafford did not fit with the idea of him that Pym and his supporters had been at pains to create, and it was not surprising that within a few days the more suggestible of the spectators were exclaiming " Alas, poor soul! " shaking their heads with pity, and murmuring that there might be two sides to the question.

This appeal to pity was accidental; it was not in Strafford's character deliberately to try to evoke such a sentiment. But the impression added to the effect of his defence as, worn, bent and weary, he fought on day by day with steady wits and an unfaltering voice.

The first week of the trial went badly for the Commons. John Pym opened the case and was ably supported by two of the best lawyers in the House, John Glyn and John Maynard. All three developed much the same argument. They urged the Lords to look upon the indictment as a whole. Although the charges individually might not seem to go so far as treason, yet the tendency of the whole was unmistakable. " It is a habit, a trade, a mystery of treason exercised by this great lord," said Maynard. In support of this general attack a remonstrance from the Irish Parliament was read in Court as though it had been evidence instead of a series of unproved accusations.

Strafford's defence was a masterpiece of precision. Disregarding the wider aspects of the indictment and refusing at this stage to be drawn into any general statement, he held tenaciously to the factual charges made against him and repeatedly demonstrated discrepancies of time and place or cast doubt on the competence and honesty of the witnesses. By the end of the first week Strafford was rapidly gaining the advantage over his opponents.[4] The King would have done well to leave it to his resourceful minister to work out his salvation in the teeth of his accusers while he, for his part, built up support among moderate men, ready for the moment when the failure of the impeachment would give him the chance of winning the initiative from Pym.

Things were moving smoothly in this direction. He had gained the support of the influential Bedford who had come so far towards the King's orbit as to consider marrying his daughter to the Marquis of Hamilton. Hamilton himself, pursuing his private policy of conciliation in Scotland, had offered his own daughter to Argyll's son.[5] These projected family connections suggested a new framework of councillors and friendships around the throne, an alliance of which Hamilton would be the pivot, between the moderates in England and the leading Covenanting nobles in Scotland. This would break down the connection between the extremists in the House of Commons and the Scots and give to the monarchy a new, broad and solid foundation. Charles had gone so far as to raise to the rank of Privy Councillor —although without admitting them to his inner cabinet— almost all his critics in the House of Lords: Bedford, Bristol and Essex, Hertford and Savile, even the incorrigible Puritans Saye and Mandeville. But he knew that their firm alliance was not to be obtained except by concessions which he still hoped to avoid, and he hankered after an alternative solution.

The Covenanting army, in occupation of the northern counties, was openly the ally of the House of Commons. In these unprecedented circumstances, it was reasonable for the King also to seek some kind of military support in case of need. He had hitherto successfully resisted the requests of the House of Commons that Strafford's Irish army should be disbanded, and he was resolute to keep it in being until the Scots withdrew theirs. He had also been told by Harry Percy that the English army officers were resentful of their treatment by Parliament and might support him in a crisis.[6]

Percy and his principal supporters, Wilmot, Ashburnham and Pollard, by drawing together a group of like-minded men and indicating their sympathy to the King had not generated a plan for a military counterstroke but they had provided the material out of which, at some future date, a military counter-stroke might be contrived.

The Queen's Master of the Horse, Harry Jermyn, would have liked to see things move at a greater pace, and somewhat contrary to Percy's judgment, encouraged the two poets, Suckling and Davenant, both irresponsibles, to consider more immediate and drastic military action for which a leader could be found in the governor of Portsmouth, Colonel George Goring. This young officer, a soldier by profession with five or six years' experience, was the feckless eldest son of one of the Queen's favourite servants, Lord Goring. As a young man he had caused his family almost as much anxiety, though for different reasons, as Harry Vane had caused his father the Secretary. Young George, the antithesis of young Harry, had never been troubled with religion; gaming and women were his undoing. His father had hoped that on his marriage to one of Lord Cork's daughters he would settle down and perhaps make a career in Ireland, but the young man took neither to his wife nor his father-in-law and very soon outraged the family by departing without notice on the best horse in the stable. He was later sent to the wars in the Nether-lands to make good. Surprisingly, he did so; he had audacity, physical endurance, a quick judgment and the power to inspire his men. He had also an insinuating charm which he used to some purpose when he thought it worth his while, because, with all his wildness, he was ambitious. In the two mismanaged campaigns against the Scots he had suffered the mortification of seeing his talents wasted and his ambitions checked by the incompetence of the high command. Since then, discontented with his post as governor of Portsmouth, he had intrigued to be made Lieutenant-General in the North where, should war again break out with Scotland, he believed he could conduct it with success. Popular with the Queen and her friends, Goring was suspect to his more experienced seniors in the army; they distrusted his ambitions and knew that although he was an inspiring leader in battle he was at other times careless and irresponsible. Both Sir John Conyers at Berwick and Sir Jacob

Astley at York were strongly opposed to his appointment in the north.[7]   For other reasons, it suited the King and Queen better to keep him at Portsmouth. The Queen cherished baseless hopes of help from France, so that the necessity of keeping a royalist commander in the Portsmouth garrison was evident.

Goring, reckless, ambitious and disappointed in his hope of the northern command, went far beyond the modest and tentative suggestions of Percy and his friends. He was for occupying London and seizing the Tower.[8] The difference between the two plans, the moderate and the immoderate, was still one of words, for neither Percy nor Goring had taken any steps to translate their ideas into action.

Discretion is rarely a virtue of amateur conspirators, and the courtier-officers, many of them wits and poets, were not by nature discreet, nor were the circumstances in which they evolved their plans favourable to secrecy. Oaths of silence had of course been taken, by some, if not all, of them; Goring, in Percy's lodging at Westminster, over tobacco after supper had put his hand on a Bible and sworn to reveal nothing.[9] But the important looks, the sidelong glances, the hurryings in and out of the Queen's apartments, advertised that something was afoot. Some time in April George Goring, dubious about the success of the enterprise, the wisdom of his associates and the advantages to himself decided to put himself right with Parliament by betraying the plot. He sought out Lord Newport and warned him of the growing conspiracy. Newport passed the information on to the Earl of Bedford, who appears to have under-valued its significance, and to Lord Mandeville, Pym's principal friend and associate in the Lords, who passed it on to Pym. Goring meanwhile went quietly back to Portsmouth and awaited the outcome.[10]

Pym made no immediate use of his knowledge, knowing that its value hinged on the time at which he chose to make it public. Article twenty-three of Strafford's impeachment had yet to be heard, and much depended on the success or failure of the Commons to prove his intention of bringing in an Irish army against the King's English subjects. The exposure of a conspiracy among the King's soldiers to seize the Tower and overawe London might come in at an apposite moment to confirm the suspicions aroused by article twenty-three. Pym held it in reserve.

On Monday, April 5th, the prosecution called Secretary Vane to give evidence of what Strafford had said at the Council eleven months before, when the Short Parliament was dissolved. Vane must have been aware that his son had provided the information on which article twenty-three was based, although he may not have known precisely what shape that information had taken. It should have been his function, as a servant of the Court, to deny the imputation that Strafford had offered the Irish army for the reduction of England; as Secretary of State he was in a position to know that no such offer had been made, that the Irish army had always been intended for Scotland. He disliked Strafford, but an ambitious man will hardly jeopardise his position for dislike alone, and to give evidence against Strafford was to endanger his future as the Queen's courtier or the King's Secretary of State. Vane, therefore, must have known that the Commons had, or thought they had, stronger means of proving article twenty-three than his words alone, and that it might be safest for him and his family, in this disastrous turn of affairs, to please the winning side.

Whatever his motives, Vane proved an unshakable witness. He declared that Strafford had advised the King to remember that he had an army in Ireland which could be used " here to reduce *this* kingdom." In cross-examination he refused to bate a syllable from the fatal phrase although its interpretation was a matter that must necessarily be left to the hearers. In his defence Strafford called three other councillors who had been present on that day, Hamilton, Cottington and the Bishop of London, all of whom categorically denied that he had advised using the Irish army against England. After a session of nearly ten hours, with battering assertion and counter-assertion, impassioned speeches from Glyn and Maynard for the prosecution, and a persuasive appeal from Strafford to their lordships to distrust mere verbal evidence " for words pass and may be easily mistaken," the critical hearing closed. No one could say with certainty whether the prosecution or the defence had the better of it, but at the next session, on April 7th, Strafford was clearly winning his case. The prosecution, leaving aside article twenty-three, turned their attention to the charges connected with his tyrannical conduct during the second Scots war, and Strafford was able conclusively to disprove, or at least to cast grave doubt on, the truth of the assertions on which their accusations were based.

All in all he had now disposed of a good number of the specific charges made against him, had created a certain sympathy for his predicament and a growing distrust of the prosecution. Neither he nor anyone else can have hoped for a violent popular reaction in his favour, but the bitter, unreasoning general hatred felt for him had given way, among Lords and Commons and among those who followed the trial, to a much more uncertain feeling. The legal arguments he had used and the weight of evidence he had been able to produce in his own defence had made the inevitable impression. The legal-minded English, knowledgeable in the law and respectful of it, did not like the idea of condemning a man to death for high treason on charges as dubious as those against Strafford had been shown to be. Broadcast in print without comment they had served well as propaganda, but argued out in the hearing of thousands they were very weak.

Pym was alive to the gravity of the situation and fully aware that article twenty-three alone gave unquestionable grounds for the charge of treason—if article twenty-three were accepted as proven, which was far from being the case. Something had to be done to strengthen the evidence of Secretary Vane. So far, it depended on nothing but his personal recollection of what had been said, and Strafford's witnesses had impugned the accuracy of his memory by giving different accounts of the incident. Pym and the committee for the prosecution therefore decided that they must buttress this inadequate evidence by producing the written copy of Vane's notes on which, in the first place, the charge had been based. All that they now possessed was a copy in Pym's handwriting of a copy made by young Vane from his father's original and since destroyed. This was poor enough but it might serve their turn.

On April 10th when the Court reassembled Glyn opened the proceedings by informing the peers that he had new evidence to submit on article twenty-three. Strafford immediately asked for a like permission to call new witnesses, not only in respect of article twenty-three but of other articles if necessary. The Lords, after some consideration, gave way to his request, a concession which reflected the doubts that most of them now felt as to the wisdom and justice of the prosecution.

This concession threw out the strategy of the prosecution who wished to reopen only article twenty-three, and were anxious to prevent the prisoner from reopening any other, lest he gain further advantages against them. Glyn, with a rash conviction that Strafford was bluffing, went forward none the less and rose to call the new witness for article twenty-three. Strafford, on the instant, announced that he had additional evidence on four earlier articles of the indictment which should be heard first.

Amid a tumult of shouting from Pym's party, Glyn offered to forego the new evidence altogether, and the Earl of Arundel, who stood the Commons' friend throughout, with remarkable acumen adjourned the Court. Strafford watched their embarrassed retreat from the hall with a sardonic smile, and the King, remote in his box, was seen to be laughing.[11] Both of them, in that moment, believed that the hour of danger was over, and the game once more in their own hands. The impeachment had failed.

John Pym had not foreseen the defeat of the impeachment, the moment at which it would crumble or the form that the defeat would take; but he had always been prepared for the possibility. On the morning of April 10th, 1641, his first attack on Strafford, doggedly prosecuted since the autumn, came to a sudden end. On the afternoon of the same day he mounted the second attack for which he had long had everything in readiness.

His spokesman in this was Sir Arthur Haselrig who that afternoon introduced into the House of Commons a Bill of Attainder against the Earl of Strafford.[12] The Bill was nothing more than a restatement of the charges put forward in the impeachment but the difference in procedure was all-important. The purpose of the impeachment was to convince a majority in the House of Lords that Strafford was by English law guilty of certain crimes for which the punishment was death. The purpose of a Bill of Attainder was to declare by Act of Parliament that Strafford's death was necessary to the safety of the state. The impeachment could succeed only if legal proofs of Strafford's guilt were forthcoming, but a Bill of Attainder could be passed as long as the majority felt that the presumption of guilt was strong enough. This change of tactics brought in once again to Pym's support those who believed Strafford guilty of an intention of treason, but were troubled at the difficulty of proving it, and did not wish to countenance an undue stretching of the law. To such men as the conscientious and logical Falkland or the learned, meticulous Selden, the Bill of Attainder provided the perfect solution.

It was possible, in support of the Bill in the House of Commons that afternoon, to introduce the written evidence for article twenty-three which had been abandoned in Westminster Hall that morning—Pym's copy of young Vane's copy of his father's notes. The occasion caused a painful outburst from Secretary Vane, who, with an air of astonishment and horror, rose in his place and denounced the treachery and deceit of his son in making copies of his papers for Pym's benefit.[13]

The elder Vane must have known that Pym had had access to his notes; the wording of article twenty-three, and the way in which he had been handled as a witness, suggests as much. His exact repetition, when supposedly answering from memory, of the phrase which appeared in the written version betrays something like co-operation with the prosecution. The inference is that the elder Vane had been prepared to let the evidence be used in drawing the charges, and to support it, in the witness-box, apparently from memory. But he had not been willing that the carelessness which had enabled his son to procure the evidence should become a matter of public knowledge.

Although the Bill of Attainder had been introduced, the process of impeachment was not fully concluded. Strafford was to speak in his own defence on April 13th. That speech, in the existing circumstances, would be an appeal to the Lords to reject the Bill which the Commons were preparing against him. Pym, in a conference with the Upper House, laid before them the copy of Vane's notes on the day before they were to hear Strafford's defence; he was thus at least certain that they had taken notice of the whole of the evidence for the prosecution before being exposed to the persuasive eloquence of the accused. The fight was still a very close one and, although Pym was fairly sure of getting the Bill of Attainder through the Commons, he was by no means sure of the Lords. A well-judged appeal from Strafford to their sense of justice and their political wisdom might easily prevent its passing.

Pym's fears were fully realised when, on April 13th, he and the other managers of the prosecution listened for two hours to Strafford's speech in his own defence. First he took the charges against him one by one and demonstrated their malice and inaccuracy, emphasising the points which had told in his favour during the trial. From this he turned to the more general aspects of the impeachment. His crime, as he saw it, was to have defended the King's prerogative with too much vigour. In the last months the mere word " prerogative " had been made to stink in the Commons as though any act committed under that shield was of itself evil. Against this dangerous exaggeration he now protested. The safety of the Commonweal, he argued, depended neither on the destruction of the prerogative nor on the excessive use of it, but on the harmony and balance between the King's authority and the subject's liberty.

" The prerogative of the Crown and the propriety of the

subject have such mutual relations that this took protection from that, that foundation and nourishment from this; and as on the lute if anything be too high or too low wound up, you have lost the harmony, so here the excess of a prerogative is oppression, of a pretended liberty in the subject disorder and anarchy. The prerogative must be used as God doth his omnipotency, at extraordinary occasions; the laws . . . must have place at all other times, and yet there must be a prerogative if there must be extraordinary occasions."

These were unexceptionable sentiments, intended to counter-act the suspicion of the prerogative which Pym had sedulously encouraged during the last months. Politically, this was the heart and centre of Strafford's defence, the belief from which his career and actions as a statesman had arisen. This was the theory that he left as legacy to those who, after him, would have to support and defend the policy of the King, and stop, if they could, the overturning acts of Pym and the extremists. But it was not the principal argument on which he depended to save his own life.

Knowing his own countrymen, he defended himself in the last resort by a direct appeal to the laws of the land. Nothing capital had been proved against him; in all their charges the Commons had failed to prove against him anything that by any existing law could be called treason. "My Lords," he pleaded, "do we not live by laws and must we be punishable by them ere they be made?" It went against every principle of English justice to create a new law in order, retrospectively, to punish a man who had offended against it. "These gentlemen tell me they speak in defence of the Commonweal against my arbitrary laws," he said, indicating the Commons. "Give me leave to say that I speak in the defence of the Commonweal against their arbitrary treason." [14]

Throughout his speech Strafford had been careful to appeal from the Commons to the Lords, to make it apparent that he trusted in the wisdom and dignity of the Upper House who were themselves, as he hinted, endangered by the arbitrary accusations made by the Commons against one of their number. He strove to arouse the jealousy of the Lords and he partly succeeded. Already, he knew, a considerable party among them were for saving his life, not out of any love for him, but because they did not wish to see a dangerous reversal of the normal order of things. For a minister and a peer of the realm to be executed at the instance of the Commons and against the known will of the King, was something new and dangerous in politics. As the full implications of the question became clear to them, the Lords as a body were drawing back from that alliance with the Commons which had marked the first months of the Parliament. The leaders in this movement were the Earls of Bristol and Bedford whose influence was now wholly bent towards the formation of a middle party and a new moderate government in which the House of Lords, and more especially their friends in it, would hold an even balance between the claims of King and Commons.

Bristol apparently did not know of, and Bedford did not seriously consider, the mysterious confederacy of the young army officers. They believed the King to be ready to extricate himself from his unhappy predicament and to buy Strafford's life by accepting their help and advice and placing them, in due course, in the foremost offices of state.

Bristol's son, George Digby, hitherto one of Pym's most reliable supporters, suddenly changed his tactics in the House of Commons. He was not the only member to have been dissatisfied with the evidence in support of article twenty-three but it seems likely that his decision to denounce it was taken in consultation with his father Lord Bristol, and his father-in-law Lord Bedford. The timing was extremely apposite. But no amount of pre-arrangement with his friends in the Lords can take away from Digby the credit for his courage in speaking out. His argument, put with all the fervour of a young and consciously eloquent speaker, was strictly legal: two witnesses were, by statute, essential before a man could be condemned for treason, but so far only one witness had been found to support article twenty-three. Sir Harry Vane's personal account of what had happened, given in evidence, and a copy, at two removes, of what Sir Harry Vane had written down about it at the time were not by any stretch of imagination *two* witnesses: there was still one witness only to article twenty-three and that did not satisfy the law. To condemn a man on such evidence was not justice but murder. "Before God," declared George Digby, "my vote goes not to the taking of the Earl of Strafford's life." [15]

Digby was a moving speaker but too much the young nobleman to make a deep impression in the House of Commons, who knew his affiliations in the Lords and were suspicious and jealous of them. It was Digby's misfortune throughout life that, although he could inspire affection and admiration, he rarely inspired confidence. The harm that his speech might do to the Bill of Attainder now before the Commons was more than counter-balanced by the thoughtful support given to it by the persuasive Lord Falkland. Falkland was one of those men who carry in their faces and manner the unmistakable marks of extreme conscientiousness. When Falkland spoke, it was not from impulse but conviction, not from any hope of gain or consideration of friendship, but from a sense of duty even, as now, of painful duty. Falkland was not vindictive; he disapproved of Strafford in the negative manner dictated by a naturally moderate temperament and a tolerant and liberal political philosophy. He may, in some other compartment of his well-regulated mind, have disliked him personally, for Strafford's predecessor in Ireland had been Falkland's father, and Strafford was inclined to think—and say aloud—that his predecessor had been incompetent. But political disapproval and private dislike would not have moved Falkland to seek the death of Strafford had his conscience not been satisfied that his death was lawful. Any legal doubts that he had were removed by the new procedure by Bill of Attainder. It was possible, he argued, to recognise treason without knowing precisely how it came to be treason, as it was possible to know a tall man from a short man without precisely knowing how many hairs' breadths made the difference between them.[16]   These things depended not on exactitude of detailed measurements, but on a clear general impression. With the argument placed before them in this fashion, the majority in the House of Commons on April 19th resolved that an intention to subvert the laws was tantamount to treason,[17] and that such an intention was clear in Strafford's case. Whether the House of Lords would accept this view, or yield to Strafford's appeal that a man could not be retrospectively condemned for offences invented afterwards, depended much on the skill and management of Bedford and Bristol.

The King was reasonably confident; he had both his moderate party in the Lords and the support of his army to sustain him. If his army friends were to be ready for a possible crisis they must be at their posts, and therefore, towards the middle of April, the loyalist officers who had long been about Whitehall were ordered to their various stations. Half a dozen of them were also members of Parliament and could not abandon their duties in the Commons without permission. Commissary General Wilmot, member for Tamworth, asked leave for them all;[18] it was quietly granted, but Pym, who still waited his time to reveal what he had learnt from Goring of their intentions, did not fail to notice this forewarning move.

The only son of the Prince of Orange, magnificently accompanied by a suite of four hundred servants, had meanwhile arrived in London. On April 20th he made his first visit to Whitehall to see his bride. It was the children's hour; the twelve-year-old bridegroom, a beautiful child in gorgeous clothes, was received on the stairs of Whitehall by his future brothers-in-law, the Prince of Wales and the Duke of York, the elder nearly eleven, the younger seven and a half. They led him to the King, Queen and Princess, but although the scene was one of indulgent smiles and prettiness, Henrietta Maria did not kiss her future son-in-law and the nine-year-old bride offered only her hand and not her cheek. The French friends of the Queen still elected to despise the House of Orange, and Henrietta Maria, although herself the daughter of a Medici whom her father had called "ma grosse banquière," encouraged her daughter to resent the inferior match that circumstances forced upon her. The little girl may have heard the wounding exclamations of the French at Court—" *Jesu-Marie, la fille d'une fille de France!* " [19]

Some said the Prince of Orange had sent over 200,000 ducats in gold to assure his son a warm welcome. Whether this was true or not, the bride allowed herself to be kissed a few days later and was reconciled to her fate by the end of the week.[20] Sir Anthony Van Dyck painted the wedding portrait, the Prince in scarlet satin and gold, the Princess in cloth of silver, a pretty pair, well brushed, well curled, demure, and holding hands.

On April 19th Charles had ordered his loyal officers to their posts. On April 20th he received his little son-in-law. On April 21st the House of Commons voted on the Bill of Attainder; two hundred and four voted for the Bill and fifty-nine against it. Of the two hundred and four who voted Strafford to death, one at least did so in the conviction that the Lords would certainly stop the Bill.[21]

On April 23rd, Good Friday, King Charles wrote to Strafford in the intervals of the day's devotions, solemnly reiterating his earlier promise. He should not suffer in life, honour, or fortune, wrote the King, and added with deep feeling—" a very mean reward from a master to so faithful and able a servant." [22]

On April 23rd, therefore, the King was quietly confident that he could save Strafford's life. On the 24th, the Saturday, Pym again sent forward to the King the urgent request of the Commons and a petition from the citizens of London that he should disband the Irish army and dismiss—once and for all— every Roman Catholic from his Court. On the 25th, Easter Day, rioters tried to break into the Spanish ambassador's house during Mass; crowds began to gather on the waterfront and about the Tower. Rumours went round: it was said that the King intended to dissolve Parliament by force, that the English army was on the verge of mutiny because Parliament had so far failed to pay it, that Pym was to be offered a place on the King's Council as Chancellor of the Exchequer.[23] The contradictory and inconsistent character of these rumours reflects the indiscreet talking of all parties rather than deliberate rumour-mongering on the part of any one of them. Trade was depressed and there was considerable unemployment among mariners; May Day, always the moment for riots, was fast approaching.

In this atmosphere the King continued to pursue his two plans simultaneously. The Earl of Bedford, with practical good sense, had outlined a scheme by which Charles could ensure the financial stability of his government in future by the imposition of a general excise on exported goods, a tax already in use in the Low Countries. To avoid the confusion and corruption of the past, he suggested that Pym, whose business abilities were transcendent, should be made Chancellor of the Exchequer to organise the excise and set the finances of the Crown at last on a firm foundation.[24] In return for this support and assistance Charles would naturally adopt a more moderate policy in religion, following the suggestions of Bishop Williams. He would eliminate the more unpopular members of his Council and draw about him, in positions of trust, such men as Bristol, Essex, Warwick, Hertford, possibly even Lord Saye. Strafford, whose life and fortune would be spared, must retire for ever from public life.

On the face of it this looked like a workable and satisfactory programme, but everything depended on the King's good faith, and Pym, differing in this from Bedford and Bristol, was unwilling to believe in it. For him, the Irish army was the touchstone of the King's sincerity. He may or may not have believed that Strafford had seriously advocated using that army against the English. But he certainly believed that the King could only disprove such an intention on his own part by disbanding the Irish army. He knew of the intrigues in the King's favour in the English army. He knew therefore that the King was not acting frankly with the Earl of Bedford and the moderates. If the King should also refuse to disband Strafford's army in Ireland, that could mean only that the King intended sooner or later to appeal to force. On April 28th Charles again returned a negative answer to a request to disband the Irish army and Pym dissociated himself from the Bedford plan.[25]

At the same time Charles made another move. He attempted to reinforce the garrison in the Tower with a hundred men under the command of an officer of his own selection. Rumours of a plot among the officers of the English army were now all over London and Edward Hyde reported to the House of Lords a prevalent belief that Strafford was about to escape.[26] The Lords took notice of it, but did nothing. Lord Newport, Warwick's half-brother and Constable of the Tower, was one of Strafford's most virulent enemies: while he remained at his post it was impossible for the King's friends to gain control of the Tower and unlikely that Strafford could escape.

Charles continued his double manipulation. On Saturday, May 1st, he fell in with a suggestion of Bedford's that he should address a personal appeal to the Lords to reject the Bill of Attainder. Bedford no doubt intended the King to elaborate the argument which Strafford himself had used and to emphasise in the strongest terms to the Lords the danger of agreeing to a measure so offensive to justice and the laws of England. In Bedford's conception the King's new position was to be built solidly upon the laws of the land; but at this critical juncture Bedford was suddenly taken ill.

Lacking the intelligent guidance of Bedford, King Charles informed the House of Lords on Saturday, May 1st, that he was not himself satisfied in his conscience of Strafford's guilt and could therefore in no circumstances agree to pass the Bill against his life.[27] A singleness of purpose, a noble blindness inspired the King's action; he knew the laws of the land and understood the legal objections to the Bill, but in the last resort, and in spite of all his communings with Bedford and Bristol, he believed that no higher law than his kingly conscience could be cited to protect the Earl of Strafford. He could have cited nothing worse, for this placing of his conscience before all earthly respects sounded to most of his hearers like a defiance rather than an appeal. Moreover, it relieved the Upper House from further responsibility.

If the King intended in no circumstances to consent to the Bill of Attainder, what did it matter if the Lords gave way to it?

Pym, in the House of Commons, was busy strengthening the position of the present Parliament against eventual attack. He had a Bill put forward to guard it against sudden dissolution. This Parliament, by a special act, was to be dissolved only by its own consent. The scrambled, emergency measure, patched up to guard against violence or against a desperate move to save Strafford's life, was to confuse the politics of England for eighteen years to come.

At Whitehall on May 2nd the King and Queen saw their daughter married, very quietly, in an atmosphere of anxiety and strain. The Elector Palatine was conspicuously absent from the family gathering. It was Sunday and popular Puritan preachers were thundering from their pulpits for the death of Strafford. Roving bands of apprentices and seamen set upon the servants of Roman Catholic ambassadors and demonstrated outside their chapels. At almost any moment now most of the foreign diplomats in London expected the King's counterstroke and feared civil war.[28]

No counterstroke came. The King had tried and failed to put troops into the Tower; he had sent his loyal officers to their action stations. But as Secretary Vane was to say, " the design has been ill-carried whatsoever it has been." [29] What had it been? In the end, nothing but talk and bragging and indiscretion, of no avail to the King but of great value to Pym.

On Monday, May 3rd, Pym acted at last on the hints that Goring had given nearly a month before. A committee was appointed to examine the now widespread rumours of unrest in the army. The unrest was genuine enough, and on the same day the Commons instructed Speaker Lenthall to write to Sir John Conyers in the North assuring him that the English army would be paid in full and all its wrongs and grievances be carefully considered.[30] Ever since the King's attempt to send troops to the Tower in the previous week, rumours of a plot had been growing in London. A plot to save Strafford, a Popish Plot, a

Gunpowder Plot—plots were meat and drink to the Londoners in the merry month of May. All shops were closed and the crowds flooded westwards to the Parliament house, crying for "Justice," asking for news of the plot, inventing news of the plot. This thronging to Parliament went on for the best part of two days while, within doors, the Commons drew up a declaration that they would live and die for the true Protestant religion, the liberties and rights of subjects and the power and privilege of Parliaments. This Protestation, as it came to be called, was tendered to all their number for signature, and on May 4th sent to the Lords for theirs.[31]

In the midst of the excitement the ordinary business of the House continued; on this flurried May 4th the committee appointed to inquire into John Lilburne's case reported that the sentence pronounced against him in the Star Chamber was "illegal and against the liberty of the subject, bloody, wicked, cruel, barbarous and tyrannical." The young man himself had on that very day again got himself arrested for shouting too loudly and prominently among the crowds outside the House. He was set free after questioning but "free-born John" was never long out of trouble.[32]

Strafford from the Tower watched the situation deteriorate and was powerless to prevent it. Some faint knowledge of the King's army plans he must have had, for when Charles tried to introduce the new troops into the Tower he had himself offered a bribe of £20,000 to Sir William Balfour, Newport's lieutenant at the Tower, to assist him to escape.[33] He would hardly have done this without a hint from the Court that his escape would be welcome to the King. The scheme had failed.

The House of Lords, irritated and offended by the King, was now surrounded by a shouting crowd of Londoners. The chances of their rejecting the Bill of Attainder were small. For the first time, perhaps, in the long months since his arrest, Strafford saw death very near. He had no fear of death in itself but he feared the consequences for the King. If the Bill could not be stopped in the Lords, would the King have the resolution, in the face of popular clamour, to stop it with his sole veto? If he failed to do so, having openly declared it a matter of conscience, could the Crown ever recover from so disastrous a surrender? Strafford fought for something more than his own life. He fought to save the King from irreparable defeat.

For the second time that year Charles was defending the life of one man against the will of Parliament and the angry people. In January he had reprieved Goodman, the priest; during the crisis of the ensuing days, Goodman's life had been saved not so much by the King's action as by his own generous rejection of the King's reprieve.[34] Goodman's fine act had placed him at the mercy of the Lords as arbiters of his fate and they had been unwilling, in the circumstances, to be less noble-minded than their victim.

Knowledge of this may have suggested to Strafford the course he now took. He released the King from a promise he could no longer keep.

"May it please your Sacred Majesty," he wrote from the Tower, "I understand the minds of men are more and more incensed against me, notwithstanding your Majesty hath declared that, in your princely opinion, I am not guilty of treason, and that you are not satisfied in your conscience to pass the bill. This bringeth me in a very great strait; there is before me the ruin of my children and family, hitherto untouched with any foul crime: here are before me the many ills, which may befall your Sacred Person and the whole Kingdom should yourself and Parliament part less satisfied one with the other than is necessary for the preservation both of King and people; there are before me the things most valued, most feared by mortal men, Life and Death.

"To say, Sir, that there hath not been strife in me, were to make me less man than God knows my infirmities make me and to call a destruction upon myself and my young children will find no easy consent from flesh and blood. To set Your Majesty's conscience at liberty, I do most humbly beseech Your Majesty (for preventing of evils which may happen by your refusal) to pass this bill. . . ."[35]

424

The Christian, the politician, the faithful servant—each had his part in this letter. Facing an almost inevitable end, Strafford was prompted by his religious faith and his personal devotion to free the conscience of the King; but in so far as the end was not yet quite inevitable, he had a faint hope left that this deliberate release of the King's conscience might, by casting the responsibility for his life or death back upon the Lords, work the King's and his own salvation.

He wrote on the evening of May 4th. On the morning of May 5th the committee for inquiry into the Army Plot, as it was now generally called, made their first report to the House and sent for various officers whom they believed to be concerned in it. During the next twenty-four hours most of those whom they wished to question fled the country or otherwise vanished from public view.[36] Only Colonel Goring remained quietly at Portsmouth. The Queen's friends could hardly have done worse: their flight seemed to prove their guilt and to justify the wildest speculations.

On 7th and 8th May the crowds were thick at Westminster. The ports had been closed and the London quays were idle. While the Commons took measures for securing the principal seaports, especially Hull, Portsmouth, and the coast of Kent, the people in the streets of Westminster talked of invasion; some said French forces had been seen in the Channel, some Spanish, some Irish.[37] When the Lords drove up in their coaches for the debate on the Bill of Attainder, they could hardly make their way through the throng furiously crying out for "Justice."

Bedford had died at the week-end. Lord Bristol had no longer any control of the House. The bishops were not voting. The King had not understood the use he might have made of Strafford's letter. Only forty-eight lords were in their seats when the Bill of Attainder was put to the vote: eleven of them, with useless courage, gave their voices against it.[38]

On Sunday, May 9th, the Bill was before the King at White-hall, and the crowds, transferring their attentions from the Houses of Parliament, now wrapped in sabbath silence, congregated about the precincts of the palace. The King remained unmoved; he was without fear. The Queen, irritable, anxious and as deeply mortified as she was disappointed by the flight of her friends and the disintegration of the Army Plot, gave way by turns to anger and tearful despair.[39] She had never fully understood the constitutional issues at stake in Strafford's trial, had never liked him personally, and was not at this time able or willing to strengthen the King's resolution to save him.

In painful anxiety the King sent for the judges to advise him on the state of the law in Strafford's case. When they had gone his doubts were still unresolved. He sought spiritual guidance. How could he consent to the Bill when it was against his conscience to do so? Strafford's letter might release him from an obligation to Strafford: it did not release him from an obligation to God. On this point and no other he called in those in whose spiritual gifts he trusted. He sent for the Primate of Ireland, Archbishop Ussher, then on a visit to London. Ussher, who received the message in the pulpit of St. Paul's, Covent Garden, sent to say that he could wait on His Majesty only when he had done his duty to God. It was the kind of answer which pleased Charles. But Ussher, when he arrived later in the day, gave it as his opinion categorically that the King should in no circumstances perform an act against his conscience. William Juxon, Bishop of London, resolved the moral problem in the same way and with the same firmness.[40]

Bishop Williams spoke round and about in a very different manner. He pointed out to the King the evils that might ensue from his refusal to gratify his people. He discoursed learnedly of the dual character of kingship, showing how the King, as a private man, may think and act in one way, but, as a King, is bound to think and act differently. The King in his private conscience could not condemn Strafford, but what of the King's public conscience? Could he load it with the fearful responsibility of bloodshed? He must go against the dictates of conscience either as a man, or as a King, whichever decision he took; as a King, was he not more answerable than as a man to God from whom his power came?[41]   The argument was subtle and well urged. It moved the King. What had been a crime against his conscience appeared to him in a new light—as a duty: with tears in his eyes he gave his consent to the Bill of Attainder. " My Lord of Strafford's condition," he said, " is happier than mine."[42]

Another Bill had been presented to him at the same time as the Attainder. It was Pym's hurried Bill prohibiting the dissolution of the present Parliament without its own consent. He passed that too.

The King gave his consent to the Act of Attainder against the greatest of his servants on the afternoon of May 10th. Strafford's execution was fixed for noon on May 12th. The interval allowed little time for second thoughts, but the King had them. On the 11th he sent the Prince of Wales, whose youth he thought might touch the peers, to appeal to the Lords for mercy.[43] It was in vain. In vain too his gnawing regret, his bitter, growing certitude that the conscience of the King and the conscience of the man were one and indivisible. He had done wrong; he had failed in his sacred trust; he never forgave himself.

The tragedy was for Charles a moral one; he never fully realised the enormity of the political mistake, or the cruelty of the personal betrayal. He had valued Strafford as a servant but never loved him as a friend, and he had not adequately understood the significance of Strafford's fate in the conflict between him and his Parliament. Towards the lonely and awful end of his own life the King was to say, more than once, that all his sufferings had come upon him as a just punishment for his sin in letting Strafford die. He never said, and perhaps never realised, that they were also the logical outcome of the political error.

Archbishop Laud, miserably alone in the Tower, perceived it, and confided with bitterness to his diary that the King whom he and Strafford had served had not been worth serving—" he knew not how to be or be made great."[44]   He saw, once more before he died, the great colleague whom he had loved and trusted, with whom he had shared his hopes and fears during that time—now so remote—when they had strenuously worked together to realise a great vision. The two prisoners were allowed no private farewell, but Laud stood at the window of his room in the Tower, as Strafford, sombre in black, went out to his death, and with trembling hands gave him a last, speechless blessing.[45]

On the scaffold itself, in the mild May sunshine, before the dense crowds who had come to rejoice in his death, Strafford spoke for the last time, saying with simplicity what he believed to be the truth:

> "In all the honour I had to serve His Majesty, I had not any intention in my heart but what did aim at the joint and individual prosperity of the King and his people. ..."[46]

The words echoed another speech, made twelve years before when he first assumed high office under the Crown:

> "To the joint individual well-being of sovereignty and subjection do I here vow all my cares and diligence through the whole course of this my ministry."[47]

He had not been selfless in his exercise of power. He had used his office to aggrandise himself and his family. Yet according to his large abilities and his narrow judgment had not swerved from his ideal. In other circumstances, with a different master, he might have done good service and might be remembered in history for what he had achieved in power, not merely for the tragedy of his end.

BOOK III CHAPTER V REFERENCES

1. *C.S.P. Ireland*, 1633–47, pp. 252, 261–5; Rushworth, III, i, p. 214.
2. *H.M.C.Ormonde MSS.*, New Series, II, p. 352.
3. *Harleian MSS.*, 6424, folio 13.
4. *C.S.P. Ven.*, 1640–2, p. 138.
5. *Breadalbane MSS., Letters*, 1639–59. Glencarradale to Glenorchy, March 9th, 1641.

6. *Portland MSS.*, I, p. 15.

7. *C.S.P.D.*, 1640–1, pp. 532, 535.

8. Rushworth, III, I, pp. 255–7.

9. *Portland MSS.*, I, pp. 16–17.

10. Nalson, II, pp. 272–3.

11. *C.S.P.D.*, 1641, p. 539.

12. *Commons Journals*, p. 118.

13. Verney, p. 37; Clarendon, III, 135–7.

14. The details about Strafford's Trial are from Rushworth's volume devoted to it; the above speech is also given at greater length in *C.S.P.D.*, 1641, pp. 540 ff.

15. Rushworth, III, I, pp. 227–8.

16. Rushworth.

17. *Commons Journals*, II, p. 123.

18. *Ibid., loc. cit.*

19. *C.S.P. Ven.*, 1640–2, pp. 142, 145; *C.S.P.D.*, 1640–1, pp. 554, 560.

20. *C.S.P. Ven.*, 1640–2, p. 145.

21. Knowler, II, p. 432.

22. *Ibid.*, p. 416.

23. *C.S.P.D.*, 1640–1, p. 560; *H.M.C. Egmont MSS*, I, I, p. 133.

24. *C.S.P.D.*, 1640–1, p. 560.

25. *Commons Journals*, II, 127, 131.

26. Rushworth, III, I, pp. 238, 254.

27. *Ibid.*, III, I, p. 239; *C.S.P.D.*, 1640–1, p. 567.

28. *Portland MSS.*, I, p. 12; *C.S.P. Ven.*, 1640–2, pp. 141–2, 147, 149.

29. *C.S.P.D.*, 1640–1, p. 571.

30. *Ibid.*, p. 569.

31. Baillie, I, p. 352; Rushworth, III, I, p. 241–2

32. *Commons Journals*, II, p. 134.

33. *Portland MSS.*, I, p. 719.

34. Rushworth, III, i, p. 166.

35. Rushworth, *Trial of Strafford*, p. 743 f.

36. *Commons Journals*, II, pp. 135, 137; *C.S.P.D.*, 1640–1, p. 571.

37. *Egmont MSS.*, I, i, p. 134.

38. *Lords Journals*, IV, p. 239.

39. *Egmont MSS.*, I, I, p. 134.

40. Hacket, *Scrinia Reserata*; N. Bernard, *Life of Usher*, p. 96.

41. *Scrinia Reserata*.

42. *Hist. MSS. Commission*, II, p. 99; XII, ii, p. 281.

43. *Lords Journals*, IV, p. 245.

44. Laud, III, p. 443.

45. *Ibid.*, p. 445; Heylin, *Cyprianus Anglicus*, p. 480.

46. Rushworth, III, I, pp. 267 f.

47. The speech, first printed in *The Academy*, June 1875, has been reprinted in whole or in part in every subsequent life of Strafford.

CHAPTER SIX

THE KING AND JOHN PYM

Summer 1641

STRAFFORD made his last solemn declaration of political faith on the scaffold on May 12th, 1641. The same day, the House of Commons authorised the publication of the late Sir Edward Coke's exposition of an opposing creed. The generation of lawyers then present in the House of Commons had grown to maturity under the powerful influence of Coke's mind and character. He had been silenced twelve years before by Charles I; his papers had been seized and the commentaries on the laws of England through which he had defended the Common Law against the Prerogative had been forcibly interrupted. The House now gave orders for the printing of Coke's *Second Part of the Institutes of the Laws of England*, which contained his commentary on *Magna Charta*.

Coke, with irresistible logic, had applied the general terms of chapter twenty-nine of *Magna Charta* to the particular instances of his own epoch. The medieval King had sworn in the following terms to his barons:

" No freeman shall be taken, or imprisoned, or be disseised of his freehold, or liberties, or free customs, or be outlawed or exiled, or any otherwise destroyed; nor will we not pass upon him, nor condemn him, but by lawful judgment of his peers, or by the law of the land. We will sell to no man, we will not deny or defer to any man either justice or right."

Coke found in these words a depth and breadth of meaning very much to the purpose. The vagueness of the royal undertaking not to " destroy " any freeman, he invested with a clear and comprehensive significance:

> " Every oppression against law," wrote Coke, " by colour of an usurped authority, is a kind of destruction . . . and it is the worst oppression that is done by colour of justice."

Imprisonment at the King's pleasure, or sending men abroad on the King's service against their will, were both shown to offend against the Charter, a point which had been confirmed under Coke's influence when King Charles had been compelled to pass the Petition of Right in 1628. By a wide, inclusive gesture, Coke managed also to cite the Charter against restrictions of trade and manufacture:

> " Generally all monopolies are against this great charter, because they are against the liberty and freedom of the subject and against the law of the land."

Such phrases as " the law of the land " and " justice or right " depended for their meaning entirely on the experience and intelligence of lawyers. Therein lay the danger to the Crown, once the legal opinion of the country was, for whatever reason, at variance with that of the King. The King had promised not to " deny or defer to any man either justice or right." This meant, so Coke averred, that the King must concede not only justice to his people but *right*, which in this case, he argued, meant *law* because law was the accepted means by which justice was to be given. The King had therefore admitted himself to be bound by the law and to the law. Coke did not add—but he certainly implied—that, given the practice of England, this meant that the King was bound not by an abstract, disembodied law, but by the opinions of lawyers. His interpretation of Magna Charta utterly contradicted Lord Chief Justice Berkeley's ruling in the Ship-money case, that *Rex* is *Lex*. It made a recent statement of Lord Keeper Finch, that it behoved not the Chancellor to do anything other than the King's bidding, look like an ignorant surrender of established principles.

In conclusion, Coke broke into eloquence:

" As the gold finer will not, out of the dust, threads and shreds of gold, let pass the least crumb, in respect of the excellency of the metal, so ought not the learned reader to let pass any syllable of this law, in respect of the excellency of the matter."

In concentrating his energies on the destruction of Strafford, John Pym had not lost his hold upon other questions of more far-reaching significance than the removal of a single minister. His well-planned attack on the power of the Crown had achieved almost complete success by the early summer of 1641. In the seven months since Parliament met, almost all the supports of the throne had been cut away. Strafford was dead, Laud in the Tower, Finch in exile; six of the judges were under threat of impeachment. The King's rich friends, in the City and elsewhere, were being harried and intimidated as projectors and monopolists. His customs revenue and the men responsible for collecting it were the subject of question and scrutiny. His Postmaster-General had been accused of abusing the public service in the interests of the Crown. The most intimate part of the administration had been damaged by the threatened proceedings against Windebanke and his flight. The Triennial Parliaments Bill was already law, and the King had consented to the Act perpetuating the existing Parliament on the same day as he consented to the Attainder of Strafford. Bills for the abolition of the Prerogative Courts—in Wales and in the North as well as the Star Chamber—were passing smoothly through the Commons, along with the Bill against the High Commission. Since the appointment of the Puritan Warwick to be Lord High Admiral even the navy appointments were out of the King's hands.

By his policy of the last six months Pym had brought the Crown under the control of Parliament and achieved political changes in England more far-reaching than those achieved in the previous year by the Estates in Scotland.

He did not advertise his achievement as a revolution and it did not appear so to him. He believed that he was restoring the ancient balance between the sovereign and the people glorified under Queen Elizabeth. Antiquarians, like Sir Symonds d'Ewes the member for Sudbury, thought they could trace the elements of this balanced government in the institutions of the Anglo-Saxons, and Sir Edward Coke's exposition of Magna Charta seemed to show that the Plantagenet kings had set their seal upon it four hundred years before.

In this revolution, which at first appeared to many as the restoration of a more authentic order, the House of Commons, except for the King's own friends and servants, had willingly supported Pym. But if few of King Charles's subjects shared his exalted view of the royal authority, fewer still wished to see that authority wholly overthrown. Once the "evil counsellors" had disappeared and the worst of them had lost his head on Tower Hill, they felt the time had come to let the King alone. The English gentry liked to exercise freely their right to grumble as much and as loudly as they pleased at the King's government but they meant no disrespect to the King's person. While they thought it best for him to govern with the help of Parliament, they regarded him as the undoubted head of the State, the fountain of justice, the apex of society and, next after God, the object of awe and veneration. The idea of the King compelled by a vulgar rabble to give his consent to a Parliamentary Bill was, in retrospect, disquieting—even to members of Parliament and Londoners when the crisis was over. It was a violation of the social order, an overturning of the accepted conventions. This terror of "overturning"—immensely strong in England's hierarchic society of social climbers—was the impulse behind the now growing opposition to Pym in the House.

With the coming of the spring and the Lent Assizes the

subsidies voted in Parliament had to be assessed and in due course collected throughout the country. But instead of being paid as usual into the Royal Exchequer they were to be forwarded by order of Parliament direct to the Guildhall to meet the debt incurred to the City of London for paying the Scots indemnity. This perturbed the gentry who doubted whether money which had been voted to the King ought to go into coffers other than his. Whatever financial follies might have been committed by the royal officials, they had no higher regard for the honesty of those into whose hands the money would fall at the Guildhall. There was at least something traditional and respectable in paying money into the Royal Exchequer, but to pay money into the hands of subjects like themselves was a disturbing innovation.[1]

Pym's anxieties had not lessened with the death of Strafford and the achievement of the political revolution. He knew the King would not accept defeat, that he had made concessions merely to gain time until he should be strong enough for a counter-attack. For the next months, therefore, Pym's policy was to safeguard the position he had won and forestall any move the King might make against it.

For his own purposes, Pym had greatly exaggerated the plot between the Court and the discontented officers of the English army; but he had not invented it. There had been a plot. In a desperate situation the King was bound to find desperate remedies. Force was in the end his only answer and force was what Pym feared. The words for which Strafford had died, that ambigious phrase of " an army in Ireland you may employ here to reduce this kingdom," had been stretched at his trial to convey a threat to England. In the summer of 1640 when Strafford spoke them, the Irish army had been intended only for Scotland; but now, in the spring of 1641 this Irish army of eight thousand men, seven thousand of them Roman Catholics, was still in existence, and Charles was very unwilling to disband it. Pym had some legitimate cause for anxiety there. To these fears of army plots in England and Ireland, a third was added.

Charles might so conduct affairs as to break the friendship between Parliament and the Covenanters: Hamilton was still pursuing his laborious policy of trying to win the friendship of Argyll, first for himself, and then for the King. Charles himself was working on the envious Rothes who, distrustful and jealous of Argyll had promised the King to use his influence to make a party for him in Scotland, and claimed that he had already gained Loudoun.[2]

Fears of this kind were never far from the minds of Pym and his chief supporters in the summer of 1641, but the most immediate and serious danger that he had to face was the resurgence of sympathy for the King and the opinion, sincerely held by the growing body of " moderates " in the House of Commons, that Charles had changed his convictions and was now ready to be respectfully guided along the path of Parliamentary government.

The King himself assiduously encouraged those who held this view by a further display of moderation. He relinquished suspect advisers without pressure from Parliament, withdrew Cottington from the Exchequer and the Court of Wards and bestowed the latter, with all its opportunities for private profit on Lord Saye. Sometime also in the course of the summer he made approaches to Edward Hyde, the able and eloquent lawyer who had been directly responsible for the bill against the Prerogative Courts. In foreign policy he became cool to his Spanish friends, arranged to send his wife's troublesome mother out of the country, and received an ambassador from the Portuguese, now in revolt against Spain.

The Queen of Bohemia heard with relief of this change of policy and of the favour that the King was now showing to her son, the Elector Palatine. Charles's more friendly attitude to his nephew was made possible by the departure of the young Prince of Orange, three weeks after his marriage to Princess Mary and a fortnight after Strafford's death; while the bridegroom was still at Court the King had found it necessary, in accordance with etiquette, to mortify his grown-up nephew by

compelling him to take second place to his child son-in-law.[3]
But as soon as the bridegroom had gone home, the Elector found
himself the object of flattering attention. Unlike his mother,
he was not deceived. The King spoke of raising troops in
England and Scotland (or using those already raised) to help him
to regain his German lands; the Elector accepted the suggestion
without enthusiasm. He believed that the King wanted the
troops for his own purposes and was using his name and the
Protestant Cause merely as a cover. He could not, of course,
voice his doubts in public, but he saw no reason why he should
assist his uncle in the deception. Although for the next months
he was repeatedly made to appear at his uncle's side when
appeals were being made on his behalf, he said little or nothing
on these occasions and maintained a stubborn air of boredom.
He had his own spies and informers about the Court,[4] had a
shrewd idea of the Queen's influence and the King's plans, and
maintained discreetly his own relations with individual members of the House of Commons.

It was of the first importance to the King to have troops at
his disposal. He might gain this end by encouraging a Royalist
faction in the English army, by retaining Strafford's Irish army,
by winning over all the Covenanters under Argyll, or half of
them under Rothes, or by a levy in favour of the Elector
Palatine; he tried to do it—in his usual diffused manner—in all
five ways at once. While the Queen encouraged the Royalism
of the English officers and stimulated the fears and hopes of the
Irish, the King soothed the moderate-minded men in the House
of Commons, courted the friendship of Argyll through Hamilton,
promised favours to Rothes if he would overthrow Argyll and
entered into a correspondence with Montrose behind the backs
of both. His policy was of an elaborate complexity, but poorly
co-ordinated.

It imposed, all the same, a heavy task on Pym who had, at
one and the same time, to hold together his majority in the
House of Commons—which depended on the support of the
moderate men—and to outbid the King for the continued

friendship of the Covenanters. The two things were incompatible; he could outbid the King with the Covenanters only by hastening legislation for the reform of the English Church on the Presbyterian model, but such drastic action, while encouraging an extremist minority, would alienate the Protestant but conservative majority in the House of Commons.

The summer of 1641 was therefore a time of play-acting and changes of mood. The King assumed the outward appearance of moderation, forbearance and devotion to the Protestant Cause while Pym tried to shake this pose without alienating those moderate men in the Commons who believed in it. Charles and Pym, men unlike in almost every respect, had in common an intense political fanaticism. The King believed that, under God, his authority was sacred and must be restored by force if necessary; Pym believed that, under God, the King was answerable to his subjects (meaning the House of Commons) and must be kept so. Both men were prepared to use any means to secure what they conceived to be right.

Immediately after Strafford's death, Pym moved to strengthen the Scottish alliance by allowing the Presbyterians in the Commons to go forward with their Bills for reorganising the Church by the abolition of episcopacy and the secularisation of colleges and cathedrals. These projects shook the intellectual centres of the land, startled ancient scholars of Oxford and Cambridge, troubled many lawyers and all conservatives. Both the universities petitioned the House against the secularisation of cathedral chapters lest the learning and dignity of the clergy should suffer by it.

The universities, except for such islands of Puritanism as Emmanuel College, Cambridge, had been deeply penetrated by fashionable Anglican theology; if Puritanism gained the upper hand, they would be more in need of help themselves than able to give it to others. Laud's beloved Oxford was in the greatest danger and, at about this time, he wrote from the Tower of London to resign the Chancellorship. " The university," he wrote, " hath great need of friends, great and daily need ... if you had another Chancellor you could not want the help which now you do." His withdrawal was an act of true devotion. "If there be any good which I ought to have done to that place and have not done it, it proceeded from want of understanding or ability, not will or affection," he wrote.[5] Long after his death, his manuscripts in the Bodleian library, the fellowships he had endowed, and the tranquil colonnades of St. John's College would be his monuments in the place which had the most of his heart and the best of his service.

The attack on the organised Church brought with it, for Pym, a tangle of political problems. On May 24th the Lords rejected the Bill for excluding the bishops from their House; this opened still further the breach between the two Houses which Strafford had tried hard to make and which the King encouraged. The Presbyterians in the Commons at once introduced the more far-reaching Root and Branch Bill for removing the bishops altogether. The more violent became the actions of the religious extremists in the Commons, the more essential was it for Pym to undermine confidence in the apparent moderation of the King. In May, to precipitate the crisis which had cost Strafford his life, he had revealed the information given by Goring about the Army Plot. In June, to divert attention from the violent religious policy of his colleagues, he maintained interest in the Plot by frequent reports from the committee which had been set up to investigate it.

On June 8th, Nathaniel Fiennes, Lord Saye's son, reported some startling details. Sir William Balfour, lieutenant of the Tower, had deponed that, at the time of the Plot, five weeks ago, Strafford had offered him £20,000 to connive at his escape. At the same time, Colonel Goring, governor of Portsmouth, had admitted attempts on the part of the Court to secure the governorship of Portsmouth for Jermyn, presumably to receive French ships and troops into the town. He hinted that Commissary-General Wilmot was deeply involved. At these revelations from the committee, Wilmot himself and George Digby rose to protest that the accusations were groundless. They demanded more proof than Goring's bare word. Other members shouted them down. Lenthall, an ineffective Speaker in a rowdy House, strove in vain to bring order out of the hubbub, but could not make himself heard. Dusk was thickening and he could scarcely see who was standing, who trying to catch his eye. Someone moved for candles. Others cried "No," for already all possibility of serious debate was at an end. Two members, none the less, brought them in unbidden. This unorthodox behaviour restored the Commons to a sense of their own dignity; the majority voted the candle-bringers to the Tower for a breach of order, and the Speaker adjourned the House.[6]

The desired crisis had arisen, and the revived rumour of an Army Plot hampered the King's new policy as much as Pym had intended that it should. To satisfy the extremists, debates in the House on the Root and Branch Bill went on, and Sir Symonds d'Ewes argued eloquently from an early Greek manuscript, preserved in the King's own Library, that St. Paul had addressed neither Titus nor Timothy with the title of bishop, the word being an impertinent interpolation of a later date.[7] But the focus of interest was elsewhere; the assertions and counter-assertions of Goring, Wilmot and Digby held all attention. Digby was by far the ablest in debate, but in action he was impulsive and indiscreet. Perhaps from vanity, in which he was not lacking, but more probably as propaganda against Pym's party, he chose this moment to publish the admirable speech he had made against the Attainder of Strafford. Incontrovertibly, to do such a thing without permission of the House was a breach of privilege and Digby might have found himself in the Tower had not the King instantly elevated him to the peerage. Pym would not permit an attack on a peer for his past misdeeds lest he should further widen the breach with the Lords.

The crisis was not over. On June 14th, the King was unexpectedly betrayed by the Earl of Northumberland. The earl had been Strafford's friend, and it is possible that angry contempt of the King for his desertion of a good servant, added to the many slights he had himself endured, had finally turned him against the Court. Family and personal ties perhaps hastened his decision. He may truly have felt, as he himself said, that a brother's honour was at stake and must be vindicated. His brother, Harry Percy, accused when news of the Army Plot first came out a month before, had escaped abroad. Northumberland now placed before Parliament the letter he had received from him, in which the story of the Plot was set forth in detail. Percy proclaimed his own and Wilmot's innocence of any evil intent; he had merely informed the King that his army was loyal and would serve him. Goring, on the other hand, with Suckling, Iermyn, Davenant and the young Lord Carnarvon, had urged on the King a plan for seizing the Tower and occupying the City of London. This, said Percy, the King had very properly rejected.[8]

The effect of this letter was all that Pym could wish. In a sense, of course, it exonerated the King, and Wilmot's steadfast assertion under examination, that it was the exact truth, should have had the same effect. But the niceties of the King's position among the interlocking plots were not exactly studied and the general impression created was that violence and mischief had been planned at Court. Goring delicately enhanced this impression, by admitting the existence of the second and more violent plot but denying his own participation.[9]

In the midst of the excitement, on June 16th, a sinister paper from Scotland was laid before the Commons by their Scottish allies. A messenger carrying a letter from the King to Montrose had been intercepted on the Border. The letter was harmless, but with it was an inexplicable series of notes, presumably a code, about an elephant, a dromedary and a serpent. These " dark memorials," it was alleged, concerned a plot, suggested by Montrose to the King, for gaining control of the government of Scotland.[10]

The King took this strange happening calmly and returned a soft answer to an insolent challenge from Argyll about his correspondence with Montrose. He did not deny the letter: " I do avow it as fit for me to write, both for the matter and the person to whom it was written." [11] But of dromedaries, elephants and serpents he denied all knowledge. The zoological incursion remained unexplained, but otherwise Charles's correspondence with Montrose had been singularly innocent and high-minded. In Scotland, as in England, a moderate party was coming into existence; Montrose had himself almost originated that party by his criticisms of the actions of the Scots Estates and his association with a few like-minded friends in the secret Cumbernauld Bond, of the previous year, to preserve the true Covenant " against the indirect practising of a few."

But Montrose had not been included in the more cautious plans of Rothes for overthrowing Argyll. He was too indiscreet and impulsive, and was left therefore to his own free-lance devices. He had got into trouble for criticising Argyll and writing letters to the King during the treaty negotiations at Ripon; reproved but forgiven by the Covenanters, he had got into trouble again when the existence of the Cumbernauld Bond leaked out a few months later. Once again he was let off with a reproof, but he had become a marked man and deeply suspect. He went boldly on his way and soon after wrote the King a budget of unsolicited advice on how to govern Scotland. The advice was unexceptionable: he strongly advocated " the temperate government," and the maintenance of the Presbyterian religion.[12]

Charles was within his rights in answering this letter with courteous thanks, and the Covenanters were most certainly stepping beyond theirs when they intercepted the answer. They had acted under the pressure of a crisis which, unknown to Charles, had been suddenly sprung upon them by the irrepressible Montrose. Towards the end of May, Mr. John Graham, minister of Auchterarder, the town which lay at the gates of Montrose's chief castle of Kincardine, had said in an Edinburgh tavern that Argyll intended to depose the King. Summoned before the Committee of Estates for this dangerous slander, he gave

Montrose as the source of it. Montrose did not deny it; he had had it from John Stewart, Commissary of Dunkeld, who had reported to him a speech made by Argyll in the previous July when he entered Atholl to subdue the royalists. Argyll (according to Stewart) had said that if the King levied war on his own people he should be deposed. A few days later John Stewart himself, before the committee, confirmed the words, whereat Argyll "broke out into a passion and with great oaths denied the whole." [13]

Argyll soon recovered himself and a few days later John Stewart admitted after long cross-examination that he had not thought Argyll was speaking of King Charles, but only of kings in general. Later, when he discussed it with Montrose, the special application to King Charles had been suggested to him. In this way the evidence against Argyll was turned back against Montrose and he now stood under suspicion of having deliberately spread false rumours about Argyll. The interception of his correspondence with the King and the peculiar notes about the dromedary—of which he denied all knowledge—were enough to justify his arrest on suspicion of conspiracy against the government. On June 11th he was sent to Edinburgh Castle by order of the Committee of Estates, and held *incommunicado*. [14]

The news of Montrose's arrest and the discovery of his correspondence with the King, reaching London at the same time as the revelations of the Army Plot, set rumours flying. The King had already announced his intention of opening the next session of the Scottish Parliament in Edinburgh and it was soon a current belief in London that he planned, on his journey northward, first to place himself at the head of the discontented English army in these parts, then to join with the Scots conspirators and so to overthrow all his enemies. [15] This rumour was a natural consequence of the double revelation—the Army Plot and the correspondence with Montrose. Fears and speculation both in London and the country were increased, as usual, by the persistent belief in a possible Popish Plot. Justices of the peace, by ordinance of Parliament, were ordered to make sure that no recusants had arms, and the resultant questioning and searching stimulated anxiety among the Protestant population and gave it new rumours to feed on. There was little or no logic in rumours that credited the King with plotting both with Catholics and Covenanters, but there was a half-truth in both beliefs, and Pym, who knew better than anyone that the King's plans were neither so complete nor so elaborate, made the rising panic an excuse to request him to postpone his visit to Scotland for a fortnight, or until the English army in the north should be disbanded and the Scots forces have gone home.[16]

Rumour gave to the plots more definite shape than they had, and Pym was willing enough to stimulate rumour and to exaggerate the importance of the revelations that had been made. All the same, certain things were happening in Ireland which justified his suspicions. The King had yielded to pressure about the Irish army, but it had been disbanded rather in name than in fact. Officers and men had been permitted to re-enlist in foreign service if they wished to do so; large companies therefore stayed together waiting for shipping to France or Spain, and the country was full of scattered bands of troops, attached to their own officers, but no longer owning any higher authority.

A situation which would have been dangerous anywhere was doubly so in Ireland where the resentment and uncertainty of the populace, after the collapse of the Strafford administration, might at any moment break into violence.

The Lords Justices, who ineffectively presided at the head of the government in Dublin, contemplated the future with apprehension.[17] Since the winter, priests had been working among the people and more landed daily from Europe. They rode about the country speaking to the disbanded troops, telling them not to go abroad to seek wars, for God would soon have work for them in Ireland. The Catholic Archbishop of Tuam, Malachi O'Queely, held meetings openly. A gathering of Catholic clergy was said to have met for consultation with the Irish gentry as near to Dublin as " the wood of Maynooth."[18] These stirrings alarmed the two elderly Lords Justices and the divided, unguided, quarrelsome council in Dublin; but they did nothing.

Rumours of these things reached England but the fear of an Irish rising, though it must have been present to Pym's mind, was overshadowed by what seemed to him more immediate dangers. His first aim was to make sure that the English army in the north was disbanded and the Scots on their way home before the King started on his journey to Edinburgh. Before the end of June the negotiations with the Scots Commissioners, which had begun at Ripon in the previous October and continued in London since Parliament met, were brought to an end and the terms of the peace treaty settled. The Covenanters and the English House of Commons seemed, in these terms, to present a united front and the King yielded with little protest. He undertook to withdraw all declarations made at any time against the Covenanters, to ratify the legislation put forward by the Scottish Parliament in the previous year, to withdraw the garrisons from Berwick and Carlisle, to indemnify the Scots for ships and goods captured by his navy, to place Edinburgh Castle henceforward in the control of the Estates, and to allow the victorious party in Scotland to proceed against whom they pleased for having provoked the war. The Scots furthermore demanded the reformation of the English Church, for which joint consultations were in due course to be held, and the exclusion of all Roman Catholics from places about the King and his eldest son. For damages sustained in the war they required a payment of £300,000, of which the first instalment was to be paid before they would evacuate England.[19]

For the next weeks the King worked hard to allay the suspicion raised by the further revelations about the Army Plot. He dismissed the Marquis of Newcastle from his post as governor of the Prince of Wales because his name had been mentioned among those thought to be sympathetic to the conspiracy. In his place he appointed the Earl of Hertford, a known moderate and brother-in-law to the Earl of Essex. He even changed the Prince's tutor, Dr. Duppa, lest he should be thought too Laudian.

The new tutor, John Earle, rector of a Wiltshire parish and fellow of Merton College, was an innocuous, open-minded theologian, chiefly famous for having published as a young man his *Microcosmographie*, a pleasing collection of "characters" which has enduring fame as a minor work of literature.

These concessions were not enough to please Pym, or to satisfy him as to the King's future intentions. In a conference with the House of Lords he gained their support for a singularly bold demand, namely that in future all appointments to the household of the Queen or her children should be made only with consent of Parliament. At the same time he pressed once more for the dismissal of all Roman Catholics and the expulsion of Rossetti.[20] The King who had already permitted the Queen's confessor, Father Philip, to be questioned before Parliament on the Army Plot, continued his gracious policy by agreeing to the departure of Rossetti. The Pope's agent did not leave in disgrace; both King and Queen bade him an affectionate farewell and he was escorted to his ship by the Venetian ambassador and his servants to protect him from any impertinences of the people.[21] All the same, he had left. It was, or seemed, a triumph for the Protestant Cause to which official expression was given some days later in a Parliamentary manifesto authorised by the King proclaiming his intention to restore the Elector Palatine to his rightful heritage.[22]

Early in July, the Bill for the abolition of the prerogative courts came up for the King's consent. He persisted for forty-eight hours, no doubt testing the state of opinion in Parliament and London, but on this issue the majority in both Houses was strong and included nearly all the moderates. On the third day he passed the Bill and made an end of the direct judicial powers of the Crown.

The Army Plot excitement was flagging although Pym spun out all through July the examinations of the officers who had been involved, so that neither the Commons nor the Londoners would be able to forget the supposed menace. A new French ambassador had arrived and been welcomed by both King and

Queen. They had given him four hours of private talk, a circumstance which provoked comment.[23] The Queen announced an intention of going to Spa for her health, perhaps accompanied by her mother, whose departure, repeatedly postponed, was planned for August at latest. The House of Commons objected and insisted on questioning the Queen's doctor. Even to this unprecedented impertinence the King gave in, and Sir Theodore de Mayerne satisfied the vulgar curiosity of the House about the Queen's morning tears, her spinal curvature and the rash on her upper lip.[24] The Commons were not reassured; they asked next about her household accounts and the safety of her jewellery which they did not wish her to take abroad. On this the Queen reversed her decision since she found it the cause of so much anxiety to her husband's subjects.[25] She had meant, naturally, to take jewellery with her to raise a loan, and the journey lost its point if she had to go empty-handed.

The frenzy against the Roman Catholics continued to rise in London. One of the Douai priests, Father William Ward, was tracked down and brought to trial. Another, Father Cuthbert Greene, attendant on the Venetian ambassador, was rudely dragged from this diplomatic protection, and both were sentenced to be hanged, drawn and quartered. The Venetian ambassador, resolute that no one should infringe the diplomatic rights of the Serene Republic, managed to save Father Greene, in spite of the offensive behaviour of Secretary Vane, who took it upon himself to lecture the King at a public audience on the wickedness of granting a reprieve to a priest on whatever grounds. Vane, who had forfeited all hope of royal favour, had become the servant and mouthpiece of his friends in the Commons and was making the most of the King's inability, as things stood, to dismiss him. Father Ward had no one to protect him, for the King could not risk a second intervention after the trouble over Father Goodman six months before. He was an old man and was offered a mitigation of a horrible death if he would abjure the Roman error. He remained constant and died with a fortitude which impressed even the Londoners.[26] But it did not soften for

long their vindictive mood; a week later, two English priests
from the household of the Portuguese ambassador were arrested.
They were rescued by the French ambassador's servants after a
street fight.[27]

The King continued his policy of conciliation. When the
bad-tempered Earl of Pembroke, the Lord Chamberlain, slapped
the foolish face of Lord Maltravers during an argument, the
King made it an excuse for dismissing him and elevated to his
place the Puritan Earl of Essex.[28] This appointment was another
move to win the support of all moderate men. By the late
summer the King had, in some quarters, so far disarmed criticism
that he was credited, or allowed himself to be credited, with the
intention of raising not only the Lords Saye and Brooke, but
Pym, Hampden and Holles to his inner council.[29]

On Scotland the King's immediate hopes were fixed. Hamilton for the last nine months had been ingratiating himself
with Argyll: something must surely come of that when Charles
reached Edinburgh in person. Rothes, although in the last
weeks he had become alarmingly ill and had had to seek rest
and health in the country air of Richmond, believed that he
had built a party for the King. All in all the possibility of getting
help in Scotland from one group or another smiled on Charles.
He even entertained the idea of uniting the Scots forces in the
north with his English troops there, to form an effective army
for his service. With this in view he had sent two officers,
William Legge and Daniel O'Neill, secretly to test the loyalty
and intentions of the principal officers in the north.

Pym, for his part, was holding to the Scottish alliance with
difficulty. "Our brethren of Scotland," who had been so
friendly in the winter, had grown cooler in their love, and Pym,
weighing one danger against another, felt that whatever the risk
of weakening his majority in Parliament, he must try to restore
the old friendship by a further demonstration against the bishops.
Early in August thirteen of them were impeached for having
countenanced the sittings of Convocation after the Short Parliament had been dissolved.[30] The gesture might do something to

restore confidence between Commons and Covenanters; unfortunately it also angered the House of Lords, a majority among whom increasingly resented the pretensions of Pym's party in the Commons. The task of holding together the whole of his disparate alliance against the King—Lords, Commons, Covenanters, and English Protestants—was becoming more problematical with every new development in the complex situation. Charles, who watched the divisions between Lords and Commons with pleasure, was meanwhile buying support and raising money simultaneously by the creation of new honours. The price of baronetcies sank in the month of July from £400 to £350 apiece. Nineteen new baronets were created in July, twenty-four in the first fortnight of August. Favours, at a comparatively low rate, rained on those who might be useful. The King overwhelmed by the variety of business, was sometimes a little confused, and on one occasion, seeing a petitioner kneeling in his path, embarrassed him considerably by bestowing an unwanted knighthood on him.[31]

All this activity perturbed Pym. He made a last-minute attempt to stop the King's journey, now finally fixed for August 10th. A small crowd gathered in the precincts of Westminster when, on the morning of that day, he came down to the House to give his consent to a further group of Bills. They clustered round the King's horse imploring him to stay, but he shook them off, saying only, with a touch of irony, that he was glad to find himself so much desired in both his kingdoms.[32]

At noon that day he began his journey to Scotland, taking with him the Elector Palatine, in whose interests he intended to ask the Scots Parliament to grant him the authority to raise and control an army. He left the Queen at Oatlands, privately giving her authority to instruct and organise his friends in and out of Parliament for a new attack on Pym in the next session. He was full of hope that the autumn would see a change in his fortunes. His own difficulties, although heavy, were at least no more serious than they had been a year before—less so, for Strafford's death and the peace with Scotland had removed two of the causes of quarrel between him and his subjects. The King hoped in the next months to win the Covenanters to his own side, to widen and deepen the breach between Commons and Lords in England and to gain for himself—from Ireland, England or Scotland—an armed striking force to have in reserve against his enemies if they tried again to raise tumults in the City.

To achieve the first of these ends, Charles relied on his own skill and judgment in dealing with his countrymen in Edinburgh. For the second and third he relied at least in part on the Queen; she was to use her influence and charm with those members of the House of Lords who might be brought to help her husband, and she was to see to it that the light-hearted young nobles, who had not hitherto taken their political duties too earnestly, made it a point of honour to attend Parliament in its next session, to defend the dignity of their House against the Commons and serve the policy of their King.

The Queen's political intervention was not to end with this salutary encouragement of the too frivolous royalist lords. She was also to keep in touch with the loyal officers in the King's army—now in process of disbandment—and hold together the framework of armed support for the King which might still be needful.

With so many strands of policy to control and so much that must of necessity be kept secret, the King recognised the need to have trustworthy servants about him. He was under the unfortunate necessity of taking Secretary Vane with him to Scotland but he instructed those who wished to communicate with him privately to do so through his cousin Lennox, whom he now created Duke of Richmond. In England he gave his special trust—and this time also justly—to Edward Nicholas. During the last eighteen months, since he had become secretary to the Council of War in the spring of 1640, Nicholas had shown himself a careful and entirely devoted servant. To him therefore in these critical weeks of absence, Charles entrusted the task of watching the actions of his enemies and reporting at length upon them, with any advice that Nicholas deemed fit.

These dispositions made, the King journeyed to Scotland. In hot, restless, plague-ridden London, Parliament sat for a few weeks longer, and Pym anxiously looked for means to hold his crumbling alliance together and above all to prevent the defection of the Covenanters. One weapon, offered months before by George Digby and since put by, was now taken up again. This was a Remonstrance which should set forth in detail all the errors of King Charles's rule. When Digby had suggested this he had been, with his father, Lord Bristol, among the critics of the King; he had now joined those who believed that all necessary reform was accomplished and complete. By an irony of fate, John Pym took up this half-forgotten idea when its author wished it buried. A Remonstrance which recalled every unpopular act, every attack on liberty in religion, every imprisoned merchant or minister over the last sixteen years, would be the best way to destroy again the confidence in the King which he and his friends had newly built up.

While the Remonstrance was discussed in a half-empty House, six Commissioners, two from the Lords, four from the Commons, were chosen to follow the King to Scotland and keep in touch with what went forward there. At Westminster Pym concluded the session with a further concession to Scots opinion. The House of Commons—much depleted because many members had gone home for the harvest or fled the plague—passed an ordinance on sabbath-keeping and idolatry. They decreed that no games were to be played on Sunday, that all images were to be removed from churches, that the Communion table was once again to be shifted from its Popish position in the East and set in the middle of the church, and that all bowing at the name of Jesus was henceforward to cease.

This ordinance, well pleasing to the Scots and to English Puritans, gravely embittered the feeling between Lords and Commons. Only a minority in the Lords were truly in its favour and even among those who were not personally out of sympathy with the ordinance there was angry resentment that the Commons should take it upon themselves to send out orders without the concurrence of the Lords.

With this quarrel in the air, Parliament adjourned for the recess. But Pym had one more innovation to make. Imitating the practice of the Scots Estates, Parliament elected a committee of fifty to look after the business of the nation during the recess.[33] They met officially at Westminster; unofficially they met at Pym's lodging in Chelsea or at the more spacious house of Lord Mandeville in the same village.

Mandeville, the eldest son of the Earl of Manchester and elder brother to the Queen's Catholic favourite, the convert Wat Montagu, had in the course of the last months emerged as the most astute and active of the Puritan lords. He sat in the Upper House during his father's lifetime by right of his own barony of Kimbolton, although he preferred to be known by his courtesy title of Mandeville. He was a heavy, humourless man, deeply and narrowly religious, without much inspiration or fire, but with something of Pym's organising ability and judgment of political advantage. Lord Saye, the Earl of Warwick, the Earl of Newport, might carry more weight in the Lords as personalities and as speakers, but Mandeville had become the organising brain of the Puritan party. The meetings between the Puritan leaders at his house—even more than at John Pym's—attracted the attention and provoked the anxiety of Edward Nicholas as, like a faithful watchdog, he tried to guard his master's house during his master's absence in Scotland. Some plot, some re-arrangement of political forces against the next session of Parliament and the King's return was evidently being perfected. Something was afoot: Nicholas did not know what. But Charles answered him almost merrily from Scotland; if Pym and Mandeville could plot a campaign so could his clever wife, and Nicholas must consult with the Queen.[34] So both sides, each working in half darkness, made their plans against the autumn.

BOOK III CHAPTER VI REFERENCES

1. Twysden, *Journal*, pp. 191 ff.
2. Rothes, p. 225.
3. *C.S.P.D.*, 1640–1, pp. 549–50, 589; 1641–3, pp. 5, 16.
4. *Ibid.*, 1640–1, p. 121.
5. Laud, *Works*, VI, i, p. 301.
6. Rushworth, III, i, pp. 282–3; *Commons Journals*; Symonds d'Ewes, *Correspondence*, Camden Society, XXIX, p. 169; *C.S.P.D.*, 1641–3, p. 6.
7. Rushworth, III, i, pp. 283–4.
8. *Ibid.*, pp. 255–7; Collins, *Historical Collection*, p. 109.
9. *Portland MSS.*, I, pp. 15–22.
10. Rushworth, III, I, p. 291; Napier, I, pp. 286, 292.
11. *Letters of Argyll*, ed. Macdonald, p. 36.
12. Napier, pp. 273 ff.
13. *Ibid.*, p. 279; Guthry, pp. 92–3.
14. *Ibid.*, p. 96; Napier, pp. 296–301.
15. *C.S.P. Ven.*, 1641–3, pp. 166, 171.
16. Rushworth, III, i, p. 291; Carte, *Ormonde*, V, pp. 248–9; *C.S.P. Ireland*, 1633–47, p. 295.
17. *Ibid.*, pp. 298–9, 302–3.
18. *Ibid.*, pp. 307–9.
19. Rushworth, III, i, pp. 264–70.
20. *Ibid.*, pp. 298–301.
21. *C.S.P.D.*, 1641–3, p. 127; *C.S.P. Ven.*, 1641–2, p. 175.
22. *Lords Journals*, July 5th, 1641.
23. *C.S.P. Ven.*, 1641–3, pp. 175–6.
24. Verney, *Notes on Long Parliament*, pp. 106–7; Norman Moore, *History of the Study of Medicine*, London, 1908, p. 176.
25. Rushworth, III, i, pp. 349–50; *C.S.P. Ven.*, 1641–2, p. 187.
26. *C.S.P. Ven.*, 1641–2, pp. 191–2; *C.S.P.D.*, 1641–3, p. 63.
27. *C.S.P. Ven.*, 1641–2, p. 198.
28. *C.S.P.D.*, 1641–3, pp. 59, 62.
29. *Ibid.*, p. 63.
30. Rushworth, III, i, p. 359; *Commons Journals*.
31. *C.S.P.D.*, 1641–3, pp. 38, 53, 82.
32. *C.S.P. Ven.*, 1641–2, p. 201.
33. *Commons Journals*.
34. *Nicholas Correspondence* in Volume IV of *The Diary of John Evelyn*, ed. Bray, London, 1859, p. 76.

CHAPTER SEVEN

SCOTLAND AND IRELAND

August–November 1641

WHILE the King travelled to Scotland, Members of Parliament, released for the recess after the heavy session of ten months, went back to their ordinary business or their ancestral acres, to their families, neighbours and servants. They had leisure, far from the quarrel and bustle of Westminster, to enlarge their doubts or sharpen their convictions in the light of local politics and local interests.

The country was restless. Soldiers, disbanded after more than a year in arms, brought home the disorderly manners of the camp. Some remained together in groups and fell to robbery. In Lincolnshire rioters pulled up the fences of new enclosures and burnt the barns of the enclosers. An organised band of poachers, nearly a hundred strong, broke into Windsor Great Park and made free with the King's deer. They had to be reasoned with, argued and bought off because they were too strong for the ordinary procedure of the law.[1] The abolition of the prerogative courts left those who administered the judicial system with a sense of incompleteness, of lack of control. The destruction of the ecclesiastical courts removed the power which had enforced the moral sanctions of society. Lawyers were having to revise their ideas of what moves were possible and what impossible in the skilful chess of the English law; no longer could one angry gentleman clinch an argument by shouting at another "I will make a Star-Chamber matter of it"; and the threat of a High

Commission prosecution could never again be held over the head of a dissolute priest, a faithless husband, or a neglectful father. No great change had yet taken place in the daily pattern of local life, with its accepted authorities, rules and customs, but the new legislation at Westminster had opened possibilities which were dimly and apprehensively discerned.

The only visible sign of Parliamentary ordinances over the last months was the removal or obliteration of all remnants of Popery from parish churches. This went forward rapidly in the more Puritan districts, but in others was neglected, and in a few was already a matter of angry dispute between justices of the peace holding different views about it. Whitewash covered over the Saint Christophers, the Dooms, the Archangels, the Patriarchs, whose painted images had survived on the walls of churches—or even been repainted—since the Reformation. Stone saints were shattered from reredos and tomb, village crosses overturned, stained glass broken. Secular ornaments were respected—the crusader and his lady, the blackened brasses, the stiff, recumbent gentlemen in gowns and ruffs and armour, couched by their wives in farthingales and canopied by armorial bearings. Nothing idolatrous could be urged against them, and besides they were often related to the squire.

These removals and destructions perturbed responsible men much less than the prevailing atmosphere of doubt and change. The monarchy, which had now for a hundred and fifty years remained stable against all shocks, had become so abject that the King had consented to the disgrace and death of ministers whom he trusted, to the reversal of his acts of justice and the destruction of his own power. Educated men could refer to history and note with interest or dismay that nothing like this had happened since the Wars of the Roses. The less educated felt that the society and especially the law that they knew was being very roughly handled. This was not what they had anticipated a year ago when they complained of Ship-money, objected to restraints and licenses, muttered over surplices, Communion rails and popery, or wished Strafford at the devil. They had wanted to go back, to reject the changes they believed the King was making. They had not anticipated that greater changes would be made under pretence of returning to their ancient rights.

The more convinced Puritan Members of Parliament, returning to their homes, were concerned to answer, or to overrule, the doubts of their neighbours. Sir Robert Harley of Brampton Bryan, who represented the county of Hereford, did not fail on his return home to espy and to order the removal of a crucifix, a wall painting and a window of stained glass at Leominster church. But the strong-minded were a minority; the greater number of the members found only reasons to deepen their doubts during the recess. Looking back on the last months, now that they had time to do so, they saw and they resented the way in which John Pym and a few others had managed affairs, had indeed managed *them*.[2]

Meanwhile the King, in reviving spirits, reviewed the Scots army at Newcastle and entertained Leslie at dinner. He spared no pains to please the Covenanting commander on whom, he broadly hinted, he would shortly bestow an earldom.[3] After the disbanding of the Covenanting army a force of four thousand was to be retained for emergencies: of this four thousand and of General Leslie the King had hopes. At six o'clock on August 14th he made his formal entry into Edinburgh, escorted by the Elector Palatine, his cousin Richmond, and Hamilton. On the 17th he came in procession to the Parliament House, with Hamilton bearing the crown and Argyll the sceptre before him. The solemnity was disturbed by the Laird of Langton who quarrelled with the Earl of Wigton for the place of usher. Charles, who was still master in details of etiquette, withdrew in anger to an inner chamber, whence he issued a warrant for Langton's arrest. The intruder thus disposed of, he entered Parliament and took his seat on the throne; his nephew the Elector occupied a small embroidered stool on his left hand but Richmond, Hamilton and the Earl of Morton, who had not yet signed the Covenant, had to be left outside.[4]

The King in a short and gracious speech asked his loyal

subjects to give what help in money or arms they could to restore his wronged nephew to his German lands.[5] The request was well received and the King's behaviour during the next days seemed to show a change of heart; he attended worship according to the Scottish fashion, allowed Alexander Henderson constant access to his person, listened to him in private and to many other ministers in public, with the greatest civility, and sat attentive while bishops and evil counsellors were denounced from the pulpit. He allowed his cousin Lennox to subscribe the Covenant; he received Argyll with warmth and looked graciously even on Lord Balmerino—whom he had sentenced to death a few years earlier, and who had been chosen by the Covenanters to preside in Parliament. He gave no favours and little attention to any of those who had in the past two years openly served him against the rebels. The bold Montrose, shut up in the castle, clamoured in vain for an open trial: " What I have done is known to a great many and what I have done amiss is unknown to myself," he challenged the Estates. " As truth does not seek corners, it needeth no favour . . . My resolution is to carry along fidelity and honour to the grave."[6] The splendid phrases fell on deaf ears; neither the King nor the Estates would agree to an open trial, in which Montrose might well accuse Argyll of treason and upset the King's present austere honeymoon with the Covenanters.

On August 28th Charles solemnly ratified the legislation of the previous year; he had now, in two of his three Kingdoms, pronounced his *fiat* upon acts which limited his authority and ran directly counter to his belief in the sanctity and inviolability of his office. To celebrate and conclude his surrender he welcomed his new friends and masters to a feast at Holyrood.[7]

The King congratulated himself on the happy impression he had made on his fellow-Scotsmen during the first fortnight of his visit, and the Commissioners dispatched by Parliament —spies, Charles privately called them [8]—felt no slight anxiety when they reached Edinburgh. The party consisted of two from the House of Lords and four from the Commons—the new

Lord Bedford and Lord Howard of Escrick, both consistent supporters of the Scots, Nathaniel Fiennes, who was the son and mouthpiece of Lord Saye, the persuasive John Hampden, Sir Philip Stapleton, a scrawny Calvinist Yorkshireman, and Sir William Armin who, like Hampden, had fought the King on every vital issue since the impeachment of Buckingham.

The fears of the English Commissioners were partly allayed by their first official meeting with the Committee of Estates, which took place privately at Argyll's house.[9]   Appearances were deceptive; the Covenanters had eaten and drunk with the King in apparent friendship, but their friendship depended on his acquiescence in their purposes. They were not willing to be used by him and were as alert as Pym and his associates to the probable intentions behind the King's apparent change of policy. Their occasional disagreements with the English House of Commons were essentially the disagreements of allies; their present friendship with the King was a cautious, diplomatic truce with an enemy.

The doubts of the Covenanters as to Charles's true intentions were shared by European observers, and the King's attempt to raise forces in Scotland, ostensibly for the Elector Palatine, was soon checked by reports reaching Edinburgh from the imperial Diet at Ratisbon.   Sir Thomas Roe, veteran diplomatist and indefatigable servant of the Protestant Cause and the Elizabethan tradition, had been sent earlier that summer to attend on the Diet and persuade the representatives of Spain and Austria that his master would go to war with them unless they would agree to restore the lands and dignities of the Elector Palatine.   Roe was distressed rather than surprised when he found that he could make no converts to this view of King Charles's intentions. The experienced diplomats who represented the European powers at Ratisbon saw very well what had happened. The King of Great Britain, with his subjects in revolt and a Parliament he could not control, was doing as any other European king would have done in his situation; he was making a bid for popularity. It was evident to them that the only use King Charles could reasonably have for an army, if he could get one, would be against his own people. This they put to Sir Thomas with an almost contemptuous frankness.[10] The unwillingness of European diplomatists to take the King's intentions seriously heightened the suspicions of his own subjects, and on September 4th the Scots Parliament refused to countenance the use of their remaining army or the levying of any more troops for the Elector until they should have further news of the negotiations at Ratisbon.[11]

This was the first serious check to the King's hopes. A graver one soon followed. He had hoped for the support and help of Rothes in establishing an agreement with the Covenanters, but Rothes, left behind in England and gravely ill at the time, died at the end of August. Charles could therefore depend only on the friendship which Hamilton had, in the last months, built up with Argyll. How far this had gone—with the usual talk of the widower Hamilton marrying Argyll's eldest daughter —no one quite knew. The two noblemen certainly appeared to be on cordial terms but some of the King's friends doubted whether Hamilton could, or would, use his influence to forward the King's plans.

The King was shortly to place before the Estates the list of the new officers of State chosen to replace those dead, exiled or excluded since the troubles started. He made his list cautiously; he retained Sir Thomas Hope, the principal adviser of the Covenanters, as Lord Advocate and he elevated Argyll's kinsman Loudoun to the important place of Treasurer. As Secretary of State he proposed to retain Hamilton's brother Lanark. But the vital place of Chancellor, left vacant by the flight and death of Archbishop Spottiswoode, he was determined to keep under his own influence. He selected for it the Earl of Morton, an ageing, moderate loyalist on whom he could rely; he anticipated no real difficulty in securing his will because Morton, whatever his politics, was the father of Argyll's wife, and family ties are strong in Scotland.

The King miscalculated. Argyll was not a man to care for

appearances when God's cause was at stake. At the name of Morton he rose to his feet in the Parliament House and denounced his father-in-law as a man crippled by age and debt and under suspicion of worse crimes. Morton replied with dignity that he was unaware what offence he had given to Argyll whom he had had the honour to know from his childhood and had partly brought up. The appeal to natural affection seemed to stir a greater bitterness in Argyll, who had not had a happy childhood. He reminded Morton that he would not have been able to attend Parliament at all but for his own intervention; he had satisfied the creditors who would otherwise have laid his father-in-law by the heels on his arrival in Edinburgh. Morton, in painful distress, asked the King to withdraw his name, but Charles would not accept defeat. He called on Parliament to vote on the list as a whole, not name by name. This suggestion fell upon an obstinate silence, broken at last by Morton's renewed entreaty to the King to withdraw his name rather than make him a cause for misunderstanding.

A prolonged deadlock followed this inauspicious beginning; agreement could not be reached and the leading Covenanters, at all hours, pressed the King with their arguments. "There was never King so much insulted," a faithful royalist reported. "It would pity any man's heart to see how he looks, for he is never at quiet amongst them, and glad he is when he sees any man that he thinks loves him." [12]

The King's disappointment and the bullying of his opponents provoked more than pity among some of those in Edinburgh. He had brought with him a number of professional soldiers or gentlemen volunteers who were to have posts in the army he hoped to raise. Several of these were from the disbanded Irish army and one at least, Lord Crawford, from the Spanish service. Their first loyalty was to the King, and they, with others of the King's servants, had become friendly with such of the Covenanting officers as they believed would also, in the last resort, serve the interests of the King, chief among them Colonels Cochrane and Urry, both veteran professional soldiers, who were critical of the growing influence of Argyll.

The King pursued his usual technique of hedging against defeat by developing a second and different policy alongside his plan for conciliating the Covenanters. He loitered on the outer edge of this Scottish Army Plot much as he had done in similar circumstances in England, and left backstairs meetings and whispering in corners of Holyroodhouse to his favoured Groom of the bedchamber, Will Murray. Once he had a private talk with Cochrane which Murray arranged but did not hear. The King knew probably no more than it was safe for him to know, but he was certainly aware of something. He was also, as his letters to Edward Nicholas in England showed, still extremely confident, announcing with satisfaction at about this time that Pym and his party " will not have such great cause for joy " when he came home again.[13]

He was however for the first time in his life, disillusioned about Hamilton's diplomatic skill and doubtful even if he had been fully loyal to him in his dealings with the Covenanters. He remarked with some asperity to Lanark that his brother " had been very active in his own preservation." [14] The King's criticism of his once most trusted servant was quickly known among the fiery young men and ambitious soldiers he was now encouraging.

In the midst of the King's wrangle with the Estates, on September 29th, news burst upon Edinburgh that Lord Ker, Roxburgh's son, had called Hamilton a traitor and sent a challenge to him by the hand of Lord Crawford. The Estates immediately summoned Ker to answer for his ill conduct; he came obediently, but was escorted through the streets by several hundred of his father's armed tenantry. He apologised to Hamilton and shook hands. The King on the same day, to conciliate the Covenanters, confirmed as Chancellor of Scotland, Argyll's clansman, Lord Loudoun.[15]

But the Covenanters had been thoroughly aroused. Ker was the first royalist who had boldly followed their own custom and brought armed retainers into Edinburgh. That royalist plots were afoot about the Court and even in their own army, they already suspected; Ker's action made them fear riot and treachery in their ranks beyond their control.

On Friday, October 8th, Colonel Cochrane came down to Musselburgh where his regiment was stationed, stood drinks to his officers and promised to make all their fortunes if they would stand by him. Most of his officers were professionals from the German wars and recognised this procedure, if not from experience, then at least from report. The professional soldier, about to change his allegiance from one General to another, or from one Crown to another, habitually sought to buy and flatter his subordinates to come with him, knowing that his value to his new masters depended on how large a force he could offer them. The great drinking parties, the persuasions, the oaths offered by the imperial general Wallenstein to his staff, when he tried to lead an army of twenty thousand men from the imperial into the Swedish camp, was but one gigantic and famous instance of a manœuvre which, in a more humble manner, was often practised by ambitious mercenary colonels in the European wars. The example of Wallenstein, who had been murdered by officers loyal to the Emperor (an Irishman, an Englishman and a Scot) was a recent event in the memory of veteran professionals. They had their code and their honour, but although some were willing to believe that a soldier's only loyalty was to his paymaster, others admitted a higher morality. Not every man could be won by drink and promises.

Robert Home, Cochrane's lieutenant-colonel, was one of these. When Cochrane, drawing him aside, dropped hints of Court favour and spoke of some private understanding with Will Murray of the Bedchamber, Home stiffened. He told his colonel that he wished to hear no more. Cochrane, only a little discouraged, returned to Edinburgh, joined company with Lord Crawford and others and drank destruction to the King's enemies far into the night.

On the morning of Monday, October 11th, Colonel Urry

and Captain William Stewart were strolling down the street when Colonel Alexander Stewart asked them to step into his lodging for a drink. Urry excused himself, but his companion accepted, only to rejoin him a little later in great agitation. Colonel Stewart had appalled him by telling him of a plot to kidnap Argyll and Hamilton out of the King's own rooms at Holyrood that night, with the assistance of Will Murray who would admit the plotters by the back stairs. He had come in all haste to warn Colonel Urry, because he knew him to be dining with Lord Crawford and the principal conspirators that day and believed that they would compel him to join them.

John Urry, an intelligent, unscrupulous professional soldier, had already heard something of the plot. He saw—as Goring had seen in the same situation in England—that the conspiracy, whatever it was, was likely to be found out, since the conspirators had made the error of trying to draw into it those who did not want to come. It was safer to be the betrayer than the betrayed: John Urry, before dinner on Monday, October 11th, told General Leslie all he knew. Together, they found Hamilton and communicated the story to him and Argyll who, according to Urry, told him to keep his appointment at dinner-time with Lord Crawford and see if he could learn more. In this Urry was disappointed, for all Crawford did was to ask him to call next day, bringing three or four " good fellows " whom he could trust. Crawford hinted that, by means unspecified, he would make the fortunes of all of them.

That afternoon, the weather being fine, Hamilton attended the King as he walked on the lawns of Holyroodhouse; he was, as often happened, to sleep in the King's room that night, but for reasons obscurely expressed, " in a philosophical and parabolical way," he asked leave of absence and, on being pressed, hinted that there were those about the King who did not love him and whose actions he feared. Charles, puzzled and annoyed, refused him leave of absence. Hamilton disregarded the King's refusal. That night he withdrew with his younger brother, Lanark, and Argyll, to his house at Kinneil about twenty miles away; hence, on the following day, Argyll gave out that there was a conspiracy against their lives, of which he implied the King himself was not ignorant.

The muddled plot misconceived between the intriguer Will Murray and some mischievous, ambitious soldiers, usually the worse for drink, had—like the Army Plot before it—turned into a valuable weapon for the King's enemies. Charles was probably innocent of any design against Argyll and Hamilton, but he had, as before in England, by silence, by hints, by granting secret audiences to Cochrane, by encouraging Lord Roxburgh, Lord Ker and Lord Crawford, prepared the way for the disaster, and he had given his trusted servant Will Murray enough rope to hang them all.

The news of the Incident—as this affair came to be called—spread quickly to the excitable people of Edinburgh. Charles came up to the Parliament House with Roxburgh's retainers as a guard against the people. This necessary precaution gave Hamilton and Argyll the opportunity to proclaim, with an air of suffering virtue, that they would not come back to the capital for fear of untoward incidents between their servants and the King's armed followers.

The popularity that Charles had briefly enjoyed vanished overnight. In vain he declared his innocence to the assembled Estates and, almost with tears, taxed the absent Hamilton with ingratitude for allowing himself to believe so horrible a falsehood as that his life or liberty was unsafe in the King's own bed-chamber. He demanded an immediate and public examination of the whole scandalous business. His opponents in the Estates, knowing that uncertainty and rumour worked for them and not for the King, hung back. The King's wild friends continued their indiscretions; the scandal multiplied. Lord Carnwath, another loud-voiced, wooden-headed warrior, was reported to have babbled of three Kings in Scotland, Argyll, Hamilton and King Charles, and to have said that the first two would be better without their heads. This childish rubbish linked well with the speeches said to have been made by Montrose's friends in May, for which Montrose was still awaiting trial in the castle. A Royalist campaign to blacken the character of the godly Argyll, and perhaps to murder him, seemed credible to many and was believed.

On October 15th, Sir Thomas Hope strongly advised the Estates to conduct the inquiry in secret because in privacy alone would men disclose all that they knew. The King protested: "If men were so charitable as not to believe false rumours, Sir Thomas, I would be of your mind," he said, "but since I see the contrary, you must give me leave to think otherwise. . . . I must see myself get fair play." The rumours in Edinburgh increased; four days later the King was stung to yet stronger words before the assembled Estates. "By God," he cried—and when the King used his Creator's name it was an invocation and not an oath—"it behoved Parliament to clear his honour." But the Estates saw no reason to clear his honour and his opponents won the day; the inquiry was held in private.

Colonel Urry and Captain William Stewart, who had between them revealed the plot, were questioned on October 12th; so was Cochrane's lieutenant-colonel, Robert Home. All three of their stories pointed to Will Murray as a central figure in the plot, and therefore most damningly to the King.

Crawford and Cochrane, with soldierly bluster, denied any plot; they had, admittedly, looked upon the alliance of Hamilton and Argyll with suspicion, and had talked—but only in theory—of what might be done to overpower them should they be found to be disloyal. This too was the substance of Colonel Alexander Stewart's account. He claimed that Captain William Stewart had misunderstood him, when they talked over their drinks, on the morning of Monday, October 11th; he had spoken of no actual plot, but only of a possible method of procedure, should Hamilton and Argyll be proved traitors.

Will Murray, examined three times, appeared as a confident man of the world—very ready to help and not in the least embarrassed. He admitted that he had arranged a private interview for Cochrane with the King but had no idea what had been said;

Cochrane had stood close by the King's bed, His Majesty having retired for the night, and the bed curtains had been drawn round them both for greater privacy. He steadfastly denied the existence of any plot and laughed off the suggestion that he had intended the kidnapping of Hamilton and Argyll from the King's rooms at Holyroodhouse. But with a quiet, insistent subtlety he emphasised a new element in the story. Crawford had muttered something about a letter from Montrose to the King. Will Murray elaborated this: he said that Montrose had managed to convey not one but three letters to the King, that the King had not shown much interest in the first two, but that the third, received on October 11th in the morning, had contained statements on which he had intended to question Montrose, had not the Incident intervened. This third letter was produced—the two others were not, and may well have been imaginary; what Montrose had written was a request that he might have leave " to acquaint His Majesty with a business which not only did concern his honour in a high degree, but the standing and falling of his Crown likewise."

The meaning of this letter is clear enough when Montrose's position during the last three months is brought to mind. He had been shut up in the castle, out of touch with current events. He knew nothing of Crawford, Cochrane and Ker, but was still brooding on the accusation that he had sought, and failed, to bring home to Argyll in May. He had once or twice been cursorily examined, he had never been tried, and a thorough search through his private papers had revealed no additional evidence on which he could be arraigned. The Committee of Estates had taken the precaution of hanging his principal witness against Argyll, the unfortunate John Stewart. Montrose was therefore desperate to see the King and to explain to him the dangers of which he believed him ignorant. His letter had no bearing on the Incident; it belonged to another, and an earlier, sequence of events.

That had not prevented Will Murray from quoting ambiguous phrases from it to encourage the military plotters. He now used it with equal skill to direct attention from himself and his friends and canalise suspicion against Montrose.

It was round Edinburgh in a flash that Montrose had offered to cut the throats of Argyll and Hamilton, seize Edinburgh Castle for the King and establish his authority in Scotland by force of arms. The palpable absurdity of this story was disregarded, not only by the King's enemies, but also by his friends. The idea of Montrose offering bloody deeds to his sovereign suited the Covenanters very well in their desire to discredit the Royalists. But once his name had been brought in, he served as a scapegoat for those Royalists who had actually done the mischief. Cochrane, Crawford, Will Murray became in the popular view, mere satellites and unimportant figures in the Incident of which the revealed architect was Montrose.

This transference of responsibility saved the conspirators from the worst consequences of their folly, but did not restore to the King the possibility of forming a Royalist party in Scotland. Moderate-minded men, who distrusted the Covenanters, now saw good reason for distrusting the King also. "It behoves you to clear my honour," Charles had declared to the Estates, but the Covenanters preferred to leave his honour under the cloud his mischievous friends had brought upon it.[16]

The cloud hung upon him as heavily in England as in Scotland. From Westminster the faithful Nicholas, appalled at the shocking versions of the Incident now current in England, implored the King to send him some clear information, to issue some official statement that could be put out to stop the mouths of the slanderers.[17] But Charles sent him no such explanation, having none to send. The Queen's little Court at Oatlands was all this time closely watched by Pym and his associates. Since August they had tried to gauge her husband's hopes and fears from her changing moods, often with confusing results. The Standing Committee of the House of Commons had at first received with equanimity the news that the Covenanters were retaining four thousand men under arms, but when they learnt that the Queen was also delighted their faces lengthened and they suspected a secret understanding between the King and Leslie.[18] They became more cheerful again as the little Queen's momentary joy evaporated; she drooped when she heard of her husband's defeat over the Chancellor's appointment and became tearful and distraught at the news of the Incident.

She had good reason for anxiety; whatever conspiracies she had encouraged or was still encouraging in her husband's name, she was herself the object of conspiracy. Lord Newport, who as Constable of the Tower had, in April, announced his intention of cutting off Strafford's head on his own authority, had since then increased the Tower garrison and uttered another fierce indiscretion. Dining in Kensington with Lord Holland, he remarked that, in the event of the King making any dangerous move, the Queen and her children should at once be seized as hostages.[19]

The attention of the King's enemies was for the moment fixed on him in Scotland or on his wife in England. They had temporarily forgotten about the unquiet state of Ireland. They trusted to the strong and confident men, the powerful Anglo-Irish who had helped them to destroy Strafford, to control any disturbances and they failed to realise the magnitude of the forces which the death of Strafford and their subsequent policy was stirring into action. They made no allowance for two things: first, that Strafford's army, even disbanded, was still a danger because seven or eight thousand discontented men cast loose upon so small a country necessarily constituted a danger; second, that Strafford's army was not the only potential force in Ireland.

Strafford, who believed with passion in law and order, had in 1639 skilfully repressed the dangerous offer of the Earl of Antrim to raise the Irish Macdonnells for the King against the Covenanters. He had strengthened and increased the Irish army because it gave him an opportunity to keep these wild forces under discipline and draw off some of them into authorised and honourable employment. This army, disbanded, scattered throughout the country a leaven of trained troops who could impart their knowledge, and distribute their equipment, to their fellow-Irishmen. Strafford's army, in its disintegration, did precisely what he had created it to prevent: it gave arms, encouragement and military knowledge to the " wild Irish."

The Earl of Antrim's plan had been ridiculous because he was himself ridiculous. But his people were not. Acting in small bands, under lesser chieftains, the Macdonnells were determined fighters. So were their neighbours in Ulster the O'Neills; so were the O'Byrnes in Wicklow, the O'Reillies in Cavan, the O'Gradies in Clare and the rest of those throughout the country whom Strafford had contemptuously called " the O's and Mac's." Their raiding had been held in check for the last forty years, but it had not ceased. Bound together by the Catholic religion, by the Irish language and by a deep sense of wrong, these scattered, disinherited people were potentially very dangerous.

The King had always hankered after Antrim's scheme and had not forgotten it. He was in touch, this summer of 1641, with Sir Phelim O'Neill, the young Irish chieftain whom Antrim had planned to have for his second in command. Phelim O'Neill that summer held at his house several meetings of the Irish gentry of Ulster. Other Irish lords of the north, MacMahon and M'Guire, were busy recruiting. The troops they raised were, they said, for Spain.[20] Messages of some kind had been exchanged between the King and O'Neill. But this Irish business was on the King's part only one of his many attempts to win allies for the rebuilding of his broken power. If Parliament knew and understood scandalously little about Ireland, Charles knew and understood even less. John Pym for his part had only studied the politics of Ireland in so far as he had had to use them to destroy Strafford. For Charles, Ireland had never been anything but a potential source of revenue and now a potential source of troops. Neither saw that the Irish were a people brought to the edge of despair who, if they once appealed to arms, would not soon lay them down again.

When Strafford fell, and Wandesford died, a government

came to an end which, although alien and exacting, had been at least reliable and, within defined limits, scrupulous and just to the Irish. The party in power in England, which had destroyed Strafford, had thus in Ireland confirmed the triumph of the adventurers, English and Scots, who were insatiable in their greed for Irish land and who recognised no rights of the Irish or the Norman-Irish which stood in their way. Strafford had tried vainly to get the King to appoint for his successor a man who had some understanding of the Irish problem and some respect for the rights—however limited—of the Irish themselves. It is significant that both his suggestions were Norman-Irish lords—Lord Dillon and the Earl of Ormonde. The King had not been able to follow his advice. Instead the two Lords Justices Sir John Borlase and Sir William Parsons, appointed with Parliamentary approval to govern for the time being, were themselves prominent men among the recent adventurers, in sympathy only with their practical and ruthless point of view.

The dominance of the Puritan party in the English Parliament, and the reassertion by the English Parliament of its power over the Irish Parliament, meant that extreme Protestantism might at any moment be rigidly enforced on Ireland with all the penal laws against Catholics and the total extinction of their religion.

To a threat of this magnitude to their land, their religion, their very lives, only one answer was possible from a people still warlike, still unsubdued, and still in a majority over the newcomers. Nothing and no one in the autumn of 1641 could have prevented the rising in Ireland. It was like no other rebellion the King had known; it was not, like the rising in Scotland, subject to political control and exploitation. It was disordered, elemental, desperate, a movement over which no single leader at any moment in its ten years' course had complete control.

In Dublin, on the night of October 22nd, one Owen O'Conolly, not altogether sober, knocked up Sir William Parsons at the castle. He declared that on the morrow, Saturday and market day, a party of Irish under the Lords MacMahon and M'Guire would seize Dublin. Parsons had MacMahon arrested in his lodging that night but M'Guire, forewarned, fled and was discovered early next morning crouching among the fowls in a henhouse in the suburbs. The city gates were closed, the market cancelled; all day and far into the night Parsons and the council questioned the prisoners. The two boisterous young chiefs were airily defiant; knowing that the seizure of Dublin was but a part of a wider plan they waited in confidence for the news the evening would bring. It came at midnight, while the anxious council was still in session; Lord Blaney, an old Welsh soldier, commander of the garrison at Monaghan, rode stumbling up the castle hill on a tired horse. The O'Neills had risen in force, had rushed his town of Carrickmacross at daybreak, had surrounded Castle Blaney with his wife and children in it, and laid siege to Monaghan. He was the first of many frantic messengers who in the next days filled Dublin with horror and dismay. In eastern Ulster the insurgents, burning farms and scattering the terrified settlers, carried all before them; they seized Newry; they threatened Belfast. From hill to hill their beacons spread news of the rising and summoned their clansmen to arms. While the government hesitated and the settlers fled, the O'Neills gathered strength. A horde, wildly estimated at twenty thousand, plunged towards Drogheda. Belfast was already cut off.[21]

The King was playing his customary round of golf on the links at Leith when, on October 27th, the first news from Ireland was put into his hand. Like Sir Francis Drake on a different occasion, he finished the game. Later that day he reported the matter with becoming gravity to the Scottish Parliament.

The news created a kind of breathless uncertainty. But no one yet perceived that this was something more than another incident in the struggle for power between the King and his subjects. Argyll knew of the King's one-time agreement with Antrim; it was he who had defended the south-west coasts of Scotland from that projected Irish invasion which Charles, two years before, had countenanced and encouraged. He can hardly have doubted that Charles knew something of this present rising. The English Parliamentary Commissioners entertained the same fear: six months earlier they had had constantly in their minds that dubious threat of Strafford's "Your Majesty has an army in Ireland." Would this Irish rebellion turn out to be simply a rising of the King's friends? It was one thing to suspect, another to act. The King's conduct was correct; he deplored the rising; he asked for help in restoring peace to Ireland. What action then could safely be taken by those who agreed with his expressed intentions but gravely doubted what lay behind them? The English Commissioners asked him to come back to Westminster to consult with Parliament, and the Scottish Estates, playing for time, appointed a committee to consider the matter of Ireland, but postponed further action till they should know the intentions of the English Parliament.

The Elector Palatine in a private letter to a friend in the House of Commons immediately passed on this decision,[22] which thus reached Westminster earlier than it could have done in the report of the Commissioners. The Elector made no comment but his anxiety that the strong alliance between the Scots and the English Parliaments should not break down shows how far he disagreed with his uncle's private policy and how much he too wondered what was really happening in Ireland. News must by this time have reached Edinburgh—although it passed without comment in the general excitement—that his younger brother Rupert had at last been released. The terms of the prince's release, settled by the English ambassador at Ratisbon, were that he would never again fight against the Emperor. But Rupert was a professional soldier; if he could not fight against the Emperor, where would he fight? There was more than a hint in the air of some employment for him in King Charles's service and this the Elector was determined to prevent.

As for the King himself, he had written to Nicholas with his usual optimism: "I hope these ill news from Ireland may hinder some of these follies in England." [23] The rebellion in Ireland seemed to him primarily an event that could be turned to account in the renewed struggle for power with his English Parliament.

The House of Commons had reassembled at Westminster on October 20th but its ranks were thin. Plague was still bad in the City and Members were in no hurry to come back. The disbanded troops seemed dangerous, and vicious words, scrawled on walls or scattered in public places, threatened Pym and Parliament. Some ill-wishing person sent him a filthy rag said to have been infected with the plague. The London trained bands under the Earl of Essex guarded the House against possible violence. The fear of violence dominated the debates. The Incident and its possible connection with the Army Plot were discussed and Pym laid before the House evidence he had obtained during the recess of the King's attempts to win the northern army wholly to his interests.[24]

News of the rebellion in Ireland was officially communicated to Parliament by Lord Keeper Littleton on November 1st. Pym immediately focused attention on the Court by putting forward a request for a list of all the Queen's servants. Her confessor, Father Philip, later in the day refused to answer questions put to him in Parliament on the ingenious excuse that he could not swear on a Protestant translation of the Bible. In sober truth, Father Philip knew nothing about the Irish rebellion but was afraid lest questioning should expose another awkward secret —the Queen's continued friendly communications with the Vatican.

The Commons, in the hope of detecting foreign machinations behind the Irish trouble, intercepted all letters from Dublin to the envoys of Catholic powers in London and broke open the despatches of the Spanish ambassador.[25] But the danger of foreign intervention in the Irish rising was less immediately serious than its possible effect on politics at home. John Pym, like the King, saw that he must use this new event in the struggle to maintain the power of Parliament against the King, and he saw at the same time the way in which the King was likely to use it. Armed forces would have to be raised to put down the

Irish revolt. The King's principal need in the struggle had been just that—the control of armed forces. It was evident to Pym that the King would not use any armed forces which were placed under his authority exclusively to put down the Irish revolt—if indeed he used them in that way at all. A year ago the King had certainly intended to use an Irish army against the Scots and—so the impeachment of Strafford implied—may have entertained a desire to use an Irish army against the English. That Irish army, disbanded, was now in alliance with the rebels; some of its officers were among the leaders of the Irish revolt. Who could say with certainty that the King had no further connection with these men? They themselves asserted that they were in rebellion not against him but only against his enemies. Early in November the news reached London that the Irish rebels claimed that the King was to land on the coast of Ulster and put himself at their head.

On November 5th the Commons celebrated their usual thanksgiving for their deliverance from the Gunpowder Treason, the Popish Plot of 1605. In the mood which this ceremony engendered Pym solemnly addressed the House on the message that they were drawing up to send to the King in Scotland about the measures to be taken against the Irish rebels. No offers or plans of theirs, no raising of loans in the City or gathering of arms and troops would be of any avail to quell the revolt, he argued, unless the King would once and for all rid himself of all " evil counsellors." He must agree to have only such men in his service and among his advisers as Parliament should choose. The demand was astonishing, so astonishing that Edward Hyde, until this time a supporter of Pym on every legal issue, rose to object. But Pym was never in theory an innovator and he had taken good advice on this question. He could cite a precedent for the request of such respectable antiquity as the reign of Edward III.[26]

Edward III notwithstanding, Pym knew he was on dangerous ground. The Lords were bound to object to attaching so outrageous a demand to the message sent to Scotland about the

Irish revolt. The King from a distance, and the Queen from closer at hand, had done their work well in the Lords. Bristol and his son Lord Digby were well instructed and well prepared to fight this new attack, and the younger royalist peers were being rounded up from their country houses by the Queen's letters.[27]

Pym in the Commons continued methodically to build up the attack as he had done the year before. Then he had had to remove Strafford and destroy the legal strength of the royal position by pulling down the prerogative courts. Now he had only one problem left but that the hardest: he must destroy the King's authority over the armed forces in time of emergency. He must get the army, once and for all, under the direct control of Parliament. The renewed attack on evil councillors was only a necessary move in that scheme. On November 6th one of his principal henchmen, Oliver Cromwell, the Member for Cambridge, a man of heavy, uninspiring presence but considerable eloquence, moved that the Commons join with the Lords in asking that the Earl of Essex, whom all trusted, should be given the command of all the trained bands in the south.[28] This was the quiet opening move in the campaign to have all military appointments placed under the control of Parliament.

Pym knew that he could only win in this last struggle if he systematically undermined all trust and faith in the King. For this reason his party went ahead day after day with drafting that Remonstrance, first suggested by Digby a year before and taken up again a little before the recess. This was to blast the King's reputation by recalling, act by act, everything in his reign that had given offence to his subjects.

Terribly aware of the danger of this Remonstrance, the Queen and Nicholas wrote repeatedly to Charles in Scotland. They implored him to return before Pym could marshal all his forces against him and get his deadly Remonstrance through the Commons. Charles, miscalculating the speed of Pym's action and the number of his supporters, wrote to Nicholas instructing him to tell all his trusted friends in Parliament that " by all means" they contrive to stop the Remonstrance.[29] He was himself on his way home to confront and, as he hoped, to outwit his enemies.

In the interim he had concluded his business in Scotland. He had worked hard to pacify the Covenanters and make them his allies when it should come—as soon it must—to an open breach with the English Commons. After making Lord Loudoun, Argyll's clansman, Chancellor he had put the Treasury into commission with Argyll as a principal commissioner, and confirmed Sir Thomas Hope as Lord Advocate. He elevated to his Council the Lords Balmerino, Cassilis and Maitland, thus entrusting the government of Scotland, in his absence, exclusively to his enemies. Of his Council at least half had been, during the last ten years, either accused or under suspicion of treason; not one of them had, since then, altered his opinions. This extraordinary conduct, which dismayed the loyalists and the sad remnant of the episcopal party in Scotland, reflected Charles's prevailing mood of optimism. He was confident that he had gained these men for his friends although he had secured nothing in return for his favours but the unconditional release of the Incident plotters, Crawford and Cochrane, and the release on bail of Montrose.

To seal these new friendships he made Argyll a Marquis and General Leslie Earl of Leven. Hamilton, who had come back to Holyrood and been restored to favour, was probably the architect of this alliance. With his usual over-confidence, he may truly have believed that these new friendships would last, and so have persuaded the King, always too easily convinced of good news, that he could henceforward count on the friendship of the Covenanters against his English Parliament.

Superficial appearances easily deceived the King; in his native land, his voice, his manner, his addiction to golf and natural fondness for Scots servants and Scots jokes, gave him a spurious feeling that he was at home again and this, in spite of disagreements, convinced him that his fellow-countrymen would, in the last resort, be staunch to him. At his Court at Holyrood, the

English Parliamentary Commissioners, with their thin southern voices and their stiff English manners—so different from the rugged fervour of the Scots—had seemed foreign, mistrustful and mistrusted. For the second time in two years, the King gambled on the strength of national prejudice. In 1640 he had been sure the English would rise for him against the Scots; in 1641 he was convinced the Scots would stand by him against the English.

He was mistaken. John Hampden, Philip Stapleton and the rest might not understand Scots jokes, might indeed barely understand Scots English; but the community of interest between them and the Covenanters went deep. The community of interest between the King and the Covenanters did not exist at all. No one knew this better than Argyll and no one knew better than Argyll how to accept and make use of each change and turn in the King's erratic policy. He got from him on this occasion the royal commission to defend the Highlands and Islands against possible attack from the Irish rebels, a commission which was to prove very useful to him in years to come.

On November 17th in cheerful spirits the King adjourned the Estates. Sir Thomas Hope pronounced congratulatory words: "a contented King is to depart from a contented country." [30] That evening Charles feasted his lords at Holyrood and the castle cannon fired joyful salvoes. Early next day he rode away from his capital city of Edinburgh to face with equanimity the problems which awaited him at Westminster.

On this first day of his journey he received a letter from Nicholas warning him at length about the Remonstrance, but Charles was confident that his friends in the House of Commons could prevent its passing. He was confident of everything. He believed that the worst of his dangers were over, that he had won the Scots and was half-way to defeating Pym. While he had heard from Nicholas of his enemies' manoeuvres, he had also heard of their difficulties. The citizens of London were growing tired of the pretensions and claims of the Commons and were displeased at the activities of the extremer Puritans. For most of them, the Protestant religion was a form of social discipline as well as a spiritual belief. They saw with grave annoyance the congregations which now gathered round self-appointed prophets who, free from the fear of prosecution in the ecclesiastical courts, stalked the streets expounding the Scriptures. Many of the preachers were humble folk—a cobbler, a hawker of pots and pipkins familiar in Cheapside, a zealous button-maker, some were even women.[31] Being moved of the Lord, they frequently scorned the appointed order of society and exhorted their betters to repent. In the face of these uncomfortable manifestations the fervour of the City for religious reformation cooled. The Puritans lost ground. At the election of the new Lord Mayor the decision hung in the balance and the King's friends among the City men, led by one of the sheriffs, secured the election of the royalist alderman Henry Gurney by a hurried, tumultuous demonstration.

Against this royalist reaction Pym fought with the double weapon of rumour and slander. He encouraged every tale of plot and conspiracy that could be used to discredit the King's friends and link them with the Popish-Irish danger. Thomas Beale, a tailor, regaled the House for several days with the details of a plot which he swore he had overheard, for the massacre of all the Parliament-men.

Sir Walter Earle, the Member for Hampshire, reported from his county that letters were passing very frequently between the Queen at Oatlands and Colonel Goring, the governor of Portsmouth. Goring, it was said locally, had mounted cannon to overawe the town but had put up no defences on the seaward side, as though he expected and would welcome a foreign landing. "The Papists and jovial clergymen" of the district were said to be "merrier than ever."[32] But Earle's report of these suspicious circumstances failed of its purpose, for Goring, alone among the conspirators whom the Queen encouraged, was a liar of such bland confidence that he could outface any accusation. He appeared in the House of Commons and made so clear and convincing an explanation of all his actions that they let him go again with the good thanks of the House for his loyalty to them.

Far more damaging to the King's prestige were the revelations made a little later in the month, concerning the whole mysterious business of the King's plan to use the northern army against Parliament in the previous summer. Sir John Conyers had clearly stated on examination by a Committee of the House of Commons, that Major Daniel O'Neill—the significance of his surname was missed by no one—had come to him from the King very secretly in the summer, and tried by persuasion and by veiled threats to get him to agree to a plan for marching on London to overawe the Parliament.[33]

Meanwhile the King approached, travelling down the Great North Road by Northallerton, York and Doncaster. On his journey he kept his forty-first birthday on November 19th; but he was travelling too fast to spare time for much ceremony. In the fruitful, peaceful land through which he travelled, he was well received. News from Ireland had hardly penetrated to it. But west of the Pennines, on the Lancashire coast, in Wales, in the region of Watling Street, the direct road from Chester to London, and farther south in Devon and Somerset, the news spread fast. The first fugitives, wives of wealthy settlers and Dublin officials, cumbered with trunks of household goods and tearful with tales of horror, had already landed at Chester and Bristol. Mariners from the southern Irish ports coming back to Gloucester, Barnstaple, Minehead, brought news which ran fast up the Severn valley, and over Devon and Somerset. From Chester, tidings from Dublin were carried over the Midlands and the Welsh marches. Ships from Belfast and Londonderry gave the lamentable story to Liverpool and Whitehaven, thence to Carlisle; to Ayr and Irvine and Dumbarton and over all the Scottish Lowlands.

The Popish-Irish-Spanish plot expanded in the telling. North Wales shuddered at a supposed conspiracy to seize Conway Castle. Near Hereford Lady Brilliana Harley, at her husband's express orders, fortified his castle of Brampton Bryan in dread of siege. Messengers from Kidderminster warned the hill-town of Bridgnorth that invasion was hourly expected and Bridgnorth, as in the Armada days, lit the alarm beacon, with a prodigious expenditure in coal and beer.[34]

All this was vague, alarmist—the uninformed reactions of doubt and fear. At Westminster they had more definite news in a stream of letters from the government in Dublin. They wanted ten thousand men, money, arms . . . . O'Neill was sweeping south; he was closing in on Drogheda. Farther west and north the M'Guires had risen and were driving all before them towards Londonderry. The O'Byrnes were out in Wicklow, the O'Reillies in Cavan. Peaceable Irish gentry gave them shelter and arms, turned suddenly on their English neighbours. . . . Gradually the council in Dublin came to understand that they were facing a co-ordinated revolt.

In Munster it had come like a thunderclap, sending Lord Cork and his four elder sons helter-skelter to raise arms and men for the defence of their ill-got possessions. For once the Boyle family had been caught unprepared. Wickedly triumphant over Strafford's fall, the old Earl of Cork could not seriously believe that a revolt of the native Irish would come to trouble him in his last days. He heard the news from Ulster while he sat at table at Castle Lyons feasting his favourite son, Lord Broghill, the Haymarket bridegroom of the previous winter who had that week brought home his bride. The fearful messenger from Dublin broke in on them with news of what had happened in Ulster. He added a further warning: he had seen armed men gathering in the villages, and gangs on the roads as he passed. He had heard strange threats and caught the glint of arms and what looked like banners.[35]

Among Lord Cork's guests was an Irishman, Lord Muskerry. He laughed the messenger to scorn; some men were cowards enough to be frightened by the sight of peasants going to market. . . . The Boyles, well pleased to enjoy their false security a little longer, accepted this view, which was precisely as Muskerry had hoped; he was himself the chief of the rebels when a few days later the revolt flared up over Munster.

The Lord President of Munster, the veteran soldier Sir William St. Leger, tried to make light of the matter. " A company of naked rogues," he wrote angrily to Dublin; if they would send him a regiment of cavalry he would dispose of the rebels before they could interfere with the hunting.[36] The Lords Justices in Dublin sent no cavalry; they hardly even sent news. The roads between Dublin and the South were cut by the insurgents. The settlers, abandoning their farms, fled in terror to Kilkenny. Each region, each man, fought for himself. The government had no troops to send, while the officers and men of Strafford's disbanded army joined with the rebels.

While the Lords Justices in Dublin wailed for help to their friends in the English Parliament, the Norman-Irish landowners, the Lords of the Pale who had once been the bulwark between the English settlements and the Irish of the south and west, behaved in suspicious fashion. For the past fifty years the aggressive new English settlers had driven these Norman-Irish Roman Catholic nobility into closer friendship with the Irish. Now the testing time had come, and if they did not immediately join with the rebels, they showed a dreadful slowness to assist the government. While Ulster farmsteads went up in flames and triumphant robber bands drove off the cattle and burnt the barns everywhere, the Lords of the Pale sent a letter to the King asking him for some security in future for the lands of the Irish, that they might not be, to all time, subject to the " quirks and quiddities " of English law.[37] It was a very sound request, but it did not suggest to the Justices in Dublin or to Parliament in England that the Lords of the Pale were making ready to defend law, order and the existing government against the insurgents.

In the North Sir Phelim O'Neill boasted and bragged to his men and to English prisoners as his forces thrust on towards Drogheda. He was no rebel but the King's true knight and faithful servant who had risen in arms to liberate His Majesty from the oppression of his enemies and those who dared to set limits upon his sacred authority.

In support of this contention he showed, to prisoners in his camp at Newry, a commission under the King's Great Seal. His supporters, up and down the land, had copies of it; by the middle of November it had reached Dublin and a priest in Bull Tavern on Merchants' Quay displayed a copy, showing how the King had given order to O'Neill to seize the castles, houses and property of Protestant settlers—" witness Ourself at Edinburgh the first day of October, in the seventeenth year of our reign." [38] That the document was, in whole or in part, a forgery should have been apparent to any dispassionate eye. Whatever Charles had done to encourage the rebels, he would hardly have authorised their actions in such terms. But the rights and wrongs of the matter were less important than the effect it made.

Before King Charles approached his capital for his second great encounter with Pym in the battle for authority, his name and fame had been entangled once and for all with the cause of the Irish rebels.

In the fear rather than the knowledge of what was happening in Ireland, the House of Commons continued to debate their Grand Remonstrance against the King's past government.

Charles had sent word of his return to his Queen and to Sir Edward Nicholas. Henrietta Maria in a flutter of happy anticipation made ready to drive out to meet him at Theobalds with the three eldest children. The loyal gentlemen of Hertford planned a reception for him at Ware. Nicholas sent word of the royal time-table to the Lord Mayor so that the City of London, under Henry Gurney's genial persuasion, should receive the King with a demonstration of loyal enthusiasm, dissociating themselves from all base suspicions of the King spread abroad by the Puritan faction. Nicholas, writing to Charles, permitted himself a word of respectful advice: if His Majesty could perhaps smile at those who received him, and " speak a few good words to them. . . ." [39]

The King was expected in London by November 24th. On

November 22nd Pym's Remonstrance was again before the House. The debate opened at midday. Edward Hyde, the Member for Saltash, asked that messengers should be sent to call in Members strolling in Westminster Hall and a handful of errant royalists were rounded up for the debate. Hyde, who had supported Pym in the attack on the prerogative courts and had been until this time a principal architect of the constitutional changes of the last year, was now to measure himself against Pym in organising the Commons. A fortnight earlier he had been startled by Pym's claim to control the appointment of the councillors round the King, and he rightly saw in the Remonstrance the opening of a more far-reaching attack on the royal power than any he had anticipated. Henceforward, he was never again Pym's man.

On this 22nd November he stood, with his friend Lord Falkland beside him, as the advocate of a moderate policy and an enemy to the Remonstrance. Hyde's attack was well conceived. He had learnt in the last year a great deal about political strategy from Pym, and his experience as a barrister had given him training in the special strategy of debate. He was careful not to oppose the Remonstrance in principle. On the contrary, he declared himself very willing that a short statement, touching only the events of the present Parliament, should be made to the King. But, he argued, it was a grave error of judgment to put forth a long, injurious catalogue of complaints covering the entire reign. This could only anger the King and alienate the House of Lords, perhaps even provoke them to issue a counter-Remonstrance.

Lord Falkland persuasively enlarged on the theme set forth by Hyde. What would people think of the Commons, he asked, if they persistently, and for no good cause, raked over events of the past better consigned to oblivion? The King had come far to meet them in the last year; they had asked nothing that he had not conceded. To receive the King on his homecoming with revived accusations of past misdeeds was to do grave injury to their cause.

Sir John Colepeper took up and developed the criticisms made by Falkland and Hyde. The clauses of the Remonstrance which attacked the King's religious policy were, he argued, bound to cause a breach with the Lords, already angry at the religious ordinances of the Commons. More serious, in his view, was the unconstitutional character of the Remonstrance—it masqueraded as a document for the attention of the King, but it was in truth addressed to the people: it was a public statement by the Commons accusing the King, a procedure as yet unheard of in the annals of England.

The irrepressible Sir Edward Dering felt no less strongly on this point. "When I first heard of a Remonstrance," he said, "I presently imagined that like faithful councillors we should hold up a glass to His Majesty ... I did not dream that we should remonstrate downward and tell stories to the people."

The criticisms made by Hyde and Falkland and enlarged by Colepeper and Dering drew the moderate men of the Commons together and linked them with the more active royalists against the Remonstrance.

Pym, who fully apprehended the growing strength and improved organisation of his opponents, answered their criticism with an overriding argument: the necessity of the times. He was willing to drop a clause of the Remonstrance here and modify one there, but the Remonstrance as a whole must go through. He reiterated his belief that a malignant party still existed and was still strong round the King. In the last month every conspiracy and every violent design had been, in Pym's words, "thrust home to the Court." While such counsels prevailed there, the religion and liberty of the subject were in perpetual danger. "It is time to speak plain English," he said, "lest posterity shall say that England was lost and no man durst speak truth."

The debate outlasted the winter afternoon and went on by candlelight. At midnight, Edward Nicholas went wearily home; he wrote to the King that the opponents of the Remonstrance were making head against Pym but for his own part he could sit up no longer.

At one o'clock the House divided. Three hundred and seven Members had sat it out so long. The division, in the flickering light, seemed almost even. It must have been with infinite relief that Pym heard Lenthall announce the numbers: a hundred and forty-eight against the Remonstrance, a hundred and fifty-nine in its favour. He had won by eleven votes.

More than eighty sleepy Members now pushed out of the House, but the night's work was not over. Geoffrey Palmer, the Member for Stamford, a strong King's man, rose to announce that the minority wished to enter a protest against the Remonstrance. Confusion broke out. The Royalists shouted their support of Palmer, Pym's following were as noisy in objection. Members sprang to their feet, tweaked each other's hair and tore ill-temperedly at each other's collars. Some rattled their swords or banged their scabbarded points menacingly on the ground. Lenthall was unable to restore peace but John Hampden, dominating the clamour with his fine resonant voice, urged that nothing further be done that night. The tumult subsided. The Speaker adjourned the House and two hundred tired men came muttering and yawning, into the empty streets of Westminster "just when the clock struck two."[40]

The King slept that night within two days' ride of London. Behind him lay his kingdom of Scotland, deceptively tranquil, deceptively content. Before him lay his great City of London, decked and prepared to do him honour, and his angry, divided House of Commons, John Pym with his Remonstrance, that declaration of distrust, Oliver Cromwell with his demand that Parliament choose the commanders of the armed forces. Far to the west lay Ireland where the fires of camp and beacon and burning homestead lit the cold November night.

It was not five years since these three kingdoms had seemed the most tranquil in Europe and their sovereign the happiest King in Christendom. The tranquillity of the kingdoms, the happiness and the power of their King had proved to be illusions.

In Scotland a formidable faction, controlling and directing the fervour of the Kirk, had bereft the King of all but the semblance of sovereignty. In Ireland the imposed framework of government had been shattered by the popular rising. In England the King had pledged himself not to dissolve a Parliament which had destroyed his judicial powers, taken over the management of his finances, and awaited his return with an indictment such as had never before been presented to a reigning English sovereign.

The crucial conflict had begun between the King and John Pym—the conflict for the ultimate source of all authority, the power of the sword.

Early on the morning of November 23rd, 1641, while the Members of the House of Commons slept off the effects of their late night, the King and his following were once more upon the road, a distinguished, orderly, elegant cavalcade, moving towards London.

BOOK III CHAPTER VII REFERENCES

1. *Nicholas Correspondence*, p. 60; *C.S.P.D.*, 1641–3, p. 117.
2. *H.M.C. Portland MSS.*, III, p. 81; *C.S.P. Ven*, 1640–2, pp. 206, 222.
3. Guthry, p. 98; *C.S.P. Ven*, 1640–2, p. 205.
4. Balfour, II, pp. 40, 44.
5. Rushworth, III, i, pp. 382–3.
6. Balfour, III, pp. 46 ff.; Napier, I, 311–16; *Wigton Papers*, p. 429; *C.S.P.D.*, 1641–3, pp. 101, 110.
7. Balfour, III, p. 54; *C.S.P.D.*, 1641–3, p. 110.
8. *Ibid.*, p. 84.
9. Balfour, II, 56.
10. *C.S.P.D.*, 1641–3, p. 70.
11. Balfour, III, p. 57.
12. Carte, *Letters*, I, p. 4.
13. *Nicholas Correspondence*, p. 79.
14. *Hardwicke State Papers*, II, p. 299.
15. Carte, *Letters*, I, p. 7; Balfour, III, pp. 82–5.
16. The incident is described in Balfour, III, pp. 95 ff; also in *C.S.P.D.*, 1641–3, pp. 137–9, 143; *Hardwicke State Papers*, II, pp. 299–300. The evidence given by those involved is in *Hist. MSS. Commission*, IV, pp. 163–70. Few accounts tally and many mysteries remain unsolved; my own view is different from earlier versions because I am disposed to regard Montrose as wholly unconcerned in the

business. Clarendon accepted the contemporary story of his dominant part in the Incident and it was taken over by later historians until further examination of the facts and documents proved it substantially untenable. Gardiner, however, accepts Will Murray's evidence of Montrose's stream of letters to the King without difficulty and presumes some connection with the plot. Montrose's name is not mentioned in evidence until Crawford brought it in on October 23rd. Thereafter he figures ever more largely, especially in Murray's evidence. From this, and from a careful examination of the chronological sequence of events, it seemed to me reasonable to deduce that the Royalists were thankful to find a scapegoat.

17. *Nicholas Correspondence*, p. 92.

18. *C.S.P. Ven.*, 1640–2, pp. 213, 215.

19. *Ibid.*, p. 272. Newport later denied the words, but he could hardly have acknowledged them; they are typical enough of the man and the situation to sound plausible.

20. Carte, *Ormonde*, V, p. 254–5.

21. *H.M.C. Ormonde MSS.*, N.S. II, pp. 1–5; *C.S.P. Ireland*, pp. 342, 344.

22. D'Ewes, *Journal*, ed. Coates, Yale, 1942, p. 77.

23. *Nicholas Correspondence*, p. 97.

24. *C.S.P.D.*, 1641–3, pp. 141, 147; Rushworth, III, i, pp. 392, 394; *Harleian MSS.*, 6424; D'Ewes, ed. Coates, pp. 18, 21, 58, 60.

25. *C.S.P.D.*, 1641–3, pp. 162, 168; *C.S.P. Ven.*, 1640–2, pp. 241, 244.

26. D'Ewes, ed. Coates, pp. 94–5, 94 n.

27. *Nicholas Correspondence*, pp. 115, 124.

28. D'Ewes, ed. Coates, pp. 97–8.

29. *Nicholas Correspondence*, p. 117.

30. Balfour, III, pp. 139–40, 162–5.

31. John Taylor, *Swarm of Sectaries*, London, 1642.

32. D'Ewes, ed. Coates, pp. 169, 170.

33. *Ibid.*, pp. 155–7.

34. *H.M.C. Portland MSS.*, III, pp. 81–2; *H.M.C. X*, IV, pp. 433–4; *C.S.P.D.*, 1641–3, pp. 170, 270; *C.S.P. Ireland*, p. 345.

35. *Egmont MSS.*, I, i, p. 152; Carte, *Ormonde*, V, p. 259.

36. *C.S.P. Ireland*, pp. 345–6.

37. Rushworth, III, i, p. 400.

38. Bowle, *Mystery of Iniquity*, London, 1643, pp. 34–6.

39. *Nicholas Correspondence*, p. 127.

40. D'Ewes, ed. Coates, pp. 183–7.

BIBLIOGRAPHICAL NOTE

THE REFERENCES given at the end of each chapter indicate the sources from which information has been directly drawn. I have followed the usual practice of giving the full name and the date of publication of any book the first time it is cited and citing it thereafter by an abbreviated title, or simply by the name of the author.

The sources cited in the references represent only a proportion of the works consulted. The material for the seventeenth century is limitless and each further advance into it only serves to show the historian how much unexplored territory lies beyond. The literature of the epoch is moreover very fruitful in historical evidence and many of my impressions and deductions are as much the outcome of leisure reading, more especially in seventeenth-century poetry and drama, as of research proper.

I have made use of two important MS. sources which have recently become available to historians. The Strafford Papers, now housed by the courtesy of the owner Lord Fitzwilliam in the Sheffield Central Library, are of the greatest value for the period of King Charles's absolute rule. The other source of which I have made great use is the Breadalbane MSS. preserved at the General Register House, Edinburgh. I am particularly grateful to the Keeper of the Records for Scotland, Sir James Fergusson, for drawing my attention to the great importance of this collection for the early Covenanting period, as also to other relatively unexplored sources in the Register House, of which I hope to make use for succeeding volumes.

The Bankes MSS. which I have occasionally cited are the papers of Sir John Bankes recently deposited at the Bodleian Library, Oxford, by Lord Bledisloe.

Harleian MSS. 6424, to which one or two references are made, is a Diary of the House of Lords during the Long Parliament, compiled by an unidentified bishop.

I am indebted to more modern scholars than I can here name either for the impersonal assistance of their writings or for personal kindness and help, or for both. The exhaustive bibliography of the epoch compiled by Professor Godfrey Davies has been my bedside book for twelve years. For the economic background I owe much to the second volume of Dr. E. Lipson's incomparable *Economic History of England* and to his comprehensive and authoritative *History of the Woollen and Worsted Industries*. Professor John Nef's *Rise of the British Coal Industry* is—appositely—a mine of information on seventeenth-century methods and administration, as well as on the coal trade itself. Dr. Mildred Campbell's *English Yeoman* is rich in suggestions.

For Parliamentary affairs all workers in this field are indebted to Professor Notestein. I would like also to record my gratitude to Professor Willson Coates for much help and for kindly lending me his transcript of part of D'Ewes Journal. Professor J. H. Hexter's *Reign of King Pym* (Yale, 1942) is extremely interesting on the management of the Long Parliament. *The Members of the Long Parliament* (London, 1954) by D. H. Pennington and the late Douglas Brunton—which appeared while this book was in the press—bears out in detail the general conviction that I had myself formed when working many years ago on the seventeenth-century section of the *History of Parliament*—that political divisions in the House of Commons did not follow any clearly defined lines of class, property or social interest. Professor J. E. Neale's great work on the Elizabethan Parliaments does much to explain, to the student of the succeeding epoch, how Parliament came to be so firmly entrenched.

For the atmosphere, moral, social and religious, of the epoch, I owe many ideas and suggestions both to the writings and the conversation of Dr. David Mathew, of Dr. Margaret Judson author of *The Crisis of the Constitution* (Rutgers, 1949) of Miss

Mary Coate, Miss Gladys Scott Thomson, and of the late Dr. W. Schenk. I would like to thank Dr. Agnes Mure Mackenzie for helping me towards a more sympathetic understanding of the episcopal position in Scotland. Sir George Clark's great work on *The Seventeenth Century* first guided my footsteps into this incomparable epoch.

The twentieth-century controversy on the economic interpretation of history is almost as fierce as the religious controversy of the seventeenth. I have learnt much from the broad vision of Professor R. H. Tawney, from the writings of Mr. Hugh Trevor-Roper and Mr. Christopher Hill, if sometimes by the stimulus of disagreement.

Finally Dr. B. H. G. Wormald's *Clarendon: Politics, History, Religion* (Cambridge, 1951) is of fundamental importance not only for the better understanding of Clarendon's work and career but for the better understanding of the key epoch 1641–3. The political developments of that critical period are but faintly foreshadowed in the present volume; they will be treated at length in the succeeding one.

Any writer dealing with the first half of the seventeenth century must take up a position in relation to the late Samuel Rawson Gardiner. Gardiner wrote in an epoch when moral certainty was not only possible but natural; we live in an epoch when it is extremely difficult either to reach or to maintain certainty about moral issues in politics. This seems to me a much more fundamental difference between Gardiner and ourselves than anything brought about by changing fashions and emphasis in research, or changing historical judgments. For him the seventeenth century was a time of confusion and distress compared to his own. For us it cannot seem so. But we are not wiser because we are more disillusioned. Gardiner was certain he knew which side was right in the Civil War and was therefore on that side, although he tried to be fair to the characters of the men on the other side—which is more than can be said for writers of the neo-Royalist school. His prejudices and his point of view are so evident that any intelligent reader should be able to detect and make allowances for them. His scholarship, on those subjects which interested him and for which the sources were available, has not its equal to-day.

INDEX

Abbot, George, Archbishop of Canterbury, 96, 97
Abel, John, 39
Abell, William, 159, 362
Aberdeen, 115, 228, 232, 233, 249, 261, 264, 269, 277, 343
Abernethy, Thomas, 229
Aboyne, Viscount, see Gordon, James
Airlie, Earl of, see Ogilvy, James
Alexander, William, Earl of Stirling, 149, 162, 312
America, 48-9, 110-11, 130, 204-5
Anglesey, Countess of, 65
Annand, William, 177
Anne, daughter of Charles I, 384
Antrim, Earl of, see MacDonnell, Randall
Argyll, Earls of, see Campbell, Archibald
Arminians, 96, 101-3
Armstrong, Archie, 201
Armyn, Sir William, 457
Army Plots, 389, 407-10, 418, 421, 422-3, 425, 434, 438-9, 440, 442, 444, 445, 472, 478; Scottish, 459-62; see also Incident
Arundel, Earl of, see Howard, Thomas
Ashburnham, John, 389, 407

Astley, Sir Jacob, 227, 242, 249, 251, 253, 263, 270, 352, 407-8
Aubrey, John, 87-8

Babington, John, 80
Bacon, Francis, 136
Bagshawe, Edward, 316
Baillie, Dr. Robert, 257, 258, 261, 273, 276, 373
Balcanquhall, Dr. John, 235-6, 237
Balfour, Sir William, 423, 438
Balmerino, Lord, see Elphinstone, John
Bancroft, Richard, Archbishop of Canterbury, 96, 101
Bankes, Sir John, 137, 176, 192, 193, 207, 217, 278, 386-7
Bastwicke, John, 108, 173-4, 370, 375
Baxter, Richard, 99
Beale, Thomas, 477
Bedell, William, Bishop of Kilmore, 78
Bedford, Earls of, see Russell, Francis and William
Bellièvre, Marquis de, 190
Bensted, Thomas, 331
Berkeley, John, 389
Berkeley, Sir Robert, 196. 205, 208, 396, 431

Bernard, Duke of Saxe-Weimar, 289

Berwick, 25-6, 234, 249, 263, 304, 348; the King at, 270, 272; Treaty at, 275-6, 288-9, 313

Blaney, Lord, 470

Blount, Mountjoy, Earl of Newport, 129, 310, 409, 421, 451, 467; his wife, 182-3

Bohemia, King of, see Frederick; Queen of, see Elizabeth

Bolton, Sir Richard, 402, 403

Book of Sports, 102-3

Borlase, Sir John, 404, 443-4, 469, 480

Boyle, Richard, Earl of Cork, 310-11, 404, 479; sons of, 310, 479

Boyle, Roger, Lord Broghill, 310, 393-4, 479

Bramhall, John, Bishop of Derry, 113, 401, 402

Bramston, Sir John, 136-7, 217

Brathwaite, Richard, 52

Brechin, Bishop of, see Whitford, Walter

Breda, siege of, 189

Breisach, 289

Bridgwater, Earl of, see Egerton, John

Brig o' Dee, battle at, 277

Briot, Nicolas, 68, 125

Bristol, Earl of, see Digby, John

Broghill, Lord, see Boyle, Roger

Brooke, Sir Basil, 266

Brooke, Lord, see Greville, Robert

Browne, Thomas, 77

Buchanan, George, 83

Buckingham, Duke of, see Villiers, George

Burke, Ulick, Earl of Clanricarde, 355

Burnet, Gilbert, 213

Burton, Henry, 107-8, 173-4, 370, 375

Busby, Richard, 255

Bushell, Sir Thomas, 37, 180

Butler, James, Earl of Ormonde, 287, 395, 403, 469

Campbell, Archibald, seventh Earl of Argyll, 187, 204

Campbell, Archibald, Lord Lorne, later eighth Earl of Argyll, 176, 189, 197, 211, 230, 231, 275, 276, 279, 441, 455, 475; character, 186-7, 296-7; and the Antrim project, 225, 228; at the Glasgow Assembly, 235, 238-42; in the first Scots War, 249, 256, 258; and the Lords of the Articles, 295; in Atholl, 341-2; in the second war, 342, 356; relations with Hamilton, 356-7, 407, 434, 436, 458; attacked by Montrose, 441-2; attacks Lord Morton, 458-9; and the Incident, 462-6; and the Irish Rising, 470-1, 476

Campbell, Archibald, of Glenorchy, 256

Campbell, Duncan, of Auchinbreck, 228

Campbell, John, Lord Loudoun, 184, 313, 323, 460, 475

Canopis, Nathaniel, 79

Carey, Lucius, Viscount Falkland, 81, 372, 379, 382, 417-18, 482

Carlisle, Countess of, see Percy, Lucy

Carnarvon, Earl of, see Dormer, Robert

Carnegie, David, Earl of Southesk 267

Carnwath, Earl of, see Dalzell, Robert

Cartwright, William, 92

Cashel, Archbishop of, 112

Cassilis, Earl of, see Kennedy, John

Castle Chamber, Court of, 144-5, 208, 287, 302-3, 400

Cavendish, Charles, 69

Cavendish, William, Earl of Newcastle, 81, 210, 271, 274, 444

Cecil, William, Earl of Salisbury, 147, 182, 313

Chancery, Court of, 143

Channel Islands, 25, 61, 111

Charles I
  his theory of government, 21-3, 61, 62-4
  his Court, 50, 60-1, 65-70, 74
  his character, 70-3, 91-2, 152-3, 321
  his collections, 67-8

  administration, 71, 336, Book I, Chapter III, passim
  colonial policy, 110-11, 204-5
  foreign policy, 123-8, 131-3, 189-90, 246, 247-8, 288-90, 309, 329, 334-5, 337-8, 385-6, 397-8, 435-6, 457-8
  Church policy, England, 41, 76, 91-5, 103, 108-9; Ireland, 112; Scotland, 114-18, 177, 196, 214-5, 221, 230, 293, 456; Roman Catholics, 119-23, 190-1, 337, 391-3
  relations with Scotland, first war, 223, 226-8, 242-3, Book II, Chapter IV, passim; second war, 303-4, Book III, Chapter III, passim; corresponds with Montrose, 356, 436, 440-1; overtures to, Covenanters, 448-9, Book III, Chapter VII, passim
  relations with Ireland, 468-71, 480-1
  relations with Parliament, the Short Parliament, 314, 322-6; the Long Parliament, 363, 388, 406-7, 410, 420-1, 435, 437, 447
  his promises to Strafford, 358, 419, 424-5
  and the Army Plots, 389, 439-40

Charles Louis, Elector Palatine, 21, 126-7, 131, 167, 168, 189, 246, 289-90, 334; and the

Weimar troops, 292, 300, 301-2; claims Princess Mary, 397-8, 422; accompanies the King in 1641, 435-6, 448, 456, 457, 471

Charles, Prince of Wales, 209-10, 321-2, 418, 427, 455

Chevreuse, Duchesse de, 247

Childe, Richard, 47

Chillingworth, William, 191

Christian IV, King of Denmark, 357

Christian, William, 60-1

Church, see under England, Ireland, Scotland, Wales

Clanricarde, Earl of, see Burke, Ulick

Clare, Earl of, see Holles, John

Clotworthy, Sir John, 372

Cochrane, Colonel, 459, 460, 461, 475

Coke, Sir Edward, 136, 387, 430-2, 433

Coke, Sir John, 148, 308, 338

Colepeper, Sir John, 371, 483

Colquhoun, Sir John, of Luss, 89

Comenius, John, 84

Compton, Spencer, Earl of Northampton, 81, 356

Con, Fr. George, 122, 190, 266, 292

Convocation (1640), 324, 331-2, 447

Conway, Edward Lord, 341, 344, 346-7, 348

Conyers, Sir John, 407-8, 478

Cork, Earl of, see Boyle, Richard

Cosin, John, 104, 390

Cottington, Francis, Lord, 148-9, 190, 204-5, 218, 249, 250, 321, 335, 410, 435

Cotton, Sir Robert, 79, 136

Courtine, Sir William, 180

Covenant, The National, 197-9, 201, 228-9, 230-1, 240, 256-7, 293, 344

Covenanters, 201, 203, 211, 218, 343-4, Book II Chapters III and IV passim; army of, 257-8, 313, 314, 339-40; relations with English Parliament, 355, 367-8, 390, 395, 397, 407, 435, 444, 447-8, 450, 456-7, Book III Chapter VII passim

Coventry, Thomas, Lord, 216, 312

Cowley, Abraham, 288

Cradock, Walter, 110

Crawford, Earl of, see Lindsay, Ludovic

Crew, John, 330

Crewe, Sir Randolph, 136

Croke, Sir George, 167, 205-6, 217

Cromwell, Oliver, 83, 370, 474, 484

Cumbernauld Bond, 343-4, 441

Dalkeith, 261

Dalzell, Robert, Earl of Carnwath, 263, 463

Danby, Earl of, see Danvers, Henry

Danvers, Henry, Earl of Danby, 48, 167

Davenant, Christopher (Franciscus a Sancta Clara), 119

Davenant, John, Bishop of Salisbury, 97, 106

Davenant, William, 66, 67, 127, 310, 389, 408, 440

Davenport, Humphrey, 193-4, 217

Davies, Lady Eleanor, 108, 256

Denham, Sir John, 194, 217

Dering, Sir Edward, 371, 380, 483

Derry, Bishop of, see Bramhall, John

Devereux, Robert, Earl of Essex, 129, 251, 264-5, 349, 355, 384, 389, 407, 420, 447, 472, 474

D'Ewes, Sir Symonds, 79, 433, 439

Dickson, David, 198

Digby, George, later Lord, 69, 371, 372, 388, 395, 416-7, 438-9, 450, 474

Digby, John, Earl of Bristol, 274, 354, 407, 416, 418, 420, 425, 474

Digby, Sir Kenelm, 77, 123, 266

Dillon, James, Lord, 403, 469

Dormer, Robert, Earl of Carnarvon, 250, 440

Dorset, Earl of, see Sackville, Edward

Douglas, Robert, Earl of, 261

Douglas, William, Earl of Morton, 455, 458-9

Dover, Captain Robert, 42

Down, Bishop of, see Leslie, Henry

Downs, Battle of the, 299, 300-1

Drummond, William, of Hawthornden, 81

Dublin, 59-60, 469-70

Dumbarton, 261

Duppa, Brian, later Bishop of Chichester, 210, 444

Dutch, diplomatic relations with, 26, 111, 125-6, 248, 289, 334-5; see also Frederick Henry, Prince of Orange

Dyck, Sir Anthony van, 67, 68, 69, 74, 249, 419

Earle, John, 445

Earle, Sir Walter, 330, 477

East India Company, 31, 180, 334-5

Edinburgh 45; Assembly at, 291, 292-3; Castle, 261, 309; riots and demonstrations in, 176-7, 183, 197-8

Egerton, John, Earl of Bridgwater, 61, 144

Elector Palatine, see Charles Louis

Eliot, Sir John, 307, 323

Elizabeth, daughter of Charles I, 309, 357, 386

Elizabeth, Queen of Bohemia, 21, 126, 132, 288-9, 357, 386, 397, 398, 435-6

Elizabeth I, Queen of England, 95, 140-1, 157, 392, 433

Elphinstone, John, Lord Balmerino, 115, 184, 456, 475

England, agriculture, 43-5, 46-8; Church, 91-112, 332-3, 380, 454; education and culture, 77-85; industries, 34-8, 51-2, 159-61; the law, 135, 137-40, 142-6, 453-4

Erbury, William, 109

Erlach, Hans Ludwig von, 289

Esmond, Robert, 144

Essex, Earl of, see Devereux, Robert

Falkland, Lord, see Carey, Lucius

Fens, 47, 211, 339

Fenwick, Sir John, 70

Ferrar, John, 321-2

Ferrar, Nicholas, 94

Ferriter, Piers, 87

Fiennes, Nathaniel, 438, 457

Fiennes, William, Viscount Saye and Seal, 259, 264, 324, 330, 349, 388, 407, 420, 447; and the Providence Company, 130, 132, 319; and Ship-money, 168-9

Finch, John, Lord, 136-7, 173, 312, 316, 317, 322, 323, 324, 368, 379, 432, 435, 451; impeached, 381-2

Fitzgerald, John, 208

Forbes, Alexander, Lord, 202

Foxe's Book of Martyrs, 82, 85, 102, 335

France, relations with, 127, 190, 334, 446

Frederick, Elector Palatine, King of Bohemia, 21, 126

Frederick Henry, Prince of Orange, 111, 309, 357, 385-6, 418

Gardiner, Sir Thomas, 362

Garland, Augustine, 140

Garraway, Sir Henry, 304, 316, 330, 335, 362

Gascoigne, William, 78

Gellbrand, Henry, 77

Glanville, John, 323, 325

Glasgow, 27, 46; Assembly at, 233-43, 278

Glisson, Francis, 77

Gloucester, Duke of, see Henry

Glyn, John, 376, 406, 412

Goodman, Godfrey, Bishop of Gloucester, 96-7, 333, 392

Goodman, Fr. John, 391-3, 424, 446

Gordon, George, Marquis of Huntly, 120, 212, 228, 243, 249, 257, 259, 292; in the first Scots War, 261, 264, 267, 278

Gordon, George, Lord, 243

Gordon, James, Viscount Aboyne, 243, 267-9, 277

Gorges, Sir Ferdinando, 204

Goring, George, Lord, 250, 408

Goring, Colonel George, 189,

250, 300, 389, 408, 409, 418, 438-40, 477-8

Graham, George, Bishop of Orkney, 292

Graham, James, Earl of Montrose, 188, 197, 228, 229, 231, 242, 293, 314; joins the Covenanters, 184-5; in the first war, 259, 262, 267, 269, 277; in the Parliament of 1639, 294-5, 298, 341; signs Cumbernauld Bond, 341-3; corresponds with the King, 356, 436, 440-1; demands trial, 456; and the Incident, 462, 465-6, 475

Graham, John, 441

Graham, Lady Katherine, 89

Grantham, vicar of, 103

Greene, Fr. Cuthbert, 446

Greville, Robert, Lord Brooke, 130, 131, 132, 168, 255, 264, 324, 330, 349, 388, 447

Grey, Henry, Earl of Stamford, 53

Gurney, Sir Henry, 362, 477, 481

Hale, Matthew, 140

Hall, Joseph, Bishop of Exeter, 97, 106

Hamilton, James, Marquis of, 116, 148-9, 159, 328, 355, 410, 455; character, 212-5; Commissioner in Scotland, 211-15, 218, 221-3, 227-30, 232-3, 277, 279; at the Glasgow Assembly, 233-43; commands in the first Scots War, 249, 262, 265, 268-

9, 270; supports Vane, 311-12; commands in second Scots War, 343, 348, 352-3; relations with Argyll, 356-7, 407, 434, 436, 458, 475; and the Incident, 460, 462-6

Hamilton, William, Earl of Lanark, 312, 458, 460

Hamilton, Sir William, 122

Hammond, Henry, 92

Hampden, John, 130, 132, 307, 330, 349, 364, 447, 457, 475, 484; Ship-money case, 168-9, 191-4, 205-6, 215-16, 217, 323

Hannah, Dean, 176

Harley, Lady Brilliana, 478

Harley, Sir Robert, 454

Harrison, Thomas, 215-6

Hartlib, Samuel, 81, 84

Harvard, John, 130

Harvey, William, 68, 77

Haselrig, Sir Arthur, 364, 413

Heenvliet, Baron de, 334, 335, 385

Henderson, Colonel, 277

Henderson, Alexander, 188, 198, 275, 276, 293; moderator of Glasgow Assembly, 236, 237-9

Henrietta Maria, Queen Consort of Charles I, 61, 66, 242, 247, 335, 445; character, 73-4; birth of her children, 252, 340; her health, 384-5, 446; and the Roman Catholics, 121-3, 183, 191, 265-6; influences appointments, 260, 311-12; in the second Scots War, 349, 350; and the Army Plots, 389-90, 408-9, 436, 477-8; and Strafford, 426; and the King's absence in Scotland, 448-9, 451, 466-7, 474, 489

Henry, Duke of Gloucester, 340

Herbert, Edward, Lord of Cherbury, 68-9

Herbert of Raglan, Lord, see Somerset, Edward

Herbert, Sir Edward, 386-7

Herbert, George, 93, 94

Herbert, Sir Henry, 67

Herbert, Philip, Earl of Pembroke, 68, 71, 147, 313, 447

Hertford, Earl of, see Seymour, William

High Commission, Court of, 101, 104, 117, 145, 175, 254, 432

Holbourne, Robert, 192, 193

Holland, Earl of, see Rich, Henry

Hollar, Wenceslas, 69-70

Holles, Denzil, 307, 323, 364, 371, 395, 447

Holles, Gervase, 395

Holles, John, Earl of Clare, 250

Home, Robert, 461

Hope, Sir Thomas, 186, 197, 222, 235, 239, 241, 273, 458, 475, 476; character, 187-8; and the Confession of 1580, 230-1, 232-3; and the Incident, 464; son of, 347

Howard, Edward, Lord of Escrick, 457

Howard, Henry Frederick, Lord Maltravers, 447

Howard, Thomas, Earl of Arundel, 68, 69, 227, 242, 251, 253, 263, 271, 272, 308, 404

Hull, 227, 230, 249, 251, 304

Huntly, Marquis of, see Gordon

Hussey, Anne, 350, 372

Hutchinson, John, 140

Hutton, Sir Richard, 167, 205, 207-8, 215-16, 217

Hyde, Edward, 140, 372, 382, 387, 395, 421, 435, 473, 482

Inchiquin, Earl of, see O'Brien, Murrough

Incident, the, 460-6

Ingram, Sir Arthur, 35, 48, 263

Ireland, army, 328, 350, 352-3, 358, 419-20, 434, 436, 443, 467-8, 471, 473; church and religion, 60, 112-13, 468-9; land question, 43, 402, 469, 480; unrest and revolt in, 443-4, 468-9, 469-71, 478-81

James, Duke of York, 322, 418

James VI and I, 23, 59, 65, 70, 83, 93, 114, 136, 149-50, 294; writings of, 62-4

Jermyn, Henry, 389, 408, 438, 440

Johnston, Archibald, of Warriston, 183, 197-9, 230-1, 236, 275-6, 293; character, 185-6

Johnston, Arthur, 83

Jones, Inigo, 22, 39, 62, 77, 79, 94, 310

Jones, Sir William, 56, 217

Josselin, Ralph, 53

Juxon, William, Bishop of London, 148, 163, 218, 410, 426

Katherine, daughter of Charles I, 252

Kelso, encounter at, 271-2

Kennedy, John, Earl of Cassilis, 184, 475

Ker, Henry Lord, 460-1, 465

Ker, Robert, Earl of Roxburgh, 188, 267

Ker, William, Earl of Lothian, 184

Kimbolton, Lord, see Montague Edward

King, Henry, Dean of Rochester, 81

King's Evil, 72, 90

Kintire, 225, 249

Knox, John, 117

Kynaston, Sir Francis, 69

Lanark, Earl of, see Hamilton, William

Langton, laird of, 455

Laud, William, Archbishop of Canterbury, 79, 83, 96, 97, 112, 201, 247, 321, 350; character, 93-4; attitude to Roman Catholics, 122-3, 183, 254; his reforms in the Church, 105-6, 109-11, 333; attacks the Walloon church, 111, 256; and Bishop Williams, 175, 195; foreign policy, 190; relations with Wentworth, 151-3, 163, 218, 427-8; and Oxford, 227, 256, 437-8; his house attacked, 330-1; impeachment of, 379-81

Legge, William, 227, 242, 447

Leicester, Earl of, see Sidney, Robert

Leighton, Dr. Alexander, 145

Lennox, Duchess of, see Villiers, Mary

Lennox, Duke of, see Stewart, James

Lenthall, William, 363, 395, 439, 484

Leslie, Alexander, later Earl of Leven, 202, 223, 234, 252, 455, 475; in the first war, 257, 261, 269, 272, 273, 275; in the second war, 346-9

Leslie, Henry, Bishop of Down, 113, 401

Leslie, John, Bishop of Raphoe, 272, 280, 285

Leslie, John, Earl of Rothes, 115, 184, 188, 197, 212, 222, 231, 258, 261, 275, 293, 313, 435, 441, 447, 458

Leven, Earl of, see Leslie, Alexander

Lilburne, John, 194, 195, 206-7, 265, 370, 423

Lindsay, Ludovic, Earl of Crawford, 459, 460, 462, 463, 464, 465, 475

Littleton, Sir Edward, 137, 192, 193, 278, 386-7, 404, 472

Lithgow, William, 46

Livingstone, William, 221

Loftus, Adam, Lord, 207-9, 287, 302, 402

London, 22, 29-33; Inns of Court, 138, 140, 251; loans from, 330, 335, 354, 355, 392; petitions from, 353, 379; plague in, 32, 472; playhouses closed, 350; riots in, 330, 349, 418, 422-3, 425-6; rivalry with Newcastle, 36, 204; soapmakers of, 160-1; Tower, 304, 409, 410, 421, 422, 440

Londonderry, 165

Lorne, Lord, see Campbell, Archibald

Lothian, Earl of, see Ker, William

Loudoun, Lord, see Campbell, John

Louis XIII, King of France, 247, 314, 322

Love, Nicholas, 140

Lovelace, Richard, 66, 253, 394

Lucas, Sir Charles, 189

McCarty, Donough, Lord Muskerry, 479-80

MacDonnell, Randall, Earl of Antrim, 60, 224-6, 249, 259, 350, 468

M'Guire, Connor, Lord Enniskillen, 468, 469-70

MacMahon, Hugh Oge, 468, 469-70

Mainwaring, Philip, 287

Maitland, John, Lord, 314, 475

Maltravers, Henry Lord, see Howard, Frederick Henry

Man, Isle of, 25, 60-1

Manchester, Earl of, see Montague Henry

Mandeville, Lord, see Montague, Edward

Marie de Medici, Queen mother of France, 247, 375, 435

Mary, daughter of Charles I, 309, 386, 397-8, 418-9, 422, 435

Mathew, Toby, 123, 183, 365

Maxwell, Robert, Earl of Nithsdale, 353

Mayerne, Sir Theodore de, 68, 446

Maynard, John, 387, 406

Merchant Adventurers, 31, 316-7

Middleton, Major John, 277

Mildmay, Sir Humphrey, 31, 42

Milton, John, 40

Mines, coal, 36-7; copper, 37; lead, 37; silver, 37, 179-80; tin, 37

Mitchelson, Margaret, 231

Monck, George, 347

Monro, Robert, 342

Montague, Edward, Lord Kimbolton and Viscount Mandeville, 250, 351, 375, 407, 409, 451

Montague, Henry, Earl of Manchester, 123, 250, 375, 451

Montague, Walter, 123, 183, 250, 266, 375, 451

Montreuil, Comte de, 334

Montrose, Earl of, *see* Graham, James

Morton, Earl of, *see* Douglas, William

Morton, Thomas, Bishop of Durham, 97, 266

Muffet, Thomas, 78

Murray, Will, 68, 149, 460, 461, 462, 463, 464

Muskerry, Lord, *see* McCarty, Donough

Napier, John, 78

Navy, 29, 249, 268, 338

Neile, Richard, Archbishop of York, 291

Newburn, battle of, 347, 352

Newcastle, Earl of, *see* Cavendish, William

Newcastle on Tyne, 36, 204, 227, 230, 234, 249, 251, 344; Charles I at, 267, 269, 455; taken by Scots, 346, 348

Newport, Earl of, *see* Blount, Mountjoy

News from Ipswich, 106-7, 132

Nicholas, Edward, 308, 320, 366, 449, 451, 460, 466, 471, 474, 476, 481, 483

Nithsdale, Earl of, *see* Maxwell, Robert

North, Court of the, 144, 432

Northampton, Earl of, *see* Compton, Spencer

Northumberland, Earl of, *see* Percy, Algernon

Norwood, Richard, 80

Noy, William, 155-7, 162

O'Brien, Murrough, Earl of Inchiquin, 60

O'Connolly, Owen, 469

Ogilvy, James, Lord, later Earl of Airlie, 257, 263, 342

Oglander, Sir John, 48, 118

O'Neill, Daniel, 389, 447, 478

O'Neill, Owen Roe, 60

O'Neill, Sir Phelim, 259, 468, 479, 480-1

Ormonde, Earl of, *see* Butler, James

Orange, Prince of, *see* Frederick Henry, and William

Osbaldeston, Lambert, 195, 254

Osborne, Sir Edward, 227, 246, 253, 336

Oughtred, William, 78, 81

Palmer, Geoffrey, 484

Parliament, English, 165-6, (1625), 64; (1626), 64; (1628), 64-5, 151, 431; (1640, April), 314, 317, 322-6; (1640, November), first session, Book III, Chapters IV, V, VI, *passim*; second session, 472-5, 476-7, 482-4; Irish (1634), 308; (1640), 320-1, 401-3, 469; Scottish (1639), 294-5, 313, 341; (1641), 455-6, 458-9, 463-4, 466

Parsons, Sir William, 404, 443-4, 469, 470, 480

Paulet, John, Marquis of Winchester, 68, 250

Peacham, Henry, 53

Peers, Council of, *see* York

Pembroke, Earl of, *see* Herbert, Philip

Pennington, Issac, 379

Pennington, Sir John, 300-1

Percy, Algernon, Earl of Northumberland, 69, 81, 148, 149, 180, 210, 226-7, 242, 252, 260; writes to Wentworth, 286; general of the army, 308, 336; deserts the King, 439-40

Percy, Henry, 149, 389, 407, 409, 440

Percy, Lucy, Countess of Carlisle, 69, 149

Perth, Five Articles of, 114

Philip IV, King of Spain, 309

Philip, Fr. Robert, 121, 445, 472

Pickering, Christopher, 216-7

Pindar, Sir Paul, 251

Pirates, 27-9, 131, 166, 182, 194, 260, 338

Pococke, Edward, 78, 256

Pollard, Hugh, 389

Porter, Endymion, 149, 335

Portland, Earl of, *see* Weston, Richard

Portugal, 435

Potter, Christopher, 391

Pritchard, Rhys, 86-7, 110

Protestation, the, 423

Providence Company, 130-2, 319, 349

Prynne, William, 107-8, 132, 173-4, 375

Pym, John, 130, 131, 132, 168, 307, 330, 352, 447; character, 363-5; ideas and policy, 366-7, 432-3; leads the Short Parliament, 323-6; friendship with young Vane, 349, 377-8; leads the Long Parliament, 369, 370-1, 374, 381, 384, 390-2, 392-3, 395, 397, 433-5; and the fall of Strafford, 372-3, 377-8, 400-1, 406, 410-5; and the Army Plots, 409-10, 434, 438, 443; policy after Strafford's death, 436-7, 438, 448; control of Court appointments, 445, 472; and the Scots, 447-8, 450; during the recess, 451, 466-7; and the Irish Rising, 468, 472-4; and the Remonstrance, 482-4

Radcliffe, Sir George, 287, 353, 359, 403

Rainborough, William, 182, 194

Ratisbon, Diet of, 457-8

Reade, Robert, 265, 320, 366, 376

Remonstrance, the Grand, 370, 450, 474-5, 481-4, 485

Reynardson, Abraham, 362

Rich, Henry, Earl of Holland, 129, 130, 147-8, 149, 210, 247, 467; commands in the first Scots War, 252, 264, 271-2, 274

Rich, Robert, Earl of Warwick, 129, 148, 167-9, 324, 330, 388, 420, 451; Admiral, 432; and the Providence Company, 130-2, 319, 349

Richelieu, Cardinal, 301, 334, 376

Richmond, Duke of, see Stewart, James

Ripon, negotiations at, 355

Roe. Sir Thomas, 180, 457-8

Root and Branch Bill, 438, 439

Ross, Alexander, 77

Rossetti, Count, 292, 335, 375, 393, 445

Rothes, Earl of, see Leslie, John

Roxburgh, Earl of, see Ker, Robert

Rubens, Sir Peter Paul, 22-4, 67

Rupert, Prince, 21, 127, 189, 246, 302, 471

Russell, Francis, Earl of Bedford, 47, 211, 349, 388, 407, 409, 416, 418, 420, 421, 425

Russell, William, later Earl of Bedford, 457

Rutherford, Samuel, 233

Ruthven, Patrick, 309

Sackville, Edward, Earl of Dorset, 205

St. John, Oliver, 130, 191-2, 193, 205, 217, 364, 387

St. Leger, Sir William, 480

Salisbury, Earl of, see Cecil, William

Savoy, Duke of, 242

Saye and Seal, Lord, see Fiennes, William

Scotland,
administration, 149-50
education and culture, 78, 81, 83, 85, 87
economic situation, 45-6, 56-7, 162
Highlands, 25, 43, 56-8, 257; religion, 113-8, 176-9, 186, 215, 229-33; see also Covenant, Covenanters

Selden, John, 146, 167, 387

Seymour, William, Earl of Hertford, 129, 331, 388, 407, 420

Shepard, Thomas, 110

Ship-money, 156, 166-9, 182, 191-4, 201-2, 227, 266, 278, 304, 316, 325, 333, 379

Shirley, James, 60, 62

Sidney, Lady Dorothy, 62

Sidney, Robert, Earl of Leicester, 81, 266, 311

Smart, Peter, 104

Smith, John, 353, 354, 384, 389

Somerset, Edward, Lord Herbert of Raglan, 69

Somerset, Henry, Earl of Worcester, 56, 250

Southesk, Earl of, see Carnegie, David

Spain,
relations with, 128, 248, 328-9, 334-5, 357, 435
bullions transported in English ships, 125-6, 190

troops transported in English ships, 276, 290, 298-9, 329

Spelman, Henry, 79

Spottiswood, John, Archbishop of St. Andrews, 114, 116, 199, 458

Stamford, Earl of, see Grey, Henry

Stanley, James, Lord Strange, 60-1, 250

Stapleton, Sir Philip, 457, 476

Stapley, Anthony, 315

Star Chamber, Court of, 143-4, 145, 146, 175, 176, 194, 206, 216-7, 254-5, 303, 432

Stewart, Alexander, 462

Stewart, George, Lord d'Aubigny, 69, 393

Stewart, James, Duke of Lennox and later of Richmond, 116, 148, 178-9, 212, 316-17, 393, 449, 455

Stewart, John, Commissary of Dunkeld, 442, 465

Stewart, John, Earl of Traquair, 150, 176, 183, 189, 197, 261, 262, 277, 314; Commissioner in Scotland, 277-8, 292-3, 303-4

Stewart, William, 462

Stirling, Earl of, see Alexander, William

Strafford, Earl of, see Wentworth, Thomas

Strange, Lord, see Stanley, James

Strickland, Sir Walter, 380

Strode, William, 307, 317, 323, 364

Suckling, Sir John, 66, 67, 251, 264, 389, 393-4, 408, 440

Syderf, Thomas, Bishop of Galloway, 183, 203

Syms, Christopher, 60

Taylor, Jeremy, 92

Taylor, John, 58

Tradescant, John, 48

Transport, rivers, 30-1, 33; roads, 33; sea, 29

Traquair, Earl of, see Stewart, John

Trendall, a sectary, 291

Trevor, Sir John, 56, 194

Triennial Bill, 391, 395, 396

Tromp, Admiral Maerten, 299, 300-1

Turriff, encounters at, 259, 267

Ulster, 223-4, 260, 401, 470

Urban VIII, Pope, 121-2

Urquhart, Sir Thomas, 78

Urry, John, 459, 461-2, 464

Ussher, James, Archbishop of Armagh, 112, 113, 181, 426

Valentine, Benjamin, 317, 323

Vane, Sir Harry, the elder, 148-9, 266, 311-12, 324, 328, 334, 352, 446, 449; evidence against Strafford, 376-7, 410, 411-12, 413, 417

Vane, Sir Harry, the younger, 349, 364, 376-8, 412, 413-14

Vassell, Samuel, 363

Venetian envoys, quoted, 30, 66,

84-6, 127, 142, 202, 378, 384, 445, 446

Vermuyden, Cornelius, 47, 211

Verney, Sir Edmund, 274

Villiers, George, Duke of Buckingham, 73, 368

Villiers, Katherine, dowager Duchess of Buckingham, 224

Villiers, Mary, later Duchess of Lennox, 69, 178

Vlotho, Battle of, 246

Wales, Church, 99, 109-10; education and culture, 86-7; social structure, 55-6

Wales and the Marches, Court of, 144, 432

Walton, Izaak, 40, 81

Wandesford, Christopher, 287, 401, 402, 403

Ward, Mary, 119

Ward, Seth, 78

Ward, Fr. William, 446

Wards, Court of, 143, 154-5, 249

Warriston, see Johnston, Archibald

Warwick, Earl of, see Rich, Robert

Wentworth, Thomas, Viscount, later Earl of Strafford, 69, 78, 193, 201; character, 151-2; administration of, in Ireland, 59-60, 112, 113, 144, 163-5, 180-1, 251, 400-1; in the North, 144; his friendship with Laud, 152-3, 219, 428; foreign policy, 190, 302, 329; and the Scots, 224, 241, 242, 260, 261, 272, 285-7; and Lord Antrim, 225-6, 259, 263; and Sir Harry Vane, 311-12; and Lord Loftus, 207-9; his return from Ireland, 263, 280, 285-8, 302-3; on the Council of War, 307-8; and his Irish Parliament, 320-1; and the Short Parliament, 304, 307-8, 314, 323-6; and the Irish army, 328, 350; General in England, 345, 348, 352-3; made K. G., 353; and the Long Parliament, 358, 368-9; impeached, 372-3, 387, 395-6, 400-6, 410-12; Bill of Attainder against, 373, 413, 427; death, 428, 430

Weston, Richard, Earl of Portland, 163

Weston, Sir Richard, judge, 194

Weston, Sir Richard, agriculturalist, 47

Wheelocke, Abraham, 78

Whitford, Walter, Bishop of Brechin, 177-8, 283, 241

Whitgift, John, Archbishop of Canterbury, 96, 101

Widdrington, Sir William, 371

Widecombe, 246

Wight, Isle of, 300

Wightman, Edward, 291

Wilkins, John, 78

Wilkinson, Henry, 391

William, Prince of Orange, 357, 386, 418-9, 422, 435

Williams, John, Bishop of Lincoln, 55, 254; charged with perjury, 97-8, 175; his *Holy Table: Name and Thing*, 103; in the Long Parliament, 405, 426-7

Wilmot, Henry, 189, 250, 347, 389, 407, 418, 438, 440

Winchester, Marquis of, *see* Paulet, John

Windebanke, Sir Francis, 148-9, 250, 265, 308, 324, 325, 335, 339, 372, 375-6

Windebanke, Frank, 339

Windebanke, Thomas, 250, 265, 270, 323, 339

Winter, Sir John, 52, 210, 266

Wiseman, Sir Richard, 216

Witchcraft, 88-90

Wool trade, 34-6, 141, 316-7

Worcester, Earl of, *see* Somerset, Henry.

Wotton, Sir Henry, 81

Wren, Matthew, Bishop of Norwich, 106-7, 173, 205, 331, 339, 381

Wroth, William, 109

York, 35, 243; the King at (1639), 260-1, 262-5; (1640), 344, 346, 348; Council of Peers at, 352-3, 354-5

York, Duke of, *see* James

MORE ABOUT PENGUINS, PELICANS
AND PUFFINS

For further information about books available from Penguins please write to Dept EP, Penguin Books Ltd, Harmondsworth, Middlesex UB7 ODA.

In the U.S.A.: For a complete list of books available from Penguins in the United States write to Dept DG, Penguin Books, 299 Murray Hill Parkway, East Rutherford, New Jersey 07073.

In Canada: For a complete list of books available from Penguins in Canada write to Penguin Books Canada Ltd, 2801 John Street, Markham, Ontario L3R 1B4.

In Australia: For a complete list of books available from Penguins in Australia write to the Marketing Department, Penguin Books Australia Ltd, P.O. Box 257, Ringwood, Victoria 3134.

In New Zealand: For a complete list of books available from Penguins in New Zealand write to the Marketing Department, Penguin Books (N.Z.) Ltd, P.O. Box 4019, Auckland 10.

In India: For a complete list of books available from Penguins in India write to Penguin Overseas Ltd, 706 Eros Apartments, 56 Nehru Place, New Delhi 110019.